Understanding immigration in Ireland

Manchester University Press

Understanding immigration in Ireland

State, capital and labour in a global age

Steven Loyal

Manchester University Press
Manchester and New York

distributed in the United States exclusively
by Palgrave Macmillan

The right of Steven Loyal to be identified as the author of this work has been asserted by him in accordance with the Copyright, Designs and Patents Act 1988.

Published by Manchester University Press
Oxford Road, Manchester M13 9NR, UK
and Room 400, 175 Fifth Avenue, New York, NY 10010, USA
www.manchesteruniversitypress.co.uk

Distributed in the United States exclusively by
Palgrave Macmillan, 175 Fifth Avenue, New York,
NY 10010, USA

Distributed in Canada exclusively by
UBC Press, University of British Columbia, 2029 West Mall,
Vancouver, BC, Canada V6T 1Z2

British Library Cataloguing-in-Publication Data
A catalogue record for this book is available from the British Library

Library of Congress Cataloging-in-Publication Data applied for

ISBN   978 0 7190 7830 9 hardback
ISBN   978 0 7190 7831 6 paperback

First published 2011

The publisher has no responsibility for the persistence or accuracy of URLs for any external or third-party internet websites referred to in this book, and does not guarantee that any content on such websites is, or will remain, accurate or appropriate.

Typeset by 4word Ltd, Bristol
Printed in Great Britain by TJ International Ltd, Padstow

I would like to dedicate this book to the memory of my father who passed away recently. He lived the experience of being a migrant – working tremendously hard and for long hours to support our whole family. He is deeply missed.

Harjit Singh Loyal
15/03/1933 – 15/10/2010

Contents

List of tables and figures

Tables

Figures

Acknowledgements

There are a number of people I would like to thank including friends and colleagues for their comments, suggestions, help, and support during the prolonged gestation of this book. These include: Kieran Allen, Andrea Berger, Louise Campbell, Alice Feldman, Matt Green, Stephen Mennell, Aogan Mulcahy, Sara O'Sullivan, Neil Rolin, and Ciaran Staunton. I would also like to thank everyone at the Immigrant Council of Ireland and the Migrants Rights Centre Ireland who allowed me to sit in on and learn from their Policy Board meetings. Thanks also to MUP for their patience in tolerating the arrival of this overdue book.

Chapter 1

Introduction

Over the last 15 years, high and sustained levels of immigration have transformed Irish society. Between 1999 and 2008 the population increased by 18%, the highest rate in the 27 countries comprising the European Union.[1] Almost 1 million Public Personal Service Numbers (PPSNs) were given to foreign nationals between 2002 and 2008.[2] Increasingly multi-ethnic and cosmopolitan, the emerging pattern of cultural heterogeneity and diversity – with immigrants from 188 countries – is unprecedented. From a nation defined by large-scale emigration, Ireland has now become a country of entrenched immigration. In the 'new' Ireland, Islam constitutes the third largest religion in the Irish State. As well as the scale of this transformation, the pace of change is breathtaking. The 2002 census recorded that just under 6% of the population was composed of non-Irish nationals. By 2006 this had increased to over 10% – a rise of 1 percentage point each year. In 2008 1 in every 6 workers in Ireland was a migrant. While some informal estimates of Poles in Ireland have stated that there are almost 200,000 living in the country, constituting over 4% of the population.

Vast socio-cultural changes have extensively transformed every level of Irish society. Migration modified the operation of labour markets; the state regulation of political and civic rights; cultural issues concerning diversity, citizenship, multiculturalism, integration, and ethno-racial domination; as well as reframing a number of socio-economic issues concerning class, poverty, unemployment, social welfare, social exclusion, housing, health care, political representation, trade union membership, national belonging and membership, and equality in Ireland.

The Irish migratory context

The profundity of these changes can only be understood against the historical background of emigration. Ireland has historically been a country of emigration like no other. From the Great Famine of the 1840s through to the 1950s, Ireland's population continued to steeply decline. Many emigrants went to the UK, the USA, Canada, Australia, and some even travelled as far as Argentina, creating a vast Irish diaspora estimated (in its most capacious interpretation) to be somewhere between 70 million and 80 million people. Such high levels of outward migration with little return migration left Ireland with one of the lowest population densities in Europe.

Significant levels of emigration had been occurring for at least 3 centuries with, for example, over 12,000 Irish recorded as living in the West Indies in the late 1600s.[3] The Great Famine of the 1840s is conventionally taken as the starting point for the population exodus. Over 2.5 million people are estimated to have left during this period alone. Following the famine and up to the First World War a further 4 million departed.[4] Such massive levels of emigration had profound effects on the size and composition of the Irish population. According to 1841 census figures the Irish population stood at 6,528,799; by 1881, however, this had fallen to 3,870,020, and by 1901 had halved. Although the population level stabilized for a quarter of a century from 1926 at just under 3 million, it reached a nadir in 1961, standing at 2,818,002. Since then the population has steadily grown, reaching 4.49 million by 2009.[5] High rates of emigration continued until the 1960s and 1970s, when, as the economy strengthened, the numbers leaving began to fall. However, the 1980s saw emigration figures rise once again.

As in all social processes there have been conflicts over the representation of emigration. Politically and emotionally charged struggles in the field of representation between historians, economists, sociologists, geographers, policy-makers, demographers, politicians, nationalists, capitalists, landlords, the media, and the Church aimed at imposing the 'legitimate' symbolic interpretation of emigration have been protracted. These have shifted according to the balance of political and ideological forces. The positive evaluations of emigration by economic Malthusians as a solution to over-population became substituted by

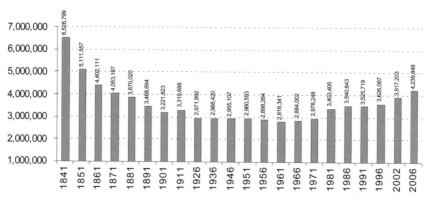

Figure 1.1 Irish population 1841–2006

nationalist and clerical characterizations of emigration as a symptom of colonialism and English misrule or responsible for the disintegration of moral life and falling church attendance.[6]

More specifically, elite political views altered according to political expediency. Thus nationalist politicians during the 1920s viewed emigration as a source of shame that would be solved by home rule. When emigration continued after the formation of the Free State politicians began instead to point to the psychological propensities of the emigrants themselves. There was, moreover, a marked divergence between what politicians rhetorically claimed and what they actually felt about emigration. The rulers of the newly independent state, concerned with issues of social order, continued to reap benefits from emigration as it transferred a young and restive population that might otherwise have questioned the failure of Irish nationalist politics. Politically the assertion that emigration resulted from the past wrongs of British colonialism helped to maintain a consensus for national development. Emigration in effect functioned as a safety valve. As a leading politician in his response to the 1954 report on the Commission on Emigration acknowledged: 'High emigration, granted a population excess, releases social tensions which would otherwise explode and makes possible a stability of manners and customs which would otherwise be the subject of radical change'.[7]

The return of mass emigration in the 1980s led to a new positive political rationalization in which the phenomenon was constructed as a rational response in a globalized economy. As the Deputy Prime Minister, Brian Lenihan, stated: 'emigration is not a defeat because the more Irish emigrants hone their skills and talents in another environment, the more they develop a work ethic in a country like Germany or the US, the better it can be applied in Ireland when they return. After all we can't all live on a small island.'[8] The 'new wave' emigration of the 1980s was represented as an exodus of young graduates seeking skills and opportunities. The normalization of emigration masked the benefits that flowed to ruling political and economic elites in the USA and Ireland. The export of tens of thousands of young Irish people in a period of economic stagnation and intense disputes over the dominant role of the Catholic Church released damaging social tensions in a context in which Fianna Fail's populist rhetoric was fading as it seemed no longer able to sustain the programme of national development.[9] It also unintentionally cemented a relationship between Ireland's political elite and US economic interests.

1996 marked a significant turning point in this context as Ireland became a country of net immigration, the last country in the EU to become so. Net emigration of 70,000 people in 1988 became fully inverted to a net immigration of 70,000 people in 2005 (see Figure 1.2). Ireland now had a higher rate of immigration than any other European country save Luxembourg.[10] The dramatic growth in large-scale mass migration to Ireland was unprecedented.

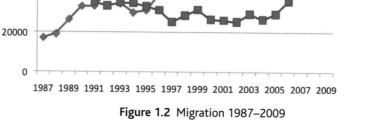

Figure 1.2 Migration 1987–2009

Source: CSO, 2009.

However, this dramatic rise in immigration was intrinsically linked to the emergence of the Celtic Tiger and subsequently fell with its demise. The recession in Ireland has seen the re-emergence of net emigration in 2009.

It would be mistaken, however, to believe that there was little immigration and settlement in Ireland prior to the 1990s. Such notions of homogeneity invariably form a central part of nationalistic state discourses. Irish society, although relatively homogeneous in terms of whiteness and Christianity, was always more diverse than it claimed to be.[11] A limited, but culturally significant, degree of Jewish immigration took place at the turn of 19th/20th centuries. It has been estimated that there were 472 Jews in Ireland from Russia and Lithuania in 1881, rising to 5,000 30 years later.[12] The majority settled in the area around the South Circular road in Dublin; others settled in Limerick and Cork. A pogrom in Limerick in 1904, incited by a fiery preacher Father John Creagh, marked the beginning of their marginalization.[13] The Irish State was deeply reluctant to accept further numbers of Jewish immigrants during the war. As S. A. Rooche from the Department of Justice noted in 1946: 'Our practice has been to discourage any substantial increase in the Jewish population. They do not assimilate with our own people but remain a sort of colony of a worldwide Jewish community. This makes them a potential irritant in the body politic and has led to disastrous results from time to time in other countries'.[14] It is estimated that as little as 60 Jews were allowed to enter the Irish State during the war years. Such a policy was justified by the Department of Justice in 1953: 'There is a strong anti-Jewish feeling in this state which is particularly evident in the aliens section of the Department of Justice. Sympathy for the Jews has not been particularly excited at the recent news that some thousands are fleeing westwards because of the recent round up of a number of Communist Jews who had been prominent in governments and government service in East Europe.'[15]

Immediately after the Irish State's ratification of the UN Convention on Human Rights (1951) in 1957 the Irish government accepted 539 Hungarian refugees into the country as Programme Refugees, following the Soviet Invasion of their country.[16] However, the state carefully ensured that those permitted entry were vetted in terms of religious and political background. Jews and communists were screened and Catholic families given preference so that fewer individual males were seen to be competing for scarce Irish jobs.[17] Accommodated in a disused army camp in Knockalsheen, Co. Limerick, and not given jobs promised by the state, they went on a hunger strike in May 1957. All but 60 had left within 2 years of their arrival.

Following the 1970s there were a number of other programme refugees who arrived in Ireland including Chileans, Vietnamese, Bosnians, and Kosovans. The state, however, played a minimal role in their uneven reception and inclusion.

Though statistically insignificant, the early treatment of immigrants reveals the three nascent and interlocking criteria that have subsequently continued to shape state policy to this day. These are questions concerning nationalism and homogeneity; questions concerning maintaining security and social order; and questions concerning economic costs and benefits of migration.

Outline of the book

This book aims to contribute to a clearer understanding of processes of immigration and settlement in Ireland expanding on an article I wrote several years ago.[18] It attempts to reflect upon and explain the development of some of the multifactorial dimensions of migration, including the change in the socio-cultural composition of the country, the implications these have for the Irish nation-state, and the processes through which selected social individuals become dominated.

A sociological approach needs to examine the social relations and interest groups involved in generating and applying the concept of migration. There are many individuals and groups involved in issues concerning migration and settlement who, depending on their social position, may perceive, interpret, discuss, and evaluate migration and its implications in profoundly exclusive and different ways. For some the radical alterations engendered in Ireland by migration are a positive thing: ethnic and cultural diversity presents opportunities for new constructions of Irish national identity, it increases diversity, or provides a flexible and highly motivated skilled and unskilled work force. For others migration is highly problematic: it challenges the sovereignty of nation-states, destroying the Irish way of life and values, and is responsible for lowering wages and working conditions.

Although the effects and consequences of migration appear pronounced in one sense, the exact contours and dynamics of migration in Ireland are not easy to discern categorically, nor are they amenable to straightforward scholarly discussion, outline, or measurement; rather, sociologically they remain contested inquiries. There are a number of reasons for this. First, a socio-genesis of migration that investigates both the grammar of the term and its use is largely absent in the literature. The construction and application of the term is often situationally determined, historically variable, and politically contested. The growth in supranational entities such as the EU, the end of the Cold War, and rise of neo-liberal capitalism have also inflected and influenced the meaning and application of the term. Semantic distinctions between 'immigrant', 'migrant', 'foreign born', 'minority ethnic', 'non-Irish national' employed and sanctioned by various data surveys, state agencies, and bureaucrats, have further blurred the possibility of gaining a precise scholarly meaning. Second, the immigrant is not a monolithic subject. The concept 'immigrant' or 'migrant' is applied to a variety of complex and varied human subject positions. Migrants are both rich and poor individuals, with a diversity of skills, and from a wide range of backgrounds. The term is usually applied to manual workers but is equally applicable, though less rarely used, to refer to highly skilled workers, businessmen, students, asylum seekers, trafficked people, returning Irish who have lived abroad, or those seeking to join separated family members. To an extent this book reproduces the ideological correlation of migrants as poor and racialized by focusing on the limited experiences of those most marginalized, rather than the more positive experiences of white Canadians, returning Irish or British nationals working in the high-tech sector, many of whom have experienced few problems whilst living here and are rarely referred to as 'immigrants'. Third, although the concept is applied to individuals, it refracts, in a condensed form, a range of structural social, political, and economic processes. The term is a manifestation or phenomenal form that represents a cipher for hidden or veiled structural processes, often constituting the conditions of possibility for it.[19] Implicit in this single category is a range of complex contradictory structural processes and presuppositions. Fourth, the nature and content of what is included in the category of 'immigration' and 'immigrant' has shifted over time and space to incorporate more and more processes within its purview from intra-state processes and movements from the country to the city, to international movement across continents. More and more countries from the South of the globe are becoming involved in the migratory process. The category therefore acquires its substantive definition from the particular historical contexts in which it is applied. This conceptual and dialectical fluidity reflects the relational and processual nature of reality.[20]

Although all social processes are by their nature conflict-ridden, heavily contested, and embodying a variety of political implications, this is nowhere more so than in relation to immigration. Migration is a politically and emotionally charged concept prone to misunderstanding, misinterpretation, and exaggeration. It is also interpreted in an overwhelmingly moral language sometimes created by the state and inflected or amplified by the media, but also assessed and perceived through popular prejudices and sensibilities. The intrusion of heteronomous valuations, common-sense beliefs, and intense emotional feelings in accounting for migration applies to all the main actors involved in the migratory process, as well as those experts who attempt to understand and account for it. Misconceptions are frequent. Thus for example, in contrast to common-sense and emotionally charged public discussions, according to official estimates the largest group of non-Irish nationals in the state are neither Polish nor Nigerian, but from the UK. And the sober reality is that prior to 2004, the largest group of immigrants entering Ireland were returning Irish.

A systematic approach to understanding migration and settlement requires not only an account of the specific contours of migration, but also an examination of the discourse of migration as part of the object of analysis. An epistemic reflexivity in which the discourse on migration becomes part of the object of research object itself is absolutely necessary. This can be facilitated by drawing on the sociology of knowledge which provides reminders about how knowledge is socially constructed, framed, and expresses social, ethical, and political interests. The diverse views of academics, migration experts, politicians, and the lay population can be interpreted as expressing various world-views and thought-styles highlighting the stated and unstated political determinations and assumptions underpinning the construction, classification, representation, and interpretation of migration.[21] Agents construct social reality and enter into struggles and transactions aimed at imposing their point of view, interests, and principles of vision determined by the position they occupy in the very world they intend to transform or preserve. Hence migrants, the state, employers, non-governmental organizations (NGOs), trade unions, and both high- and low-skilled workers may perceive and evaluate processes of migration in different ways. The phenomenon may carry divergent meanings for different political groups, be they social democrats, nationalists, libertarians, conservatives, capitalists, left-wing revolutionaries, or cosmopolitans. Moreover, the nature and practices of the central actors involved, including the state, employers and trade unions – have changed over time. For example, changes in the State's immigration policy have been strongly determined by international geo-political shifts, such as the opening of continental borders with EU expansion, and the increasing restrictiveness imposed on migrants and borders after the 9/11 terrorist attacks.

Within an uneven context of power, the majority of groups involved in this struggle over the representation of migration have failed to undertake this indispensable step of reflexivity. Given that the state plays a fundamental role in defining, shaping and structuring perceptions of migration *tout court,* through its world-view realized in discourses, categorizations, practices etc., social analysts can unwittingly absorb these conceptual instruments which construct social reality, so as to 'think with the State' in their analyses of migration. This use of what Bourdieu calls 'prenotions' or 'preconstructions' that 'convert social problems into sociological problems',[22] is not only embodied in the use of state vocabularies to describe pertinent social relations, but is reflected in the methodological correlation of a society with a nation–state or what has more recently been called 'methodological nationalism'.[23] The framework for understanding migration is the sovereign nation–state which, through discourses of nationalism, presupposes a homogenous demarcated population whether civically, ethnically, culturally, racially, or linguistically. Modern states are *nation-*states that aspire to total national forms of homogeneity and migration necessarily disturbs this ideal. It is imperative, therefore, for sociologists to subject state thought to critical reflection.[24] Because lay and scholarly discourses about migration have performative and political implications they need to be interrogated and analysed rather than unwittingly used as tools or parts of the explanation. Migration needs to be conceptualized in a manner that does not presuppose the nation–state or nation–state thinking as a tacit frame of reference. Theoretical approaches to migration in the social sciences need instead to look at humanity as a whole[25] or at least examine the global interstate system and the changing relationships between states as shaping understandings and practices of migration.

For the most part everyday understandings of migration have tended to employ a polarized Manichean analysis in which the social world is seen in the structure of a myth wherein the observer approves or disapproves of migration. Hard and fast evaluative distinctions are made between the indigenous population and problematic migrants or foreigners, or sub-divisions within migrants between 'good' (i.e. hardworking) and 'bad' (i.e. 'welfare scroungers' or 'bogus asylum seekers') migrants. Such ideological biases also enter into academic discussions of migration and settlement. The state may be seen as all-powerful and corrupt while the migrant is seen as a virtuous though powerless victim defended through a moralizing and self-righteous lexicon. [26] As Bourdieu rightly notes, 'good intentions make for bad sociology' and accounts containing such 'a logic of the trail' necessarily undermine any scientific analysis of the subject. Not all migrants are powerless or necessarily 'good', nor conversely are all state actions egregious *de facto.*

Rather than employing morally loaded accounts imbued with sharp moral dichotomies or value polarities of 'good' and 'bad', sociologists of migration need to look at the changing balance in structural and power relations. Conflict between differentially positioned individuals should be seen as a 'normal' though changing aspect of social relations. The sociological question pursued in this book is not specifically about who is right or wrong in this controversy but what structural characteristics of specifically positioned individuals impel them to act in the ways they do. Sociologists, as Elias rightly notes, need to examine the structural characteristics which bind social individuals, and sometimes groups, to each other in a specific way so that the members of one group feel impelled, or have sufficient power resources, to treat those of another group collectively as inferior.[27] These shifting social structures are intrinsically tied to psychic structures whereby modes of interaction and interdependence between individuals are modulated in class ways through differentiated structures of feeling.

Theoretical underpinnings

The central aim of this book is to uncover the complexity of migration processes in Ireland. Although this entails an analysis of a specific object of research – Ireland – its findings are meant to be generative and generalizable. The intention is not only to examine Ireland as a particular empirical case but also to demonstrate the operation of certain invariant social processes. Historically a country of entrenched emigration and relative cultural and religious homogeneity, Ireland provides almost a quasi-laboratory context for examining and analysing the impact of immigration that can add a significant new dimension for understanding migration more generally. Nevertheless, immigration into Ireland has its own specific characteristics including the short-time span within which it occurred and the profile of the immigrants – predominantly of European and East European extraction, young, and many with high skill levels.

The term 'migrant' homogenizes a very disparate group of individuals from different religious and cultural, gender and generational, class and educational backgrounds. These factors, together with their level of linguistic competence, differentiated immigration status and the racialization and discrimination they have faced, combine with broad state processes of regulation and capitalist demand to create a complex and varied array of immigrant experiences. As migrants a Polish builder, Indian software engineer, Filipino domestic worker, Somalian asylum seeker, and American pharmaceutical CEO may share very little in common. Fitting the diversity of these experiences into a single analytical straightjacket is highly problematic. However, an attempt is made in this book to provide a theoretically informed empirical and sociological analysis of migration which has some policy relevance.

Sociological frameworks, as well as the frameworks within which individuals understand their everyday world, including migration, have themselves to be explained, and here the sociology of knowledge provides a vital service. Of some explanatory relevance throughout this book, though rarely made explicit, is the opposition between conservative and natural-law thought-styles and world-views. In various ways, these thought-styles are evident in the first principles chosen, the theoretical framework adopted, the ontological presuppositions about human nature, and the methodology employed in all social science. However, they also permeate analyses and evaluations of migration, for example in accounts of how and why people migrate – from an emphasis on individuals in micro economic and rational choice approaches, to an emphasis on the social nature of migration in the writings of network theories and Marxist writers. The influence of these world-views is also evident in the evaluation of cosmopolitanism and nationalism; in discussions about access to and acquisition of citizenship; of belonging and rootedness – from the family to the state to humanity; whether different cultures integrate over time or are naturally antipathetic or incommensurable; in debates about restricting migration or arguing for more open borders. Liberal thought-styles that emphasize humanity, reason, and an expansionary cosmopolitanism as a framework for understanding the nature of social relations can be contrasted with conservative thought-styles which place a stronger emphasis on community, family, experience, a suspicion of outsiders, and entrenched and exclusive cultures. Such opposed accounts have found exemplary polar expression in the work of political philosophers such as Rawls and Oakshott, but more recently in popular books about migration: Philippe Legrain's *Immigrants: Your Country Needs Them* and Christopher Caldwell's *Reflections on the Revolution in Europe*, respectively.

Such world-views and their political and ideological implications have been used in this book as a way of understanding both scholarly and lay accounts of migration, and after critical reflection, as a means for analysing migration. The transcendence of the dualisms of Enlightenment and post-Enlightenment thought and the liberal and conservative thought-styles was of course the basis for the sociology of Marx, Weber, and Durkheim. While emphasizing the inherently social nature of humans (though Weber remains an exception), all three recognized at the same time their modern individuation; all three sociologists acknowledged the importance of theory, yet expressed it through empirical work; all employed contextual historical explanation, yet also acknowledged the trans-historical dimensions of the social world; they were all critical of modernity, yet also adopted a resolute monism by seeing both the positive and negative aspects of modernism as intertwined.

There are certain immanent threads linking the diverse arguments made throughout this book. Stated in abstract terms these first principles (or principles of philosophical anthropology) have emerged as part of a theoretical attempt to synthesize what are usually considered to be rival procedures or sociological frameworks and applying these to substantive processes. This includes a materialist emphasis on the dynamics of the global capitalist economy, and on production relations and productive activity generally, combined with a more symbolic approach that is acutely aware of the significance and constitutive power of beliefs, status, and recognition in social life.[28]

In contrast with the large majority of other accounts, this book aims to provide a theoretically informed empirical analysis of migration which does not rely on abstract reified categorizations or the conceptual dichotomies on which the sociology of migration frequently relies. These include oppositions between the individual and society, between theory and empirical analysis, materialism and idealism, agency and structure, micro and macro levels, and between asylum seekers and migrant workers. In order to avoid these oppositions, the approach adopted here begins with an ontology based upon the category of *social* human beings and their practices. The fact of human sociality understood in terms of a profound mutual susceptibility of and between interacting non-independent social individuals is presupposed as an axiom throughout this analysis. From the assumption of the intrinsically social nature of individuals follows an understanding of human social identity as socially bestowed, socially sustained and socially transformed. Moreover, as Durkheim recognized, the very conceptual frameworks in accordance which individuals think are socially and communally constituted.[29] Social individuals are deeply interdependent agents, not only in respect of their forms of shared and aligned cognition, language and knowledge, but also in respect of their actions. The ontological interdependence of agents can be highlighted in two major respects. First, agents enter a field of interaction in which they are tied to other participants through their mutual susceptibility to the evaluations of other socially interacting individuals. What is relevant here is the need to emphasize the importance of social recognition, conferred through esteem or status, as a universal characteristic of all human beings. A second factor determining the ontological interdependence of social beings is the acknowledgement that humans are productive beings. Humans require cooperation in order to produce their means of subsistence through their productive activity. As Marx notes, through their relations of production, social individuals produce their material life.[30] The productive activity of human beings is a fundamental condition of all social life. The production of material life includes the production of material objects as well as the production of social relations, the latter encompassing family forms and gendered social relations. These twin determinations are analytically separated here for theoretical purposes, but in the analysis provided by this book, they are examined in conjunction with one another, though prioritized in different ways depending on the research question at hand.

In addition to Marx, and Durkheim's emphatic emphasis on the social nature of humans, the book also draws sparingly on the work of Norbert Elias and

Pierre Bourdieu. Elias's account of the formation of the modern state, of inter-state relations, and of how these were linked to the development of the personality structure of the individual is used to inform an analysis of supranational and inter-state processes involving migration and how these are tied to the social perception of migrants. Elias's discussion of shifting power balances, and processes for understanding the process of migration and nationalism generally, is also relevant. From Bourdieu the book borrows the notion of habitus as a system of acquired dispositions, and it emphasizes social practices, and reaffirms the close connection between everyday culture and power. It also shares his methodological concern with providing a relational analysis rather than focusing on individuals or groups or of taking the existence of groups in this case national groups or 'communities' for granted, and draws on his arguments about the power of state classification in shaping the objective position in social space of migrants, as well as their self-perception and perception by others.

Although there has been a large increase in the volume of research on immigration in Ireland, a number of these analyses, in parallel with dominant explanations of migration in the social sciences generally, have tended to be occupied with specific ad hoc issues concerning immigration and settlement, and to be dominated largely by cultural forms of analysis.[31] While it is useful and eminently sensible to know about culture, such an exclusive focus leaves a number of questions unanswered. With one or two exceptions there has been little systematic discussion of the constitutive role of the state[32] and the economy. By contrast, economic approaches have tended to be equally one-sided, providing only a partial picture of the social nature and ideological underpinnings of migration. In order to try to remedy and move beyond some of the deficiencies in the literature, I have adopted a cultural materialist analysis of immigration and settlement. Migration is an empirically complex and multi-modal process which should not and cannot be flattened out on an economic anvil. How an economy operates is an aspect of society. The presence of asylum seekers and individuals migrating for family reunification is testimony to this. As part of a critique of the dominant focus on economic individual actors, the role of networks, the experiences, hopes, and practices of the migrant, and issues of family reunification, are emphasized throughout this book. Markets are instituted, controlled, and regulated within society. The economy is always and everywhere embedded in wider social relationships, being simultaneously shaped by them and shaping them.[33] Material processes not only have symbolic outcomes but are intrinsically entwined with ideological processes, and can only be separated for analytical purposes. An attempt has been made not to down-play the importance of ideas and beliefs in the constitution of the social world. The objective world consists not just of material processes but of conscious human beings, and of social institutions, characterized by rule-governed behaviour, speech-acts, collective intentionality, self-referentiality, human agreement, and shifting meanings. That is, the social world is also composed of 'institutional facts.'[34] This book aims to highlight similar concerns to those that John Berger eloquently stated in his brilliant analyses of labour migration in the 1970s, although his notion of unfreedom needs to be qualified:

> To outline the experience of the migrant worker and to relate this to what surrounds him – both physically and historically – is to grasp more surely the political reality of the world at this moment. The subject is European, its meaning is global. Its theme is unfreedom. This unfreedom can only be fully recognized if an objective system is related to the subjective experience of those trapped within it. Indeed, finally, the unfreedom is that relationship.[35]

The book also attempts to furnish an analysis of state policies and discourses on migration and the contradictions between different state imperatives including economic, nationalist, and those pertaining to security issues. As part of this it provides a critical account of the categorical schemas used by the state and how they have both objective and subjective effects on immigrants. In contrast to the natural sciences, the objects of which remain impervious to what is said about them, the object of the social sciences is composed of conscious, reflexive subjects who can become affected by discourses about them. Although the focus of this book is very much on the objective structural processes of immigration, there is also a lesser focus, because of limitations of space, on the existential and subjective experience of the immigrants, especially as revealed in interviews. An attempt is made to examine the implications for those who are classified, and labelled as migrants, understood as a master or exclusivley determining status, on the treatment and self-percpetion of the migrants themselves. Assessing these in their manifold complexity is a difficult enough undertaking which is further exacerbated when intertwined with discussions of nationalism and belonging, citizenship and ethno-racial domination. These subjective identifications are highlighted as part of discussing the lived experience of migrants, the marginal position occupied by them in Irish society, and the social suffering engendered by state policies. Their experiences are very diverse, but for a number of non-EU nationals the domination and discrimination they suffer is compounded 'on the ground' by the actions of government officials, bureaucrats, frontline service providers, and Irish nationals. It is also expressed in the operation of the asylum and direct provision system and through labour market segmentation and workplace exploitation.

The book began while the Celtic Tiger was in full flow but was completed after the onset of an acute economic recession. The Celtic Tiger is a bygone era and the future development of migration will almost certainly develop along a different socio-economic track. Nevertheless, and bearing in mind earlier qualifications to an exclusively economic approach, a core argument of this book is that, although they are analytically distinct and irreducible processes, it is impossible to understand migration in Ireland without reference to the development and passing of the Celtic Tiger economy and the neo-liberal state policies that underpinned it. The Celtic Tiger was not merely a backdrop for understanding migration, but inextricably and reciprocally linked with the structure and development of immigration processes in Ireland. It provided the dynamic lived material and ideological conditions within which migration was interpreted and perceived by the host population. In some ways the labour demand generated by the Celtic Tiger was analogous to the acute requirement for foreign labour in Western Europe and the Low countries following the Second World War. However, there is one crucial difference. In contrast with the predominantly corporatist Keynesian Fordist compact that existed during that time, the Celtic Tiger represented the unfolding logic of an increasingly deregulated global economy characterized by changing employment relations, a flexible labour market organization, the retrenchment of the social state, and an unrelenting championing of a possessive consumer individualism. Migrant labour was a central constituent in these processes. Together with increasing levels of urbanization, a shift in class struggle and composition, religious affiliation, altered patriarchal gender relations, and a reconfiguration of the Irish we-image and we-ideal[36] in-migration constituted a central facet of a rapidly changing Ireland.

Central to establishing and defining the parameters within which migration has unfolded is the shifting historical situation and power balance between state, capital, and labour, their discursive repertoires, vocabularies and practices, and how these became configured under a neo-liberal social order and social partnership. Stated briefly, immigration into Ireland may usefully be understood in terms of a tension between four analytically distinct – though substantially overlapping – generic processes that assumed a specific form in the current conjuncture:

1 Capitalism – a logic of capital accumulation which points towards open borders and the free flow of capital: this imperative has come to the foreground as a consequence of the labour market dynamism of the Celtic Tiger.
2 The nation-state – which classifies, codifies, and monitors its population conjoined with a restricted narrative of ethnic and national identity and maintenance of sovereignty and security.
3 International law – within the field of international relations, a minimal commitment to constitutional liberalism and the rule of law and international human rights obligations – this expresses itself in support various forms of international law.

4 Labour and migrant mobilization – the level and extent of trade union and NGO activity, and ethnic group mobilization in Irish society.

Migration and the representation of migration in Ireland are the outcomes of a complex, concrete, historical, and socio-political dynamic between these 4 processes.

Given that the object should determine the method and not the other way around, the approach used here is multi-levelled with various specific research problems or questions determining the appropriate mode of analysis in each chapter. As well as drawing on historical analysis, survey analysis, and global data sets the book draws on some 80 in-depth interviews and 400 surveys carried out with Polish, Chinese, Indian, Lithuanian, and Nigerian migrants that were undertaken as part of a joint research report on integration involving a large collective group of researchers.[37] These interviews were supplemented by a further 20 in-depth interviews with asylum seekers from various nationalities living in direct provision centres around Ireland. The book also draws on various NGO reports, government documents, and my experience of working with and interacting with migrants.

Given the theoretical centrality placed on long-term processes for understanding contemporary social relations the book begins with a long-term analysis of migratory processes before providing a short inventory of the different theoretical approaches used for understanding migration. Though analytically separate the two processes are related: thinking about migration often follows empirically existing migratory processes and state assessments of that process. As well as criticizing these theoretical frameworks the chapter aims to provide an alternative theoretical position that emphasizes the centrality of social relations and social networks and their linkage to economic and state processes. Chapter 2 examines the indispensable role that state formation, state categorization, and state policy play in structuring migration. It examines state formation and the plethora of different, and sometimes contradictory, functions that the state undertakes. Differentiated state categories contribute not only towards determining patterns of migration but also to how migration is assessed, perceived, and understood. Classificatory schemas also shape how migrants are treated by government officials and service providers and how they perceive themselves. Chapter 3 extends this discussion of the state by examining the emergence of exclusionary national physical borders and conceptual and ideological boundaries within the state. By contrast to most other European countries the arrival of asylum seekers preceded that of labour migrants and firmly shaped subsequent immigration policy. Chapter 4 examines their arrival and the Irish State's attempts to deal with them in terms of processing claims. It examines the degree of neutrality and objectivity in the State's assessment of claims for refugee status. Chapter 5 extends this discussion by looking at the lives of asylum seekers in direct provision centres in Ireland and how these operate as what Goffman calls 'total institutions' at once regulating their actions and behaviour, stripping their sense of self, and simultaneously forming segregated institutions for their ongoing surveillance. In Chapter 6 the role of the Irish judiciary as formally independent from the state and as a bulwark for protecting migrant rights against the excesses of state power is analysed. Chapter 7 looks the phenomenon and institution of citizenship in Ireland and specifically examines the Citizenship Referendum of 2004 and how it was used as a means by the state for restricting membership in the nation, and regulating its ethno-national composition.

2004 was an important year in Ireland in terms of migration: not only did the Citizenship Referendum effect a re-ethnicization of citizenship, but a month earlier EU accession state nationals had been permitted to enter and work in the Irish State. The state, which stands simultaneously inside and outside of the logic of capital, has both encouraged and restricted migratory movements according to its instrumental and strategic requirements. Chapter 8 examines this as part of the Irish State's attempt to structure the labour market to meet the needs of capital for a flexible and cheap labour force while simultaneously shaping its ethno-national composition. It examines the labour market segmentation of immigrants and attempts to account for these processes by looking at a number of complex interlocking processes operating at the micro, meso, and macro level. These include capitalist demand, the role of employers, the state regulation of migrant labour, social networks, and migrant dispositions. It also discusses how immigration has dramatically transformed the class configuration of Irish society.

The strengthening of the power of capital, aided by the expansion of neo-liberal state policies, has entailed a corresponding weakening and fragmentation of the power of labour, especially under the aegis of social partnership. In Chapter 9 the structural factors engendering the wide-scale exploitation of migrant workers are examined. This involves examining the conjunctural balance of forces between capital, state, and labour. The chapter looks at various labour sectors as well as the pronounced exploitation of male and female migrants in various sectors of the economy and the role of the state and trade unions in modulating this naked exploitation. Chapter 10 looks at the state and the public's reaction to increasing immigrant diversity in the country and examines the level of integration and discrimination they experience.

Ireland became an archetypal surface for the global economy where free-floating capital met increasingly mobile labour.[38] The insatiable demands for labour, initially engendered by American translational investment, and further spiked by the deregulation of property and financial services, led to a unique confluence and embedding of foreign transnational capital and foreign labour on Irish soil. Facilitated and amplified through the operation of social networks, these capital and migratory movements were strongly influenced and mediated by nation-building concerns, state categorization, and state surveillance. As one of the most open economies in the world, English speaking, and deregulated, staggering Irish growth rates exemplified fast growing lush foliage. However, the economy was in many ways an exotic plant blooming in a thin soil. If ever a country was vulnerable to the mobility of capital, it was Ireland. The boom was not deep-rooted in anything necessarily specific about Irishness or Ireland, and just as foreign direct investment had decided to come to source a cheap, educated, and flexible labour force in a country with staggeringly low corporate taxes, they decided to leave to go elsewhere for the same reasons. With the collapse of the construction industry and the financial sector, the recession has highlighted just how vulnerable Ireland was to the fluidity of capital. The book was completed in 2010, just as capitalism had faced its worst economic crises since the Great Depression. It concludes by reflecting on the recession and how it has created a wholly different framework within which migration is taking place, is assessed by the state and indigenous population, and will develop in the future. Immigration has slowed dramatically and since 2008 Ireland has once again become a country of emigration. However, the Irish economy cannot function without immigrant labour and immigration, albeit to a more limited level, will continue in the future. In addition, issues concerning family reunification and the social inclusion of migrants who remain rather than return, as well as their children, will become more prominent.

Notes

1 The rate of natural increase of the population in Ireland was 9.8 per 1,000 in 2007 compared with an EU 27 average of just 1.0 (Table 7.6). Central Statistics Office, *Measuring Ireland's Progress 2008* (Dublin: CSO, 2009).

2 The CSO says that 967,800 foreign nationals aged 15 and over were allocated PPSNs between 2002 and 2008. CSO Foreign Nationals: PPSN Allocations, Employment and Social Welfare Activity, 23 Dec (Dublin: CSO, 2008).

3 G. Kirkham, in R. Kearney (ed), *Migrations: The Irish at Home and Abroad* (Dublin: Wolfhound Press, 1989), p. 16.

4 D. Fitzpatrick, *Irish Emigration 1801–1921* (Dublin: Economic and Social History Society of Ireland, 1984), p. 3.

5 CSO, Population and Migration Estimates, April 2009: /www.cso.ie/ releasespublications/documents/population/current/popmig.pdf.

6 J. MacLaughlin, *Historical and Recent Irish Emigration: A Critique of Core-Periphery and Behavioural Models* (London: University of North London Press, 1994), p. 22; J. Lee, *Ireland 1912–1985: Politics and Society* (Cambridge: CUP, 1990).

7 Cited in Lee, *Ireland 1912–85*, p. 381.

8 Ibid., p. 36.

9 K. Allen, Immigration and the Celtic Tiger: a land of a thousand welcomes?, in Gareth Dale and Mike Cole (eds), *The European Union and Migrant Labour* (Oxford/New York: Berg 1997), pp. 149–75.

10 P. Mac Éinrí, *Labour Migration in Ireland* (Dublin: ICI, 2003), p. 17.

11 B. Rolston and M. Shannon, *Encounters: How Racism Came to Ireland* (Belfast: Beyond the Pale, 2002).

12 D. Keogh, *Jews in Twentieth-Century Ireland: Refugees, Anti-Semitism and the Holocaust* (Cork: Cork University Press, 1998).

13 Ibid., p. 28.

14 Ibid., p. 161.

15 Ibid., p. 221.

16 E. Ward, A big show-off to show what we can do: Ireland and the Hungarian Refugee crisis 1956, in *Irish Studies in International Affairs* Vol. 7 (1996).

17 B. Fanning, S. Loyal & C. Staunton, *Asylum Seekers and the Right to Work* (Dublin: Irish Refugee Council, 1999).

18 S. Loyal, Welcome to the Celtic Tiger: Immigration, Racism, and the State, in C. Coulter & S. Coleman, *The End of Irish History: Critical reflections on the Celtic Tiger* (Manchester: Manchester University Press, 2003), pp.74–95.

19 In this book 'immigrant' and 'migrant' are used interchangeably to denote persons who are non-Irish nationals and who do not have an automatic right of residency in the country. Given the recent nature of immigration into Ireland the term can currently be used interchangeably with non-Irish national. Some immigrants have of course applied for naturalization or citizenship. The increasing number of second generation children of immigrants will make this assumption increasingly problematic.

20 D. Sayer, *The Violence of Abstraction* (Oxford: Blackwell, 1987).

21 In his essay on conservatism, Mannheim usefully distinguishes specific thought-styles, a notion which he takes from the history of art and contrasts a bourgeois liberalism with its 'natural-law' style of thought and a counterposing conservative thought-style, which arose in historical opposition to its antonym. Mannheim's distinction between thought-styles provides a useful set of analytical tools which are employed throughout this book. See K. Mannheim, *Conservatism* (London, Routledge, 1986).

22 In *The Craft of Sociology* Bourdieu et al. note: 'The need to break with preconstructions, prenotions, spontaneous theory, is particularly imperative in sociology, because our minds, our language, are full of preconstructed objects, and I think that three-quarters of research simply coverts social problems into sociological problems…More generally, many instruments used to construct social reality (like occupational categories, age groups, and so on) are bureaucratic categories that no one has thought through.' P. Bourdieu, J.C. Chamboredon, J. Passeron, B. Krais, *The Craft of Sociology: Epistemological Preliminaries* (Verlag, Walter de Gruyer, Kluver, 1991) p. 249.

23 A. Wimmer & N. Glick Schiller, Methodological nationalism and beyond: nation state building, migration and the social sciences. *Global Networks. A Journal of Transnational Affairs* 2: 4 (2000), 301–34.

24 'As Thomas Bernhard says in *Alte meister*, we are more or less "servants of the state", functionaries, insofar as we are products of the educational system, teachers… And to break away from pre-thought objects you need a terrific energy, an iconoclastic violence', Bourdieu et al, *The Craft of Sociology*, p. 249.

25 N. Elias, *What is Sociology?* (London: Hutchinson, 1978).

26 Cited in C. Caldwell, *Reflections on a Revolution in Europe*, p. 86.

27 N. Elias & J. Scotson, *The Established and Outsiders* (London: Sage, 1994).

28 This dichotomy has recently been restated and re-entrenched in debates concerning redistribution and recognition. See N. Fraser & A. Honneth, *Redistribution and Recognition* (London: Verso, 2003).

29 'The nature of the concept, thus defined, bespeaks its origin. If it is common to all, it is the work of the community... it is unquestionable that language, and consequently the system of concepts which it translates, is the product of collective elaboration. What it expresses is the manner in which society as a whole represents the facts of experience', E. Durkheim, *The Elementary Forms of Religious Life* (ed. R. Nisbet) (London: Allen & Unwin, 1976) p. 434.

30 K. Marx, *The German Ideology* (London: Lawrence & Wishart, 1987).

31 For two comprehensive overviews of the literature see R. Lentin and R. McVeigh, Irishness and racism: An E-reader, *Translocations*, Vol. 1 No. 1, August 2006; and P. Mac Einri and A. White, Immigration into the Republic of Ireland: a bibliography of recent research, *Irish Geography*, Vol. 41, No. 2, July 2008, pp. 151–79.

32 The work of R. Lentin and R. McVeigh, *After Optimism: Ireland, Racism and Globalization* (Dublin: Metro Eireann Publications, 2006) is one exception. For a critique of their work see B. Fanning, Against the 'Racial State', *Studies: An Irish Quarterly Review*, Vol. 96, No. 381, March 2007.

33 K. Polyani, *The Great Transformation* (Boston: Beacon Hill, 1944).

34 See J. Searle, *The construction of social reality* (London: Penguin, 1995). For a more insightful and sociological discussion of the self-referentiality of institutional facts see Barnes, Social life as a boot-strapped induction, *Sociology*, 17 (1983), pp. 524–45.

35 J. Berger and J. Mohr, *The Seventh Man* (London: Penguin, 1975), p. 8.

36 See N. Elias, *The Society of Individuals* (Oxford, Blackwell, 2001).

37 *Getting On: From Migration to Integration, Chinese, Indian, Lithianian, and Nigerian Immigrants' Experiences in Ireland* (Dublin: Immigrant Council of Ireland, 2008). Research for this report was carried out by 12 researchers in teams of three which included a lead researcher, a UCD doctoral student and a community researcher. Research among Chinese migrants was led by Alice Feldman (UCD), supported by Diane Nititham and Hong Liu. Research among Indian migrants was led by Steve Loyal (UCD), supported by Nanette Schuppers and Jophy K. Cherian. Research among Lithuanian migrants was led by Mary Gilmartin (NUI Maynooth), supported by Jane-Ann O'Connell and Donata Leahu. Research among Nigerian migrants was led by Bettina Migge (UCD), supported by Theo Ejorh and Susan Okigbo. The final report was written by the 4 lead researchers.

38 The emotional equation of greater power with greater human value is not new as Elias points out. See N. Elias and J. Scotson, *The Established and Outsiders*, p. 29. The increased level of economic and power resources and national standing in the European and global economy provided the basis for a significant process of national re-imagining and a more positive we-image of Irish-ness to develop than had hitherto existed during the 1980s.

Chapter 2

The history and theory of migration

This chapter begins by providing a historical account of migration in order to demonstrate the long-term nature of migration, to show the wide varieties of migration, and to illustrate both the continuities and discontinuities in patterns of migration. The second part of the chapter then examines how migration has been theorized. It argues that many of the theoretical approaches to migration have significant insights yet remain flawed in various ways either because of their ontological presuppositions or for ideological reasons. Nevertheless, a synthesis of some of the most important insights is possible within a more reflexive sociological approach. This synthesis is facilitated by an examination of interviews with non-Irish nationals who migrated to Ireland.

A short history of migration

The number of recorded international migrants is growing rapidly. In 1960 it was estimated that there were 76 million international migrants. By 2000 this had reached 175 million so that 1 in every 35 people on earth was an international migrant.[1] According to the UNHCR there are currently approximately 200 million migrants constituting roughly 3% of the world's population.

Because of the low levels of social scientific detachment characterizing the study of migration, how migration is theorized, conceived, and explained has tended to follow the predominant processes of migration extant at the time, or be adversely shaped by changing state evaluations, representations, and constructions of migration. A methodological tendency to focus on short-term processes and to generalize from single case studies has meant that long-term historical and comparative analyses of migration that allow a broader focus for understanding human movement have generally been sidelined in favour of what Wittgenstein calls a 'one-sided diet'.

Migration in history

Although processes of migration are considered the exception within the context of a global modern nation-state system, they were for a long time the rule. William McNeil (1979) has persuasively argued that when our ancestors first became fully human they were already migratory. Having left what is considered humanity's cradle-land – tropical East Africa – and moving first to the Near East and eventually to Oceania, it is believed that the great migration was completed by 8,000 BCE. Around 11,000 BCE peoples on all continents were still hunter-gathers.[2] Moreover, much early agriculture was itself migratory – slash and burn – and included the development of pastoral nomadry from about 3,000 BCE.

However, it was in Western Europe from the 16th century onwards that migration began to play a significant role in global processes of modernization and industrialization. In Europe, as Marx notes in his discussion of primitive accumulation in *Capital*, the dissolution of feudal relations of personal domination in which individuals were tied to the land promoted the migration of labour from rural to urban areas.[3] Migrants subsequently moved from cities across national borders. Even today cities are used by rural migrants as springboards for more far-reaching forms of international migration.

From the end of the Middle Ages, the development of European states and their colonization of the rest of the world under capitalism gave a new impetus to international migrations of many different kinds. The enslavement and deportation of conquered people was a frequent early form of pre-capitalist labour migration, and colonization is itself a largely overlooked form of migration in which the spread of economic power and political influence abroad is consolidated. As Lydia Potts (1991) has shown in her remarkable book, the development of slavery, the coolie system, and indentured workers generated huge population movements from Latin America, Asia, and Africa both before and after the onset of capitalism.[4] Between 1509 and 1519, for example, 60,000 Indians were forcibly transported from the Bahamas to Hispaniola under Spanish-American colonial rule to be deployed in gold and silver mines that constituted the backbone of the Spanish empire. Mortality rates were extremely high with only 800 of these Indians still living by 1519.[5]

During capitalism, and especially between 1700 and 1850, the enslavement of African peoples was the main method by which European societies appropriated foreign labour power for their colonies in order to meet labour demand. Although formerly abolished in the UK in 1807 and in the USA in 1865, African slavery continued to expand in the 19th century, reaching its peak between 1832 and 1862 where slave labour became synonymous with a plantation economy and the production of agricultural goods including tobacco, rice, sugar, and, importantly, cotton. When the transatlantic slave trade ended it had produced the largest 'forced' migration in the history of the world. African labour power was deployed with considerable variation and levels of intensity in the Caribbean, Brazil, and the Southern states of the USA. Estimates of the number of slaves imported into North America range from 10 to 20 million.[6] The total number of Africans affected including all those who perished during slave raids or transportation is thought to be between 40 and 200 million. The British slave trade in the West Indies was equally profitable. The income Britain received from trading in the West Indies was estimated to be as much as 4 times higher than the income it gained in its trade with the rest of the world.[7]

The expansion of capital, trade, and goods between 1820 and 1914 engendered a second period of extensive migratory movements. Two distinct, though tangentially connected, movements are of note: the emergence of what Potts calls a 'coolie system' in which labour moved predominantly from India and China to work on various estates and plantations; and the movement of approximately 52 million workers from Europe to America and Oceania between 1820 and 1932.[8]

As Steinfeld (1991) has demonstrated, there are significant theoretical and historical problems with making sharp conceptual and historical distinctions between free and unfree labour, consensual and non-consensual manual labour, slavery, indentured servitude, and free labour.[9] In contrast to an ideal typical and discursive notion of a progressive unfolding of individual rights, freedom of movement, and ability to sell labour power, capitalist social formations have persistently used slave or constrained forms of labour power in their development.[10] Corrigan (1990) has argued that ascriptive forms of constraint, and non-wage forms of coercion, are not 'feudal relics' but actually increase with the expansion of capitalism.[11] Mixed forms of labour regime that include slavery, bondaged workers, and capitalist labour still exist today though the proportions of these different labour forms vary geographically.

Under the coolie system workers were transported long distances by employers under a multiplicity of binding contracts which were juridically enforceable. Coolie labour from India, China, Japan, Java, and Oceania working in poor conditions was used in America and the Caribbean, South Africa, Mauritius, Australia, as well as in other British colonies. About 30 million Indian workers left their country as coolies to work on European colonial plantations working as indentured labourers in the Empire.[12] Though predominating as a system of labour recruitment in India another 5–6 million Chinese, Japanese, and Melanesians were employed as coolies. The colonial state played a central role in recruiting this subaltern labour supply, often rationalizing the system via various religious and moral arguments.[13]

Following the European division of Africa between colonial powers after 1884, the slavery and the coolie system were superseded by colonially 'forced labour' from Africa deployed in plantations, ranches, and mines. Exceptionally high mortality rates were not infrequent. For example it is estimated that 8 million people were killed in the rubber plantations in the Congo Free State, then under Belgian rule, over a 25-year period from 1885.[14]

The interlocking of several processes during the 19th century also led to an increase of labour movement within Europe, the USA, and Oceania. These included rapid industrialization; population growth following improvements in health and nutrition; the growth of transoceanic shipping and transatlantic railways; and the rapid reduction in transport costs between 1820 and 1860. In contrast to previous forced migrations, which frequently employed physical force and violence, these migrations were engendered by endogenous economic processes. It is estimated that about 52 million Europeans migrated to various countries in the Americas between 1820 and 1932, with 32 million going to the USA and a further 3.5 million going to Australia and New Zealand.[15] Between 1820 and 1914, approximately 25.5 million people from various European countries including Great Britain, Germany, France, Italy, and also Russia, emigrated to the USA as it underwent industrialization.[16]

Migration also increased dramatically within Europe during the 19th century. There were more than 700,000 Irish in England in 1851. Approximately 1,127,000 people from Belgium, Spain, and Italy registered in France in 1886. They were joined by migrants from the Maghreb, who were employed in building the Paris Metro, or working in the mines in the North or in various industries in Marseille.[17] The number of foreign workers in Germany rose sharply following the formation of the 1871 Empire. Though employers required cheap and willing labour in the Prussian East, fears that this would lead to political destabilization ensued. Weber talked about the 'Polinization of the East' of 'Ruhr-Poles' working in coal-mining and agriculture.[18] By 1910 there were 1.2 million foreign workers employed in the German Empire, working in virtually every sector of the German economy.[19]

However, following this unprecedented period in the free movement of goods, capital, and labour, more and more countries began imposing restrictions on immigration by the end of the 19th century. Further restrictions ensued with the First World War. A relative decline in the numbers of global migrants during the inter-war period and during the Great Depression ended with the onset of the Second World War. Germany used Jews, gypsies and Romanies, and prisoners of war, many from Russia, as slave labour in factories. It also drew upon forced recruitment in France, Belgium, and Holland so that by the end of 1942 almost 6 million slave labourers and prisoners of war were working for the German war economy.[20]

The huge displacement of populations engendered at the end of the war meant something in the order of 4 million migrants resettling in the USA, Argentina, Brazil, Israel, Canada, and New Zealand, another 1 million in

Europe, as well as significant numbers in Africa and Asia. The consequences of such mass displacement were consolidated by shifts in geo-political power crystallized in Bretton Woods and during the Cold War. Decolonization and the formation of new states such as Pakistan also led to large population movements.

Following the Second World War Western European states reintroduced large-scale foreign labour recruitment to aid capitalist reconstruction. Germany, Belgium, Switzerland, the Netherlands, Sweden, Luxembourg, and the UK all introduced formal recruitment programmes, drawing on a Southern European reserve army of labour to bring in an estimated 13.5 million foreigners.[21] Colonial ties brought Turkish workers to West Germany; Algerians, Tunisians, Portuguese, and Moroccans to France; and Indian, Caribbean, Pakistani, and Irish workers to the UK. Emblematic of this recruitment process was the German *gastarbeiter* system, which facilitated, by the state, established recruitment programmes with Italy, Spain, Turkey, Morocco, Portugal, Tunisia, and Yugoslavia during the 1950s and 1960s.[22] Here, as elsewhere, state policy conceived of migrants as temporary labour units that could be utilized during periods of economic expansion and disposed of when no longer required. Temporary visas placing stringent restrictions on labour market access and conferring minimal civil and political rights were issued to migrants. However, following the onset of recession in 1973 and a freeze in labour recruitment, few of the almost 2.5 million foreign workers recorded in the German State, especially those from Turkey, were willing to return. They had instead become permanent settlers. Although recruitment programmes were suspended, high levels of family reunification – with women and young and older family members arriving – dramatically altered the demographic composition of the migrant population. Between 1974 and 1988 the number of Turks in Germany doubled. Self-enclosed 'Turkish communities' – socio-economically marginalized and disenfranchised – remain to this day.

The end of large-scale labour migration following the 1970s recession, and the resultant extensive restructuring of the world economy, had a profound effect on the subsequent pattern and modality of migration. Increasing capital exports and a broad move to services from a manufacturing base in many developed countries saw a decline of labour recruitment in Western Europe. In such a context a relative shift in capitalist demand from generic foreign labour to specific types of skilled labour also took place. A diversification and widening in international migration saw former emigration countries on the periphery of Europe, such as Italy, Spain, and Portugal, become countries of immigration while the number of migrants from Asia, Africa, and Latin America increased markedly. At the same time oil-rich Middle Eastern countries began recruiting unskilled workers during the OPEC boom. These workers were initially recruited from neighbouring Middle Eastern and Arab countries, including Egypt, but later from the Asian continent – India, Pakistan, Sri Lanka, and

Bangladesh. Dubai for example, where 90% of the current labour force are foreign workers, operates on the basis of a remarkably static hierarchic caste-like division overseen by an absolute monarchy. Populated by an enormous marginalized foreign underclass from India, Pakistan, and Bangladesh, many immigrants from these countries work in almost indentured conditions.[23]

The end of the Cold War had a further dramatic political and ideological effect on the perception and conceptualization of migration. With the dissolution of former Soviet states another modality of migration – those applying for asylum or refugee status – began to predominate. In addition to increasing the politicization of migration, Western states stepped up immigration restrictions, thereby unintentionally creating and generating a further socio-political category of 'illegal' migrants.[24]

Theorizing migration

Migration is a generic concept covering a wide variety of complex, multilayered processes entailing human movement and involving economic, political, social, and cultural aspects. There has, however, never been a straightforward definition of the term. The number and type of processes covered under the term have diversified. In addition, increasing globalization has meant that the geographical range of countries and continents from which and to which migrants move has also expanded. Former countries of emigration have become countries of immigration, while the size of the movement from the South to the North of the globe has grown considerably. Since the 1960s, for example, net migration from developing countries within Asia, Africa, and Latin America to European and OECD countries has trebled.[25] In 2009 about 70 million international migrants moved from a developing to a developed country.[26]

Given the intensity and breadth of global communications and networks of modern transportation links, it is remarkable that only 3% of the world's population migrate. This is even more surprising in an increasingly globally unequal world where it is estimated that the richest 20% of the global population receives 80% of all income while the poorest 20% receives just 1%. The vast majority of the world's population therefore tend to live and die within the narrow geographical zone within in which they were born. This restriction is not simply explicable in terms of restrictive borders. Despite the championing of free movement within the EU a mere 2% of Europeans lived in another EU state prior to EU expansion in 2004, and even after accession only 1 in every 175 EU accession state nationals moved to another EU country. Rather this phenomenon highlights the importance of peer context, ethno-cultural familiarity, and perhaps most importantly, something often unstated: the rootedness and disposition of individuals to remain within their family or group context.

The acute absence of a comprehensive theoretical framework to account for and explain the reasons people migrate is one of the most glaring deficits characterizing the whole field of migration theory. Instead, a variety of divergent conceptual and analytical frameworks co-exist. These are often rooted in entrenched disciplinary divisions in the social sciences – between anthropologists, sociologists, demographers, geographers, economists, historians, and political scientists.[27] But equally others are a product of political and ideological world-views. Moreover, explanations of migration have generally proceeded through various problematic conceptual and methodological dichotomies, many of which have reproduced and reconfigured debates concerning micro–macro, agency–structure, hermeneutical–causal, ideal/cultural–political/economic explanations.

In his analysis of the laws of migration, E. G. Ravenstein provided perhaps one of the earliest modern approaches for explaining migration.[28] Drawing on census data, Ravenstein outlined 11 major principles of migration. These included that: migrants preferred to travel short distances; those travelling long distances usually moved to centres of commerce or industry; the natives of towns were less migratory than those of rural areas; women migrated more within their country of birth, and men outside their country of birth; migration increased in volume as industries and commerce developed and transport improved; and that the major causes of migration were economic. In terms of the latter, Ravenstein noted that there were many reasons for migration: 'Bad or oppressive laws, heavy taxation, an unattractive climate, uncongenial social surroundings, and even compulsion (slave trade, transportation)… [but] none of these currents can compare in volume with that which arises from the desire inherent in most men [sic] to "better" themselves in material respects.'[29]

Ravenstein's arguments have been highly influential in the field of migration.[30] The economic basis of migration constitutes the central platform from which rational-choice accounts of migration have developed. Central to the rational-choice approach is the figure of *homo economicus* – an independent individual, with a fixed preference schedule, rationally weighing the costs and benefits of leaving one area to move to another in order to maximize his or her utility. The choice is primarily based on whether the immigrant will gain higher economic returns in the country of destination. Such models, incorporating a balance-sheet of opportunity matrixes, are often, though by no means necessarily, associated with a push–pull framework whereby the causes of migration are seen as a combination of push factors impelling people to leave their areas of origin, and of pull factors, attracting them to other countries. Push factors in the country of origin may include excessive demographic growth, low living standards, lack of economic opportunities, and political repression; while pull factors in the destination country include demand for labour, availability of land, good economic opportunities, and presence of greater political freedoms.[31]

Although rooted in economics, where the construction of predictive models of migration is pervasive, the approach retains a position of orthodoxy in the field of migration generally. Employed by political scientists, policy-makers, the media, and – because of its proximity to 'common sense' – the general public, the model possesses a near-universality in government immigration policy. Its validity and popularity are partly based on the self-evident and platitudinous truth it reveals: that individuals move in order to acquire more money.

The plethora of problems associated with atomistic and individualistically inspired approaches to the social sciences – whether they derive from Schumpeter or Weber's methodological individualism, neo-classical marginalism, or from rational choice theory – have been widely acknowledged by sociologists. Explanations based on the ontology of the individual are politically loaded, de-historicized characterizations that overemphasize the actions of rational, self-interested, individuals. Such models ignore the social, historical, and political structural factors that influence and shape individuals' actions and decisions. Their image of the human is of *homo clausus,* of a 'closed off' individual, rather than *homines aperti* as socially interdependent, and as wholly rational and without emotive content.[32] Because of its abstract nature the rational choice approach also fails to analyse the ways in which individuals are positioned in various ways. Individuals are subject to various socio-economic determinations so that they embody specific roles and statuses in society that provide them with different forms of power, outlook, and capabilities shaping whether or not they migrate, and the modality of their migration.

By contrast, more structurally inclined approaches have rightly emphasized more macro causes for migration, and simultaneously emphasized the importance of power relations. Linking immigration to the structural requirements of modern industrial economies where the pull factors include economic, demographic, and social developments and push factors comprise unemployment, poverty, and underdevelopment, the macro needs of the capitalist system for labour power are identified as playing a central role in engendering migration.[33] A broad-based focus on state-mediated global political economy and the relationship between labour migration and capital accumulation is fundamentally necessary for understanding any contemporary process of migration. The state plays a vital role in organizing labour migration not only by recruiting workers, but also in the political and legal sphere by conferring differentiated residence and status rights facilitating their expulsion once they are no longer required during recessionary periods. Structurally oriented approaches are not all cut from one cloth. Marxist interpretations of migration, which emphasize the economic needs of capital and the reduced costs of reproducing labour power, have often been conjoined with a world system theory approach that emphasizes the unequal distribution of geo-political power across nations. The logic of capitalism, it is argued, not only perpetuates inequalities but, following the penetration of developed capitalist economic relations into essentially traditional pre-capitalist economies, engenders emigration from less developed economies into more developed countries. Since the cost of educating the migrant worker is met by the sending country, this constitutes a further source of income transferral and of 'brain drain'. Hence, for example, 30% of doctors educated and trained in Ghana, at considerable cost, have moved to the USA, Britain, Canada, and Australia. As a result Ghana only has 6 doctors per 100,000 of its population as compared to a figure of 220 per 100,000 people characterizing the latter countries. There are currently more Ethiopian doctors practising in Chicago than in Ethiopia, and more Malawian doctors practising in Manchester than Malawi.[34]

Historical-structuralist approaches have in turn been criticized for their use of functionist explanations that pay scant attention to individual motivations. Teleological explanations in which capital requires a reserve army of labour attribute social systems with purposes, whilst ignoring the intentionality and hermeneutic standpoint of actors. There remains 'a conceptual discontinuity between the units of analysis (systems of production and associated classes) and that which is being explained (the movement of people)'.[35] Moreover, some structural accounts have difficulty with accounting for non-economically motivated forms of migration. This includes asylum-seekers and those migrating to be reunited with family members, especially since in Western industrialized countries, family reunification is arguably the most prevalent form of migration.

Despite their different presuppositions, moral framework, first principles, and levels of analysis, both rational choice and historical structuralist approaches share some theoretical and empirical limitations, though significantly less so in the latter's case. Both approaches are often framed according to political and metaphysical concerns, rather than scientific or empirical criteria. In addition, they suffer from inadequately conceptualizing the appropriate balance between free and determined action or agency and structure. Microeconomic approaches have overemphasized the importance of individual agency, presupposed an overly knowledgeable actor, and similarly painted actors as exclusively self-interested. Conversely, historical-structuralist theories have exaggerated the power of social structures and global economic forces in generating and determining migration. The question of agency also plays a central role in delimiting the categorization of different types of migration. Thus, for example, Petersen talks of 5 broad classes which he designates as primitive, forced, impelled, free, and mass migration:

> In primitive migrations the activating agent is ecological pressure, in forced migration it is the state or some functionally equivalent social institution. It is useful to divide this class into impelled migration, when migrants retain some power to decide whether or not to leave, and forced migration, when they do not

have this power. Often the boundary between the two, the point at which the choice becomes nominal, may be difficult to set. Analytically, however, the distinction is clear-cut, and historically it is often so.[36]

A dualism is similarly prevalent in the pervasive distinction between economic migrants and asylum-seekers that has its roots in state classifications. It expresses the political-economic division that Marx identified as a central feature of modern capitalist society wherein civil society ceases to be directly political. People's different material positions no longer coincide with their differentiated political powers or statuses as they had, for example, under feudalism. The political sphere comes to represent the sphere of universal and general interest where fundamental individual rights are enshrined. By contrast, the economy, as part of civil society, comes to represent the site of contingency and accident, a private matter and sphere of freedom – the freedom to sell one's labour power, own property, etc. Discussions about agency and structure, free and voluntary actions are also integrally linked to moral discussions about conferring and attributing responsibility to actors for their actions.[37] Underlying the asylum-seeker/economic migrant distinction is a morally loaded agency/structure binary that attempts to account for the motivations of the migrants or more broadly how the act of migration should be conceptualized and evaluated in terms of assigning responsibility.

People who leave their country of origin for reasons of political persecution are said to be 'pushed', or forced to leave whereas people who leave for economic reasons or the attraction of the destination country have chosen to do so or are 'pulled'. These assumptions, which are reproduced in a number of theories of migration, media discourses, and political speeches, allow the possibility of assigning responsibility (and blame) in evaluating an individual's reason for migrating. Although central to state thinking, such an evaluative moral framework has also been adopted and reproduced by those sympathetic to migration as indicated by journals such as *Forced Migration* that are concerned largely with asylum issues.

However, the sharp distinction between asylum-seeking and economic migration is flawed in a number of respects. Not only does it take the division between the economy and polity as a de-historized fact, but the construction of

Political Sphere	Economic sphere
General concern	Particular concern
Causal universal processes	Accidental, contingent processes
Institution of causal connection	Institution of responsible action

Figure.2.1 The political and economic sphere and migration

what constitutes 'constraint' or 'forced' action is ideologically loaded. Economic migration can also be seen to take place within certain constraints including poverty, and the need to work in order to subsist. Rather than talking of free and forced migration (or even free and forced labour) it may be more useful to talk of differentially constrained forms and institutions of migration (and labour).

One way of transcending the agency structure dualism characterizing the sociology of migration is to begin with an ontology based upon the category of *social* human beings. There is therefore an urgent need to reconceptualize and understand migration by emphasizing the fundamentally social nature of humans, but in a way that recognizes the importance of economic, status, and even emotional forces playing a role in explaining it. Network theories of migration that have looked to social networks, the household, and family context as important frames within which the decision to migrate has been made are especially useful.[38] Membership in networks includes ties of kinship, community, friends, strong and weak acquaintances that create migration streams and migration chains. The choice of destination for migration, for example, though economically structured, is strongly based on historical and colonial ties between countries. For example, Irish missionaries sent to Nigeria working as teachers or founding schools and churches provided early forms of contact with a number of Nigerians who subsequently migrated to Ireland or came as asylum-seekers.[39] Behind the vast complex multiplicity of individual migrations social network theory alerts us to the distinct patterns in which certain groups from certain countries or regions migrate to a specific range of destinations in other countries. Almost 40% of the population in the town of Gort arrived from one village in Brazil, Vila Fabril, where the meat industry went into decline whilst meat plants in Gort suffered acute shortages of workers. Networks facilitate migratory processes by decreasing the risks and costs of moving and offering a support network that provides specific and detailed information and practical knowledge about the types and availability of jobs, wages, conditions, and accessing accommodation in the receiving country.

The existence of migration chains and migration paths between determinate sending and receiving countries implies that broad macro economic and material processes inducing migration are always and everywhere mediated by smaller-scale social networks, as well as geo-political ties, and transport and communication links. This means that we simultaneously need to recognize both the micro and the macro context of migration.[40] The explanatory role of social connections is by no means always secondary; in some instances it plays a bigger part than economic criteria in determining certain types of migration such as, for example, family reunification. Hence, the abstract sociological obsession with adjudicating whether the individual or the social being provides the ground for empirical study often hides the crucial driving role that family plays both in social life generally and in determining the shape and nature of migration.

Migrants often make their decision in the family context, under family moral and emotional pressure, or because of the economic necessity to send remittances to family members. The rationale to leave or stay in the destination country is shaped by their family and material circumstances. In addition, social networks sensitize us to the continually expanding and self-perpetuating nature of migration processes. For example the first wave of Cantonese-speaking Chinese nationals who arrived in Ireland almost half a century ago were predominantly from Hong Kong, then part of the British Empire. Largely concentrated in the restaurant sector, they provided a context within which a more recent second wave of Mandarin-speaking nationals – usually students from mainland China (and predominantly the Fujian and North Dahlian districts) came to Ireland, often to work in these restaurants.

Network approaches, have, however, for the most part continued to operate with a rigidly rational actor at their core rather than profoundly social, mutually susceptible, individuals. And although there has been some recognition of the importance of status competition and distinction as a factor in explaining or shaping patterns of migration, it has, on the whole, been absent.[41] Such approaches have also generally downplayed geo-political power structures and capitalist economic processes that foreground the mobility of capital and class inequality in an unequal global order. The inequalities between advanced capitalist societies and developing societies, between the North of the globe and the South, are vast and are growing, especially within an increasingly interdependent global economy. In the modern context Bretton Woods institutionalized what Trotsky called 'combined and uneven development'. The structural adjustment policies (SAPs) and fiscal discipline including devaluation, privatization, enforced shrinkage of the public sector, and the ending of subsidies and protectionist tariffs, imposed by the International Monetary Fund and World Bank during the 1980s, produced further inequality between developed and developing countries by under-developing the latter. 'An economy', as Berger notes, 'is underdeveloped because of what is being done around it, within it and to it.'[42] Not only have such SAP policies led to the rise of what Davis calls 'Megaslums' in which more than 1 billion of the earth's urban poor live in slums at the edge of Third World cities, but they have precipitated massive forms of rural–urban migration.[43] Yet, it is important at the same time to note that the vast majority of these impoverished masses of migrants cannot afford to participate in international migration and also have limited international social networks.

Taken together, the different explanatory frameworks discussed above have, with different frequencies, all provided important insights into why and how people migrate. They point to more complex processes than are acknowledged in the majority of rational choice approaches or push–pull frameworks. As Massey *et al.* acknowledge in their review of the various theories:

> It is entirely possible that individuals engage in cost–benefit calculations; that households act to diversify labour allocations; and that socio-economic context within which these decisions are made is determined by structural forces operating at the national and international levels. Thus, we are skeptical both of atomistic theories that deny the importance of structural constraints on individual decisions, and of structural theories that deny agency to individuals and families.[44]

Which of these forces is in operation or the dominant variable accounting for why an individual migrates is an empirical question.

However, many of these theoretical frameworks also problematically employ state concepts and arguments in their discourse. The enormous power of the state is not only external and objective but, through its imposition of classifications, equally internal and subjective: it works through individuals. Rather than looking at humanity as a whole, or looking at a global interstate system as the framework for interpreting migration, the focus of sociologists has generally been on a specific nation conceptualized as co-extensive with society. Such an erroneous correlation has long been questioned in sociological analysis generally,[45] and more recently characterized as 'methodological nationalism.'[46] This nationally reductive focus has a number of implications that have been rightly criticized by Abdelmalek Sayad (2004).[47] It is impossible, Sayad argues, to write an adequate sociology of immigration without simultaneously outlining a sociology of emigration: the two components form 'indissociable aspects of a single reality'.[48] In order to have a greater understanding of migration, he argues that we need to understand the contradictions and cleavages of the sending societies. This is also in terms of the early socialization experiences of the migrants which are so important in structuring their subsequent life. As Berger writes:

> To try to understand the experience of another it is necessary to dismantle the world as seen from one's place within it, and to reassemble it as seen from his [sic]. For example to understand a given choice another makes, one must face in imagination the lack of choices which may confront and deny him. The well-fed are incapable of understanding the choices of the under-fed. The world has to be dismantled and re-assembled in order to grasp, however clumsily, the experience of another. To talk of entering the other's subjectivity is misleading. The subjectivity of another does not simply constitute a different interior attitude to the same exterior facts. The constellation of facts, of which he is the centre, is different.

However, he adds:

> One must interrogate his situation to learn about the part of his experience which derives from the historical moment. What is being done to him, even with his own complicity under the cover of normalcy?[49]

An understanding of the country of origin of the migrant as well as his or her country of reception not only avoids a residual ethnocentrism in which it is implied that an immigrant's life begins when he enters the host nation, but facilitates an account of migration which avoids yielding to a problematic in which the adaptation of the migrant to the host society is prioritized. Sayad (2004) has also usefully highlighted the need to understand processes of migration in terms of power relationships, not only between the emigrant and the receiving state, but, importantly, as inter-state relations that bear the imprint of past relations of colonialism – as for example an Irish cleaner and her English employer working in the UK.

Ideologically loaded state categorizations and differentiations of migration simplify the interpretation of the complexities of social and political life. Despite the plethora of complex and opaque reasons that people have for migrating, including making money, leaving a politically unstable area, studying, experiencing a different culture, or joining a family member, these reasons are transformed and funnelled into a limited number of official and state-designated categories and channels which constitute the only acknowledged and classifiable forms of entry.

Accounting for the reasons why people migrate not only entails subjecting state thought to critical scrutiny, it also involves examining the social conditions in which the analyst or researcher constructs and imposes his or her interpretations on the phenomenon. The imputation and avowal of motives by migration experts are social phenomena themselves that need to be explained. The attribution of motives depends upon the existence of socially accepted vocabularies of motives which vary historically, but also across cultures, social structures, and across situations within given cultures.[50] Hence, if we look at the USA historically, religious motives have gradually become replaced by 'individualistic, sexual, hedonistic, and pecuniary vocabularies of motive'.[51] Similarly, the rise of Freudian and Marxist theories of imputation which posit unconscious drives or economic motives to explain action, themselves needs to be explained.

We can illustrate some of these theoretical concerns by examining the concrete experiences of Lithuanians, Nigerians, Indians, and Chinese nationals who came to Ireland. In research undertaken by the Immigrant Council of Ireland, a diversity of reasons were given for migrating that varied according to national, class, status, and gender backgrounds. A distinction, however, needs to be made between the rationales given and what people actually do. Migrants' accounts should not be taken uncritically, and in some ways the reasons they proffer constitute a new speech-act separate from the act of migration itself.[52] As one Lithuanian respondent pertinently remarked:

> Everybody analyses the reasons why people left, right? And this reason has to be a trigger for you to go, right? Let's call that trigger the money thing. And everyone kind of goes for the money. But when people settle down and start living in Ireland you start establishing the real reason why people really left their

country and went to Ireland. Because the reasons seem to be different after a couple of years and you realize the money might have been the trigger but the real reason was that you were either looking for adventure or you were looking for a different environment or you were bored with what you were doing with your life or maybe you wanted to challenge yourself. You know, these kind of personal subconscious reasons come out after you settle in the country and start living the quality life. (Anna, Lithuania).

Though the rationalizations and accounts that migrants in Ireland gave were diverse and varied, they could be reduced to several categories including predominantly to work but also to reunite with other family members; to acquire skills, including language skills, to be used back in their country of origin; students talked about getting a summer job to fund future travel or pay for their studies; and some also talked about coming to Ireland for a change of lifestyle.

Responses varied according to nationality and legal status. However, with the exception of Chinese respondents (83% of whom stated they primarily arrived for education and training compared to only 22% of Nigerians and 10% of Indians), the vast majority came to work. When asked whether they had any contacts prior to arriving in Ireland, over half of all Lithuanians and more than one-third of Indians and Nigerians, and nearly 40% of Chinese, had contact with friends already in Ireland at the time of their arrival.[53] These reasons were elaborated upon in interviewees and we can take Lithuanian migration as an example. Although the first group of Lithuanians to arrive in Ireland were probably the Lithuanian Jews arriving at the turn of the 20th century, the majority arrived after 2004. Given the stagnant economic conditions following Lithuania's entry into a market economy, many came to Ireland to get jobs or higher wages: 'Back home there are no job opportunities, I can do more here' (Petras, Lithuania). However, others also came to send remittances to family members, save enough money to start a business back in Lithuania, get work experience, learn English, join family members, or simply experience other ways of living: 'I just wanted to see different countries I said because I was young and I was full of power and could do lots of work and I said I want to try to go to another country for probably 2 years and then go to a third country and after that come back to the homeland and then to work for 5 to 6 years' (Renate, Lithuania).

Their decision to come to Ireland was not only a consequence of the access provided to accession workers to live and work in the UK, Sweden, and Ireland, but also shaped through formal recruitment programmes set up by companies based in Ireland, such as McDonalds or Tesco, who placed adverts in Lithuanian newspapers as part of a strategy of acquiring labour. The Irish government was also keen to recruit people through trade fairs, for the expanding IT sector but also for au pairs, bartenders, and service workers. In addition, recruitment agencies in Ireland and Lithuania – such as the World Lithuanian Agency – played a significant role in recruiting workers or at least encouraging them by advertising various job opportunities in Ireland. Hence, if a migrant did not know about Ireland as a destination before, they were made aware of it by various companies and agencies that encouraged them to travel there for work. Prior to May 2004, many Lithuanians appear to have travelled to Ireland alone. After that date an increasing number came with families and from a slightly older age cohort. Arriving with partners or their families partially abated the loneliness and dislocation: 'it made it easier to come with someone' (Jurgit, Lithuania). One couple who had been offered a job by a Lithuanian friend managing a petrol station noted: 'many people come and hope to find a job, we couldn't do this' (Laura, Lithuania). Given the financial cost, including paying agency fees, moving to Ireland was a risk for many who came and it was a bigger risk for those who didn't have a job prior to arriving: 'I just came, it was a risk because it involved a lot of money, not only the ticket which was quite expensive but also the rent, the deposit, everything, moving in buying basic stuff you will need' (Marius, Lithuania). 36% of Lithuanians had a definite job offer prior to arrival, but 41% also noted they came just for the experience of living in Ireland. The initial limited social network played a crucial role in their migration, providing invaluable support and information and introductions to broader social networks of Lithuanians. The development of commercial air transport links – Aer Lingus, Ryanair, and Air Baltic all currently offer direct flights to Vilnius – in reaction to consumer demand was also an important factor in facilitating the growth in Lithuanian migration. The promise of the city for earning a living also often served as a stepping stone for rural Lithuanian migrants before they travelled to Ireland.

Conclusion

Why people migrate is a central question in the study of migration. However, finding an answer to what appears to be a simple question is difficult given the long history and diverse forms of migration that have existed. There are and have been many reasons why people have migrated. At the level of tautology it could be argued that people migrate in order to improve their living conditions.

Broad generalizations, however, tend to be of little empirical value. Each country of migration experiences migration in a different way and even within countries and regions there can be stark differences. Yet there are, nevertheless, some universal global mechanisms operating in these particular processes. Global economic inequality, socio-political instability, unemployment, and hardship provided the context for a significant number of migrants who came to Ireland.

However, social networks, the premium placed on maintaining the family as a material, social, and emotional unit in lesser individualized and poorer countries societies, has also been an important factor shaping migration. Hence, although many migrants left their countries to find work, an equally large number did so to join family members. In 2004, for example, labour migration only accounted for more than 40% of immigration in a handful of OECD countries.[54] Most forms of migration into Ireland became mediated by social networks which provided information about jobs, travel, or evading administrative traps, as well as offering material and socio-cultural support. When these became consolidated they constituted self-sustaining and expansive entities. Current migration can therefore be seen as being shaped by material and cultural processes: economic forces, government policy in terms of migration laws and policies, political events, social networks, colonial history, geography, and family ties.

Given the diverse variety of forms of migration and range of explanatory variables available, a general theory of migration capturing the full complexity of migration may not be possible. Instead what can be provided is a loose, non-reductive, and flexible theoretical framework centred on social individuals variously positioned and connected in specific cultural and material contexts. In this framework the decision of an individual to migrate needs to be placed simultaneously within the context of a world economic system that produces social conditions leading to emigration, but also a geopolitical framework and family and network context. The explanatory weight of each of these factors varies depending on the empirical case at hand. Given the high level of migration initiated by the Celtic Tiger boom, it is clear that economic factors played a major role in generating migration. However, in the context of the recession family reunification issues may become equally as important.

Notes

1 World Economic and Social Survey, *International Migration* (New York: UN, 2004), p. 25.
2 J. Diamond, *Guns, Germs and Steel* (London: Vintage, 1998), p. 16.
3 K. Marx, *Capital* (London: Penguin, 1976).
4 L. Potts, *The World Labour Market* (London: Zed, 1991). The following account draws heavily from her book.
5 Ibid., p. 15.
6 Ibid.
7 Ibid., p. 45.
8 World Economic Social Survey, *International Migration*, p. v.
9 J. Steinfeld, *The Invention of Free Labour: The Employment relation in English and American Law and Culture, 1350–1870* (Chapel Hill: University of North Carolina Press, 1991).

10 For a discussion see R. Cohen, *Migration and its Enemies: Global Capital, Migrants and the Nation-State* (London: Ashgate, 2006); and J. Steinfeld, *The Invention of Free Labour*

11 P. Corrigan, Feudal relics or capitalist monuments? Notes on the sociology of unfree labour, in P. Corrigan, *Social Forms/Human Capacities* (London: Routledge, 1990), pp. 54–101.

12 L. Potts, *The World Labour Market*, pp. 68–70; H. Tinker, *Banyan Tree: Overseas Emigrants from India, Pakistan and Bangladesh* (Oxford: Oxford University Press, 1977).

13 Cohen, *Migration and its Enemies*, p. 25.

14 E. Morel, *King Leopold's Rule in Africa* (New York: Funk and Wagnalls, 1904), p. 237.

15 World Economic and Social Survey, *International Migration*, p. 3.

16 L. Potts, *The World Labour Market*, p. 131.

17 Ibid., p. 134.

18 See Klaus J. Bade, From emigration to immigration the German experience in the nineteenth and twentieth centuries, p. 10, in K.J. Bade and M. Weiner (eds) *Migration Past, Migration Future* (New York: Berghan Books, 1997), pp. 1–38.

19 Ibid.

20 L. Potts, *The World Labour Market*, p. 140.

21 Cohen, *Migration and its Enemies*, p. 46.

22 S. Castles & M. Miller, *The Age of Migration* (London: Palgrave, 2009).

23 See J. Hari, The dark side of Dubai, *Independent*, Tuesday 7 April 2009.

24 A. Geddes, *The Politics of Immigration and Migration in Europe* (London: Sage, 2004).

25 UNDP, *Human Development Report 2009* (Geneva: UN, 2009).

26 Ibid.

27 C. Brettell and J. Hollifield, Migration theory, in C. Brettell and J.Hollifield (eds) *Migration Theory: Talking Across Disciplines* (London: Routledge, 2000) pp. 1–26.

28 E. Ravenstein, *The Laws of Migration* (New York: Arno Press [1885: 1887], 1976).

29 Ibid., p. 286.

30 E. Lee, A theory of migration, *Demography* 3: (1966) 47–57; A. Zolberg, The next waves: migration theory for a changing world, *International Migration Review* 23:3 (1989).

31 Castles and Miller, *The Age of Migration*.

32 N. Elias, *What is Sociology?*, p. 125.

33 N. Harris, *The New Untouchables* (London: Penguin, 1995).

34 P. Legrain, *Immigrants: Your Country Needs Them* (London: Little Books, 2007), p. 186.

35 C. Wood, Equilibrium and historical-structural perspectives on migration, *International Migration Review*, 16:2 (1982), pp. 306–7.

36 W. Peterson, A general typology of migration, *American Sociological Review* 23: (1958), p. 258.

37 B. Barnes, *Understanding Agency* (London: Sage, 2000).

38 For example the decision-making model has been modified in the work of the 'new economics of migration', which focuses on the family as a decision-making entity rather than an individual agent and which incorporate the idea of risk rather than simply aggregate income as a crucial factor in the decision to migrate (Stark and

Bloom, 1985). This is equally the case in some network theory approaches (R. Bach and L. Schrami, Migration, crises and theoretical conflict, *International Migration Review*, 16(2) (1982) pp. 320–41; D. Massey, R. Alarcon, J. Durand, H. Gonzalez, *Return to Aztlan* (California: University of California Press, 1987); D. Massey, J. Arango, G. Hugo, J. Taylor, Theories of international migration: a review and appraisal, *Population and Development Review* 19 (1993); D. Massey, J. Arango, G. Hugo, J. Taylor, An evaluation of international migration theory: the North American case, *Population and Development Review* 20 (1994).

39 'The Irish people who came to Nigeria lived an exemplary life. You couldn't fault them… And they always told us that Ireland was a country of the welcomes. So we always had it at the back of our minds that, if we ever had a cause to live abroad, it was going to be in Ireland, the country that these wonderful people came from. So it was a conscious decision to come here. We worked towards that' (Akun, Nigeria).

40 R. Collins, On the micro foundations of macro sociology, *American Journal of Sociology* 86 (5) (1981).

41 The one exception, and perhaps the most systematic attempt to emphasize the social nature of humans and their pursuit of strategies of honour as an integral part of the migration process, is found in the work of A. Sayad, *The Suffering of the Immigrant* (Cambridge: Polity, 2004).

42 J. Berger & J. Mohr, *The Seventh Man* (London: Penguin, 1975) p. 21.

43 M. Davis, *Planet of Slums* (London: Verso, 2007) pp. 23, 25–6, 48.

44 Cited in Cohen, *Migration and its Enemies*, p. 130.

45 N. Elias, *What is Sociology?*; M. Mann *The Sources of Social Power, Volume 1* (Cambridge: Cambridge University Press, 1986).

46 A. Wimmer and Glick Schiller, 'Methodological nationalism'.

47 A. Sayad, *The Suffering of the Immigrant*.

48 Ibid., p. 1.

49 Berger, *The Seventh Man*, pp. 93–4.

50 C.W. Mills, Situated actions and vocabularies of motive, *American Sociological Review*, 5, pp. 904–13 (1940).

51 Ibid., p. 910.

52 Mills, Vocabularies of motive, p. 901.

53 Although most of those surveyed travelled to Ireland alone, including around 50% of Indians and Lithuanians, nearly 80% of Chinese, and almost 70% of Nigerians.

54 T. Shelley, *Exploited: Migrant Labor and the New Economy* (London: Zed Books, 2007), p. 19.

Chapter 3

The state of migration and the bureaucratic field

This chapter examines the role of the state in constructing and regulating migration. It begins by analysing how state policies in relation to migration are not fixed or clear-cut but rather shifting and contradictory. Both state laws and policies and state forms of classification have significant impact on migratory processes. The second part of the chapter looks at the bureaucratic impacts of differentiated state forms of classification on the everyday lives of immigrants.

A productive side-effect of interrogating immigration processes is that it provides a shorthand introduction to the sociology of the state. The contours and nature of the state, however, remain highly disputed. Certain features of the state become magnified when dealing with immigration. Modern democratic states are complex and contradictory entities. States are simultaneously capitalist states, nationalist states, and liberal states. It is in the shifting balance between these various political logics – *liberal democratic* (including international human rights), *capitalist* and *nationalist* (including maintaining social order) in relation to immigration that modern states express their symbolic and material relations.

The classical sociological theorists all provided penetrating, though selective, insights into the state. For Durkheim, the state was above all an 'organ of social thought' elaborating definite representations for the collectivity: 'the special organ whose responsibility it is to work out certain representations which hold good for the collectivity.[1] It both partially constituted society's sentiments and ideals, the moral order, and reflected the universal interests of those over whom it governed by promoting moral individualism. For Weber the state was able to claim a monopoly of legitimate violence with the aid of a regularized administrative staff as well as a paid army over a delimited territorial area. As he added: 'the modern state is a compulsory association which organizes domination'.[2] Marxists have been more concerned with the economic functions of the state as a relation of production, distinguishing between its ideological appearance as serving the general interests of society as a whole, and its essential relations that function to promote the specific needs of the bourgeoisie. Its repressive aspects geared towards the maintenance of social order and property have also been acknowledged.

These three classic sociological conceptions of the state point to a central dilemma. The state remains recalcitrant to any tightly constructed conceptual or functional definition. Modern Western democratic capitalist states carry out a multiplicity of tasks in addition to their political function of governing and the production of legislation, and these include binding rule-making, maintaining security, sustaining international relations (including warfare), and the regulation of the market and labour power. To rephrase this when taking migration as our object of analysis, modern states are at once liberal democratic, nationalist, and capitalist states. Weber recognized this diversity in state functions when he noted that that there were no activities that the state had not been involved in 'from the provision of subsistence to the patronage of the arts'.[3] The problem of achieving an adequate working definition of stateness is further exacerbated by four factors:

1 the possibility of defining a state in terms of either its institutions or its functions;[4]
2 the historical shift in the nature of the state so that modern states have relatively little in common with traditional states other than a shared nomenclature;
3 the constitutive power of state thinking forms a doxa – providing unquestioned and implicit background assumptions and categories framing the analysis. The fundamental dilemma confronting the sociology of the state is to analyse the state without *uncritically* or *unwittingly* deploying the nation-state's own categories, schemes of perception, ideology, and structuring principles;[5]
4 the shifting relation between state and capital.

State formation has to be intrinsically linked to broader social processes including the development of capitalism and class formation. Historical discussions of state formation do shed further light into the structure of its modern practices. As Tilly notes:

> The singling out of the organization of armed forces, taxation, policing, the control of food supply, and the formation of technical personnel stresses activities which were difficult, costly and often unwanted by large parts of the population. All were essential to the creation of strong states; all are therefore likely to tell us something important about the conditions under which… states come into being.[6]

The socio-genesis of the absolutist state entailed a monopolization of the means of violence and taxation that played a central role in modern state formation. A virtuous circle in which greater pacification facilitated trade and economic growth, in turn underpinning the economic and military power of a central authority, accelerated the concentration and consolidation of state power. The broad-based collection and concentration of taxes led to a shift away from what Anderson calls 'parcellized sovereignty' to the development of an increasingly unified territory both in reality and in the consciousness of members within the state.[7] A key aspect of this process included the formation of a rationalized administrative apparatus in the towns, and a corresponding increase in the power, intensity, and reach of the state.

States have both material and ideological aspects. The 'objective' institutional features of the state, which includes the civil service, the government, the legislature, judiciary, the police, the army, the courts and prisons, schools, the welfare state, and various authorities that administer the life chances, and shape the destinies, of those within its territorial area through their *practices*, need to be conjoined with the symbolic and ideological role of shaping and constituting people's social identities, and their thinking. In shaping people's ways of thinking, acting, and feeling, the state has a symbolic and expressive dimension, as well as a materialist and instrumentalist one. Social structures, as Bourdieu points out, exist in both the 'objectivity of the first order', constituted as objective social positions and in 'the objectivity of the second order', in the form of systems of classification, and subjective bundles of dispositions and cognitive schemata which inform people's thoughts, feelings, and conduct. Social divisions are therefore inscribed in both the material order vis-à-vis differential distributions, and in the symbolic order, through discourses and cognitive classifications. Discourses and schemes of classification, through the fostering and reproduction of restricted narratives of ethnic and national identity and nationalism, but also through the codification, the collection, control, and storage of information as a means for monitoring and regulating a circumscribed population, become instilled in individuals and in their practical relation to the world. As Bourdieu notes:

> An exploration of objective structures is at one and at the same time an exploration of the cognitive structures that agents bring to bear in their practical knowledge of the social worlds thus structured. Indeed there exists a correspondence between social structures and mental structures, between the objective divisions of the social world – especially the division into dominant and dominated in the different fields – and the principles of vision and division that agents apply to them.[8]

The state accomplishes three functions through its official institutional discourse:

> firstly; it performs a diagnostic function, that is, an act of cognition which enforces recognition and which quite often tends to affirm what a person or a thing is and what it is universally, for every possible person, and thus objectively. It is an almost divine discourse, which assigns to every one an identity. In the second place, the administrative discourse, via directives, orders, prescriptions, etc., it says what people have to do, given what they are. Thirdly, it says what people really have done, as in authorised accounts such as police reports. In each case, it imposes a

point of view, that of the institution, especially via questionnaires, official norms. This point of view is set up as a legitimate point of view, that is, as a point of view which everyone has to recognise at least within the limits of a given society. The representative of the state is the repository of common sense.[9]

Thus states have monopolized not only physical force, taxation, and the means of movement, but also the legitimate use of symbolic force, including the power to name, to categorize, and to define objects and events. The power of state nomination allows the state to create social divisions, to reify individuals, to shape people's social destinies, and to reproduce their social identities, including their national identity. Official state categorizations constitute both the different legal status of migrants in terms of rights, usually defined in contrast to citizens but also how both the indigenous population and migrants perceive themselves and others. Through nomination the state consecrates social divisions between citizens and aliens, nationals and non-nationals, economic migrants and asylum-seekers, and EU and third country nationals in both the objectivity of material divisions and the subjectivity of cognitive schemas and classifications. The state's monopoly of the official definition of identities shapes group life chances so that 'the fate of groups is bound up with the words that designate them'.[10]

As the dominant force in the field of power, and controlling the field of the nation and citizenship through legislation, the state assigns identities, authorizes accounts, and actively encourages some forms of social life and thinking whilst downplaying and repressing others. Through legislation and social policies, states attempt to define and sanction acceptable types of social behaviour and activity, including migratory behaviour. This ability to regulate social life also depends in part upon the state's capacity to sustain and impose categories of thought through which institutions and individuals make sense of the world. These three functions for Bourdieu presuppose the state being able to produce and impose categories of thought, which are subsequently applied to the social world. It is a form of 'world-making'[11] Political struggle is therefore a cognitive struggle for the power to impose the legitimate vision of the social world – that is, the power to (re)make reality by establishing, preserving, or altering the categories through which agents comprehend and construct that world.[12] The state therefore provides categories and accepted ways of thinking that people, including government bureaucrats, administrators, doctors, politicians, the media, NGOs, employers, and migrants inherit and necessarily make reference to, thereby recursively reproducing the classificatory system.

All states classify and assign migrants into specific legal and political categories – or differentiated immigration statuses. These categorizations have profound effects on the lives of the migrants. They raise the problem of representing migrants and immigrant experiences outside of these categories. Processes of official classification condition the level of entry for all migrants as well as the variations within each of the immigrant status categories, they reify individuals, and shape how migrants are seen by others and see themselves. As a social fact immigration can only be grasped and interpreted through categories of state thought which operate with a distinction between citizens and others. As Sayad (2004) notes:

> It is as though it were in the very nature of the state to discriminate… to make the distinction, without which there can be no national state, between the 'nationals' it recognizes as such and in which it therefore recognizes itself, just as they recognize themselves in it (this double mutual recognition effect is indispensable to the existence and function of the state), and 'others' with whom it deals only in 'material' or instrumental terms. It deals with them only because they are present within the field of its national sovereignty and in the national territory covered by that sovereignty.[13]

Official classificatory schemes are not neutral taxonomic forms representing the world but arbitrary divisions that have evaluative judgements inscribed into them. The socio-genesis of some of the most salient historically constituted and acquired categories is rooted in Irish legislation and policy documents, in state bureaucratic circulars, and in legal discourses. It is with and through these classificatory divisions incorporated in everyday thought and action, and in and through the minds of specific actors, that migration becomes interpreted, perceived, and actualized in practices.

The Aliens Act of 1935 instituted a grounding constitutive binary division between 'citizens' and 'aliens' wherein the word 'alien' referred to a person who was 'not a citizen' and not entitled to be within the state without permission. The 1935 Act did not explicitly or comprehensively discuss the status of non-citizens or aliens in the Free State and not every non-Irish national was defined as an 'alien'. Within the context of complex relations with Britain, and the establishment of a Common Travel Area, the Irish State exempted UK and some Commonwealth states nationals from the restrictions imposed on those deemed to have alien status.[14] Following the introduction of the Irish Nationality and Citizenship Act of 1956, the citizen–alien binary became supplemented and reworked through a further legal state binary distinction between 'nationals' and 'non-nationals.' The latter was defined as 'a person who is not an Irish citizen'.[15] Supporting earlier normative and performative oppositions a further constitutive and regulatory classificatory operational division came into force after Ireland's entry into Europe in 1973 with the creation of a central division between EU and non-EU (or EEA) nationals within the broader national/non-nationals dichotomy. Finally a further paired qualifier for migration arose after the accession of new states in May 2004 with a categorical differentiation between EU15 members and EU10 states. The development and increased circulation and use of these binary oppositions saw a mixing of political-legal distinctions between citizens and aliens, legal distinctions between asylum-seekers and economic migrants, geographical distinctions between EU and non-EU, all overwritten and associated with colour-codified and racially hierarchized populations.

Individuals are defined by the state, as Marx noted in his characterization of feudalism, 'in a narrowly national, religious or political determination.[16] The state allocates a highly differentiated hierarchy of rights and entitlements to migrants by assigning various immigration statuses.[17] Though the content of citizenship has changed over time, and has become increasingly 'emptied' in modern neo-liberal states in terms of the substantive meaning of rights, the concept still serves as the basis for rights and entitlements in the state. Citizenship is a social status that provides access to a broad range of rights and resources thereby functioning as both a medium and outcome of social closure by the state.[18] These rights and resources include access to a complex array of civic, social, political, and economic rights, and even intangibles such as a feeling of belonging or collective identity.[19] Materially and politically they include: access to social welfare, to education, to fair treatment in the labour market and workplace, to social services including the health service, the right of residence, as well as the right of individuals to vote, to have family members live with them, and to be treated equally and free from discrimination generally.[20] Rather than providing all residents with the same civil, political, social, and economic rights state bureaucratic classification schemes discriminate and empower in different ways. These statuses have considerable effect in shaping both the migrants' objective position in social space, and their own self-perception. This is not merely an ideological imposition but rooted in the body and the unconscious. It is about 'everything that native insertion into a nation and a state buries in the innermost depths of minds and bodies, in a quasi-natural state, or in other words far beyond the reach of consciousness'.[21] 'The power of naming transmutes or reclassifies the person named, functioning almost as a rigid designator shaping his or her life chances. So that the fate of groups is bound up with the words that designate them.'[22] From its vantage point the Irish State assigns each group its place in the social order.

Thus, the Irish State has constructed and affirmed a restricted number of channels permitting the entry of non-Irish nationals to enter, live, and work in Ireland and reinforced these through the employment of saliently defined social and categorical boundaries. However, these formal categorizations tied to legal and migrant status are not exhaustive in fully determining the treatment and life chances of migrants in Ireland. Ethno-racial domination and racism also play a key role. Nevertheless, legal status plays a central role in structuring an individual's social trajectory. Immigrant status is used by Irish state service providers as the basis for making judgements about individual entitlements to social, political, and economic support. These differentiated categories in turn enter public consciousness as key categories for seeing and perceiving the social world. It is important to note however that in practice there is no clear-cut dichotomy between citizens and non-citizens in Western immigrant states but rather a continuum, with different legal statuses conferring different rights to different categories of migrants sometimes referred to as 'denizens'.[23]

All EU citizens and European Economic Area (EEA)/Swiss nationals (excluding those who joined the EU in 2007 from Romania and Bulgaria) are entitled to unrestricted access to live in Ireland for the purpose of employment or self-employment, or if they are financially self-sufficient.[24] In the context of an acute labour shortage, Ireland, together with the UK and Sweden, was one of the few EU states to allow EU10 nationals to work and reside immediately following accession in 2004. Consequently, unlike a great many other European states, the majority of non-Irish nationals in Ireland were from the EU. According to the 2006 Census, they constituted over 65% of immigrants in the country. EU migrants have similar rights to Irish citizens. They and their family members can work and reside indefinitely within the state. However, they cannot vote in national elections unless they are nationals from the UK. Their access to social welfare is also restricted by the Habitual Residence Condition. Paradoxically, they have an additional right to Irish citizens – all family members of EU workers can join them to live with them. Paradoxically, Irish citizens, if they have non-Irish national family members who want to live with them, must apply to the Department of Justice, Equality and Law Reform (DJELR) for Ministerial discretion.

By contrast to their broad-based rights, all individuals from non-EU countries have more restricted forms of entry through various migration mechanisms that stratify their access to the labour market and their residential and welfare rights. Non-EU nationals can enter through various legal channels including the work permit system, the green card system (formerly the work visa/authorization system), intra-company transfer system, student visa system, and the asylum system. The rights these statuses confer constitute a bewildering and ever-changing complexity of entitlements that few people, including most state officials and bureaucrats in Ireland, fully understand or comprehend. The principal means for non-EU nationals to enter Ireland to work is through the work permit system. Work permits were initially renewable on an annual basis and residence stamps had to be acquired every year. They were non-transferable and tied to specific jobs. The employer had to pay an application fee of €500 but this was usually passed on to the employee. A labour market test meant that employers had to demonstrate that it had not been possible to fill the vacancy with indigenous labour or with EEA workers by advertising the post through FAS or in a newspaper for at least 3 days. Spouses of work permit holders were not allowed to work. The Department of Enterprise Trade and Employment (DETE) could take about up to 2 months to process a permit.

Following February 2007, permits were issued on a bi-annual basis and either the employee or the employer could apply for them. If this was the first work permit the employee had to stay with the employer for at least 12 months. Spouses of work permit holders could now apply for a spousal/dependant work permit. After 5 years permit holders were eligible to apply for long-term residence. Work permit holders could also apply to INIS (Irish Naturalisation and Immigration Services) to have their family join them after 12 months as long as they demonstrated sufficient supporting income.

A further legal immigration mechanism, aimed specifically at recruiting skilled migrant workers, was introduced in 2000. Migrants coming through a work authorization/work visa system were given more flexibility than work permit holders. Work visas/authorizations were issued for 2 years and allowed the employee to move jobs within a specified sector. Holders of work visas were permitted to apply for family reunion after 3 months and those on work authorizations, immediately. After February 2004, spouses of workers under the work visa/authorization scheme, especially nurses, had a right to work. Spouses have to apply for a work permit but they do not have to pay the €500 permit fee.

Following the publication of the Employment Permits Bill in 2006, the work authorization/visa system became replaced by what was designated a 'green card system'. Under this scheme a green card would be granted to the employee for an initial period of two years after which time it would 'normally be renewed indefinitely'. Green card holders do not have to undergo a labour market test. The fees for the green card – €1,000 for a new permit and then €1,500 for an indefinitely renewable permit issuable after a two year period – were to be paid by the applicant. Application for the green card was restricted to certain occupations with a requisite salary level. First, those earning over €60,000 or more in all occupations were eligible to apply. Second, those earning between €30,000 and €59,999 in certain delimited occupations could also apply. No green cards would be issued for salaries under €30,000. Those on green cards who were on their first employment permit were not allowed to move jobs within the first 12 months other than in exceptional circumstances.

In addition to these 2 work-focused migration systems, individuals can also come through an intra-company transfer or a business permit system.

By contrast, asylum-seekers are not permitted to work. Those who arrived in the State after April 2000 are provided for through a system of dispersal and direct provision. Under this system they are housed around the country in hostels, prefabricated buildings, and mobile homes and receive €19.05 per adult and €9.52 per child per week in addition to the provision of fixed meals and basic accommodation. Their residence in the country is not tied to a visa but is renewable every 12 months. Those given refugee status have similar rights and entitlements to Irish citizens but they cannot vote and legally have 'no nationality'. They and their family members, however, do have a right to work. Individuals granted refugee status can be joined by their spouse and unmarried children under 18. However, if they apply for naturalization as Irish citizens they lose this right. Some asylum seekers can be given 'humanitarian leave to remain' at the discretion of the Minister for Justice, Equality and Law Reform if they fail to gain refugee status but have sufficient grounds for remaining in Ireland (for example, due to an illness or because their form of persecution is not covered by the Geneva Convention). Others can also be granted 'subsidiary protection' since Ireland's implementation of the Asylum Qualification Directive. Persons granted refugee status, subsidiary protection, or humanitarian leave to remain are normally given a 12-month residence permit, which is renewable.

An Irish-Born Children Scheme (IBC) was introduced following the Citizenship Referendum of 2004. In order to clear a backlog of applications, residency was granted to individuals who were parents of Irish-born children born before 1 January 2005. The residency rights of individuals who have IBC status are akin to those on humanitarian leave to remain but are reviewed after 2 years rather than 1. Immigrants who became parents of Irish-born children are allowed, and are in fact obliged, to work as they are required to become 'economically viable to remain in the state'.[25] Like the status of persons with 'leave to remain', the legal status of parents of Irish-born children is discretionary and remains uncodified, leaving migrants in an uncertain position about their rights.[26]

Non-EU migrants can also enter Ireland through student visas. Initially all could work in the State. However, after 2006 only students who were registered on a full-time course (i.e. non-language institute based students) were permitted to work for up to 20 hours during term time. Students have no statutory right to family reunification. Other non-EU migrants who do not have any of the above legal statuses and who are not tourists are categorized by the State as 'illegal' or 'undocumented' migrants. They have no *de jure* status and therefore officially have no rights or entitlements in Ireland. Informally, however, they may have access to emergency medical services.

The bureaucratic field

'In a modern state the actual ruler is necessarily and unavoidably the bureaucracy, since power is exercised neither through parliamentary speeches nor monarchical enunciations but through the routines of administration.'[27] The emergence and formation of a bureaucratic apparatus, as Weber noted, is integrally linked to state formation and state building which in turn was a constituent of part of a process of nation-building, capitalist production, class consolidation, and social domination. The rationalized state bureaucracy is a central part of the state institutional apparatus responsible for implementing public policies and achieving state goals. As a material expression of the state, and an outgrowth of politics, the bureaucracy implements state policies and serves as the main instrument for achieving and maintaining 'stateness' and reproducing and regulating nationalism and capitalist social relations.[28] However, though integral to state policy and a central aspect of its power configuration, the bureaucracy is nevertheless partly autonomous from various governments and politicians. Together with the drafting of government legislation and the implementation and interpretation of both legislation and policy, the bureaucracy functions as a central site for the production, affirmation, and interpretations of rules, jurisdictional areas, laws and administrative regulations, categories and classifications, and varied forms of discursive imagery used by the government and subsequently by people in everyday life. These latter discourses and categorical schemas are reproduced and amplified through the education system, political discourses, media, NGO reports, and filter into everyday life to become folk, or common-sense taken-for-granted schemas for perceiving and interpreting the world. They in turn become inscribed in the ways people think, act, and feel about immigration.

Bureaucracy in Ireland

The Irish State inherited the British State's highly centralized bureaucratic and administrative structures.[29] Unlike the British system, the Irish State lacks inter-departmental strategy units ensuring cross-cutting departmental policy-making. British State departments are also better staffed and contain various specialist agencies, facilitating policy implementation in the context of a predominantly cautious outlook by civil servants.[30] By contrast, the Irish bureaucracy has historically been characterized by a certain rigidity and ineffectiveness in adapting to social change. It constitutes a collection of administrative agencies operating in antagonistic cooperation. The uneven allocation of fixed governmental budget by the Department of Finance has further fuelled inter-bureaucratic competition for funds.

In order to provide a more nuanced and empirically accurate account of modern government and state policies and to try to account for the dualism of the state in terms of its repressive and penal aspect and its protective and social aspect, Bourdieu has introduced a distinction between the 'right hand' and the 'left hand' of the state that can be usefully adopted here. According to Bourdieu, government departments that have historically high levels of public spending, and which bear the trace of past social struggles, can be contrasted and be seen in competition with ministries involving fiscal and penal areas of government. The application of this viewpoint to the concrete practices of the Irish State has some explanatory utility. Various State departments can be placed on a political continuum ranging from the Department of Education, Social Welfare, Environment, and Health, constituting the 'left hand' of the state competing against Department of Justice, and Enterprise, Trade (DETE), the Department of Justice, Equality and Law Reform (DJELR) and Employment and Department of Finance on the right.[31] The ideological and material retreat from the state's social functions as guardian of the public interest with responsibility for social housing, universal and affordable health care, public transport, social inclusion, social support, and equality to the encouragement of private interests, private enterprise, deregulation, and fiscal and budget cuts follows the neo-liberal shift. The move expressed ideologically through a neo-liberal trope of no rights without responsibilities, and an exaggerated stress on economic and social individualism also indicates a remaking and reshaping of the state itself.[32] It is a process that has been for the most part consolidated under social partnership.[33]

If Bourdieu's political framework is accepted, the two core departments responsible for immigration in Ireland – the DJELR and the DETE – are both part of the right hand of the state. The DJELR has overall responsibility for national immigration policy, asylum, deportation, family reunification, residence, and naturalization and citizenship policy. And through the Garda National Immigration Bureau oversees the control of entry of migrants into the state, the duration of their residence, and, when necessary, their deportation. An insular, reactionary and xenophobic world-view, especially in its treatment towards outsiders trying to enter the state, has historically been institutionalized within the context of state partition. The DJELR's over-riding concern with national security, social order, and population control has meant that it historically has been anti-foreigner in its collective culture with its overall practices and organizational procedures embodying a form of 'institutional racism'.

By contrast, historically the central functions the DETE have entailed responsibility for facilitating the expansion of markets, regulating and supplying an adequate and requisitely trained workforce, fostering economic enterprise, and intensifying competition and productivity. Though the internal structures, cultures, and officers of this Department are diverse, the Department's *modus operandi* does nevertheless, coalesce around a narrow operational culture based on economic maximization. It has responsibility for issuing work permits, work visas/authorizations, and green cards. Its policies and industrial vision have been strongly shaped by external influences including membership of the EU and WTO and by the activities and needs of US multinationals.

Irish immigration policy has therefore essentially been a compound of these delimited and reactionary world-views: economic maximization and labour commodification combined with anti-foreigner sentiment, ethno-racial and cultural preference, and concerns about national security. They have been recently expressed in two central pieces of immigrant legislation: the Employment Permits Act of 2006 and the Immigration, Residence and Protection Bill. The first, compiled by the DETE, was concerned with acquiring a skilled labour force and accordingly calibrating the intake of migrant workers. The latter was concerned with regulating the State's borders and the provision of visas, instituting accelerated deportation procedures, and controlling migrant residence in the State. The different practices engendered by these divergent ideological world-views can at times cause tension or rifts between the two departments over the interpretation of immigration policy and its implementation in practice. This conflict arising from self-interested concerns is heightened by short-term policy objectives that lead to incoherent policy formation. However, although Bourdieu's analysis of the left and right hand of the state has some utility when the State is looked at at a concrete level of abstraction, it can exaggerate the way the State operates as a contradictory unity. Despite their different world-views the two departments share an overriding concern: providing a flexible, compliant, and disposable labour force for the expansion in the power of the Irish State.

Caught in an iron cage

Speaking of the highly centralized 19th century French State, and presaging Foucault, Marx noted that it 'enmeshes, controls, regulates, suppresses and regiments civil society from the most all-embracing expressions of its life down to its most insignificant motions, from its most general modes of existence down to the private life of individuals'.[34] Many non-EU migrants in Ireland find themselves enmeshed in a reifying, bureaucratizing, administered world. A strong populist nationalist ethos pervades the whole bureaucracy and its functionaries.[35]

In sociology no-one has produced a more powerful depiction of modern bureaucracy than Max Weber. Although Weber was correct in the general thrust of his discussion concerning the mechanization and impersonal character of bureaucratic work as the basis of a reorganization of the social habitus and 'the settled orientation of man', his analysis is inapplicable in two senses in the context of Irish bureaucratic domination. Firstly, Weber's description of modern bureaucrats as undertaking an 'exact execution of the received order, in which all personal criticism is unconditionally suspended and the actor is unswervingly and exclusively set forth carrying out the command' is overstated.[36] All organizations require a degree of flexibility to operate. Bureaucrats are not simply automatons that are part of a rationalized administrative machine strictly following orders based on rational principles, and bureaucratic rules are not formulas that bureaucrats can blindly follow on every occasion. No law or administrative circular relating to migration can stipulate what will occur in future cases and it is up to the bureaucrat to decide, within lesser or broader parameters set by ministers and general secretaries, how to apply these protocols on an ongoing basis. All rules have to be interpreted and applied 'creatively' in different contingently unfolding contexts on an ad hoc basis.[37] In addition, there is a considerable gap between what is formally declared to be policy and what actually happens: between what is said and what is done. Frontline bureaucrats have various levels of discretion in interpreting and applying on-the-ground state-level migratory policies formulated at an abstract level. This discretion is not only a power invested in the Minister of Justice in relation to granting naturalization, permitting family reunificaton, or granting 'humanitarian leave to remain', but also a power inscribed in lower level bureaucrats for processing migrant visas, work permits, GNIB cards and stamps, accessing social welfare, and allowing discretionary payments to asylum-seekers. However, the level and form of discretion have tended to vary within and between the two departments responsible for migration. The processing of work permits in the DETE up until 2004 at least largely occurred on a very liberal basis with very few applications rejected or refused. After this date the DETE became more restrictive and less flexible in its interpretation of whether an applicant met the necessary requirements for acquiring a permit. More recently, with the onset of the recession, the issuing of work permits has become even stricter. However, this policy has not been consistent. The DETE has often given permits to companies who have had problems recruiting indigenous workers, for example in the meat industry, even though those jobs were deemed ineligible for a permit. By contrast, and given its different ethos, the DJELR has generally been highly restrictive, inflexible, and illiberal in interpreting rules concerning the provision of visas, asylum applications, and residence permits, and in the issuing of GNIB cards.

Secondly, Weber is mistaken in his view that state bureaucratic interventions are inevitably connected to a process of democratization that involves the 'levelling of social and economic differences'.[38] Although bureaucrats may claim that their judgements are based on technocratic, abstract, and neutral principles, they are rarely unbiased or autonomous in the application of these rules and policy measures. Weber's claim that 'the "objective" discharge of business primarily means a discharge of business according to calculable rules and "without regard for persons"... in general, of all pursuit of naked economic interests', may be applicable on a qualified basis to the workings of DETE,[39] but it is less so with regard to the DJELR. The treatment of migrants does not follow rational abstract norms and principles of formal equality, but possesses a degree of selectivity and ad hocness based on 'doing business on a "case to case" basis' that discrimintates between migrants and renders them categorically unequal and results in their domination.[40]

For a non-Irish national entering Ireland as a migrant constitutes an insertion and encasement into an iron cage of bureaucratic processing that embraces and shapes their 'private life' and structures their life experiences. Different migrants have differentiated rights and entitlements that determine their access to resources and shape life chances within the state. Depending on their legal status the law can be everywhere for some migrants, permeating their daily existence. This is nowhere more apparent than in the provision of legal and residency status. Enmeshed in a complex web of rules the migrant, as a human being, with social and cultural needs, all but disappears in the conjoined world-views and practices of the DETE and DJELR entailing commodification and restrictions on movement. The discriminatory and arbitrary decision-making that migrants face from state departments and bureaucrats is bolstered by the fact that the latter are not covered by equality legislation. As depersonalized objects of policy and administration, migrants are reified through a powerful complex bureaucratic process aimed at maintaining control and regulating their presence and activities within the state. The effects of this bureaucratic processing can range from minor hindrances and irritations in waiting for GNIB stamps to be renewed, to profoundly humiliating and incapacitating experiences at airports. Two interrelated factors have determined this. Firstly, the operation of the frontline immigration system was in some senses deliberately made inaccessible and unresponsive in order to deter certain migrants, especially asylum-seekers, from entering the State. Secondly, however, the rapid increase in the numbers of immigrants conjoined with the State's unwillingness and reluctance to acknowledge that migrants would be arriving en masse and for a long duration meant that the State failed to employ or relocate sufficient numbers of staff in immigration services areas. Combined with a regular ad hoc change in rules and the introduction of more and more (often contradictory) circulars from the DETE and the DJELR, the immigration system is characterized by extraordinary levels of confusion. This has meant that the frontline system for dealing with GNIB cards, or asylum-seekers, visas, and naturalization has not only been discriminatory and arbitrary in its treatment of migrants but has also provided a very poor level of service.

Stamp collecting

The bureaucratic processing of non-EU migrants is evident in a number of areas, but is particularly pronounced in the issuing of stamps in residence cards. As part of its power of surveillance and control over non-Irish nationals, all non-EEA migrants not visiting as tourists must register with the GNIB within

3 months of arriving in Ireland. Immigration authorities, however, have the right to refuse stamps and to refuse the right of residence to certain categories of persons on a case-by-case basis. The migrant's papers are photocopied before a stamp outlining rights and entitlements is put in their passport, and a registration card containing their photo and stamp number is issued. The stamp number constitutes a material signifier of rights and status within the State. It represents a legible marker for the management of dispossessed categories in terms of juridical rights pertaining to duration of stay, access to work, family reunification, and access to welfare. Stamp 1 is given to non-EEA nationals on a work permit, on a green card, those who have been granted permission to operate a business in the state, and working holiday authorization holder. They are entitled to work but only on a temporary but renewable basis. Stamp 1A is given to a non-EEA nationals training as accountants who are ineligible to work in any other job. Stamp 2 is given to a non-EEA national attending a full-time course of study. The person can take up casual employment of 20 hours per week during term time and 40 hours during holidays but has no recourse to public funds and must leave by the specified date. Stamp 2A is given to a non-EEA national attending a course not recognized by the Department of Education and Science. The person cannot enter into employment and has to leave by the specified date. Stamp 3 is given to a non-EEA visitor, non-EEA retired person of independent means, non-EEA Minister of Religion and Member of Religious Order, or non-EEA spouse/dependant of employment permit holder. The person cannot work and has to leave by the specified date. Stamp 4 entitles the holder to work in the State without having to acquire an employment permit. Because of the high level of rights and low level of subsequent bureaucratization it entails, it is referred to by immigrants as 'the golden stamp'. Stamp 5 is for Irish citizens with dual nationality; and Stamp 6 is for those with indefinite leave to remain or 'without condition as to time' and is applied to a number of different migrant groupings within the immigration system.[41] As well as determining the migrant's subsequent life trajectory with reference to accessing the labour market, residential rights and welfare resources, the stamps also determine the degree to which the migrant becomes further enmeshed in a bureaucratic apparatus.

Although initially free, the GNIB began to charge €100 for registration after 2005, increasing payments to €150 after 2008. The GNIB card has to be renewed every year. For a family of 3 or 4 on a low wage this can be costly. Such fees have also proved lucrative for the State, contributing over €37,000,000 to its income. The payment of the fee, which bears no relation to administration costs when added to the long and frustrating process of queuing at GNIB offices, often led to resentment among migrants. As one interviewee commented: 'they start charging… for a GNIB card, €100, every time… So, it is more of like a money-making thing. So, they want to make money on your head and then still try to treat you shit' (Kumal, India). Another was not displeased at the charges per se but the poor service:

> I'm not complaining about how much the government are making per visa... I did pay at one stage €100 per visa and on average there are anywhere between 400 and 500 people everyday at the GNIB. Think I you can do the maths, it's very straightforward. So if they're getting that normally why don't they improve the service? Why don't they process more visas for people? There's one counter open and there's 20–30 people standing there. It's not that they don't have the infrastructure, they have 20 counters, out of that four are working, What happened to the other 16? Get the staff, get it working, they can well afford it (Inderjit, India).

Migrants generally lack the 'know how' that circulates in indigenous Irish social networks and rarely understand the rules governing various bureaucratic procedures. Together with language difficulties this can exacerbate tensions with frontline service personnel. Issues are further compounded by the length of time needed to process requisite papers, visas, cards, including queuing for services, and inconsistent advice from frontline staff and sometimes even racism. In one report 18% of those migrants who had contact with the immigration services reported being badly treated or receiving poor service, the highest level of discrimination for any state institution.[42] As one interviewee stated: 'I won't even like to mention it on a recording because I've had some of the worst behaviours of my life at GNIB actually. I mean I've been told by one officer at GNIB that I should be grateful that he is allowing me to stay here.' (Surinder, India). Others noted how the immigration system treated all immigrants as potentially 'illegal' or criminals: 'I think most of the Irish immigration system treats the immigrants as criminals... rather than welcomed' (Kumal, India). Moreover, before the opening of the Burgh Quay office, only limited numbers of GNIB cards were stamped each day meaning that migrants had to queue very early in order to get a number to be seen: 'When you're standing in the cold, I did that at one stage, I did that, yeah. I stayed with my friend in Dublin who just stays somewhere in Temple Bar, really close to GNIB, walked there at 3 o'clock in the morning. Stood there just for my written visa' (Surinder, India). Though other migrants have since recognized an improvement in the service:

> I can't be complaining most of the time, it's actually got better. Initially 7 years ago I've actually queued to get my immigration. I've actually had to queue from 2 in the morning to get an immigration slot here, and the immigration thing was only open from 8 to 12. And if you are around 100 in the queue they wouldn't even look at you... I've actually had to stand in the rain, cold, freezing temperatures, from 2 till 8 and then they're open. And then the re-entry thing and the immigration thing. It's changed completely, which is one great thing that has

happened. It was an absolute nightmare, I used to dread the time when we had to just go there (Suresh, India).

For some migrants, especially those who have to acquire an entry visa, the bureaucratic process begins even before they enter the country. Bureaucratic impediments vary from having to queue at GNIB offices which can take all day, to acquiring a travel visa, to the monthly delays in acquiring a work permit, a working visa, an entry visa, or to the 2 or 3 year wait for asylum applications, naturalization, or long-term residence. The question of delays is especially acute for those who are lonely and want family members to be with them. As one Indian national noted about acquiring a visa for a family member:

> They ask you for certain things and you provide those things and still tell you 'no'. In the case of people who apply for visa to visit Ireland, it is a nightmare most of the time. Three years ago my mother was twice refused an Irish visa to visit me. I had to get an Irish person to intervene before they could give my mother a visiting visa. What were they looking for? They were looking for a bank statement, which I had because I was working at the time. I had even bought a home at the time but my mother was still refused the visa. So the criteria are not really clear-cut. Many a time it depends on whom you meet at the counter... because we met 2 different people, the problem would be solved in two different ways... My own visa was delayed 6 months... It's a terrible process' (Inderjit, India).

Taken-for-granted activities such as travelling also become increasingly complex and difficult. For an Irish citizen to travel to France he or she simply needs to book a plane ticket and to arrive at the airport with a passport. By contrast a non-EU migrant is required to produce:

> a photo ID which costs €35, a re-entry visa to Ireland, a residence permit showing they live in Ireland, a Garda immigration card, travel insurance, confirmation of a hotel booking, a bank statement, a letter from their employer, and two pay slips. In addition the individual will have to take time off work to queue at the French embassy and the Department of Justice's Immigration and Citizenship division at Burgh Quay, which could take up to 8 hours.[43]

The State constitutes a structure of domination. Out of indivisible continuities and family resemblances between individuals the State constructs and imposes rigid classificatory divisions, primarily between citizens and aliens, but also other hierarchically ordered sub-divisions between migrants depending on geographical and ethno-racial and cultural criteria, and skill levels. These administrative divisions inscribed in classifications then become 'common-places' which are used by the State in various ways primarily to allocate rights. Such politically loaded classificatory schemas are not only reproduced and used by bureaucrats in their differential treatment of migrants, but can also be taken up by the indigenous population as frameworks for interpreting, defining, judging, and treating migrants in their interaction. Finally, migrants can themselves adopt these schemas as part of their self-definition, thereby solidifying and affirming these arbitrary and symbolically violent state designations.

The State finds itself in a contradictory position in respect of migrants. Despite a need to maintain a culturally and ethnically homogeneous population, immigration is economically necessary for the development of the economy. The Irish State's response to this dilemma – as we shall see in the rest of the book – has been to employ a cultural ethnic preference policy by allowing in predominantly white European accession state migrants while restricting the entry of non-EU nationals for highly skilled labour. However, for various reasons this has not always been possible in practice.

Notes

1 These representations are distinguished from other collective representations by their higher degree of consciousness and reflection; Durkheim, The concept of the state, in A. Giddens (ed), *Durkheim, Politics and the State* (Cambridge: Polity, 1996) p. 40.

2 Weber, Politics as vocation, in H.H. Gerth and C. Wright Mills (eds), *From Max Weber: Essays in Sociology* (London: RKP, 1970), pp. 77–128.

3 M. Weber, *Economy and Society: An Outline of Interpretive Sociology* (Berkeley: University of California Press, 1979), p. 54.

4 M. Mann, The autonomous power of the state: Its origins, mechanisms and results, *European Archive of Sociology*, XXV (1984), pp. 185–213.

5 P. Abrams, Notes on the difficulty of studying the state, *Journal of Historical Sociology*, 1:1 (1988), pp. 58–89; P. Corrigan and D. Sayer, *The Great Arch: English State Formation as Cultural Revolution* (Oxford: Blackwell, 1985).

6 C. Tilly (ed) *The Formation of National States in Western Europe* (Princeton: Princeton University Press, 1975) p. 71.

7 P. Anderson, *Lineages of the Absolutist State* (London: New Left Books, 1974).

8 P. Bourdieu, *Practical Reason* (Cambridge: Polity, 1998), p. 1.

9 P. Bourdieu, *In Other Words* (Cambridge: Polity, 1990), p. 136.

10 P. Bourdieu, *Distinction: A Social Critique of the Judgement of Taste* (London: Routledge, 1994), p. 481.

11 N. Goodman, *Ways of Worldmaking* (Indianapolis: Hacket, 1978).

12 In terms of the latter, the potential to impose a 'vision of divisions', is the, 'power of making social divisions and hence the political power *par excellence*' (Bourdieu, *Distinction*, p. 468).

13 A. Sayad, *The Suffering of the Immigrant*, p. 279.

14 B. Ryan, The common travel area between Britain and Ireland, in *Modern Law Review* 2001 64:6, November 2001) p. 862.

15 Ibid.

16 Cited in D. Sayer, *Capitalism and Modernity: An Excursus on Marx and Weber* (London: Routledge, 1991), p. 12.

17 Some of these migration statuses are likely to change with the enactment of the Immigration, Residence and Protection Bill 2010.

18 R. Brubaker, *Citizenship and Nationhood in France and Germany* (Harvard: Harvard University Press, 1992). As Joppke rightly points out, citizenship also provides a social identity. Citizenship between de- and re-ethnicization, *Archives Européennes de Sociologie* 44(3) (2003), pp. 429–58.

19 In his discussion of the evolution of the concept of citizenship, Marshall argues that the term can be usefully divided in terms of civil, political, and social rights. Marshall, *Citizenship and Social Class* (London: Pluto, [1950] 1987).

20 Although many migrants do not gain full formal citizenship, many still have access to some (though not all) important social and economic rights.

21 P. Bourdieu, Preface, in Sayad, *The Suffering of the Immigrant*, p. xiv.

22 Bourdieu *Distinction*, p. 481.

23 T. Hammar, 1990 *Democracy and the Nation State: Aliens, Denizens, and Citizens in a World of International Migration* (Aldershot: Gower, 1990).

24 In 2004, in order to prevent 'welfare tourism' the Government introduced the Habitual Residence Condition, which meant that an EU worker had to be in the State for 2 years before being allowed to access various forms of social welfare.

25 Immigrant Council of Ireland, *Family Matters: Experiences of Family Reunification in Ireland* (Dublin: ICI, 2006), p. 22.

26 Parents of minor Irish children or those on the Irish Born Child scheme can apply for family reunification but there applications are generally not accepted ICI, *Getting On*, p. 22.

27 Weber, *Economy and Society*, p. 1393.

28 O. Oszlac, State bureaucracies, in T. Janoski, R. Alford, R. Hicks, M. Swartz (eds), *The Handbook of Political Sociology* (Cambridge: Cambridge University Press, 2005).

29 A. S. Cohan, *The Irish Political Elite* (Dublin: Gill and Macmillan, 1972).

30 D. O'Brien, *Ireland, Europe, and the World: Writings on a New century* (Dublin: Gill and Macmillan, 2009).

31 Bourdieu, *Acts of Resistance* (New York: the New Press, 1999), p. 2.

32 L. Wacquant, *Urban Outcasts* (Cambridge: Polity, 2008).

33 K. Allen, *The Celtic Tiger*.

34 K. Marx *Surveys From Exile* (London: Pelican, 1973), p. 186.

35 R. Collins and T. Craddon, *Irish Politics Today* (Manchester: Manchester University Press, 2001).

36 Gerth & Mills, *From Max Weber*, p. 253.

37 As Wittgenstein notes in *The Philosophical Investigations,* the cumulative application of rules provides a precedent for future application, but it cannot determine it. *Philosophical Investigations* (Oxford: Blackwell, 1973).

38 Gerth and Mills, *From Max Weber*, p. 224.

39 Ibid., p. 215.

40 Ibid., p. 224.

41 It is applied to non-EEA family member of EEA citizen, non-EEA spouse of Irish citizen, refugee, non-EEA person granted family reunification under the Refugee Act, a programme refugee, long-term residents, persons on a working visa,

a non-EEA parent of Irish citizen child where parent was granted permission to remain in the State, non-EEA family member of EU citizen.

42 F. McGinnity, P. O'Connell, E. Quinn and J Williams, *Migrants' Experience Of Racism And Discrimination In Ireland: Survey Report* (Dublin: ESRI, 2006), p. 48.

43 Allen, K. *Citizenship and Racism: The Case against McDowell's Referendum* (Dublin: SWP, 2004), p. 9.

Chapter 4

State borders and boundaries

During the 18th century in a context dominated by mercantilist economics that associated a large population with greater economic growth and prosperity, European monarchs were more concerned about who was leaving their territory than who was entering it. Nowadays, of course, the opposite is the case. States invest considerable resources in developing infrastructure and strict surveillance measures designed to regulate borders and maintain sovereignty and control over the type and flow of non-national migrants entering their territory. For Davis, 'the Border, *strictu sensu,* is a state sanctioned system of violence: physical, environmental, economic, and cultural'.[1] State borders engender two important interconnected effects: symbolically they contribute towards the ongoing reproduction of nationalism and national identity, and materially they structure who will be allowed on state territory. Citizenship is involved in both processes. The construction of symbolic boundaries and material borders is an ongoing accomplishment that has shifted historically, and been shaped by a number of factors including inter-state relations, nationalistic self-understandings, technological innovations, and state power and world-view. More recently, a strong developmental spurt towards policing external borders has ensued, driven and determined by the USA, following 9/11.

State borders have determinate effects. Three Irish examples can illustrate this. In December 2001 8 Kurds hoping to seek asylum in Ireland died in a trailer in Wexford en route from Belgium. On a 53 hour journey they suffocated after they ran out of oxygen. Many of these migrants had solely aimed to start a better form of life, escape poverty, or send remittances. Though the traffickers are usually blamed, tight immigration and border restrictions mean that traffickers and smugglers – sometimes tied to criminal organizations – become necessary to facilitate the entry of migrants into Europe.[2]

A prominent Nigerian priest, who arrived in Ireland in 2008 on a tourist visa to visit his relative, was arrested by the Garda National Immigration Bureau for attempting to enter the country illegally through Dublin Airport. It was decided that he had given false reasons for trying to enter the State and he was taken to Cloverhill prison, strip-searched, placed in a cell with four other inmates,[3] and notified that he would be deported the following day. Since all his papers, including his visa, were in order, the decision to refuse permission to 'land' was based on two criteria. Firstly, the priest's response to questions concerning his relationship with the host who had invited him – whether he was his cousin or not – and secondly, the diminutive amount of luggage he had in his possession. After the Nigerian Ambassador intervened to clarify his identity the priest was released. The Minister of Justice defended his arrest and refused to apologize for the incident, arguing that the detention was justified since the State had complied 'with all the necessary legal and administrative procedures'.[4]

Borders have different meanings for different people. For the state and citizens they are a source of protection; for immigrants of exclusion and discrimination. Citizens can freely reside and enter and leave a territory. By contrast, those defined as 'aliens' or 'foreigners' are restricted in various ways in entering and residing in the state. Consequently, the meaning of borders diverges for both groups. For the former, borders are a 'gateway', a source of protection or security, whereas for all others they constitute a constraint or impediment preventing access to work or family reunification and therefore may be experienced as a state-sanctioned system of symbolic, cultural, and physical violence.[5]

These different perspectives can be illustrated in a third example, a case involving a Pakistani businessman in 2003. Having paid over €1,500 for a ticket and visa from the Honorary Consul in Karachi, a Pakistani businessman was refused entry by an Immigration Officer at Dublin airport in January 2003. Instead, he was arrested and taken to Mountjoy Prison and detained overnight in a holding cell with 3 others before being forcibly removed from the State. A refusal order that was stamped in his passport meant that he was further detained and interrogated for 4 days on his route back to Karachi in the UK and Kuwait. The businessman described the situation thus:

> Upon arriving at the Dublin Airport the Immigration Officer presented me a form to fill in where in one point was where to stay in Dublin: I replied 'Any suitable hotel'. The second question was any relative in Dublin? The reply was 'no'. He then verbally asked me to show him money if any. I presented £1100 on the spot for required 10 days. His attitude was harsh and without speaking anything he sent me to jail.[6]

The Immigration Officer saw the situation very differently. 'I found it very hard to believe that the subject was indeed a tourist. He had no contacts in Ireland and appeared to be at a loss to explain exactly why he is in Ireland.' He refused the immigrant entry because the individual had 'intent to deceive'. The officer also pointed to the fact that the person had not booked a hotel – though the immigrant claimed he could not do so because of a lack of credit card system where he lived. He was deemed to be entering the State for reasons other than those formally stated on his visa, that is, 'to see Ireland'.

Far from being exceptional, these cases are emblematic of anterior structural and historical processes concerning the maintenance of borders that have been in operation for a considerable time both in Ireland and elsewhere.

Border history

Contemporary migration is defined primarily by reference to the crossing of international borders by foreign individuals. As Zolberg notes, it is: 'the control which states exercise over borders that defines international migration as a distinctive social process.'[7] This conception has become so commonplace that its recentness masks two constituent aspects of the definition. Both national borders and their traversal by individuals are processes that emerged and developed within shifting contexts of social, economic, and political contestation. The construction of social space and spatial practices are, as Lefevre points out, an outcome of ongoing relations of political and economic domination, control, and power.[8] Both the free movement of individuals, firstly on a local, then on a national scale, and the ideology that accompanies this movement, were an outcome of long-term processes involving industrialization, and the rise of capitalism. Equally, the emergence of strictly defined national borders was inextricably linked to state formation, rising nationalism, and technologies of surveillance. Though separated here analytically, and expressing partly divergent logics that sometimes follow different historical trajectories, these processes also overlapped significantly and reinforce each other depending on context.

In the first of his ground-breaking lectures on migration given to the Royal Geographic Society in 1885, E.G. Ravenstein focused principally on the rural–urban movement of individuals. This correlation of migration with small-scale urban movement was not an anomaly. Rather, his analysis reflected the predominant nature of migration as intra-state movement that existed during the 19th century. International migration with the state playing a comprehensive role in controlling this movement did not emerge fully until early into the 20th century. However, administrative restrictions and blockages on the physical movement of individuals have existed for hundreds of years, finding expression in slave societies, the medieval world, and in modern times so-called forms of 'state socialism'. There were attempts to prevent international movement, especially against conquest, in early feudalism. According to Cohen (2006) the notion of the passport originated in the 11th century when 5 ports of exclusive entry were introduced following William the Conqueror's conquest of England, as an attempt by the latter to prevent others emulating his capture of the country.[9] However, the major focus of rulers during earlier periods of history was on the restriction of local movement. Attempts to regulate population movement during feudalism took place in societies predominantly rural and local in character, characterized by high levels of violence, and 'parcellized sovereignty', where functions of the sovereign state were 'disintegrated in a vertical allocation downwards'.[10] Although there was some variation within feudal (and absolutist) Europe characterized by uneven development, the tight administrative restriction on the movement of peasants between kingdoms and parishes under serfdom paralleled the physical restriction on movement that slaveholders had over their slaves. The denial of access to resources to those from the lower orders took place in several countries. In England, a statute of 1381 ensured that everyone needed a license to leave a kingdom with the exception of peers, soldiers, and certain merchants.[11] Such restrictions were redoubled during the 15th and 16th centuries with the development of poor relief systems such as the Speenhamland system designed to prevent the poor from moving to parishes offering this service. Elsewhere various edicts and laws in Prussia not only tied servants more firmly to masters, but prohibited the movement of 'masterless rabble' from the lower orders – including beggars, gypsies, vagabonds, and vagrants – or required them to have travel documents to pass through lands or from the countryside to the cities. In the USA, in *antebellum* Massachusetts where the poor were the responsibility of local towns, the increasing number of poor migrants also led to local legislatures issuing regulations preventing their settlement.[12]

State formation and centralization resulted from the centripetal forces unleashed by competition struggles between kings and local magnates. The development of a specialized and centralized state administrative apparatus for ruling was crucial in underwriting the collection of taxes used to finance a regular army, which in turn was used to collect more taxes in a virtuous circle. Over time various dominions became consolidated into an overarching singlular national-state enjoying a monopoly of coercion over a well-defined territory.[13] The shift from local territorial dominions to a national centralized state was to transform and dramatically lengthen the administrative reach of the state. The monopolization of the means of violence, internal pacification, and taxation that developed through the operation of a monopoly mechanism and state warfare also strengthened the state's claim to the absolute right to have a monopoly over the regulation of individual movement. In Western Europe, prior to the French Revolution, administrative restrictions on movement were part of the state's attempt to track and control their subjects in order to extract taxation, maintain social order, prevent access to poor relief or funds, and to have access to military conscripts.[14] Within the context of an expanding bureaucracy the increasing use of censuses and documents were integral to a state policy of increasing its surveillance capacity and control over the population, often to collect taxes. Examining an earlier period of history, Scott

(1998) highlights the connection between state-building and the invention of permanent surnames in 14th- and 15th-century England, allowing the state to keep track of the payment of taxes. As he notes, although the imposition of surnames dates back to the Qin Dynasty in China, such processes really got underway in Western Europe during feudalism: 'Many of the 14th century surnames were clearly nothing more than administrative fictions designed to make a population fiscally legible.'[15]

The poor increasingly became the responsibility of a nascent state increasing its administrative role vis-à-vis local authorities and thereby expanding its administrative jurisdiction and bureaucratic power. In addition to fiscal concerns, the poor constituted a threat to the social order and so, from the state's point of view, necessitated the imposition of restrictions on the movement of gypsies, vagrants, and demobilized soldiers. The inspection of documentation and the need to carry it also increased. It was also these oppressed groups who were predominantly stigmatized as outsiders. Thus in France, just before the Revolution, the term 'foreigner' largely referred to those outside the city trying to access poor relief.[16]

The formation of an increasingly central bureaucratic state over time also meant a shift in a preoccupation with movement between local jurisdictions, to a concern with movement across borders – outsiders of the interior became replaced by those from the exterior.[17] The shift from the local to the national regulation of movement, that is, a move in focus from the control of settlement in towns and urban spaces centred on class (and the undesirable poor) to a state preoccupation with nationality and citizenship, was not, however, a straightforward or sequential process. Rather, the two processes remain entwined. Concerns over class and poverty and rural migration were conjoined with those of nationality and citizenship. Hence, at a time when a weaker form of territorialization was prevalent during the 18th century, nearly all colonies in the USA were concerned about policing the entry not only of immigrants *per se* but of 'undesirable immigrants' – the dissolute, infirm, and older immigrants as well as rural migrants.[18] Such processes of state regulation have continued well into the early part of the 20th century.[19] European colonizers prevented the large-scale movement of the rural poor into cities by withholding substantive urban citizenship rights including land ownership and permanent residence. In East and Southern African cities various pass laws and vagrancy ordinances passed by the British penalized informal workers, while Africans in Nairobi, Dar-es-Salaam, and Lusaka could only enter as temporary labour before returning to their rural locales. A parallel disciplining of migration from the countryside took place in India, consigning these rural migrants into slums or shanty towns located on the peripheries of cities, making the British 'arguably the greatest slum-builders of all time'.[20] The French State equally prevented migrants in their African colonies having a 'right to the city', forcing them into slums such as Medina, Teichville, and Poto-Pot. Latin American countries imposed formidable, if less effective, restrictions on rural movement in Mexico and Venezuela just before and after the Second World War. East European Socialist states, with the partial exception of Yugoslavia, made placing institutional restrictions on geographical mobility a central part of state policy, until their domino-like collapse in the 1990s. More recently China has continued to impose severe restrictions on rural–urban migration. The *hukou* (household registration) system effectively functions as an internal passport system, and though restrictions have been partly loosened, over 140 million rural peasant migrants[21] working largely in sweatshops in Pearl River Delta, and in construction in Beijing and Shanghai, are believed to be part of a 'floating population' living on the fringes of cities with no entitlements to housing or state services.[22]

Early state forms had much lower levels of population penetration than modern states, which have greatly extended both the intensity and the scope of their surveillance capacities into the most intimate aspects of everyday life. The increase in surveillance capacity that occurred both in terms of the direct supervision of the activities of individuals, and in terms of the accumulation of coded information, has been central to maintaining and consolidating state sovereignty. National groups are not simply 'imagined communities' but are codified through documents indicating a person's nationality. As Gerard Noriel rightly claims, the material manifestation of modern citizenship and nationality is the passport.[23] Passports presuppose the establishment of bureaucratic control, surveillance, citizenship, and large-scale identification of individuals which allow states to differentiate and distinguish between citizens or subjects and outsiders on the ground. The institutionalization of the passport indicated both the consolidation of nationalism within a territorial state and the development of international cooperation between nation-states controlling the movement of mutually exclusive nationals.

Though passports and various documentary and identity papers to track and control citizens for taxation and conscription, and maintain social order, formally existed prior to the French Revolution, their requirement for travel was rarely implemented. Calls for the removal of passports in both France and Germany continued into the late 18th and 19th centuries, and for most of the latter, the passport was an irrelevancy. Restrictions on freedom of movement between states remained loose even in the 1820s and 1830s. It was not until the last quarter of the 19th century that the regulation of immigration began to take a new stronger and more comprehensive form, culminating in the early 20th century, when the strict enforcement of the passport fully returned with the 'revolution in identity papers' that came with the First World War.[24] Henceforth, civilians became targets of mass conscription and propaganda with each country drawing the boundaries of citizenship ever tighter and seeking to rigorously control the entry of 'non-nationals' by making distinctions between their own citizens and others via documents. This was part of an attempt to effectively 'embrace' their citizens.[25] Passports became standardized after the Second World War.

Nations and borders

The meaning, function, and number of state borders has shifted historically. According to O'Dowd there are four functions or ways of understanding borders: as *barriers, bridges, resources,* and *symbols of identity.*[26] Borders based on natural or physical boundaries have long existed; however, the emergence of sharply delimited and regulated territorial boundaries – as opposed to blurred and more permeable frontiers between kingdoms or countries – is, as indicated above, intrinsically connected with nation-state formation, nationalism, and imperialist rivalry. As a bounded power container, the state, theoretically at least, had the power to maintain absolute and sovereign control over its borders and who or what could pass across them.[27]

Borders and boundaries exist both in the objectivity of the first order and in the subjectivity of the second order. Through nationalism, territorial state borders are historical developments that are intertwined with and reciprocally reinforce social and psychological boundaries operating through classifications schemes and cognitive distinctions. Physical closure to outsiders solidifies and manifests a form of social and psychological closure.

In a mutually reinforcing process the operation of borders allowed the state to undertake a process of nation-making by structuring the composition of the population predominantly according to restricted ethno-national, ethno-cultural, or ethno-racial criteria in a way that was unimaginable in the past. Nationalist ideology promoted the construction of beliefs based on demarcated, bounded, and differentiated nations and peoples of different origins and histories heretofore predominantly defined around class and status.[28] A central historical function of borders has therefore been to keep a selection of categorically defined individuals outside the territory by discriminating against them on selective grounds, something that has, over time, become a normal and natural aspect of a state activity. Territorial state boundaries guarded by immigration border control play a central role in nation-making as an ongoing material and symbolic process, representing a physical embodiment of the imagined community. State borders carry a high degree of symbolic capital – they effectively came to represent a symbol of national identity and belonging and provided a framework within which to interpret the state, territorial membership, and population and the interpretation of their actions and movements.

The movement across borders into different territorial space and a different socio-cultural order can also mean a shift in social identity of the individual. For individuals whose dominant definition and social status may be derived from a composite of various social roles and modes of identification including occupation, religion, gender, age, or class, they become 'migrants' with a formally ascribed social status distinct from citizens. As Kearney notes: social identity can only be formed by being bordered with respect to contrasting identities in a system of relationships and distinctions – that is ordered by some form of social, political, cultural, legal, or possibly spatial geographical politics, formally or informally, that construct the border in question. Similarly, identities are changed upon crossing a border because of the classifying power of some order or constellation of orders, be they formal or informal, that construct that border. Said differently, borders are classificatory devices imposed by some order that defines the identities of persons who are within their borders, beyond them, and who cross them (and of course, individuals and groups are also active in the construction of their own identities).[29]

Notwithstanding the complex dialectic of state categorization and self-identification, the migrant social status usually carries degraded valuations that may become associated with being an 'outsider', not fully belonging, a potential drain on resources, and temporariness. The redefinition of the identity of the individual into 'migrant' has important implications for their subsequent social trajectory and destiny – not just in material terms but also subjectively and biographically. The concept and social status of migrant or non-national become in effect rigid designators.

Irish borders

We can see the operation of these historical and global forces entailing border formation in the context of the Irish State. The contested nature of partition has meant that the issue of borders and territory has been highly politicized. As an island, Ireland combines naturally formed sea borders with a border created through the force and violence of national struggles. The cross-border violence ensuing from partition played a fundamental role in shaping the Irish State's security-conscious world-view. However, the view of the border as a State necessity was always ambivalent since it cut across a nationalist view which saw the border, as it existed, as a colonial imposition dividing a united territory. Given its geographic contours, Ireland has considerable power in controlling entry into the territory and maintaining immigration controls. Irish entry ports, including Rosslare Harbour, Shannon, Cork, and Dublin airport, offer material openings into the State that express concentrations of state power at the edge of the state territory, so to speak. Moreover, although restrictions on outsiders are stipulated in laws and codified in various formal documents including visa applications and passports, they only take 'real' effect at borders and ports of entry. The material infrastructures and procedures constituting the border (entry ports, passport control, immigration checks) also provide physical embodiments of a bounded imagined community. This sovereignty of borders enshrined in laws has been powerfully backed by the judiciary. As Justice Gannon notes:

> That it is in the interests of the common good of a State that it should have control of the entry of aliens, their departure and their activities and duration of stay within the State is and has been recognised universally and from earliest times. There are fundamental rights of the State itself as well as fundamental rights of the individual citizen, and the protection of the former may involve restrictions in circumstances of necessity on the latter. The integrity of the State constituted as it is for the collective body of its citizens within the national territory must be defended and vindicated by the organs of the State and by the citizens so that there may be true social order within the territory and concord maintained with other nations in accordance with the objectives declared in the preamble to the Constitution.[30]

As was the case elsewhere, just who is considered an 'alien' or an 'outsider' and who is freely permitted to enter the state has shifted over time. Borders are selective in their constraining effects, and this selectivity varies according to contingent historical, political, or economic factors. These shifts have been illustrated in the operation of the Common Travel Area (CTA), and more recently in the freedom of movement of accession state EU nationals. In terms of the former, despite ideological and political animosity towards Britain, there has, since the founding of the Irish State, been an absence of immigration controls between the Ireland and the UK. The need for bi-national trade and contestation over the 6 counties played a considerable role in the creation of the CTA. However, practical considerations involving policing a 280 mile long border that cuts across over 180 roads were also important.[31] The CTA has meant that a passport was not needed to move between the two jurisdictions, but also that both countries were effectively policing each other's borders. However, following a rise in the number of asylum applications in Ireland and a belief that many were coming via the UK, the CTA was modified. As the director of Irish Naturalization and Immigration Services noted:

> While Ireland has a sovereign immigration regime, there are some external drivers for our approach. A key element to be considered in Ireland's case is the Common Travel Area with the UK and in particular our largely un-policed land border with Northern Ireland. In short, we have not only to protect our own State but have a responsibility to our neighbours, as they do to us. This is the price we pay for the ease of movement between the two jurisdictions. A lot of undesirable people want to get to the UK and it is pretty easy to see that a person seeking to enter the UK 'under the radar' would consider coming through Ireland if they thought that they would escape detection.[32]

The operation of the CTA has had two major implications for Irish immigration policy. Firstly, changes in immigration law in the UK have often been mirrored by changes in Irish law. This includes the list of countries deemed to require a visa and permitting the immediate entry of accession state nationals to live and work in Ireland, and also subsequently barring Bulgarians and Romanians from doing work in the State. Second, the CTA has discouraged Ireland's entry into the Schengen European Travel Area.

The major division determining entry into the State is between EU and non-EU (or EEA) citizens. Although in theory all foreign nationals can be stopped, in practice because of European membership it is difficult to detain EU nationals. Together with the CTA and UNHCR regulations relating to the protection of refugees, the free movement of EU nationals significantly undermines state sovereignty. Again as the Director of the Irish Immigration and Naturalization Services has noted: 'The unfortunate reality is that it is very difficult to prevent an EU citizen from entering the State, even when they have a criminal record… This is a fact of life in all EU member states.'[33]

Since the 1990s the State has developed an encompassing administrative and surveillance infrastructure to deal with immigration. A stepping up in the policing of borders with and expansion in personnel and monitoring equipment, including immigration officers, cameras, fingerprinting facilities, and internal building design designed to regulate the flow of individuals, all permit greater regulation control over movement. A central aspect of this process is a more stringent and thorough examination and inspection of identity papers and passports of incoming individuals. Immigration officers are invested with considerable powers to arrest, detain, allow, or refuse individuals permission to land. Despite some minor modifications in the Immigration Acts of 2003 and 2004 the law regulating entry into the Irish State goes back to the 1935 Aliens Act and the Aliens order of 1946. This allows immigration officers empowered by the Minister of Justice, and usually members of the Garda Siochana, to refuse entry at the borders of the State, to enter any vessel and demand documents or detain any person in the State who is a foreign national.[34] The Aliens Order not only prohibits foreign nationals from entering or leaving the state, but also requires persons to comply with provisions covering registration, change of address, and employment. The Order provides 15 grounds according to which an individual can be refused leave to land. Since the 1999 Immigration Act, this includes the belief that the individual poses 'a threat to national security', 'public policy', or has an 'intention to deceive'. These have been extended in the 2004 Immigration Act. Under section 4.3 of the Immigration Act 2004, permission to enter the State can be denied and the person can be detained and searched. As 'frontier guards of national identity',[35] immigration officers have considerable grounds for refusing to issue a visa, ranging from a lack of specificity in the application to a fear that the granting of a visa may result in a cost to public funds or resources.[36]

Non-EEA nationals are required leave to enter the State by reporting to an immigration officer at an Irish port of entry, stipulating their reasons for entering the State. The latter include both visa-holding and non-visa-holding nationals. The countries selected to require visas by the Irish State mirror those selected by the British State or are those deemed to pose 'a risk'. This includes countries with high levels of asylum applications, those believed to have a propensity towards 'illegal' immigration, or countries perceived to contain a significant number of criminals who emigrate. Because an increasing number of countries require visas to travel to Ireland as well as because of a rise in migration generally, the number of visa applications has risen sharply from 30,000 in 1999 to 80,000 in 2008.[37] Moreover, a large number of visas are declined.[38] The cumbersome and bureaucratic process of securing a visa does not, however, guarantee entry into the State but merely allows the individual to present themselves in order to obtain permission from an immigration officer to enter.

The power of boundaries to function can only be effected on the ground through the ongoing and contingent decisions of immigration officers about allowing entry. However, the processes followed by immigration officers in applying and interpreting the law to persons seeking leave to enter the State can be complex and contradictory. The differentiations between insiders and those deemed threatening or burdensome outsiders is generated and reproduced through various mechanisms including state categorizations and immigration policies. Immigration laws are poly-vocal texts that have to be interpreted and applied. In determining entry, hierarchically ordered, codified state taxonomies and classificatory schemes are drawn upon, applied, and their application extended on an ongoing and contingent basis by immigration officers. Their authorized position in social space allows them the power to define the situation vis-à-vis allowing the immigrant to enter and considerable discretion. Interpretative work in selecting and classifying migrants has existed as long as borders have existed. For example, as Luibhead notes in relation to early Chinese migration to the USA:

> although Chinese immigrants were targeted for exclusion since the inception of federal immigration control, deciding who was Chinese was never a simply a matter of empirical fact – it was always a moment of social construction. Immigration officials initially relied on the notion Chinese people came from the country 'China' in order to enforce the Chinese exclusion law of 1882. But they eventually had to reckon with the fact that Chinese people also came from the Americas, and they had to decide whether to admit people who claimed Chinese ancestry but South or Central American nationality (since the former were prohibited but the latter were not). Officials also had to decide how to classify and

process immigrants with one Chinese and one non-Chinese parent. The immigration service's changing constructions of Chinese identity drew on existing US racial taxonomies. But they also helped to extend and rework these taxonomies in particular ways and served as sites where people challenged such racial taxonomies and the inequalities they sanctioned.[39]

In Ireland nationality and skin colour play a key role in determining entry, and anecdotal evidence suggests that racial profiling is prevalent. Assertions about terrorism, criminality, and illegal immigration have provided the context for ethnic profiling on a European-wide basis. Over 32% of British Muslims have reported being subjected to discrimination at airports since 9/11.[40] In the UK following the 7 July terrorist attacks Asians were 4.1 times more likely, whilst black people 4.5 times more likely, to be stopped and searched under the Terrorism Act 2000 than white people. As one commentator noted, they were 'guilty by pigmentation'.[41] Bodily characteristics, gestures, clothes, and attitude may all be used by immigration officers in their intuitive and practical anticipation of who is 'coming in illegally'. The shift to opening borders to EU nationals, deemed to be predominantly white, has resulted in an increasing racialization and use of ethnic and racial profiling at the borders. Individuals who are not white are increasingly likely to be stopped and questioned while others are often waived through passport control. As a spokesperson for An Garda Siochana noted to an enquiry from the Irish Human Rights Commission as to their rationale for adjudicating decisions and refusing entry, officers depend on their experience: 'It is important to understand the knowledge which immigration officers have with regard to the deception which immigrants engage in with a view to creating an impression that they are bona fide visitors, when, in fact, they intend to remain illegally in the State'[42] There exists a negative framing of certain nationalities that are more likely 'to deceive'. Masked by legal-rational bureaucratic criteria, the judgements of immigration officials are seen by migrants to be based on selective and discriminatory intuition rather than formal universal scrutiny of everyone entering the State. Officers' prejudiced knowledge, beliefs, and stereotypes constitute acts of construction implementing schemes of thought and expression that project attributes upon certain selected immigrants that are not immanent to the immigrant themselves. There are currently no grounds for reviewing immigration officers' decisions to evaluate whether they are consistent with the State's legal obligations. Nor are there any clear regulations or codes of conduct for immigration officers. The State has also consistently prevented immigration officers from coming within the remit of the Garda Siochana Ombudsman Commission so as to become accountable for their decisions. Nor is there any right to appeal a decision.

Approximately 16 individuals a day are refused entry into the State.[43] Moreover, immigration officers have become stricter in enforcing entry requirements. The number of people refused leave to land in Ireland has risen on a yearly basis. In 2004, 4,477 were refused; in 2005, 4433; in 2006, 5,366; and in 2007, 5,854. The countries of origin of those who are refused entry have also shifted.[44] Some nationalities have been specifically targeted, reflecting the State's priorities concerning risks based on propensity to overstay, crime, and security. Following a dramatic growth in numbers settling in Gort the State specifically targeted Brazilians entering Ireland. In the first half of 2006, 547 were refused permission to enter the State, more than any other nationality.[45] Those arriving from Africa and Asia or countries with high asylum applications were also reported to be especially subject to ill-treatment or aggressive interrogations.[46]

With an increase in migration the Irish State has invested in the material strengthening of the boundary. The use of expanding European-wide electronic surveillance mechanisms has augmented the State's capacity to screen immigrants, even those with no documents. These include the fingerprinting capacity provided by EURODAC but also the Automated Visa Application and Tracking System (AVATS) system and enhanced cooperation with other international, and especially EU, States – including transnational border agencies such as Frontex. The State has also invested in strengthening its surveillance capacity with the development of the Irish Border Information System (IBIS). Passenger information collected by carriers prior to departure is to be sent to the Irish Borders Operation Centre facilitating the 'monitoring, interception, questioning and arrest of individuals'. This is part of a wider 'Entry/Exit scheme of Integrated Border Management' for the sharing of immigration data.[47]

Creating undocumented workers

The operation of borders is inextricably connected to the concept of 'illegality'. As a social construction an illegal migrant is considered both symbolically and materially as someone who is 'out of place', *atopos*. All non-EU migrants have the potential of becoming so. As borders become stricter and legal means of entry into a country reduced, the number of migrants who become 'illegal' increases. However, most migrants enter Ireland on a legal basis. They subsequently become 'illegal'.

Discussions about undocumented or 'illegal' migrants have become increasingly charged since 9/11, with many states echoing a US discourse that correlates unauthorized migration with terrorist activities. This in turn has fuelled an emotionally charged and morally loaded public outrage towards, and criminalization of, migrants. The concept of 'illegal immigrant' is, however, of relatively recent provenance.[48] Earlier migration was relatively less restrictive than contemporary forms of regulation which use a developed surveillance capacity, and unauthorized migrants were somewhat benignly designated as 'spontaneous migrants' and, depending on the political conjuncture, seen as less of a threat, and even sometimes allowed to work. According to Duvall, the term 'illegal migrant' was initially used by the British State to designate Jewish migration into Palestine; invoked again, though infrequently, during the 1960s and 1970s with the introduction of restrictive legislation designed to stop migration; and becoming popular during the 1980s and 1990s. Since by their very nature they do not appear in official statistics, it is difficult to assess the exact or even approximate number of undocumented migrants. The level and extent of undocumented migrants in a country will therefore depend on a number of factors including the level of labour market regulation, the changing nature of the economy, and with labour markets imposing flexibility and contract work, but also the ease and access that states provide for individuals to become citizens or to regularize their situation, and, of course, the restrictive nature of immigration regulations and how they are interpreted and enforced. The International Labour Organization (ILO) suggests that about 10–15% of migrants in most OECD countries are undocumented,[49] while the EU commission estimates that between 350,000 and 500,000 undocumented migrants travel to Europe every year to join about 8 million irregular migrants in Europe. It is more likely, however, that figures vary from country to country depending on institutional conditions. It has been estimated that only 1–2% in Sweden have an irregular status while 15% in Germany do so.[50] Figures in Ireland are even more difficult to ascertain. In 2002 the GNIB estimated about 10,000 'illegal migrants' were in the State.[51] However, the International Organization of Migration posited a larger figure of between 15,000 and 50,000 irregular migrants residing in Ireland.[52]

For the state, 'the illegal migrant' constitutes the profane which threatens the sacredness of citizenship through contagion.[53] It is the state that gives permission to reside in its territory, and it is the state, via bureaucrats and civil servants, that provides the authoritative definition of who and who is not undocumented. The point is that a person becomes undocumented or illegal when the state deems them to have become so and classifies them as such. This is not merely a question of semantics, of states simply distinguishing between legality and illegality, a process integrally tied in with the juridical field and police apparatus, but a process that has significant material outcomes in terms of an individual's access to rights and resources, and ultimately to their physical presence or removal via deportation from the country.

Individuals can be or become undocumented for a number of reasons involving a variety of factors which can be placed on a continuum of lesser to more constraining forces. Some irregular migrants arrive without a visa, others come as tourists and overstay their residence permit, others come on student or work visas which may expire, while others may have been forcefully and deceptively brought here against their will, or 'trafficked'. A large number of undocumented migrants are failed asylum-seekers who fear or are unwilling to go back to their country of origin. Many of those who are here initially on a legal basis may become undocumented through policy change or legislative ambiguity. The entry of Romania and Bulgaria into Europe in January 2007 meant that citizens from these two countries could travel freely into Ireland but not work unless they were self-employed or had a work permit. This led to large numbers working illegally.[54] The picture here is of a process in which individuals move between different legal, political, and social statuses determined by the State. Some may begin legally, become classified as 'illegal', but subsequently become reclassified as 'legal'. An asylum-seeker who, having failed to meet the State's legal definitions, can become undocumented, but may then leave the country and apply for a work permit and again become legal.

Most evidence, however, suggests that the majority of the undocumented in Ireland are either failed asylum-seekers or have initially arrived on work permits that have not been renewed. According to the MRCI, of the 1,000 migrants who entered the country legally in 2006, one quarter had become undocumented by the time they sought the support of the MRCI, and over 60% of those who had lost their legal status had experienced exploitation.[55] Although a small minority choose to remain irregular for various reasons, the majority of undocumented prefered to have a regular status, pay taxes and contribute to the State by working.

If and when they do access employment, undocumented workers tend to take up work in the informal economy in jobs that are usually shunned by the local population because they are considered to be at the bottom of the social ladder, badly paid, and with poor working conditions. Hence many take jobs in hotels, mushroom farms, construction, the cleaning industry, retail, domestic work, or in factories.[56] Despite the poor working conditions and precarious nature of their labour contract which in effect creates an underclass, many are grateful to accept what work is available and so they rarely complain. This makes undocumented workers especially vulnerable to exploitation.

The Irish State has an ambivalent relationship to undocumented migration. During the boom the State generally turned a blind eye to undocumented workers. Moreover, while continually supporting the rights of undocumented Irish in Ireland, the State has been reluctant to meet international human rights obligations or provide regularization for undocumented migrants in Ireland. However, in September 2009 it announced the beginnings of a small-scale time-bound bridging visa policy. This was largely a prelude to 'clearing out' the system before introducing the Immigration and Residence Protection Bill, which contains more restrictive deterrence measures backed with harsher penalties in the context of a recession. The number of undocumented workers in Ireland is likely to increase in the near future. Tougher border policies and increased restrictions on entry and channels of entry will coalesce with many work permit holders not having their permits renewed during the recession.

Deportations

Despite international and economic restrictions the state deals physically with anomalous categories of undocumented migrants. As Durkheim recognized, cultures deal with anomalous sacred and profane categories in several ways: by assigning the anomaly into one of the two binary categories of sacred and profane, by destroying the anomaly, by avoiding the anomaly, or by declaring the anomaly as dangerous. In Ireland the state can provide the undocumented migrant with a bridging visa, subsidiary protection, or expel and deport them. Under 'section 3' of the Immigration Bill of 1999 an individual residing without permission can be removed by a deportation order. The person is given notification of the order and has 15 days to make a submission to the Minister of Justice as to why he or she should not be deported, or to leave the state voluntarily. If the State declines to offer subsidiary protection a deportation order is served.

The vast majority of deportations that are effected involve failed asylum-seekers, who are either sent back to their country of origin or transferred under Dublin Convention/Dublin II regulations. This has been facilitated by the strengthening of the State's electronic surveillance capacity including the introduction of the EURODAC fingerprinting framework.[57]

There is, however, a sizeable difference between the number of deportation orders signed and the number actually effected. In 2008 only 162 of the 779 deportation orders signed were effected. The number being deported each year since 2004 has, decreased. Deportation is a difficult process for the State to undertake. The cost of deportations is one factor accounting for the decrease in numbers being deported. The booking of flights, being returned to long-distance destinations such as Nigeria and China, sometimes involving transit flights, having to book flights at short notice and the cost of Garda escorts all contribute to this.[58] It is estimated that it cost the State €6,837,998 to carry out 1,598 deportations between 2004 and 2008.

Claims of absolute state power of control over the entry of foreign nationals and territorial management and enforcement as a 'spatial strategy' or practice are often ideological claims at variance with actual practice. States have significant power to control the movement and residence of non-citizens, but in practice their control is constrained by two major factors. Firstly, as liberal democracies they are under international human rights obligations which prevent the unconstrained violation of human rights. These are increasingly posed as rights to family reunification. Deportation is seen as cutting across human rights and is therefore not seen as a feasible solution to unwanted migrants. Together with human ingenuity and persistence, these rights allow individuals some leeway in escaping immigration restrictions or 'passing' by them. In reaction, states have attempted to reassert control in various ways: by ignoring rights, by making

Table 4.1 Number of deportation orders 2004–2008

Year	Deportation orders effected	Transfer orders effected
2004	599	65
2005	396	209
2006	302	294
2007	139	225
2008	162	271
Total	1598	1064

Source: Parliamentary questions 31/03/2009

both *de facto* and *de jure* entry into the state more difficult, or by constraining membership of the nation through naturalization.

Secondly, for capitalist liberal democracies, borders need to remain porous to economic flows and labour power in order to be competitive and for overall economic development. The contradiction between the free flow of goods, services, and finance and the restrictions imposed on the movement of people has remained a fundamental feature of capitalism. However, the balance between these processes – of the permeability of the transnational flows of goods and services and the restriction of immigrant labour – has shifted continually depending on the prevalent conjuncture and the relative power of interest groups within the state. The DJELR's exclusionary security and national concerns have sometimes come into direct conflict with the DETE's economic fiscal and business priorities based on the free movement of goods and services. The DETE, for example, has shown considerable concern about the hindrances faced by non-EU businessmen trying to enter the State. The clampdown on the 200,000 foreign students coming to learn English and the €0.5 billion this generated every year had significant monetary implications.[59] However, it may be more useful not to see issues of security and the free movement of individuals as opposed from the State's point of view but as sometimes reinforcing one another. As Davis notes: 'Economic globalization and free trade, per the model of NAFTA, tends to strengthen, not weaken the institutional apparatus of borders, and to deepen the existential and juridical divides between "legal" and "illegal" beings.'[60] What Davis notes about the Mexican border is applicable with equal force to the Irish State. 'Realists, of course, understand that a cheap labour flux without the unnecessary quotient of fear and uncertainty imposed by illegality might cease to be cheap labour'.[61]

States need to strengthen their powers of controlling the population but also need to be seen to be doing so. After the unprecedented and unexpected arrival of large numbers of individuals from the accession states, the Irish government has sought to reassert its sovereignty over asylum-seekers, failed refugees, and undocumented migrants.

The introduction of the Immigration, Residency and Protection Bill 2008 by the State was central to the State's future strategy to maintain, reassert, and expand its sovereignty. As the title of the Bill noted, it is 'An Act to restate and modify certain aspects of the law relating to the entry into, presence in and removal from the State of certain foreign nationals and others'. The preamble of the Bill states that its primary objective is to control and manage the coming into and presence in the State of foreign nationals in the national interest. It aims to enhance its ability to control and manage its borders and the regulation of immigrants entering and residing in the country. It constitutes a legal means for the State to extend its administrative reach, and through legislation, reassert its power of control the ethno-racial composition of the population. The Bill would replace all previous legislation on immigration, residence, and asylum, as well as to deal with areas such as visas, entry into the state, long-term residence permits, removal from the state, and the protection of asylum-seekers and refugees. Its emphasis is very much on the regulation of the state's borders and national security and 'deterring those who have malevolent intentions of seeking to come to the State'. Considerable text has been devoted to augmenting Garda National Immigration Bureau powers to refuse permission to land on the grounds of 'security of the State, public policy, public good and public health'. This is backed by high levels of ministerial discretion. Immigration officers will also be enabled to 'detain and examine' anyone whom they 'reasonably suspect to be a foreign national' with no time limit given to this detention or necessary access to a lawyer. The Bill also restricts access to State services and legal aid to irregular migrants. Accelerated procedures for the removal and deportation of irregular migrants and failed asylum-seekers will also be put in place so that they can be deported without notice. In effect the new Bill aims to bring in summary deportation without notice and to prevent access to remedy and complaints procedures such as the Employment Appeals Tribunal or the Equality Tribunal. Those deported may also become liable for their deportation and detention costs.

The Bill also proposes to strengthen the State's surveillance capacity. Biometric information (visual images, fingerprints, or eye scan) will be included in residence permits and ID cards which non-EU citizens will be required to carry at all times. If they do not and cannot prove their identity, they are likely to be arrested. In addition to the excessive cost and practical policy of implementing such a scheme, research in the UK has indicated that black people are several times more likely to be stopped and asked for their ID than whites, hence reinforcing discrimination by singling out those who are perceived to 'look foreign'.[62] The Immigration Bill further expands the already extensive grounds for refusing leave to land as well as increasing the reasons for expelling immigrants.[63]

The Bill also aims to curtail citizenship through marriage. The right of foreign nationals to marry in the State will be severely restricted in the new legislation. The Minister's rationale for this is his claim that this is to cut down on 'marriages of convenience' but this is backed by no empirical or statistical evidence.

Contrary to the State's belief, most evidence shows that increasing immigration restrictions, by employing more guards to police borders, and introducing more electronic surveillance measures are both highly costly and generally ineffective. Migrants who are determined to enter a country will continue to do so, often aided by traffickers who have devised countless methods to evade immigration officers.[64] More restrictions generally mean that non-EU and non-white migrants will suffer in various ways.

Although the 2008 Bill was withdrawn and replaced by the Immigration, Residence and Protection Bill 2010 to take account of the several hundred amendments tabled by opposition parties, the new Bill retains much of the content of the older version.

The state is an ever-changing and contingent project, produced by practices of statecraft that both draw upon and reproduce a world-view that assumes the territorial state to be a natural and inevitable order. State regulation of boundary enforcement and immigration control is expanding in Ireland. In the context of the recession and the forthcoming enactment of the Immigration Residence and Protection Bill, boundary enforcement, inflexibility towards renewing residence stamps, and an intensified policing of borders will more than likely lead to an increase in the number of undocumented migrants in Ireland.

Notes

1 M. Davis, Foreword, J. Nevins, *Operation Gatekeeper* (London: Routledge, 2002), p. x.

2 J. Harding, *The Uninvited: Refugees at the Rich Man's Gate*, (London: Profile Books, 2000).

3 As his cousin noted his humiliating treatment: 'the pain was that he was made to take away all his clothes before the other inmates of his room and the other warders around. He said that nobody had seen his nakedness since he became an adult. This man does not like violence of any form this is a huge embarrassment to him'. *Irish Times*, 13 September 2008.

4 *Irish Times*, 4 October 2008.

5 M. Davis, Foreword, in J. Nevins, *Operation Gatekeeper*, p. x.

6 Irish Human Rights Commission, *Report on an Enquiry into the treatment of a prisoner refused Leave to land in the State* (Dublin: IHRC 2009), p. 45.

7 Cited in M. Kearney, The anthropology of transnational communities and the reframing of immigration research in California: the Mixtec case, in M. Bommes and E. Morawska (eds), *International Migration Research: Constructions, Omissions, and the Promise of Interdisciplinarity* (2003), p. 71. Although the development of nation-states

for the most part led to the dissolution of city/countryside relations such forms of control over rural movement to the cities still exist; see M. Davis, *Planet of Slums* (London: Verso, 2007).

8 H. Lefevre *The Production of Space* (Oxford: Blackwell, 1991).

9 R. Cohen, *Migration and its Enemies*, p. 4.

10 P. Anderson, *Passages from Antiquity to Feudalism* (London: Verso, 1996), p. 148.

11 J. Torpey, *The Invention of the Passport* (Cambridge: Cambridge University Press, 2000).

12 K. Parker, State, citizenship, and territory: The legal construction of immigration in Antebellum Massachusetts, 19 *Law and History Review* 583 (2001); J.Steinfeld, Subjectship, citizenship, and the long history of immigration regulation, *Law and History Review* 19: 645–53 (2001).

13 N. Elias, *The Civilizing Process* (Oxford: Blackwell, 2000); Tilly, *The Formation of Nation States*. As Tilly notes, there were over 5,000 autonomous political entities in 15,000 but only 25 states survived by 1900.

14 Torpey, *The Invention of the Passport*.

15 James Scott, *In Seeing like a State How Certain Schemes to Improve the Human Condition Have Failed* (New Haven, CT: Yale University Press, 1998), p. 68.

16 Torpey, *Invention of the Passport*.

17 The concept of nation played a lesser role as an explanatory factor than class for a significant time. The intermarriage of aristocrats across European countries was the norm for a long time.

18 J. Steinfeld, Subjectship, citizenship, and the long history of immigration regulation, M. Baseler, *Asylum for Mankind: 1607–1800* (Cornell: Cornell University Press, 1998), pp. 72–3.

19 I draw the following data from M. Davis, *Planet of Slums*.

20 Ibid. p. 52.

21 Kam Wing Chan, Internal labour migration in China: trends, geographical distribution and policies, *www.un.org/esa/population/meetings/EGM_PopDist/Chan.pdf*.

22 Davis, *Planet of Slums*, p. 60.

23 G. Noiriel, *The French Melting Pot* (Minnesota: University of Minnesota Press, 1997).

24 A. Torpey *The Invention of the Passport*.

25 Ibid.

26 L. O'Dowd, The changing significance of European borders, *Regional & Federal Studies*, 12:4, 13–36 (2002).

27 A. Giddens, *The Nation-State and Violence*.

28 N. Elias, *The Germans* (Oxford: Blackwell, 1996).

29 M. Kearney, The anthropology of transnational communities, pp. 72–3.

30 J. Gannon, in Osheku v. Ireland [1986] I.R. 733 at 746.

31 B. Ryan, The common travel area between Britain and Ireland, 2001, p. 858.

32 Pat Folan, Crime Security and the Irish Immigration System, paper given at 11th Minorities, Crime & Justice, Conference October 2008 available at http://www.oireachtas.ie/documents/report/AnnualConferenceReport11.pdf (2008) p. 9.

33 Pat Folan, Crime Security and the Irish Immigration System, paper given at 11th Minorities, Crime & Justice, p. 9.

34 Though they may interview people on trains and buses which are in close proximity to the state borders such as in Northern Ireland, the decision in whether to allow or refuse entry usually takes place at a port of entry initially in a passport booth but also in an interview room, *Report on an Enquiry into the treatment of a prisoner refused Leave to land in the State*, p. 27.

35 Cohen, *Migration and its Enemies*, p. 4.

36 Irish Human Rights Commission, *Report on an Enquiry into the treatment of a prisoner refused Leave to land in the State*, pp. 29–301 Crosscare, *Invisible Pathways: A critique of how the Irish immigration system can contribute to people becoming undocumented* (Dublin: Crosscare, 2009) p. 26.

37 *Irish Times*, 26 March 2009. Visas can be short stay (C Visa) or long stay (D), can be single entry or multiple entry. The issuance of a visa is at the discretion of a visa officer.

38 INIS publishes the reasons why they were refused. Other than missing documentation the most frequently cited reason is because they do not believe the person has enough finances – 'finances shown have been deemed insufficient', or obligations to return home have not been deemed sufficient.

39 E. Luibhead, *Entry Denied* (University of Minnesota Press, 2002), p. xii.

40 Open Society, Ethnic profiling in the European Union, Pervasive, Ineffective and Discriminatory, 2009:7 available at www.soros.org/initiatives/justice/focus/equality_ citizenship/articles_publications/publications/profiling_20090526/profiling_200905 26.pdf.

41 Daniel Moeckli, The impossibility of terrorist profiling, in *Open Democracy*, 12 September (2008).

42 Irish Human Rights Commission, *Report on an Enquiry into the treatment of a prisoner refused Leave to land in the State*, p. 54.

43 Crosscare, *Invisible Pathways*, p. 26.

44 In 2003 prior to accession of the 4,827 refused leave to entry 560 were Polish, 484 were Lithuanian, 408 Brazilian, 387 Nigerian, 268 South African, 261 Romanian, 247 Latvian and 114 Chinese. In the first two weeks of that year 'intention to deceive' was the main reason leave to land was refused Irish Human Rights Commission, *Report on an Enquiry into the treatment of a prisoner refused Leave to land in the State*, p. 56.

45 *Irish Times*, 7 February 2008. Two incidents gained media attention. Three students from Brazil studying in Portugal were held in Mountjoy Prison for two days after attempting to spend a weekend in Ireland, before being deported; and 50 Brazilians trying to enter for an international football match were also refused permission to land as Gardai suspected them of trying to stay on in Ireland to work illegally.

46 See also *Irish Times*, 19 April 2008, in which 8 Chinese solicitors were turned back because suspected of going on to the UK.

47 D. Aherne, Ahern Announces New Border Control System, at www.justice.ie/en/ JELR/Pages/PR09000014).

48 F. Duvell, *Illegal Immigration in Europe. Beyond Control?* (London: Palgrave/Macmillan, 2006), p. 3.

49 International Labour Organization, *Towards a Fair Deal for Migrant Workers in the Global Economy*, International Labour Conference, 92nd Session, 2004 (Geneva International Labour Office, 2004).

50 Duvall, *Illegal Immigration*, p. 7.

51 *Irish Times*, 2 November 2002.

52 National Economic and Social Council, *Migration Policy* (Dublin: NESC, 2006), p. 18.

53 M. Douglas, *Purity and Danger: An Analysis of Concepts of Pollution and Taboo* (London: RKP, 1966).

54 Although just 11 new work permits were issued to Romanians between January and March of that year, 5,291 received PPS numbers to work. See *Irish Times*, 6 March 2007.

55 MCRI, *Life in the Shadows: An Exploration of Irregular Migration into Ireland* (Dublin: MRCI: 2007), p. 22.

56 Ibid., p. 45.

57 During 2008, in the context of the operation of the EU Dublin II Regulation, some 3,402 sets of fingerprints of asylum applicants were sent to EURODAC with 359 hits confirmed. ORAC 2008 Annual Report.

58 As the Minister of Justice noted: 'While it is important to keep deportation costs to a minimum, to not remove persons who have no valid basis for being in the State would call into question the integrity of the entire asylum and immigration systems.' Parliamentary Questions, 30 March 2009.

59 *Irish Times*,19 April 2008. An Indian national who had won a prize from Tourism Ireland in a competition designed to promote Ireland and their opening of an new office there, the latter were concerned about its the racism and harassment the individual faced from immigration officers.

60 M. Davis, Preface to Nevin's *Operation Gateway*, p. xi.

61 Ibid, p. x.

62 Open Society, Ethnic profiling in the European Union, p. 9.

63 For these grounds see IHRC, *Report on an Enquiry into the treatment of a prisoner refused Leave to land in the State*, pp. 29–30.

64 Cohen, *Migration and ites Enemies*, p. 210; Legrain, *Immigrants*.

Chapter 5

The migrant as asylum-seeker

This chapter examines the arrival of asylum-seekers and the processing of asylum claims. It argues that both stages of the application processes are flawed and that political rather than objective criteria have consistently been used in deciding whether asylum-seekers are given refugee status.

By contrast to European patterns of migration where labour migration preceded the arrival of asylum-seekers, early debates on migration in Ireland were primarily centred on asylum-seekers and refugees. Prior to the rapid entry of accession state nationals after May 2004 there was generally a direct and exclusive correlation of immigrants with asylum-seekers in the public mind. This was despite the fact that asylum-seekers constituted less than 10% of the non-EU nationals who entered the State between 1995 and 2000.[1] Their numbers were significantly lower than the numbers of returning Irish and other EU immigrants. However, asylum-seekers became a focus of state and public attention primarily because they were not white. The racialization of primarily Nigerian asylum-seekers through anterior racist and racializing European civilizing discourses had important implications for how migration in Ireland was subsequently framed and interpreted. The semantic correlation of immigrants with non-white, welfare-dependent asylum-seekers constructed as work-shy and prone to criminal activity was an ideological effect of social relations of domination, specifically those involving state and media discourses.

The entry of migrants into the asylum system was characterized by the transformation of humans into legal subjects with a determinate and restricted status. Legal rules and administrative guidelines constituted an inescapable presence into which they were included but from whose interpretation and control they were excluded. By contrast to others living in Ireland for whom the law remains a distant abstraction, for 'asylum-seekers' as a category, the law is everywhere, paradoxically structuring their life chances at an intangible remove but also punctuating their lives on a daily basis, constituting a web-like enclosure in which they are caught and made dependent.[2] After arriving asylum-seekers become confronted by a system of bureaucratic intrusions, impediments and indignities. A significant part of their lives subsequently become organized and regulated by a regime of legal rules invoked by officials claiming jurisdiction over their choices and decisions. This was especially evident following their settlement into direct provision centres.

The sudden and rapid arrival of asylum-seekers into the State in the mid-1990s led to a reactive and restrictive discourse premised on the notion of a 'crisis' that functioned as a moral panic. Such a reaction was not peculiar to Ireland but mirrored wider global, and especially European, trends and practices. During the 1970s the number of asylum-seekers arriving in Western Europe rarely rose over 100,000, with the vast majority of these coming from Eastern Europe.[3] However, numbers grew rapidly in the 1980s and 1990s. The UNHCR estimated that there were approximately 10.7 million refugees in 1984, a figure that more than doubled to 27.4 million a decade later.

The causes of the shift in the modality of migration and increase in numbers were complex and diverse. Continuing crises in the world economy meant that large numbers of asylum-seekers began arriving in the 1980s from a broad array of economically unstable, developing (often post-colonial) countries with weak political structures in Asia, Africa, Latin America, and the Caribbean. These countries were characterized not only by inter-ethnic, religious, or tribal struggles, but also by environmental degradation, and 'low intensity democracy'.[4] Between 1989 and 1994 there were 94 conflicts in 64 worldwide locations primarily within, rather than between, states and involving intense fighting between power-seeking militias and paramilitaries.[5] The geo-political involvement of Cold War superpowers in strategically attempting to shape or maintain the trajectory of weak, vulnerable, and often authoritarian states, and the balance of power within them, functioned to exacerbate their political instability. While aggressive economic policies geared towards liberalization, structural reform, adjustment, and debt enhancement – initiated by supranational trade organizations such as the IMF and the World Bank – undermined the development of any nascent economic or political infrastructure within them. Burgeoning transit opportunities and choice of destination of those seeking asylum were also mediated by cheaper travel, expanding global communication networks, and the growth of trafficking and smuggling organizations. Nevertheless, the vast majority of asylum-seekers and refugees tended to move to neighbouring countries with less than a third travelling to Europe.

These sending countries were not only economically marginalized and marked by high levels of poverty but from the point of view of the West, contained predominantly non-white populations deemed to be ethnically and culturally distant from European values. However, not all asylum-seekers were non-white. The break-up of the Soviet Union and the former Yugoslavia in the late 1980s and early 1990s witnessed protracted local and national ethnic conflicts producing over 2 million refugees, with over 400,000 going to Europe.

By the end of the Cold War asylum-seekers were no longer viewed by Western states sympathetically or used as ideological ballast to highlight the totalitarian nature of communist regimes. Instead, during the 1990s most European states reacted to the growing flow of asylum-seekers by either seeking to contain them within their continent, or region of origin, or what was more frequently the case, restricting their access into their target nations. Intense hostility to these increasing numbers was matched by anxiety-ridden ideological constructions of asylum-seekers as opportunistic and unnecessary burdens on the finite resources of the state, and as a threat to cultural and national homogeneity. In some cases the state responses were coordinated such as through the signing of the Schengen Agreement in 1990. Equally, the 1992 Maastricht Treaty established concepts such as 'safe third country', 'manifestly unfounded' applications, and developed accelerated procedures for processing claims and enacting the rapid deportation of aliens;[6] whilst the Dublin Convention enshrined a policy of 'first country of application' in which asylum-seekers would be sent back to the first European country they had arrived in. The Treaty of Amsterdam 1999 initiated the creation of a Common European Asylum System that determined which state was responsible for reviewing asylum applications and also establishing commn minimum standards in the reception and treatment of asylum-seekers. The removal of borders within Europe was simultaneously established with the harmonization of asylum policy as part of an attempt to create a 'Fortress Europe'. In other cases states individually, though with collective effect, pursued a diverse range of restrictive policies including tightened border surveillance, fingerprinting, and formulating legislation aimed at fining airline or ferry carriers who brought undocumented immigrants into the country. The introduction of the Illegal Immigrant Trafficking Bill 1999 in Ireland in which fines of £1,500 and 1 year's term in prison could be imposed on carriers, was to co-opt transport companies into the State's surveillance system. If these measures did not pre-empt the arrival of asylum-seekers they were also increasingly turned away at ports of entry and denied their right to claim asylum. In addition to enacting stricter laws of admission, signing bi-lateral readmission agreements such as that between Ireland and Nigeria, states also imposed narrower and stricter interpretations of what constituted 'refugee status'. New bureaucratic discourses concepts such as 'clearly fraudulent' emerged that placed the burden of proof on the asylum-seeker and incrementally emptied the concept of refugee of its original humanitarian thrust. The cumulative effect of these changes meant that the acceptance rate for asylum-seekers in the EU fell from 50% in 1987 to 10% 10 years later.[7]

The Irish State's attempt to discourage asylum applications entailed introducing a series of restrictive measures aimed at garnering populist support. Negative public feelings towards asylum-seekers were circulated and legitimized by the State and media, sometimes in combination with various political actors and State departments that drip-fed emotionally charged and often unsourced negative stories about asylum-seekers through the media. These rhetorical tactics constructed a specific 'crisis' through which asylum-seekers were to be understood and interpreted. Asylum-seekers and refugees were not only effectively portrayed as biologically and culturally different, but as 'bogus' claimants responsible for increasing unemployment, welfare fraud, the housing and health system crises, or rising crime levels. The underlying message, reinforced by government discourses and politicians, was that ethno-culturally distant and unscrupulous asylum-seekers were utilizing scarce resources that would otherwise be given to the indigenous population. As Ivor Callely, Fianna Fail TD, asserted, 'rogue' asylum-seekers were 'carrying on in a culture that is not akin to Irish culture' and 'should be kicked out'.[8] A few days later he added an oft-repeated distinction that echoed an earlier historical distinction between the deserving and undeserving poor: 'We must ensure that genuine refugees obtain appropriate support. However, it is unfair that large numbers of asylum-seekers – over 3,000 – who may not be genuine, and who are probably attracted to Ireland because of its welfare state, are enjoying its welfare provisions, including supplementary welfare benefits and medical cards.'[9]

The power of the state and media as information-providers, agenda setters, producers of negative assumptions and stereotypes, and their power to shape public opinion, was vividly demonstrated in their negative portrayal of asylum-seekers. Beginning in 1997 sensationalist and banner headlines in the media emphasizing various 'refugee crises' or 'floods', 'swamping', and 'influxes' were especially evident in the Independent Group of Newspapers. Headlines such as '5,000 refugees flooding Ireland', 'Floodgates open as a new army of poor swamp the country', 'Tax-payers to face bills of 20m-plus for refugee flood', 'Crackdown on 2,000 "sponger" refugees', and 'Garda purge on bogus refugees' were emblematic.[10]

Perception plays a central role in constituting reality. Such headlines could be contrasted with the positive media representation and subsequent treatment that the 1000 Albanian Kosovan programme refugees received in 1999. Their plight was used as a rationale by the EU and NATO military for an intense bombing offensive in Serbia. Front-page newspaper headlines such as 'Welcome' in the *Evening Herald*, greeted their arrival and promoted more positive treatment. Prior to the NATO invasion many regularly had their applications for Convention refugee status turned down.

The negative framing of asylum-seekers was part of a vicious cycle that fuelled xenophobic public opinion, which in turn led to pressure on politicians and provided justification for them to enact even stronger restrictive policies aimed at deterring their arrival. However, despite talks of 'influxes', 'floods', and 'deluges', the State's reaction was disproportionate to the actual numbers entering the country. In absolute terms, Ireland in 2000 received the lowest number of asylum-seekers within the EU, with only 2.4% of the total number of applications. However, while the absolute figures may be low, it did have the 5th highest number of asylum-seekers per capita.[11] In 1992, Ireland received only 39 applications for asylum. By 1996, this figure had risen to 1,179, rising to 7,724 in 1999 before peaking at 11,634 in 2002. By 2003 it began to fall, reaching 7,900, and in 2008, a total of 3,866 applications for refugee status were received, representing the lowest annual number of applications since 1997 and almost a 70% decrease on the 2002 figure. In 2009 the figure fell again, to 2,689. This pattern is shown in Figure 5.1.

In total between 1992 and 2008 there were just over 80,000 applications for asylum. The top 5 countries of origin of asylum-seekers arriving between 1992 and 2008 were Nigeria, Romania, Moldova, Democratic Republic of Congo, and Somalia.[12] What was of enormous significance was that relatively few asylum-seekers came from Europe or were not white: in 1998, 60% of asylum-seekers were from Africa.[13]

In everyday discourse the term 'immigrant', 'asylum-seeker' and 'refugee' are often used interchangeably. The term 'refugee' derives from the Latin *refugee* – to flee – and is believed to have first been applied to the Huguenots who fled France in the 17th century, some of whom arrived in Ireland. The increasing control of borders following the First World War was matched by huge population displacements exacerbated by the Russian Revolution.[14] However, its modern legal usage follows the UN General Assembly's establishment of the United Nations High Commission on Refugees (UNHCR) in 1951. In international law the term 'asylum-seeker' designates someone seeking refugee status.

By becoming signatories to the 1951 UN Convention – which Ireland signed in 1956 – nation-states agreed to grant special protection on an international

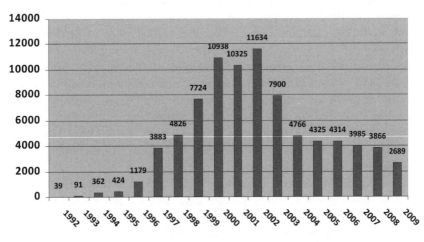

Figure 5.1 Number of asylum applications 1992–2009

basis to citizens of a state that could not guarantee their human rights or physical security. This remit for protection was later extended beyond Europe to encompass refugees from all over the world with the signing of the 1967 Bellagio Protocol, as the problem of displaced people became more global.

The refugee system was constructed within a specific ideological and historical conjuncture entailing massive post-war upheaval that subsequently shaped its configuration and definitional boundary of who counted as a 'refugee'. Within a system of nation-states with fixed borders, the UNHCR's principal aim was to guarantee and provide international protection and assistance to individuals who had become displaced by the Second World War. As a standardized model to deal with mass displacement the concept of 'refugee' became institutionalized as a way of labelling and treating individuals as a distinct type of person. However, any interpretation of the nature, patterns of refugee flows, and definition of refugees prior to 1989 involves reference to the Cold War context that determined these processes. The ideological underpinning of refugee status was intrinsically linked to individuals escaping repressive communist states for the free West. For example, all but 925 asylum-seekers from a total of 233,436 who gained refugee status in the USA between 1956 and 1968 were from communist states, and even by 1986, 90% of those granted refugee status were from these states. By contrast, refugees from states friendly to the USA were usually denied such status.[15]

With few direct non-European international flights to Ireland and relatively small numbers of asylum applications – which were nevertheless still overwhelmingly rejected – the State initially dealt with asylum-seekers through the 1935 Aliens Act. However, a steady increase in numbers following the early 1990s led to the publication of the Refugee Act in 1996, which became the act of law which the Irish government uses to guide its asylum procedure and to interpret the 1951 Convention. Initially formulated while a more liberal-minded rainbow coalition was in office, the Act has an unusually broad and progressive definition of an asylum-seeker: 'A person who, owing to a well-founded fear of being persecuted for reasons of race, religion, nationality, membership of a particular social group or political opinion, is outside the country of his or her nationality or, owing to such fear, is unwilling to avail himself or herself of the protection of that country.'

Though published in 1996 the Act was not fully enacted until November 2000 as a result of significant opposition to it from the incoming Fianna Fail/Progressive Democrat coalition.

Theoretically at least, each signatory to the 1951 UN Convention has to operate according to that body's specified guidelines and principles. In practice, however, each state has significant latitude in interpreting and implementing its asylum and refugee policy. In Ireland the asylum process, housed in the DJELR, contains 3 major bodies: the Office of the Refugee Applications

Commissioner (ORAC), Refugee Appeals Tribunal (RAT), and the Reception and Integration Agency (RIA). The asylum determination process itself involves a complex and protracted process entailing 4 major stages. In the 1st stage an applicant applies for asylum either at a port of entry or, as is more commonly the case, at the ORAC office, filling in a questionnaire indicating why they should be granted refugee status. In the 2nd stage, following an interview, a recommendation is made to the Minister of Justice, Equality and Law Reform as to whether the applicant should be granted refugee status. If the application is rejected the applicant enters a 3rd stage in which he or she may present an oral or written appeal to the RAT. If the appeal is unsuccessful the applicant may, in what is a 4th stage, apply to the Minister for 'leave to remain' on humanitarian grounds or for subsidiary protection. If he or she is still refused they will receive a Section 3 letter, to which they have 15 days to appeal, after which they will be asked to leave the country or face deportation.

Recognition rates for asylum-seekers vary considerably between most OECD countries though they generally fluctuate around a low baseline. Mirroring wider restrictive practices introduced in Europe in the mid-1990s aimed at discouraging their arrival, and once here, their residence, the proportion of asylum-seekers granted refugee status in Ireland remains small. The government's initial liberal interpretation of asylum cases in the context of low numbers of applications changed dramatically following a sharp rise in applications in 1997. In 1995, 57% of applications processed were given one form or another of refugee recognition, by 1998 this fell to 13% of all applications processed.[16] Since then the State's recognition rate of asylum applications has rarely risen over 10% in any one year and viewed over a longer time-span is considerably lower. Between 1992 and 2007 just over 5% of applications were granted refugee status,[17] self-validating the government's consistently asserted claim that 90% of asylum-seekers were 'bogus'.

In both absolute and comparative terms the Irish recognition rate became very low with asylum-seekers less likely to gain refugee status in Ireland than in most other European countries. For example, in 1998 the recognition rate for Nigerians and Romanians, 2 of the countries with the largest applications

Table 5.1 Numbers granted refugee status at first instance 2001–7

Year	2000	2001	2002	2003	2004	2005	2006	2007
Number granted refugee status at first stage		456	894	345	430	455	397	376
As a percentage of cases finalized		6.6	10.7	4.25	6.2	8.7	9.4	9.8

Source: ORAC

made in that year, were 1.1% and 1.4% respectively while the UNHCR's average rate was 7.3% and 2%.[18] In 2009 in the context of the recession, Ireland had the lowest rate of granting refugee status in the EU (with the exception of Greece) with a recognition rate at first instance of 4%. This compared with acceptance rates at first instance of 26.9% in the UK and 47.9% in Denmark. By July of 2010 Irish recognition rates had become the lowest in the EU falling to an extraordinarily level of 1.38%.[19]

A significant backlog of over 9,000 applications had built up over a few years.[20] With an inadequate asylum infrastructure in place to deal with them – the DJELR only had about 20 people working in this section and resources were low – the State's response was a mixture of panic and hysteria expressed in contradictory and incoherent policies. Slow processing, bureaucratic inertia, and poor service and treatment were underwritten by the DJELR's entrenched denial that Ireland was becoming a country of immigration. A lack of concern by politicians about their conditions – since asylum-seekers could not vote – became combined with a view that a fair and efficient system would constitute a 'pull factor' to more asylum-seekers. The State's central concern was to demonstrate that Ireland was not 'a soft touch'. In conjunction with this standpoint the State introduced an array of exclusionary mechanisms and procedures in order to curb rising numbers of applications. As part of rendering the process of acquiring refugee status more difficult, a greater number of applicants began to be refused for failing to meet what was an arbitrary and shifting criterion for refugee status. Speed and rapidity at the expense of fair procedure became normalized. The State also introduced a dual-track system for determining refugee status – a 'manifestly unfounded procedure' supplemented the normal determination procedure based on the 1951 Convention. Cases to which such accelerated determination procedures could apply were those that 'were so obviously without foundation as not to merit full examination at every level of the procedure'. From 1999, this procedure was increasingly generalized. In 1999, 133 claims out of a total of 7,724 claims were perceived to be 'manifestly unfounded' (1.7%); by 2000, this had risen to 2,263 out of a total of 12,037 claims (18.8%). According to the Irish Refugee Council such procedures were being used on exceptionally broad grounds, with little basis in natural or constitutional justice, or international human rights law. In 2004 the state replaced the 'manifestly unfounded' procedure with a priority application procedure in which nationals from Nigeria, Romania, Bulgaria, Croatia, and South Africa – who represented about 40% of asylum applications – were designated by the State as 'safe countries' and would have their cases processed within 18 days and appeals undertaken within 15 days. In 2008 almost 30% of applications were processed under the Ministerial Prioritization Directive. The fast track procedure meant many applicants needed to be housed in Dublin to facilitate deportation. Nor would any oral appeal be given for their asylum hearing.[21] An increasing use was also made of Dublin and Dublin II Convention grounds wherein claimants who had made a prior application in another country were to be referred back to that country.[22]

The refugee determination process

From the point of view of the State the simplest way of reducing numbers was through introducing greater restrictions in the interview and appeals process. Rather than following 'objective' or neutral dictates of decision-making as the State claims, the processing of asylum applications, at both the first and second stages, has fundamentally been politically determined and ideologically driven. In both procedures patterns of social exclusion persist in the assumptions and principles of ORAC and how it operates. Since the dominant ethnic and economic group has all the institutions of the state in its control – from the education system to the media and the legal system – and decides how and to whom these resources will be allocated, it also controls issues tied to ethnicity and power. Such institutional bias is clearly evident in the asylum interview. Evidence from asylum applicants suggests that not all receive a balanced or impartial hearing but are instead collectively framed negatively.[23] Theoretically, at least, the mechanism and procedure for assessing whether an individual should be recognized as a refugee appear straightforward. Expert officers determine the applicant's credibility by assessing whether the arguments and assertions made correspond to what actually happened and, if they do, whether these events fall within the definition of refugee contained in the Refugee Act. If both grounds are satisfied refugee status is conferred. Contradictions or inconsistencies in the claimant's narrative or failure to acquire corroborating discursive or oral sources are usually taken as evidence that the applicant is lying. In such circumstance the applicant is refused recognition and by default classed as 'bogus' or 'really' an 'economic migrant'. In practice, however, the task of ascertaining whether someone should be given refugee status is infinitely more complex and arbitrary, requiring a great deal of discretion, imputation, guesswork, and presuppositions.

First, because of an initial difficulty in acquiring staff within the context of a steep rise in applications, many of the initial investigating officers were retired gardaí or former civil servants.[24] In contrast to a number of other European states where examining officers have a legal background or university degree, there was no statutory provision relating to the training and skill-sets of these officers. Irish assessors in the determination of asylum claims had little formal knowledge or understanding of law, or a human rights background knowledge of many countries of origin of asylum-seekers. Second, the categorization of asylum-seeker as a refugee is predicated on the possibility of clearly distinguishing political persecution from other (especially economic) causes of migration. However, the majority of the countries from which asylum-seekers arrived were characterized both by acute political instability, warfare, or democratic deficits, and by widespread poverty and economic underdevelopment. The United Nations' category of persecution includes within its definition both those who are being persecuted for belonging to a particular social group based on race, religion etc., and those holding certain political opinions. This throws up a complex cluster of questions including: What constitutes membership of a particular social group, persecution, and state protection? It is, for obvious reasons, exceedingly difficult to ascertain whether someone held or holds certain political opinions or not.

State bureaucrats are expected to decide the 'correct' classification of an asylum-seeker by attributing various motives to him or her. However, imputations tell us as much about the investigator as they do about the asylum-seeker. Instead of attempting to interpret what the 'real' motives of asylum-seekers are, whether they are 'telling the truth' or 'lying', and ascertaining the content of their private mental states, sociologists need to study those imputing these motives by approaching conduct socially and from the outside. As Mills argues: '[r]ather than fixed elements "in" an individual, motives are the terms with which interpretation of conduct by social actors proceeds. This imputation and avowal of motives by actors are social phenomena to be explained.'[25] Motive imputation and attribution depend upon the existence of socially accepted vocabularies of motives which vary historically, but also across cultures and across situations within given cultures. To unearth the structured distribution of alternative explanatory concepts in terms of their specific carriers, their historical genesis and their contextual employment is a difficult exercise.

The State, politicians, and media played a central role in widely diffusing ideologically loaded classifications, evaluative discourses, and politically charged vocabularies of motive pertaining to asylum-seekers. It is difficult for investigating officers and bureaucrats, especially when reinforced and partly constructed by elite bureaucrats in the DJELR, to remain unaffected by powerful political and media discourses that are circulating. Hence, the criminalization of asylum-seekers, and especially those from Nigeria framed as 'illegal', 'criminal', 'drug-pushers', 'bogus', 'fraudsters', 'rapists', and as a collective drain on social and economic resources, became 'common knowledge'. A central and widely accepted claim circulated by the State and media was that migrants were falsely posing as asylum-seekers when in fact they were 'economic migrants' here to exploit Ireland's comparatively generous welfare system. Statements from the Irish government that the Irish welfare regime was attracting 'economic migrants' became commonplace. John O'Donohue, the former Minister of Justice, Equality and Law Reform, in a speech to the Irish Business and Employers Confederation stated: 'In the early years of this decade and prior to that, our relatively high unemployment rates and low social welfare payments ensured that illegal immigrants invoking the asylum convention targeted the more prosperous countries – even small ones like Denmark and Finland. Let us be clear about it. Our current economic boom is making us a target.'[26] Similarly Noel O'Flynn, a TD for Cork, announced in more populist rhetoric:

> We're against the spongers, the freeloaders, the people screwing the system. Too many are coming to Ireland and too many to Cork in my view… I'm saying we will have to close the doors. The majority of them are here for economic reasons and they are thumbing their noses up at Irish hospitality and demanding everything under the guise of the Geneva Convention while the taxpayer is paying for it all.[27]

The attributions of investigating officers were often framed in terms of cultural preconceptions and stereotypes about various nationalities, and predicated on a delimited worldview in which it was assumed that asylum-seekers were trying to evade the system of migration controls and therefore 'guilty until proven innocent'.[28] Here a paradox was evident. In law each application for asylum had to be considered individually. Yet asylum-seekers were collectively framed as illegal, a threat to the social order, or a burden on the states social and economic resources. Moreover, the term 'illegal asylum-seeker', as used by the media, and increasingly by politicians, was a *non sequitur*, since all individuals under international law are legally entitled to apply for asylum.

It could be argued that by drawing upon various politically and emotionally loaded vocabularies of motive, determining officers simply collected information from various sources which substantiated and supported their initial negative collective framing of asylum applicants. Such a procedure can be understood in terms of a 'documentary method of interpretation'. As Garfinkel states, this was a process in which 'Not only was the underlying pattern derived from its individual documentary evidences, but the individual documentary evidences, in their turn, are interpreted on the basis of "what is known" about the underlying pattern. Each is used to elaborate the other.'[29]

The power of legal rules and practices to dominate those to whom they are applied is derived in part from the incomplete yet authoritative representation of law's categories and abstractions by officials authorized to say what a refugee is, and how the term should be defined.

The interview also embodies a sharp power differential between the interviewee and the state-sanctioned interviewer. It is the investigator, as Bourdieu argues, who starts the 'game' and sets up its rules by assigning to 'the interview its objective and use'. This 'asymmetry is reinforced by a social asymmetry since the investigator occupies a higher place in the social hierarchy of different types of capital', including, in this case, cultural and linguistic capital. The use of inadequate interpreting staff merely exacerbates this differential.

Translation difficulties were highlighted in a Nasc report: 'three or four times the [Department of Justice] interviewer said that the translator was not doing a good job' (Fatima, Pakistan). Another interviewee stated that the interpreter provided for their second interview spoke poor English: 'the interpreter was no good... didn't speak English well, so I spoke myself'.[30]

The asylum interview, which can last anywhere from 15 minutes to 4–6 hours, and depending on whether accelerated and fast track procedures are employed, not only entails a large ethno-cultural power difference, but is driven by the principle of establishing contradictions and minor inconsistencies in the applicant's account, rather than applying a 'benefit of the doubt' principle. As one former member of the RAT noted, interviews 'have all the hallmarks of a Garda interview in a station... they bear all the hallmarks of a narrow and prejudiced state of mind.' Referring to asylum-seekers, he added, '[t]he legal standards applied to them are lower than would be applied to Irish people and their fundamental rights are not observed during the asylum process'.[31] Through the exercise of symbolic violence, the officer wields considerable power in deciding whether the asylum-seeker's account 'counts'. Hence, the determining officer's basis and criteria for adjudicating credibility and ascertaining consistency in the applicants' descriptions of why they have applied can be frivolous and arbitrary, even when the applicant's country is afflicted with severe human rights problems. As another former member of the Refugee Appeals Tribunal noted: 'I recall an applicant who alleged that he had been a child soldier in Sierra Leone during the civil war. His credibility at first instance had not been accepted partly due to the fact that he could not recall the different colours of the various bank notes in his country. On appeal, the Presenting Officer on behalf of the RAC fairly stated that he was not relying on this ground as a general inquiry among his colleagues had elicited that many of them could not name the colours of the Irish bank notes.'[32]

In a report by Nasc the majority of asylum applicants claimed that they sensed that the interviewer had made his decision prior to the interview:

> interviewees felt staff seemed to be going through the motions and held preconceived notions about the people they were interviewing: 'they already had something in their mind' (James, Ghana) and assumed you were 'probably lying' (David, Burundi). There appeared to be a widely held perception among the asylum-seekers interviewed for this research that the interviewers from the Department of Justice assumed people were lying. Fatima (Pakistan) stated that her interviewers openly accused her of lying, stating that they did not believe what she was telling them. There was also widespread belief that the interviewers were trying to 'trick' the interviewees, or 'catch them out': 'no matter how often, they ask the same question just to confuse you' (Margaret, Nigeria)... there appeared to be an impression among the interviewees that the interviewers, and those who make the decisions, are looking for any reason, no matter how trivial,

to refuse claims for asylum: 'they will find something unimportant and make a big deal of it... [they are] looking for any reason to refuse you'.[33]

In another report by the Immigrant Council of Ireland, asylum-seekers talked of the unfriendliness of the interviewing officers and of being yelled and repeatedly spoken to in an aggressive manner. As one Nigerian noted:

> The first was that the interviewer was stressed, he came up late. I was waiting and when he came he was complaining of his car having a problem and I waited for an hour. Then he just like he wasn't prepared for the interview and... Yeah, so most of the interviewing time he asked me... from where I came and this and that you know that your country has been blacklisted... That was the word he used and again... [Then he said] 'Do you know that your country has been blacklisted in asylum applications? Well let's see what will happen.' (Peter, Nigeria).

One week later his application was refused by the DJELR. On taking this up with his solicitor at the Refugee Legal Services (RLS) he was told 'that nobody wants to accept Nigerians in this country'.[34] Evidence suggests that assessing officers are especially suspicious and dismissive of Nigerian applications even prior to hearing their cases.

Even when applicants have managed to establish credibility with reference to having experienced persecution they ran up against an increasing tendency of investigators to use the 'internal relocation' criteria to reject their application. Hence, if someone was deemed to be experiencing persecution in one region located within a country they were asked why they had simply not moved to another region within the same state. One Nigerian was asked why he didn't remain in Africa: 'And then again it's that whatever you're saying is just like why can't you take asylum in an African country? Seek asylum in Ghana or go to Togo Republic? I said that this is where I feel free and this is also my right' (Joseph, Nigeria).

The Refugee Appeals Tribunal

The heteronomous bureaucratic evaluations affecting the 1st stage of the asylum process were in theory to be kept in check by the 2nd stage of the application process – through an independent appeals mechanism, the Refugee Appeals Tribunal (RAT). Established in October 2000 as part of the Refugee Act, the RAT consists of a chairperson and 35 members, the majority of whom were part-time and appointed on a 3-year basis. The RAT has generally operated with a more liberal interpretation of refugee. In 1998 for example more than two-thirds of those who were refused at first stage were successful on appeal.[35] The overall number of cases decided in favour of asylum-seekers by the RAT between 2001 and 2007 was 16.2%; this compares to the 5.8% given recognition at first stage.[36]

However, despite the appearance of autonomy from the state the selection procedure for membership of the committee entails an evident bias. A proportion of those selected for the RAT were chosen because of social connections or political affiliations.[37] Moreover, a number of judicial reviews have highlighted that frivolous criteria for refusing cases can also be present in RAT judgements. As a judge discussing the refusal of an application noted in a judicial review:

> The third ground advanced by Counsel upon which this applicant seeks leave to apply for judicial review, relates to a question put to the applicant at the oral hearing before the Refugee Appeals Tribunal as to what the weather was like in Somalia in the previous five years. The applicant replied that it was hot and that it was usually hot in Somalia. The conclusion reached by the Member of the Refugee Appeals Tribunal in her decision was that there had been a prolonged drought in Somalia during this period and therefore any native of Somalia would be aware of such a catastrophe and the failure of the applicant to refer to this drought in his answer cast further doubts on his credibility. It was submitted by Counsel for the applicant that the inference drawn from the applicant's reply that he was unaware of this drought and was therefore not, as he claimed, a native of Somalia or had been away from his country of origin for at least five years was unfair, unjustified, irrational and unreasonable.[38]

From its inception the RAT maintained an unwarranted high level of secrecy and operated in a non-transparent and unaccountable manner, steadfastly refusing to: publish how it reached its decisions; disclose how cases were distributed to various members of the tribunal; provide statistics pertaining to how many appeals were upheld or rejected by specific members. Withholding such data prevented defence lawyers from advising their clients on how to construct their asylum cases. More importantly, it masked the wide level of inconsistency and the level of discretion exercised in decision-making of tribunal members. It can be argued that the inconsistencies in decision-making between the members of the tribunal resulted from two interrelated processes: the remuneration structure of the tribunal; and the ideological standpoint of its members.

Unlike members of other state tribunals, those working for RAT were paid on a case-by-case basis, with their fee determined by the type and number of cases that were heard. The structure of the financial reward system induced tribunal members to hear as many cases as quickly as possible, creating a trade-off between financial remuneration and the time needed for reflection and due process. Some members listened to 5 or 6 appeals a day: between 2000 and 2005 the tribunal made an extraordinary 23,107 decisions and between 2001 and April 2006 it spent €7.1 million.[39] The incentive to speed through cases was reinforced by ministerial pressure to clear a massive backlog of cases. As Michael McDowell, the Minister of Justice, declared:

> the nonsense that lies behind a huge amount of these bogus claims… I'm making it very clear that you will be going home within 10 weeks of making a claim in

Ireland, and I would much prefer to have a system where I could have an interview at the airport, find out the cock and bull stories that are going on [and put them] on the next flight. But unfortunately the UN convention requires me to go through due process in respect of all these claims.[40]

Since the Minister of Justice was also largely responsible for appointing and reappointing tribunal members, the latter did not remain impervious to his need for expediting cases quickly and with negative decisions. One member is said to have remarked in the law library that he 'never let one of them in.'[41] The 2 highest earners in the Tribunal, Jim Nicholson, a former trainee lawyer with Michael McDowell, and Ben Garvey, were reputed to have an almost 100% refusal rate for asylum applications. They also both received considerable financial rewards. Between 2000 and the end of November 2007 Nicholson heard over 1,000 cases, earning over €840,000 – about 10% of the total earned by the other 33 members – while Ben Garvey earned €561,184 up to April 2006.

High refusal rates and the assignment and allocation of cases by the RAT chairman on the basis of who had high refusal rates, created a lack of faith in the system for those representing asylum-seeker interests and to a massive increase in the number of judicial reviews undertaken by applicants. Many of these reviews were settled out of court, indicating State culpability. Settlement also suited the State since it prevented these cases from being aired publicly and stifled the creation of judicial precedent. In 2005, 295 High Court challenges to tribunal decisions were settled out of court while the tribunal won 16; in 2006, 358 were settled while the tribunal won 26; and in 2007 the tribunal concluded 260 cases, settling 193.[42]

Two judicial review cases are especially noteworthy for the significant repercussions they had on the operation of the RAT. Following the case of A and Ors v the Refugee Appeals Tribunal in 2005 the RAT was required to publish its most significant decisions in order for fair procedure to operate and to remain in accordance with European Court of Human Rights law. In the Nyembo case, the applicant asked to be reassigned because of an apprehension of bias pertaining to Jim Nicholson. The case was settled in November 2007 before the relevant documents could be produced and Nicholson subsequently resigned.

Declining numbers

The reduction in recognition rates for asylum-seekers took place simultaneously with a fall in the number of applications. After peaking in 2002 at over 11,000, applications began to fall rapidly, dropping to under 3,000 by 2009. Although the State has seen this fall as a successful outcome of the introduction of a number of punitive measures, principally reducing the level of social welfare asylum-seekers received, and adopting a hardline approach in its decision-making, the drop has to be attributed to a broader set of processes. The introduction of pre-emptive policies preventing the possibility of making an asylum application by refusing asylum-seekers leave to land, greater policing at ports and airports especially between Ireland and the UK, and increasing fines to €3000 for airlines carrying passengers not entitled to enter the State in 2003, were all factors. However, by far the largest factor was a broader global fall in asylum applications and changes in the countries of origin of asylum-seekers. Between 1980 and 1989 there were 2,289,454 applications for asylum in industrialized countries whereas between 1990 and 1999 this number increased to 6,215,140 applications. The spike was caused by generalized and persistent violence that resulted from a number of global processes including de-colonization in Asia and Africa, the break up of the Soviet Union, as well as acute conflict in countries such as the former Yugoslavia, Somalia, and Rwanda. The changing configuration of international conflicts meant a relative dissipation in specific global political and ethnic conflicts between 2001 and 2006, and a 50% fall in the total number of asylum-seekers arriving in all industrialized countries, reaching its lowest levels in 2 decades. Hence, between 2001 and 2004 asylum applications fell by 40% worldwide, and 25% at a European level.[43] The accession of EU states also meant a sharp decrease in numbers. Cumulatively these processes meant that less than 1% of worldwide asylum applications were made in Ireland in 2009.

Moreover, migration rarely occurs spontaneously or accidentally between countries. A complex set of factors underlies Ireland as a destination for asylum-seekers. The rise of the Celtic Tiger economy, Ireland's international profile, and increasing transport routes were all factors. The Common Travel Area also allowed relatively easy access between Britain and Ireland. However, Ireland was not chosen specifically as a destination by a large number of asylum-seekers, who instead wanted simply to enter Europe more generally. Agents and traffickers played a key role in determining Ireland, initially at least, as a destination. However, these initial arrivals were soon augmented by the existence of complex social networks.[44] Between 1992 and 2008, 30% of all applications in Ireland were from Nigeria. The initial impetus for Nigerians arriving here, many routed through the UK, were colonial and missionary connections between the states. Many Irish priests taught in Nigerian schools.

The State's regulation of migration has been idiosyncratic and contradictory. At the same time as bringing in large numbers of migrant workers for jobs initially through a liberal work permits regime, and then through the accession state mechanism, it has simultaneously prevented asylum-seekers from working. In the context of sustained pressure from businesses anxious to meet acute labour shortages, the State granted a temporary relieve to asylum-seekers who had been present in Ireland for 12 months on or before 27 July 1999, to work. However, given the absence of institutional support and training, lack of recognition of qualifications, and employer racism and discrimination, take-up was extremely limited with only 67 work permits issued in the first 5 months of the scheme when over 2,000 asylum-seekers were eligible.[45]

Notwithstanding this temporary arrangement and in contrast to all other European countries with the exception of Denmark, the State has denied asylum-seekers the right to work. The government's initial rationalization for this policy was premised on the belief that allowing asylum-seekers to work would serve as a further pull factor, attracting larger numbers of applicants; it would be more difficult to deport them if their applications failed, and they would take jobs from indigenous workers. These were spurious arguments. Firstly, it inflated the degree of choice that asylum-seekers had about where they made their application. The country of destination for asylum-seekers is more frequently shaped by social networks and transportation links than by rational economic interests. Thus for instance both Norway and its neighbour Denmark received the same number of asylum applications in 2000, even though the latter did not grant the right to work.[46] Secondly, there appears to be no correlation between countries which permit asylum-seekers the right to work and the number of deportations that actually take place. This means that even if asylum-seekers are allowed to work, this did not prevent their eventual deportation. Finally, migrants rarely displaced local workers. Rather, during the boom they tended to take up occupations that an increasingly qualified Irish workforce were no longer willing to do – such as cleaning, domestic work, or waiting tables, or jobs that Irish workers could not do – doctors, working in information technology, or as engineers.

In the context of a severe skills shortage in the Irish economy, the State prevented asylum-seekers from working, thereby keeping them trapped in poverty, isolated from mainstream society, and wasting their lives. The policy of denying them the right to work as part of maintaining state control and ethno-racial regulation of the population, especially of non-EU foreigners, has continued to this day, and is unlikely to change in the context of a recession. This was despite a call for the Irish State to fall in line with broader European policy from the EU Commissioner in his Human Rights 2007 report:

> The Commissioner recalls that European Council on Refugees and Exiles has recommended the introduction of provisions allowing temporary work permits for asylum-seekers. In addition to strengthening the autonomy of asylum-seekers and providing revenues for the receiving country, access to the labour market may actually facilitate reintegration into the country of origin by making it possible for the asylum-seeker to return home with a degree of financial independence or acquired work skills. For these reasons, the Commissioner calls upon the Irish authorities to consider providing asylum-seekers with temporary work permits, possibly in the context of the legislative change proposed.[47]

Although the State's reluctance to allow labour market access in part illustrates the irreducibility of state to economic needs and reveals its concern with population control and maintaining a ethno-racially circumscribed population, the picture is perhaps more complex. Restrictions on employment frequently result in asylum-seekers taking up work in the informal economy. Many asylum-seekers work in the informal economy in poor conditions, with few rights and entitlements, and on low wages.

Despite the former Taoiseach's claim that 'Ireland's system compares with the best in the world in its fairness, its decision making, its support services for asylum-seekers',[48] the structure of the asylum system demonstrates both the logic and practice of domination, and the mechanisms by which such domination is disguised and reproduced through an ideology based on fair and due process. Although ORAC is to be subsumed under the Irish Naturalization and Immigration Service (INIS) and the Refugee Appeals Tribunal to be abolished under the Immigration, Residence and Protection Bill and replaced with a Protection Review Tribunal, the general operational structure and world-view of these bodies will remain unchanged.

As the falling numbers demonstrate, asylum-seekers arrived in Ireland within a global context of war and poverty. A more humane reception would not have served, as the State argued, as a greater pull factor. There is also a strong case to be made for more open borders.

Conceiving asylum-seekers as a threat to the social order and instituting policies aimed at discouraging and deterring their entry, the state has systematically attacked one of the most vulnerable and dispossessed groups in Irish society. Their disempowerment means that asylum-seekers do not have access to redress through official political decision-making processes or the media. The effects of state power and the colossal structural violence imposed upon asylum-seekers will be examined further in the next chapter.

Notes

1 *Irish Times*, 30 January 2008.
2 A. Sarat, The law is all over: Power, resistance and the legal consciousness of the welfare poor, *Yale Journal of Law and the Humanities* (1990).
3 P. Cullen, *Refugees and Asylum-seekers in Ireland* (Cork: Cork University Press, 2000) p. 9.
4 A. Zolberg, The next waves migration theory for a changing world.
5 P. Marfleet, *Refugees in a Global Era* (Palgrave: Macmillan, 2006), p. 41.
6 P. Cullen, *Refugees and Asylum-seekers*, p. 13.
7 Ibid., p. 14.
8 *Irish Times*, 26 November 1997.
9 *Irish Times*, 28 November 1997.

10 A. Pollack, An Invitation to Racism? Irish daily coverage of the refugee issue, in D. Kiberd (ed), *The Media in Ireland: The Search for Ethical Journalism* (Dublin: Four Courts, 1999).

11 P. Faugnan and M. Woods, *Lives on Hold: Seeking Asylum in Ireland* (Dublin: Social Science Research Council, 2000); Comhlámh Refugee Solidarity Group, *Refugee Lives* (Dublin: Comhlámh, 2001).

12 The top 6 applicant countries for 2008 were Nigeria 26.1%, Pakistan 6.1, Iraq 5.3, Georgia 4.7, China 4.7, and Democratic Republic of the Congo 4.4.

13 Faugnan and Woods, *Lives on Hold: Seeking aAsylum in Ireland*, (Dublin: Social Science Research Centre, University College Dublin, 2000), p. 14.

14 D. Joly, *Haven or Hell?: Asylum Policies and Refugees in Europe* (Basingstoke: Macmillan, 1996).

15 Marfleet, *Refugees in a Global Era*, p. 155.

16 Faugnan & Woods, *Lives on Hold*, p. 15. This differs from the number of yearly applications because of the lengthy processing times.

17 Thus from over 76,513 applications for asylum only 4,113 applications were granted refugee status.

18 Faugnan & Woods, *Lives on Hold*, p. 16.

19 *Irish Times*, 10 July 2010.

20 Cullen, *Refugees and Asylum-seekers*, p. 29.

21 As the *Irish Times* noted: 'Asylum-seekers subject to fast-tracking are housed in Dublin and have to sign-in at their hostels at 5pm daily, except on Sundays. The penalty for missing the 5pm sign-in is a EUR 3,000 fine or 12 months' imprisonment, or both'. *Irish Times*, 30 December 2004.

22 In 2005, of the 5862 cases finalized 439 were Dublin II, in 2006 of the 4784 cases finalized 540 were deemed to fall within Dublin II, in 2007 of the 4152 cases finalized 368 were Dublin II convention, see www.orac.ie/pdf/PDFStats/Annual%20Statistics/ORAC_2005_Annual_Statistics.pdf.

23 Nasc, *Hidden Cork*; B. Toner, *Wanted: An Immigration Policy* (Dublin: Working Notes, Jesuit Centre for Faith and Justice, 1998).

24 Cullen, *Refugees and Asylum-seekers*, p. 29.

25 C.W. Mills, Situated actions and vocabularies of motive, p. 904.

26 John O'Donohue, speech to the Irish Business and Employers Confederation, Dublin, September 1999.

27 *Irish Times*, 29 January 2002.

28 B. Toner, *Wanted: An Immigration Policy*, Working Notes.

29 H. Garfinkel, *Studies in Ethnomethodology*, p. 78.

30 Nasc, *Hidden Cork*, p. 31.

31 J. Finlay, *Irish Times,* 4 December 1999.

32 McDonagh, http://www.lawlibrary.ie/documents/publications/April05.pdf (2005), p. 45.

33 Ibid., pp. 31–2.

34 ICI, *Getting on, from migration to integration*, 2008.

35 P. Cullen, *Refugees and Asylum-seekers*, p. 30.

36 *Irish Times*, 12 March 2008.

37 *Irish Times*, 6 June 2005. For example, two former Fianna Fail Ministers, David Andrews and Michael O'Kennedy, are on the tribunal.

37 F vs. Refugee Appeals Tribunal, 8 May 2008.

38 *Irish Times*, 10 April 2008.

40 Michael McDowell, address to an Oireachtas Justice Committee in 2005, http://www.rte.ie/news/2005/0518/asylum.html.

41 *Irish Times*, 8 July 2008.

42 There have therefore been almost 1,000 settlements between 2004 and 2007 costing an estimated €20 m. *Irish Times*, 18 March 2008.

43 www.unhcr.org/cgi-bin/texis/vtx/news/opendoc.htm?tbl=NEWS&id=441929762.

44 Irish missionaries played a strong role engendering this migration by providing positive stories about Ireland and its welcoming nature either in their role as priests and/or as teachers.

45 B. Fanning, S. Loyal & C. Staunton, Asylum-seekers and the right to work, p. 10.

46 Irish Refugee Council, *Asylum-seekers and the Right to Work* (Dublin: RC,, 2001), p. 4.

47 Council of Europe, Report by the Commissioner for Human Rights, Mr Tomas Hammarberg, on his visit to Ireland (Starsbourg: Council of Europe), p. 108 at wcd.coe.int/ViewDoc.jsp?id=1283555&Site=CommDH&BackColorInternet=FE C65B&BackColorIntranet=FEC65B&BackColorLogged=FFC679.

48 Bertie Ahern, *Irish Times*, 20 December 2007.

Chapter 6

The direct provision regime

This chapter looks at direct provision (DP) from the asylum-seeker's point of view. It examines the objective unfolding of direct provision and the subjective experience of those asylum-seekers trapped within the system. As individuals in a country to which they have had no previous connection, encasement in the direct provision system heightens their pyscho-social dislocation, reinforces their physical placelessness, and strips down their sense of self. Direct provision centres (DPCs) in effect function as total institutions, imposing a new spatial configuration on asylum-seekers' lives. Drawing on Goffman and Bourdieu this chapter outlines the damaging psycho-social effects that direct provision has on their lives as a system that radically alters their taken-for-granted living environment in terms of material living and subsistence, time perception, eating, social interactions, autonomy of action, recognition and status, and social expectations.

Like all sociological processes the direct provision system can be interpreted from different vantage points. Two of the most salient and starkly opposed are the viewpoint of the state and that of the asylum-seekers who live in the centres. Giving the state's point of view, a former Minister of Justice noted: 'I am satisfied that direct provision is a fair, humane and cost effective way of meeting the accommodation and ancillary needs of asylum-seekers and the Government has no plans, at this point in time, to change the system.'[1] By contrast, as an asylum-seeker on hunger strike noted: 'People outside the walls of Knockalisheen don't know how we live. It's a prison. Animals should live here, not humans. It should be destroyed.'[2]

In *Asylum* (1991 [1961]), Goffman examined the various modalities of attack and violation on the territory of the self and the multiplicity of factors that resulted in the increasing loss of control that individuals exercised over the self. The insertion of individuals into total institutions in which: 'a large number of like-situated individuals, cut off from the wider society for an appreciable period of time, together lead an enclosed, formally administered round of life' strips individuals of an otherwise socially recognized and validated autonomy.[3] Integral to this process of social degradation is the imposition of restrictions on undertaking actions that had previously served as markers of individual self-determination and autonomy. Assaults on the self include the degradation and defilement of self-esteem caused by role dispossession, a fall into a lower social status, and a concomitant sense of powerlessness and inefficacy. The total institution strips the individual of his or her identity, replacing it with a devalued sense of self.

Goffman's account of the violations on the self in the context of social relations in disequilibrium has strong parallels with Bourdieu's early writings on the sociology of Algeria. This is especially evident in Bourdieu's conceptualization of *hysterisis* to designate the adverse psycho-social effects resulting from the habitus formed under one set of social conditions confronting and attempting to adjust to a new and radically different set of social conditions. The result for both thinkers is the same – a dislocated, indeterminate, fragmented, and fractured sense of self engendering acute psycho-social suffering in the individual.

Asylum-seekers in Ireland

Asylum-seekers residing in Ireland are not permitted to leave the State, enter into employment, or carry out any form of business prior to the final determination of their case. Those who entered Ireland before April 2000 were generally in receipt of full Supplementary Welfare Assistance (SWA) payments which stood at about £72 for a single adult and £13.20 per child per week in 1999.[4] They were also free to choose their accommodation and, usually with the aid of the local health board, the vast majority – over 90% – settled in Dublin. Those who arrived after April 2000, however, were to be subjected to a qualitatively different form of state governmentality provided for through a system of direct provision, and geographically dispersed throughout the country. The process of direct provision and dispersal is overseen by the Reception and Integration Agency (RIA), which is part of the Department of Justice. The DP system has no statutory basis, thereby allowing it to evade equality legislation. Under the system asylum-seekers are housed around the country in various buildings including hostels, hotels, prefabricated buildings, and mobile homes, and are provided for with fixed meals. They are not entitled to SWA payments but, instead, receive a nugatory €19.10 per adult and €9.60 per child per week. This amount was established in 2000 and despite inflation remains unchanged. For a single adult this constitutes about 3% of the national average industrial wage. In addition, they are entitled to a medical card and sometimes exceptional needs payments of approximately €150 for maternity supplies and clothes once or twice a year, though this is at the discretion of the Community Welfare Officer. Child benefit for asylum-seekers was withdrawn in 2004 with the introduction of the Habitual Residence Condition (HRC).

As of the end of April 2008 there were approximately 6,850 asylum-seekers from 96 different nationalities, dispersed in 62 centres throughout the State. This included 2 reception centres, 58 accommodation centres and 8 self-catering centres. The majority of asylum-seekers in DP (68%) are from Africa, and a further 20% from Asia. In terms of national breakdown, the majority are from Nigeria (30%), the Democratic Republic of Congo (7%) and Somalia (4%). Age-wise, the population is relatively young, with just over 50% between 18 and 35 and about 30% aged 17 years or younger. Many are in families (3,882), though there are also 2,283 single males and 873 single women. The duration of their residence in these centres varies, though over two-thirds have been living in DPCs for over a year and almost a third for over 3 years (see Table 6.1). Since the DP system was put in place over 49,100 asylum-seekers have passed through it.

There were manifold political impulses underlying the creation of the direct provision system. After 1997 media and political campaigns began a sustained campaign of defining asylum-seekers as 'spongers' responsible for crime, the housing crisis, a threat to the social order, and as a general social malaise affecting the country. The result of these political and media discourses, together with an ever-quickening rise in numbers, was a ratcheting up the restrictions against asylum-seekers and a rise in racism towards them. Both the government and media made much of the putative difference between 'genuine' refugees of whom there are few, and 'bogus' refugees, of whom there are too many. Government and media statements frequently referred to the way that the generous Irish welfare regime was attracting 'economic migrants'. With the welfare state under pressure to change organizationally under the weight of a rising neo-liberal ideology, asylum-seekers were conceived as an unnecessary financial burden that needed to be kept out of the welfare system. The implication was that an overly generous and prosperous Ireland, the land of a hundred thousand welcomes, was being systematically abused by unscrupulous and fraudulent asylum-seekers draining the country's resources.

Table 6.1 Length of stay in direct provision in 2008

Duration	Number
Less than 1 year	2133
1–2 years	1635
2–3 years	1362
3–4 years	848
Over 4 years	953
TOTAL	6931

Source: Sean Aylward, letter 24 April 2008 to public accounts committee

The Department of Justice Equality and Law Reform (DJELR) argued that the large number of asylum-seekers who had arrived in Ireland in the last 3 months of 1999 had stretched the State's social, economic, and infrastructural capacity. In the context of an increasingly deregulated housing policy, the Eastern Health Board, which was responsible for allocating accommodation in Dublin, pointed to the limited availability of rooms and stated that it had to turn asylum-seekers away. State-fuelled hysteria, amplified and extended through the media, portrayed the arrival of asylum-seekers as constituting a 'crisis' bordering on a national emergency. In response the State introduced a policy of dispersal and direct provision which involved housing and feeding asylum-seekers in a mix of accommodation solutions including hotels, prefabricated units, and mobile homes, located around the country.

Although the sudden upsurge in numbers and acute shortage of accommodation in Dublin were used by the State as the rationalization for the introduction of DP, the decision has to be understood within a broader historical and structural context. Historically, 3 broad analytically distinct though substantively overlapping restrictionary criteria have determined the Irish State's treatment of immigrants: economic costs or benefits, questions of ethno-national/racial and religious homogeneity, and security and law and order considerations. The direct provision system constituted a manifestation and compound of all 3 of these exclusionary practices. The institution of the DP system has to be understood within the context of an overarching attempt to deter the arrival of asylum-seekers by reducing living conditions and welfare payments to the absolute minimum, and simultaneously as part of a radical intervention into the lives of asylum-seekers as a mechanism to discipline, control, and regulate their presence within the State. The introduction of DP is also inexplicable without acknowledging its prior establishment in the UK in 1999. The existence of the Common Travel Area has largely meant that for operational and practical reasons Irish migration policies often mirror those in the UK. A fear that asylum-seekers (conceived as self-seeking, individual, rational actors), would choose Ireland over the UK, if the former offered more generous social welfare payments, was a central factor underpinning the Irish State's decision. As John O'Donohue noted: 'if my scheme is more attractive than the British scheme, it must stand to any kind of logical reasoning that I would have a disproportionate number coming here from Britain.'[5] In the UK, asylum-seekers were denied access to the welfare system but instead given £35 in vouchers to be spent in designated shops. The Irish State went one better by offering £15 (€19.10) a week, albeit in cash form. The welfare and poverty needs of individuals living in the State thereby became subordinated and relegated to the economic, xenophobic, and security needs of State.[6]

As Wacquant has noted: 'to forget that urban space is a historical and political construction in the strong sense of the term is to risk (mis)taking for "neighbourhood effects" what is nothing more than the spatial retranslation of economic and social differences.'[7] The State's introduction of DPCs in various areas led to a mixture of local anger, xenophobia, and elitism. These local challenges echoed earlier objections to the construction of traveller sites and accommodation.[8] The State was prevented from establishing centres by local oppositional interests in Ballsbridge, Donnybrook, Macroom, Myshall, Rosslare, and Ballina. In Ballsbridge, for example, an affluent residents' association from Pembroke road took up a successful legal challenge to have a DP closed. One member of the group stated that the area was 'becoming saturated with unwanted elements who are a threat to the settled community'.[9] In other cases local opposition involved pickets, blockades, and even murder threats. Locals in Myshall threatened to shoot the owner of the centre, who subsequently had to be placed under police protection.[10] At a local protest meeting held in Rosslare, 400 locals out of a population of 2500 met and stated that asylum-seekers constituted an unspecified threat to children who were 'hanging around schools'.[11] The view that the presence of visibly different migrants would have a negative economic impact on the tourist industry became a common complaint from other rural areas which depended on tourism. As Ballina's town's mayor, a FF councillor noted: 'If you have 300 to 400 people that are put in a situation by the Government that they're left with €9 a week, they have very little to do. Those people are going to spend their time on the balconies and on the banks of the river. It's not going to be something that will encourage people to come and fish here.'[12] However, such opposition has to be contextualized in some cases. A lack of consultation by the State, and a feeling that a marginalized group was being dumped into their area, was compounded by conflicts over the provision and allocation of scarce resources. In the case of the protest at a hotel in Rosslare the hotel had served as a local pub and was used by community groups as a soccer club and disco. Equally, opposition by some travellers was based on the fact that they had been waiting 12 years to be provided with toilets and running water for their halting site and that these had been provided in relatively short space of time for asylum-seekers.[13] Such views reflected how economic considerations were intermingled with straightforward forms of ethno-racial discrimination and xenophobia. They demonstrated how ethno-racial stereotypes, attributions and explanations were employed by individuals to make 'practical' sense of their everyday lives.[14] As an ideology racist discrimination constituted an explanation of the problems these groups experienced. It offered an explanation for the housing crisis, lack of jobs available, and continuing poverty which many marginalized groups faced.

Direct provision as total institution

Despite general standards being set by the Reception and Integration Agency concerning accommodation, the facilities and resources provided by the various centres, and their management styles, vary greatly. Differences between the centres are manifest in a number of ways:

- in terms of disciplinary regimes, through the prohibitiveness of house rules – some strictly enforce rules while others are more flexible (for example if a resident is away for more than 3 consecutive nights, whether he or she has their asylum claim and assistance withdrawn)
- some allow visitors and others do not
- the quality of the accommodation and room – some have ensuite rooms whilst others share a single bedroom with 3 or 4 others
- the availability of crèche facilities
- access to services and amenities including a laundry room, kitchen facilities, or even appliances such as fridges or kettles.

Two of the biggest factors distinguishing DPCs are the quality and variety of food provision and their geographical location. Whether a DPC is situated in a remote rural area or in or nearby a major city structures asylum-seekers' access to a range of facilities and resources as well as determining the interaction with mainstream society.

Direct provision centres are disciplinary and exclusionary forms of spatial and social closure that separate and conceal asylum-seekers from mainstream society and ultimately prevent their long-term integration or inclusion. They are, as Goffman notes with reference to total institutions, 'forcing houses for changing persons; each is a natural experiment on what can be done to the self'.[15] With a number of graduated sanctions designed to modify people's conduct, DPCs bureaucratically process asylum-seekers, stripping them of any vestige of autonomy and self-determination and corroding their sense of self and self-esteem. By regulating, manipulating, and constraining the behaviour of those living there, DPCs simultaneously dehumanize, degrade, and control them. This material and psychological dispossession and dismantling of the self takes place in a dual sense. The move from one national context into a different socio-cultural context can have profoundly unsettling and destabilizing effects for migrants, especially if they have suffered from trauma. The move into the self-enclosed disciplinary social order of a DPC amplifies this dislocation even further.

The DPC encompasses and intervenes in the asylum-seeker's whole existence: from eating to sleeping, undercutting their individuality and destroying their dignity and self-determination. An individual is, as Goffman notes:

cleanly stripped of many of his accustomed affirmations, satisfactions, and defenses, and is subjected to a rather full set of mortifying experiences: restriction of free movement, communal living, diffuse authority over a whole echelon of people, and so on. Here one begins to learn about the limited extent to which a conception of oneself can be sustained when the usual supports for it are suddenly removed.[16]

Living in DPCs means that individuals can no longer maintain their earlier sense of self structured in their former community of origin but instead the negatively socially valued category of 'asylum-seeker' becomes their master status. In DPCs, human needs are organized so that nearly all aspects of the asylum-seeker's life takes place under one roof. Taken-for-granted social and spatial divisions between sleep, work, and play are also broken down. Daily activity is carried out in the company of a large group of others who are brought together into a single rational plan designed to fulfil the aims of the institution. Asylum-seekers arrive at a DPC with a 'presenting culture', a way of life and form of activities derived from, and made possible by, certain stable arrangements from his or her home world or country, and therefore a fundamental constituent of a central part of his or her habitus and self-understanding. Upon entrance to the centre, however, he or she is immediately stripped of the support provided by these former social/structural arrangements, and his/her territorial self becomes mortified as it is progressively assaulted. They no longer have access to resources and institutional supports permiting them to sustain a 'normal' dignified sense of self to others. This process of mortification involves a number of features. A process of 'trimming' or 'programming' in which the individual becomes coded into an object that can be worked on and disciplined by the institutional logic of the centre had already been initiated with the individual's entry into the state, and his or her registration as an 'asylum-seeker'. This is consolidated as the DPC further regiments and violates the individual's informational preserve by creating a personal dossier of information, recording activities and out-of-the-ordinary actions, available and accessible to staff.

Employment

Asylum-seekers' lack of a right to work condemns them to unemployment and to a resigned idleness. This enforced passivity, a form of 'civil death', is compounded by their inability to access adult education or training programmes.

In mainstream society, employment has at least 4 interrelated functions. First, it provides access to social contexts of interaction, aiding social integration and inclusion. With no opportunity for employment, asylum-seekers are disembedded from the outside world, trapped and geographically separated from the social world, and captive in DPCs that are often situated in remote locations. Their material misery and social insecurity are refracted through the loss of group ties on which their psycho-social stability was previously based. Those who are single can especially experience acute isolation. As one female resident, a single mother from Nigeria who had few friends or contacts, remarked about her situation: 'I feel very very lonely' (Abagabe, Nigeria). However, even those in families face new social tensions created by their stressful and inhospitable living conditions. Their geographical confinement to the centre, lack of finance, or limited access to villages and public life means relations within familes become heavily strained by the pressures of constrained co-presence and clustraphobic living: 'I have been here 3 years and 1 month and never go out. Christmas, Easter, everything here, this place, nothing else, nowhere else' (Sergei, Kosovo).

Second, work provides a sense of identity and social status. Living in DPCs enhances role dispossession and destroys the positive valences for self that follow from contributing through work or activities. For males, losing one's identity as breadwinner or the ability to look after one's family can especially be difficult. Unemployment disrupts the differentiated role schedule which existed for many prior to their entry into the direct provision system. Individuals can no longer move fluidly between a variety of roles – father, mother, husband, wife, mechanic, nurse, consumer, etc. – which had previously provided various forms of identitification, but instead become frozen in their role as 'asylum-seekers', which becomes their dominant state-enforced identity. Even prior to their entry into DPCs, asylum-seekers had already been negatively framed in a degraded status as 'bogus' or 'sponger'. Their lack of social power to challenge this persistent misframing can mean becoming enmeshed in a 'frame trap' that structures and reinforces the treatment towards them by others. In their daily life they become constrained to take on a degraded stigmatized status which detracts from their sense of human worth: a status they consider alien and which has symbolic implications that are incompatible with their own conception of self, but from which it is difficult to dis-identify. As a young male respondent from Afghanistan noted: 'Most of the time I eat, sleep and watch TV' (Abdul, Afghanistan). Although some wish to escape from the dead, heavy-hanging time framing their lives, through what Goffman calls 'removal activities', they instead spend their time watching television, dwelling on their lives and misfortune, or indulging in escapist or fantasy thinking. Schutz insightfully discussed the role played by fantasies, especially for people unable to alter their material circumstances:

> When my attention becomes absorbed in one of the several fantasy worlds, I no longer need to master the external world. There is no resistance by objects surrounding me which have to be subdued. I am exempted from the urgency of the pragmatic motive under which I stand in the everyday natural attitude. The intersubjective standard time of the everyday life-world no longer governs me. The world is still limited through what is present in my perception, memory and

knowledge. Events and situations over which I have no control do not force alternatives upon me between which I must choose. My productive ability is not circumscribed by external circumstances. But also, as long as I live in fantasy worlds, I cannot 'produce' in the sense of an act which gears into the external world and alters it. As long as I tarry in the world of fantasy I cannot accomplish anything, save just to engage in fantasy. However, under certain circumstances I can sketch out in advance the course of fantasy as such (I will imagine the fairy gives me three wishes), and I can then fulfill this project.[17]

Over-thinking can also lead to depression and insomnia for many:

Everyday you are doing the same thing: you have no education, no sport, something to do, activities, you have nowhere to go, I don't know. You get depression; you get very upset all day watching TV; you know, it's not good. I tried to ask last year for permission to work but you never get it. And I drink you know, because that €19 a week I drink that, without drink I cannot sleep, or with tablets, I'm taking sleeping tablets. (Sergei, Kosovo)

Some take up drinking and smoking as a result of boredom or to overcome insomnia: 'I'm thinking many many things… I can't sleep if I didn't take medicine or I didn't take alcohol, I can't sleep… because you're thinking too much' (Abbo, Uganda).

Third, employment provides a source of income and finance. Denying asylum-seekers the right to work leads to acute poverty. The inconsequential weekly subsistence received from the State debars them from purchasing items which others ordinarily take for granted in everyday living. This includes food but also phone cards to contact relatives living abroad and abate their lonliness, and bus tickets to travel to the city. Pecuniary factors also hinder the purchase of toiletries and cosmetics, products allowing individuals to exert some control over their self-presentation before others. The inability to buy apparel, clothing, and cosmetics, means that asylum-seekers are stripped of identity equipment usually used to present the self-image to others. Moreover, in modern society, being seen as a consumer is also a central part of personhood and self. '[T]here is the curse of being poor in the midst of a rich society in which participation in the sphere of consumption has become a sine qua non of social dignity – a passport to personhood if not citizenship (especially among the dispossessed, who have nothing else at their disposal to signal membership.'[18] The sense of helplessness and exasperation is particularly acute for single mothers bringing up children, especially following the withdrawal of child benefit payments. One respondent expecting her second child expressed her desperation in an emotional reflection:

I'm just sick and tired… I was crying up to now. I sometimes feel like committing suicide because I don't know what to do or where to go… I don't know what to do, I can't go back to my country, I'm sick and tired, I don't know, I'm just sick and tired. That's why I'm scared because if I have this baby here that's another problem... it's going to be double the problem staying in the hostel, living with 19.10 and 9.60. How am I going to cope? (Abagabe, Nigeria)

Stripped of adequate financial resources, asylum-seekers become dependent on staff for minor supplies or help to undertake activities that they had previously executed on their own. In one DPC, lacking laundry facilities for example, inmates are only permitted to hand in one item of clothing to staff a week to be washed and only given one toilet roll a week. As adults who had usually exercised some degree of self-determination this radical dependence disrupts their personal economy of action and control or command over the world. They perceive having to make continual requests or to seek permission as demeaning and constituting a further insult to their dignity, and they yearn for respect or recognition. They have been demoted to a suppliant child-like status that is keenly felt when requests are refused: 'I have been here three years and you ask for a new pillow you never get it, new sheets, nothing, never' (Sergei, Kosovo).

Fourth, employment provides a sense of purpose: a minimum material security required in order to have assurance about the present and to plan and construct a future. The general temporal framework and outlook of those living in DPCs is comparable to the experiences of the unemployed and uprooted Algerian peasantry in the 1960s:

> the whole of their existence was lacking that which normally constitutes its main framework: the daily work at one's customary occupation, with its temporal and spatial rhythms, the demands it imposes, the security it offers, the future that it allows one to envisage and plan for... They inevitably become reconciled and accustomed to a parasitic and vegetative form of existence.[19]

Time can only be defined relationally so that time for work only takes on meaning by reference to time for leisure. Without work functioning as a signpost or measure, the day loses rhythm and in some ways time stops:

> when we speak of underemployment – it means simply that what happens is not what we expected. Unlike the time of others in society, their time is valueless. The nature and the number of events that we keep to constitute time sequences, hence their tempo, depend on the principle of selection that we use implicitly and that underlies the ideas we have about work and, therefore, about life itself.[20]

Contrasted to full and well-filled time, time becomes empty or lost time. The experience of duration is of empty, homogenous, wasted time involving basic activities. Time is perceived and reified as something that has been stolen from their lives, something that has to be written off. Over half of asylum-seekers in DPCs are aged between 18 and 35 and perceive themselves to be wasting the most important or formative years of their lives. As a 25-year-old asylum-seeker noted: 'This is what's making me upset, this is the time for our study and our work and after this time, then it will be too late for study' (Abdul, Afghanistan). Another tied his wasted life to entrenched institutionalization:

> Everyday, everyday what am I going to think after 3 years if they give me a bad decision? I lose 3 years for nothing. How do I explain my youth, I was 26 when I arrived, you know in this country, I'm 29 now. For three years I've been idle, for me now even to work it's difficult because I'm lazy now I've been sitting for three years, sleeping, sitting, eating' (Sergei, Kosovo).

Denied the opportunity to work some asylum-seekers take up odd jobs or work in the black economy, sometimes at absurdly low wage rates. One Nigerian talked about the intermittent work she got as a babysitter. She was picked up from the DPC early in the morning and dropped back off by 6 in the evening and paid €5 for the day's babysitting.

Accommodation and living

Crammed together in purpose-built, prefabricated buildings, or disused hostels, the standard of accommodation for asylum-seekers varies greatly. Many live in sub-standard accommodation in cramped and overcrowded conditions.[21] One house that functioned as an extension of a DPC contained three families and accommodated 14 individuals, including 9 children. There was no shared living room and just one kitchen. Because of the constant noise and stress from the younger children, parents found it difficult to sleep, and the older children were unable to study:

> The main problem is that we don't like to live here. We live in a 3 bed house. How many families can live there? When we sleep the young kids cry. The thing is I have 2 boys and I girl, she is 14, and the brothers are 13 and 7. There are 3 kids all in one room when they sleep. There are 9 kids in the house and they scream and Fatima is in the house, she studies in the second year and it disturbs her studies... I am diabetic, I can't rest because there are so many children, because they are screaming my sugar level goes up. (Mohamhed, Pakistan)

In other centres catering primarily for single adults, between 4 and 6 single individuals shared one room. In Viking House, for example, 90% shared a room with at least three others.[22] Denied privacy, individual territories of self are both constricted and violated. The boundary the individual places between their being and the environments is invaded. The DPC allows for no private space permitting the concealment of ordinarily private activities, or for an individual to rest his or her 'front stage'. Individuals are also exposed to what Goffman calls 'social contamination' from others. In confined spaces it is no longer possible to hold objects of self-feeling – such as one's body, actions or thoughts, and/or possessions – clear of contact with what are perceived as contaminative things or people. Differentiated by class and gender, nationality, and age, asylum-seekers come from diverse backgrounds, religions, and often have few common ties of attachment other than sharing a spatial location. Their lived experiences and dispositions can differ markedly. Individuals and groups who would by choice wish to remain apart or hold themselves above others are forced to live together. Different ages, ethnic and racial groups are mixed together. Lack of a communal language, restricted space, and a lack of privacy, combined with acute feelings of frustration and powerlessness about their irredeemable situation, can sometimes lead to tensions between roommates, but also with other residents they may encounter on a regular basis. Tensions can sometimes take the form of prejudices about others' living practices, stereotypes, or negative characterizations of lifestyle. As one Pakistani noted about the Nigerians he lives with: 'Then you have to share the kitchen with Nigerians... The Nigerian lady when she cooks I can't bear the smell and the wife and kids feel like vomiting. She is a different kind of Muslim so she cooks very different food' (Mohammed, Pakistan).

Tensions also arise from being forced to accept and adjust to other people's different sleeping patterns:

> I have problems and I've been visiting a psychiatrist for 2 years now. I had a little bit before but not so much. Since I share kitchen, bedroom, and toilet with people you know and I'm sleeping in one room not even 20 m squared. And I have a small room. That room I stay, lie, and watch TV since the last 5 months. The room I have is like a shell. (Sergei, Kosovo)

Insomnia for some leads to depression in others.

Relations with staff

There is a diversity in the management and operational styles of DPCs. Some DPCs have inflexible management styles, arbitrary restrictions, and operate through a culture of intimidation. Others are more flexible, with understanding and compassionate staff who work hard to try to satisfy the needs of the residents. Notwithstanding these differences, there exists a fundamental hierarchic split between a large managed group of disempowered asylum-seekers and a small group of relatively powerful supervisory staff, with each category often dealing with the other in terms of stereotypes.

Staff and management wield power in a number of formal and informal ways. If, as Weber noted, the management of the modern office is based on keeping written documents, then the recording of (usually transgressional) activities is one of the most important ways in which management of the DPC operate a punishment and sanctioning system. Forms of punishment and reward are usually applied to children or animals, and although they also exist in the adult world they have a specific application. In DPCs staff often reprimand residents' behaviour, sometimes in an arbitrary fashion that expresses their power. Residents can be punished by threats to transfer them to a worse DPC or by blocking a transfer request to what is deemed a more satisfactory centre, especially one of the 8 self-catering centres or one close to a large city.[23] Some residents have an exaggerated sense of the existence of superior facilities in other centres. Through informal networks DPCs have been hierarchically ranked. For example, a centre in Athlone located in a mobile home site and containing small cramped caravans, worn and broken gas cooking and heating facilities, is ranked low. By contrast, many rank Mosney highly because of the greater facilities in the centre – such as self-catering – and because of its proximity to Dublin, which allows access to shops, amenities, or because friends or relatives usually reside there. As one respondent noted: 'I want to move to Co. Meath, Mosney; there you get your own kitchen, they don't give you a house to share with somebody' (Ravinder, India). Another, who was transferred after fighting with another inmate, highlighted his sense of injustice of being prevented from getting transferred to Mosney, having spent 2 years in Athlone:

> I lived in Athlone nearly 2 years – accommodation caravans. I fought there and got transferred. I tried to get into Mosney, Mosney, Mosney... we fought each other. He was not even here 2 years but got a plus for reporting people to social welfare. He got sent to Dundalk. Dundalk is self-catering. You get your own bedroom, you get good light. (Sergei, Kosovo)

For poorly resourced and sometimes agitated staff, some asylum-seekers are perceived as overly demanding, instrumental, self-seeking, and ungrateful for being allowed to stay in the country. Some residents are also seen as overly rude and aggressive in their incessant requests to alter existing organizational ways of doing things, and their constant demand for goods and facilities. By contrast, asylum-seekers see staff as condescending, unsympathetic, and mean-spirited, particularly when asking for assistance in acquiring objects or resources, or when articulating their grievances. In other cases staff are perceived as intimidating, disciplinarian, and aggressive in their approach.

Duration

Durkheim indicated the integral connection between time and social practices when he noted that the 'foundation of the category of time is the rhythm of social life'.[24] All societies operate with systems of time reckoning, sequencing, and duration. However, these vary both historically and across cultures, so that like space, to which it is inextricably linked, timing activities express and reinforce ideological and material relations of power and domination. Discussions of time in the social sciences are complex and contested, often invoking untenable and simplifying binaries such as those proposed by Levi-Strauss between linear and cyclical, cumulative and non-cumulative, reversible and irreversible, or between clock and natural time.[25] Instead, analyses of time need to examine the shifting balances between these dichotomies in timing activities.[26]

Time is not merely an environment for social activities but is inextricably constitutive of them. An individual's expectations, perceptions, and attitudes towards the future play a central role in organizing their short- and long-term plans, their future tasks, interactions, and for framing their everyday experience. Consequently, the radical alteration in social relations characterizing life in DPCs has profoundly altered asylum-seekers' experiences and attitudes towards time. At its root the change in their time horizon is a result of their structural disempowerment and wholesale psycho-social dislocation in a new institutional order.

For most Western employed adults a temporal perspective characterized by future need orientations, reached by drawing on past resources, is the norm. Everyday life is pervaded by clock time and punctuated by sharply demarcated activity routines involving employment, leisure, or family time. The nature and the expectations surrounding activities structure and shape the tempo and pace of everyday life. Through the enactment of various daily routines time progresses relatively smoothly from the past through the present to the future. Reflecting their acutely different existential conditions and material positions, asylum-seekers operate with a markedly different temporal perspective. The temporal discalibration caused by moving from one system of temporal reckoning to another is an outcome of their wide-ranging and entrenched powerlessness in DPCs. The pattern of time, the way it moves from the past, through the present, to the future is elliptical. The endemic logic and rule-bound nature of DPCs instill a specific temporal horizon in the residents that determines the rhythm of their lives. Their temporal horizon is a manifestation of their inability to control the world, to predict its outcome, waiting for a decision on their application, and the ensuing feelings of powerlessness. For many, the future has evaporated or is 'on hold'. There is instead a presentist orientation to life. As one asylum-seeker remarked, the period of waiting for a decision can be more painful than returning home:

> So I have to wait all this time and this waiting time is killing me. My life's in danger, I know, if I go back I might be killed. But this situation that I'm living here is more dangerous than that time, because most of the time I feel mad, lonely, doing nothing, eating nothing, lots of pain, better if I go once and decide where is my family... That's what's killing me... I think I will accept death to die in my country. Before I go mad in here and I do something stupid. (Abdul, Afghanistan)

Their inability to control the temporal organization of their day-to-day lives, their long-term projects or aspirations, results in a focus on everyday activity and on the proximate future. Long-term planning or the establishment of concrete goals for a distant future is forsaken for a preoccupation with the necessities of a subsistence life. The outcomes of events and their lives are instead seen as subject to fate or providential outcome. Things are predetermined by a deity or by the stars. In such a cosmology of predetermination it is futile to engage in major life-impacting choices. Since they conceive themselves not as self-determining individuals empowered and actively shaping their future but, rather as passive effects of opaque social forces, to which they remain dependent, many adopt an attitude of fatalism and resignation to the passage of time.[27] Individuals stand a great distance away from Heidegger's speculations on authentic being: they are not already futured, or essentially futural beings, in which the future is real in the present, taking on projects which they have been thrown into, but rather exist in the very nadir of inauthenticity. This is not because they refuse to choose or unthinkingly exist within the now of 'the they', but because of their structural position of dispossession. Their life is geared towards immediate survival and meeting necessities in a suspended present. The result of the lack of control in determining their environment and choices is alienation:

> Oh when I think about my future I have nothing in my hands, have nothing, I have nothing, there's no future for me. You get you get cancer, you get sick, or you smoke, smoke, thinking It makes your sugar level go up, I have diabetes. I'm getting fat sleeping, getting up, thinking, thinking, thinking. I am a human being, a human beings cannot keep for long. (Sergei, Kosovo)

With little money to spend, everyday life is geared to the repetition of mundane events and activities. The monotony of the living environment rarely changes. Few consider mastering, saving, or using up time: 'we get up, eat and sleep' (Abdul, Afghanistan). Idle or with little to do other than walk through the village or town closest to the centre, some go window-shopping with no intention or means for buying anything. Events flow slowly and repetitiously. The pace of life, its tempo, drags. Daily activities and routines are predictable and monotonous. Many sleep irregular hours, during the day, or go to bed at 4 or 5 in the morning.

The focus on day-to-day matters and foreshortened future perspective is not simply a material reflex of disempowerment and limited opportunities, but also functions as a defence mechanism within a context that does not permit any wider or longer-term perspective on the future. Some fantasize about a positive outcome to their asylum application as a resolution to their current existential contradictions, while others dwell on their past life which they have forsaken.

Some start their residence in DPCs with a great sense of hope, and even engage in a number of activities to pass the day and provide comfort. Because of the protracted length of time it takes to get a decision – almost 50% of asylum-seekers have been waiting 2 years, and a quarter 3 years or more – many become resigned, inactive, and depressed. However, sooner or later the fantasy shield breaks down as a reality shock breaks in, and when it does, the result is invariably traumatic and has strong affective and emotional effects. The long-term disruption and evaporation of a future perspective, the breakdown of self-image, and failure of self-claims to be recognized or validated, can also lead to estrangement from others. Having waited so long and endured such precarious conditions, many feel unprepared for a negative decision: 'It's taking a long time, at the end of the day if they are going to take a long time and they are going to refuse me what am I going to do? Am I not going to commit suicide at the end of the day?' (Abagabe, Nigeria).

Direct provision centres provide an encompassing social world for the asylum-seeker. As an organization set up to meet certain goals, it ends up controlling and regulating a large part the asylum-seeker's time and day. The individual's personal economy of action in which he or she chooses to fit certain activities into one another, or balances needs and objectives in a personal way, is destroyed. In DPCs the individual's line of activity becomes subject to a greater degree to regulations imposed from above, and his or her autonomy of action or planning the day becomes restricted as major phases of the day's activities become tightly scheduled. This occurs in a number of ways. Firstly, through the imposition of strict mealtimes. Because they cannot afford to buy their own food, residents need to go to breakfast, lunch, and dinner according to the stipulated times set by the centre. Some DPCs do not allow residents to take food out of the canteen either to eat in their bedroom or later at a more suitable time. Some even check bags to make sure individuals are not doing so.

Dietary provision

Given their empty schedule, eating becomes a major component of the day and takes on a disproportionate significance in structuring people's days. However, the poor quality and lack of variety of food leads to considerable anger. One of the most frequent complaints about DPCs concern the standard and type of food provided.[28] Most centres do not have any cooking facilities or allow food preparation to take place, thereby stripping the individual of a further aspect of their personal autonomy of action. Although required to produce an 'ethnic' dish, many DPCs do not do so. This can be for a number of reasons: because of the cost, the difficulty of acquiring ingredients, or because of the wide variety of different nationalities dwelling in the centres. Instead, rice and potatoes are given as staples every day and are supplemented with cheap homogenous processed foods lacking nutritional value, such as chips, chicken nuggets, or fish fingers:

> I'm not the only one who complains. You can talk to other people. I'm telling you 5 days a week its fish fingers, chicken nuggets and rice, 5 days a week, 5 days a week. The only good thing here is salad... If you don't want to be fat you can eat salad, the only thing. Bread is not fresh, it's 3 or 4 days old. The food that was made last night they give the next day as well. If it is for lunch they give for dinner. (Sergei, Kosovo)

Another, talking about her mother, noted:

> She doesn't get good food here. It's like it's really bad for your health. The food we get here is always fried. We don't get proper soups or proper things... we don't get good food to eat at all, all we get is oily food, it's like we all have cholesterol problems like my dad... mashed potatoes, chips, everyday, now we are so bored we don't even want to look at the French fries. (Jaswant, India)

The consumption of heavy food, or the lack of variety in food, results either in weight gain – some have gained up to 40% – or weight loss, as people become discouraged from eating.[29]

Mental health

Some asylum-seekers had acute psychological problems before arriving in Ireland.[30] The majority, however, have either developed psychiatric problems or exacerbated pre-existing ones as a result of living in these centres. Exiled and aliened from the present, asylum-seekers adopt different strategies to cope. Some live through day-dreams and fantasies. Others undergo situational withdrawal or succumb to depression. Various reports have shown the detrimental mental health effects of direct provision.[31] It has been estimated that 90% of asylum-seekers suffer from depression after having spent 6 months in the State.[32] Asylum-seekers are also 5 times more likely than Irish citizens to be diagnosed with a psychiatric illness.[33] A large number of residents in DPCs have been prescribed anti-depressants or sleeping tablets; others for more serious issues such as long-term psychosis. As one asylum-seeker from Afghanistan, who had become separated from his family, noted:

> In the last few months, I feel very lonely, lots of sickness you know, lots of pain in my head, lots of stress. Well I go to my GP and I explain the situation, because sometimes I was going mad with this, why is it happening to me? I don't like to see anyone, I don't want to talk to anybody, I don't want to eat, and I have lots of pain in my head and lots of stress about what happened to my family, my father, my mother, my brother, my sister. (Abdul, Afghanistan)

Stress and depression can be caused by dwelling on one's circumstances or by loss of sleep, but also by assaults on the self. These processes often reinforce each other.

The political economy of direct provision

Although Bourdieu and Goffman focused on the material and psychological dislocation and the social suffering engendered by an abrupt shift into adverse social conditions both, though Bourdieu to a greater extent, were keenly aware of the economic and financial conditions which underpinned such processes. As Goffman noted: 'the various rationales for mortifying the self are merely rationalizations, generated by efforts to manage the daily activity of a large number of persons in a restricted space with a small expenditure of resources'.[34] Given its increasing shift towards neo-liberal policies, the Irish State has chosen not to fund the DP system directly and therefore become responsible for ensuring the health and well-being of asylum-seekers, but instead to lease out contracts to private companies. However, such provision has not been cheap. With the exception of 2006, direct provision cost approximately €83 million a year to run between 2001 and 2007.

Furthermore, a small, select cluster of private contractors have been responsible for running the majority of DPCs: in 2005, 8 companies ran over 50% of the centres.[35] One company, Bridgestock Ltd, ran 8 centres and was responsible for accommodating over 20% of the 6,844 asylum-seekers dispersed across the State. During 2007 it increased its profits before tax by over 600% on an annual turnover of over €6.1 million.

In order to secure greater profits and under pressure from the Reception and Integration Agency to reduce its costs, the quality of service provision for asylum-seekers has consistently been reduced. The RIA was pleased to announce that it had reduced costs from €38.60 per person per day in 2000 to €28.35 in 2006 even in the context of consistent yearly inflation.[36]

Notwithstanding the social and juridical division between those arriving before and after dispersal and direct provision, asylum-seekers have the least access and entitlements to social and material resources of all individuals living in Ireland. Those on direct provision represent the poorest of the poor. Together with undocumented migrants, one of which may often become, they are the most disempowered group in Irish society, lacking the most basic fundamental civil, political, and economic rights and mired in a suffocating matrix of poverty, psycho-social alienation, and geographical exclusion.

The original impetus for the direct provision system, the creation of a repressive subsistence system which met the minimum requirements for living, was to discourage the arrival of asylum-seekers and welfarism, but simultaneously to control and regulate their presence once here.

How can we account for the continued extreme marginalization and experience of grinding poverty of asylum-seekers in the State? Issues of power are of course central. For the State they constitute an unwanted imposition on the national order, here only because of the requirement to meet international obligations. Asylum-seekers, unlike other working migrants, do not have the capacity to withdraw their labour, and lack the power or access to voice their concerns and needs and to react to negative media and political representations.

However, these negative experiences are not shared by all asylum-seekers, and life in a total institution is not one-dimensional. There are forms of resistance even in total institutions – places where even the institutional hand of the State doesn't reach. A number do remain remarkably positive given their dire predicament. Yet, to talk about asylum-seekers employing what Scott calls 'weapons of the weak' or to portray them as engaging or employing tactics to subvert rituals and traditions that are imposed upon them by institutions, as claimed by De Certeau for example, would be to overstate their resistance, and in some ways romanticize their bleak predicament. Their precarious social and economic position tends to lead to individualization and to low levels of solidarity. For the most part people remain isolated or interact only with their family. Children, who are allowed to attend school, appear to have a more positive view of living in DPCs.

There are generally few mechanisms for seeking redress or forums where complaints can be heard as a result of poor treatment or injustice, especially when compared to the number of mechanisms available for punishing residents.[37] Some DPCs have residents' committees but attendance is invariably low. There are exceptions to this overall submissive resignation, and there can on occasion be a revolt. Because of poor food and conditions, 200 asylum-seekers in the Meelick DPC went on hunger strike in January 2007. Ironically, it was in the same former Army barracks, in Knockalisheen, where the first group of Hungarian Programme Refugees had gone on hunger strike in 1957 because of dire conditions and neglect by the State. Equally, 41 Afghan asylum-seekers occupied St Patrick's Cathedral in May 2006 – as an act of defiance against the unfairness of the asylum system which would inevitably deport them. A protest in Mosney in 2010 against reallocation was also of note. However, these were on the whole desperate actions of those who were disempowered.

In the current political conjuncture, direct provision has become a 'commonplace', namely, an idea or reality which one takes for granted and in relation to which one argues, but not over or against which one argues. DPCs are panoptican-like institutions for controlling the presence, and facilitating the monitoring and eventual deportation of, failed refugee applicants. Despite some 700 amendments that were tabled in the Immigration, Residence and Protection Bill 2008 none concerned improving the position of asylum-seekers or overhauling the DP system. Rather, the new legislation aimed to expedite the processing of asylum claims, establishing detention centres, and accelerating procedures for deportation.

As stigmatized inhabitants in DPCs asylum-seekers effectively remain invisible, shunted to the borders of society. They have subsequently been *de facto* excluded from the remit of the Minister of Integration, remaining outside of the purview of social partnership and its rhetoric of social inclusion. In the context of the recession they are unlikely to be given the right to work. As a result, little will probably be done in the foreseeable future to ameliorate their predicament and therefore they will probably remain one of the most destitute fractions and dominated groups in the Irish State, suffering the daily violence of stigmatized socio-economic exclusion.

Notes

1 Michael McDowell, *Irish Times*, 17 May 2005.
2 Serwan Tabhri, Iran, *Irish Times*, 30 January 2007.
3 E. Goffman, *Asylums; Essays on the Social Situation of Mental Patients and Other Inmates*, (London: Penguin [1961], 1991), p. 11.
4 P. Cullen, *Refugees and Asylum-seekers*, p. 22.
5 John O'Donohue, *Law Society Gazette* (June 2000): 9.
6 The change in welfare policy led to temporary tension between the DJELR and the Department of Family and Social Affairs responsible for providing social welfare.
7 L. Wacquant, *Urban Outcasts*, p. 9.
8 B. Fanning, *Racism and Social Change in the Republic of Ireland* (Manchester: Manchester University Press, 2002), p. 104.
9 *Irish Times*, 4 August 2000.
10 *Irish Times*, 1 October 2003.
11 *Irish Times,* 8 April 2000.
12 *Irish Times*, 2 April 2008.
13 *Irish Times*, 31 March 2000.
14 R. Miles, *Racism* (London: Routledge, 1989).
15 Goffman, *Asylums*, p. 22.
16 Ibid., p. 137.
17 A. Schutz & T. Luckmann, *The Structures of the Life World* (London: Heinemann, 1974), pp. 28–9.
18 Wacquant, *Urban Outcasts*, p. 30.
19 P. Bourdieu, *The Algerians* (Boston, MA: Beacon Press, 1961[1958]), p. 179.
20 P Bourdieu, The Algerian subproletariat, in I. W. Zarman (ed), *Man, State and Society in the Contemporary Maghreb* (New York,: Prager 1973), p. 84.
21 Nasc, *Hidden Cork*.
22 WAP et al, *The Needs of Asylum Seeker Men Living in Viking House Direct Provision Centre*, p. 32.

23 However, asylum-seekers have a misperceived sense that staff can aid them in transferring to these DPCs, especially since this is only permitted by the RIA in exceptional circumstances on medical or health grounds.

24 Cited in S. Kerns, *The Culture of Time and Space, 1880: 1913* (Harvard: Harvard University Press, 2003), p. 32.

25 C. Levi Strauss, *Structural Anthropology* (London: RKP, 1967).

26 N. Elias, *Time an Essay* (Oxford: Blackwell, 1990).

27 Nor do they have a coherent self-narrative or high levels of self-esteem to think that they can make a difference in the world. Paul Ricoeur, *Oneself as Another*, translated by Kathleen Blamey (Chicago: The University of Chicago Press, 1992).

28 Mandahar, M. et al., *Food, Nutrition and Poverty among Asylum-Seekers in North-West Ireland* (Dublin: Combat Poverty Agency, 2006).

29 Ibid.

30 Spirasi, 1999: Nasc, 2008.

31 M. Begley et al., *Asylum in Ireland, A Public Health Perspective* (Dublin: Department of Public Health, UCD, Congregation of Holy Ghost Fathers, 1999); WAP, 2006; Nasc, *Hidden Cork*, 2008.

32 Nasc, *Hidden Cork*.

33 Department of General Practice, NUIG, 2007.

34 E. Goffman, *Asylum*, pp. 49–51.

35 Three of the largest companies operate a large number of all the centres and earned €37 m between them: East Coast Catering, Millstreet Equestrian Services, and Bridgestock. East Coast Catering, which owns 3 centres, made over 13 m for one centre alone – a 370-bed reception centre, Balseskin, in North Dublin, between 2002 and 2006. *Village Magazine*, 18 May 2006.

36 Letter to T.D. Jim O'Keefe from Reception and Integration Agency, 25 October 2005.

37 B. Fanning, *Racism and social change in the Republic of Ireland*, p. 104.

Chapter 7

The juridical field and immigration in Ireland

Discussions of the juridical field in Ireland usually involve reference to the criminal justice system as a whole including the courts, the Gardai, the prison system, and judges and decision-making. In this chapter the focus will largely be on the latter process and specifically the role that the Supreme Court plays in supporting state sovereignty despite conveying an impression of autonomy from the state. The chapter will examine the question of judicial independence before analysing how the judiciary modified their views about the sanctity of the family in Ireland in the context of increasing claims for residence rights by non-Irish nationals.

A central function of the law is to protect individuals from the arbitrary power of the state. Although the Irish system of law appears as independent from the state, it ultimately serves to reproduce both its own, and the state's, legitimacy and interests. Judicial pronouncements give changing meaning to key terms involved in immigration and migration rights; they also influence shifts in migratory practices. Like the state, to which it is umbilically tied, the law possesses the authority to impose a validated principle of knowledge of the social world. Through its structure and practices the judiciary, it will be argued, is integrally involved in creating and reproducing the social domination of migrants in Irish society. Within the context of the large-scale emigration that characterized the Irish State during the 1980s, and to a lesser extent in the early 1990s, judicial decisions concerning the defence of individual rights and the protection of the family unit tended to conflict with state attempts towards restricting migrant residence. However, as the numbers of migrants entering the State grew rapidly, a shift took place in judicial decision-making whereby it began to conceive of migrants, in consonance with the State world-view, as a collective threat to sovereignty. In this new context, the judiciary became less willing to defend individual, human, or substantive rights and the integrity of the family as a sacred institution.

In modern capitalist society, following a growth in the societal division of labour, the law appears to constitute an identifiably distinct realm both institutionally and ideologically. In its ideal incarnation law constitutes the arena of general public concerns and interests existing over and above sectional interests and effectively operating as an arbitrator between them. By contrast to feudal society, where a person's material circumstances implied different political and legal statuses and there existed no formal separation between polity, economy, and law, all individuals in modern liberal states are conceived to be formally equal before the law.[1] According to the principle of the separation of powers, the legislature creates and passes laws, the executive puts them into operation, and the judiciary interprets them. Hence, although formally connected to the state, and an organ of the state defined in its broad sense, the judiciary is generally perceived to be independent from state interests. It is rendered autonomous from extra-juridical social, economic, political, and cultural influences and determinations by a number of mechanisms: by judicial subservience to the constitution; by legal precedence; and by neutral and independent judges drawing on the totality of social facts available and applying their technical and impartial expertise in reaching a decision. The formalist view of the absolute autonomy of legal thought and action is not just an idealized model propagated and held by those in the legal field in order to confer legitimacy upon themselves – social actors working within the juridical field – but is also something shared and accepted by the public generally.

However, the standard viewpoint of law's autonomy needs to be strongly qualified. Despite the operation of the separation of powers, and though relatively independent, Irish law ultimately operates is in a way that is irreducibly an expression of, and cipher for, state interests. The judicial system in Ireland is at once relatively detached from the state, yet intrinsically connected to state power.

The juridical autonomy from the state, though in some ways real and substantial, should therefore not be overstated. As theorists of legal realism have shown, the idealized and theoretically constructed formal model of a neutral impartial judiciary constitutes an inaccurate depiction of how the law actually works in practice. The law cannot escape from the broader fundamental struggles in society including class, 'race'/ethnicity, and gender conflicts, though it claims to. It is, they argue, more realistic to see the principle function of the judiciary as supporting the government and state, in serving the interests of dominant political and economic forces. Law courts, and the decisions reached within them, more often than not function to reproduce the status quo and prevailing power relations. Consequently, the exercise of juridical power operates in close connection with the operation of state power.

However, the operation of the law is not simply a corrupted or a refracted mirror of politics. An instrumentalist view of the Irish judiciary in which law and legal action are seen as simple reflections of dominant political and economic group interests is equally as one-sided as the formalist view which propagates its absolute neutrality and independence from the state. Rather than seeing the law as sharply separated from the state via an institutional division of labour, or reducible to it, it may be more accurate to examine it as part of a field of forces.[2] In this view, the juridical field has a relative autonomy from the state that varies according to the historical conjuncture.

The role of judges

Judges have a variety of functions to play in the juridical field: they adjudicate between parties in civil and criminal disputes; they impose penalties or prison sentences; they also interpret the law. In the High and Supreme Court they decide whether laws are in conformity with the constitution. These judgements are crucial in structuring Irish immigration and settlement policy, and the future treatment of migrants and non-Irish nationals. Decisions reached in the higher courts have important implications for whether immigrants can stay in the country, be joined by family members, but also determine their access to resources and services in the state.

The appearance of neutrality is a central ideological process in sustaining judges' legitimacy and facilitating the self-reproduction of the juridical field and its concentration of power. The appearance of neutrality is maintained and masked in a number of ways. Firstly, the legal habitus of the judge is characterized by ascetic and aristocratic attitudes that have been gained through professional training as legal education.[3] And although this training reinforces a hierarchical view of the world, the dispositions and attitudes acquired give the impression of a sense of objective disengagement and of the judge simply as an impartial arbiter of rational arguments between equal individuals organized according to formal and logically coherent rules. Second, as Bourdieu argues:

> The appearance of neutrality is reinforced by the use of a specialist technical language that embodies an impartial rhetoric. The use of a linguistic style including passive and impersonal constructions is combined with: recourse to the indicative mood for the expression of norms, the use of constative verbs in the present and past person singular, emphasizing expression of the factual, which is characteristic of the rhetoric of official statements and reports (for example 'accepts', 'admits', 'commits himself', 'has stated') the use of indefinites and of the intemporal present (or the 'juridical future') designed to express the generality or omni-temporality of the rule of law; reference to transsubjective values presupposing the existence of an ethical consensus (for example, 'acting as a responsible parent'); and the recourse to fixed formulas and locutions, which give little room for any individual variation.[4]

A specialized linguistic style is part of the 'power to form', to formalize and codify everything, simultaneously establishing a rigid division between lay people and professionals, who alone have the logical and ethical competence to interpret a complex body of judicial norms.

Since the appearance of absolute autonomy from the state is a central facet for providing its legitimacy as a neutral arbitrator of the truth, issues of impartiality and independence are taken very seriously by those working in the juridical field. Overt political sentiments, explicitly using common sense charged or discriminatory vocabularies in place of codified law-speak, are invariably sanctioned by peers.[5] Overt sentiments of racism or hostility towards immigrants are always immediately sanctioned by peers. Two examples are illustrative. A District Court judge reviewing a case involving a Nigerian driving without insurance stated in his summary of the case: 'I don't think any Nigerian is obeying the law of the land when it comes to driving. I had a few of them in Galway yesterday and they are all driving around without insurance and the way to stop this is to put you in jail'. This was emphatically challenged and rebuked by colleagues. In another instance a Higher Court judge, Justice Paul Carney, was forced to apologize after claiming knife crimes were 'out of control' because of a failure of immigrants to integrate into Irish society.[6]

Judges, however, on the whole, have class backgrounds, interests, and interactional networks that are similar to those of the state elite. Moreover, judicial appointments in Ireland operate through a thoroughly politicized patronage system in which recruitment practices are determined by political sympathies and affiliation. As Bartholomew notes:

A former Taoiseach made the statement that 'all things being equal' a person's politics is controlling in such appointments. All Irish governments have to a greater or lesser degree been politically motivated in the making of judicial appointments. The English used Judges as patronage and the new government after independence named judges that agree with its aims.[7]

The establishment of a Judicial Appointments Advisory Board (JAAB) in 1995 aimed to remedy this. However, the JAAB does not provide judicial recommendations on the appointments of senior judges nor is the government obligated to take on any of its recommendations. Consequently, political factors can trump meritocratic criteria in determining judicial selection or the two criteria can be fused. This process is evident in the appointment, political outlooks, and membership of the current Supreme Court. Many of the appointments took place while Fianna Fail and the Progressive Democrats were in power so that both parties tended to favour candidates with similar ideological or political viewpoints or sympathies. For example, the current Chief Justice John Murray (appointed in 2004) served as Attorney General and was appointed by a Fianna Fail-led government. Both Joseph Finnegan and Richard Johnson were also appointed whilst Fianna Fail were in power. Adrian Hardiman (appointed 2000) was a founding member of the Progressive Democrats. Nicolas Kearns and Fidelma O'Kelly Macken (appointed 2005) were appointed while Michael McDowell, a Progressive Democrat, was Minister Of Justice and are associated with the PD party. Only Susan Denham (appointed 1992), who was partly appointed because she was a Protestant and the first female Supreme Court judge, is seen formally as independent.

However, as Chubb notes, it does not necessarily follow that these judges, even those who may have overt political affiliations, would be politically biased in their professions and judgements once on the bench.[8] Moreover, some judges join parties in order to build social networks, for patronage, and to further their careers rather than for straightforward ideological reasons. However, it will be argued here that the appointments system does have some effect on the ideological perspective of the Supreme Court and judicial outcomes so that judges on the whole only maintain a partial autonomy from extant political viewpoints. When Supreme Court judgements are seen with regard to immigration and residence, there has been a tendency for state-centred ideological world-views to enter into judgements, albeit in codified or refracted form.

The power to form

For Foucault the fundamental structural questions concern the power of who declares the law, and what the law is stated to be. This elicits a number of ancillary questions:

> Who among the totality of speaking individuals is accorded the right to use this sort of language? Who is qualified to do so? Who derives from it his own special quality, his prestige, and from Who in return, does he receive not just the assurance, at least the presumption, that what he says is true? What is the status of individuals who – alone – have the right, sanctioned by law or tradition, juridically defined or spontaneously accepted, to proffer such a discourse?[9]

Judges play a major role not just in interpreting the law but also in making the law. Although the majority of law, including law concerning migrants, is statute law passed by the Oireachtas, case and common law based on precedent constitutes a secondary form of law-making, especially where legislation is absent.[10] The principle of *stare decisis* means that judges from the Higher Courts have extraordinary power as quasi-law makers in Ireland. The existence of weakly codified jurisprudential case law based on precedent, and the need to apply it to future concrete cases, effectively confers considerable power on judges, as authorized interpreters.

The contingency of all legal situations requires the 'creative' application of rules and the interpretation of law. All rules require interpretation. However, the implications of rules are indeterminate.[11] Because of the infinite empirical complexity and richness characterizing all social situations, 2 identical cases where the same rule is to be applied rarely exists in the real world. The question of whether 2 cases are alike, or differ, is a difficult one, philosophically and empirically. Discussions of intransitive relations of sameness have recognized that 2 similar past situations or cases may have some generic continuities but also certain discontinuities. Judges therefore have considerable latitude in selectively deciding whether to focus on the continuities of two cases or dwelling on the discontinuities. Thus, in attempting to distinguish the rationale for a judgement from similar immigration cases involving a different set of moral implications judges, can conveniently assert 'the ground relied on by the plaintiff was not the same as that advanced in the present case'.[12] As Bourdieu notes: 'Precedents are used as tools to justify a certain result as well as serving as determinants of a particular decision; the same precedent, understood in different ways, can be called upon to justify quite different results'. Moreover, the legal tradition possesses a large diversity of precedents and legal interpretations from which a judge can choose the most suitable to apply to a particular case, within limits of course.

Consequently, practicing judges can make decisions that draw on unstated extra-juridical and moral political considerations relatively quickly and subsequently fit the law in to justify their decision. Like lay actors generally, judges often draw on unstated background assumptions, what Oakshott calls 'instinctual morality', commonsense or general knowledge, rather than explicit reasoning or 'didactic morality' in their decision-making.[13] The operation of case law and *stare decisis* therefore means that decisions are made on unique cases but these decisions or judgements do not necessarily spring or issue strictly from within the 'law' itself, as immanent logics inherent within it, or from 'universal reason' rationally emerging and actualizing itself.

This dual indeterminacy of the interpretation and application of rules, taken with judges' authorized and elevated position in social space and the performative and symbolic power of their discourses, is what allows judges to significantly influence the social world. Their decisions and discourses function as speech-acts or what Searle calls 'declaratives'.[14] These judgements have major ramifications for the lives of migrants in terms of, for example, permitting continued residence in the state, family reunification, or deportation. But they also embody an important symbolic effect. Judicial decisions and case summaries – which both construct and address the lay population as specific subjects – play a crucial pedagogic and moral role in shaping how migrant matters are perceived, interpreted, and evaluated generally. By articulating what is permissible legally, and by implication morally, judges frame how migrant issues should be posed, understood, and resolved in the collective imagination.

The judicial power to decide in areas of immigration policy, refugee status, residency rights, family reunification, arrest and deportation, access to social welfare, and citizenship has been revealed in a number of judgements reached in the High and Supreme Court. Given the structural hierarchy between the various courts, judges in the District, Circuit, and High Courts are acutely attentive to judgements reached in the Supreme Court. This is not only to remain conversant with jurisprudential issues for professional reasons, but in order to assess the rationale and ideological underpinning of the decisions reached so that their own judgements will not be overturned at appeal. This process effectively locks in and structures the ideological–political framework of the Supreme Court as the general ideological world-view of the entire court system.

Several decisions, especially in the Supreme Court, have been of major consequence for the operation of migration and patterns of immigrant settlement in Ireland.

The sanctity of state sovereignty and its correlation with the common good has been accepted and reproduced by the Supreme Court for a considerable time. The most forceful summary of this power was reached in the J. Gannon in Osheku v. Ireland judgement that has been approvingly quoted by the Supreme Court on a number of occasions:[15]

> The control of aliens which is the purpose of the Aliens Act, 1935, is an aspect of the common good related to the definition, recognition, and the protection of the boundaries of the State. That it is in the interests of the common good of a State that it should have control of the entry of aliens, their departure, and their activities and duration of stay within the State is and has been recognized universally and from earliest times. There are fundamental rights of the State itself as well as fundamental rights of the individual citizens, and the protection of the former may involve restrictions in circumstances of necessity on the latter. The integrity of the State constituted as it is of the collective body of its citizens within the national territory must be defended and vindicated by the organs of the State and by the citizens so that there may be true social order within the territory and concord maintained with other nations in accordance with the objectives declared in the preamble to the Constitution.[16]

To maintain sovereignty and the common good – the two are often interlinked in many judgements – to control entry, activity in the State, and, especially exit, the State requires wide powers to deport aliens. As Justice Costello noted in the case of Pok v. Ireland I.R.L.M: 'In relation to the permission to remain in the State, it seems to me that the State, through its Ministry for Justice, must have very wide powers in the interest of the common good to control aliens, their entry into the State, their departure and their activities within the State.'[17] Moreover, this power is intrinsic to stateness. As Justice Keane notes: the right to 'expel and deport aliens who are in the State' exists 'by virtue of its nature and not because it has been conferred on particular organs by the State'.[18]

Nevertheless, in many earlier Supreme Court judgements made in the 1980s and early 1990s involving immigrant residence, such a view of state sovereignty was offset with a concern about individual rights and protecting the family as a unit. However, shifts in the balance from protecting the individual to enhancing state sovereignty soon became evident as in a number of landmark cases, as the volume of immigrants entering the country increased. This was not an abrupt or straightforward shift in emphasis, but rather uneven and protracted. The fundamental issue in the Minister for Justice v. Laurentiu concerned the limits to secondary powers that the Minister for Justice was entitled to for regulating migration, especially through deportation. It was argued by Laurentiu that Article 5 of the Aliens Act 1935 contravened Article 15 2. 1 of the Constitution so that the powers conferred by the Aliens Act of 1935 to the Minister of Justice should have been rendered void following the introduction of the Constitution. The majority of judges rejected the appeal stating that the executive power of the State to deport was not free-standing but dependent upon legislation. However, some of the dissenting judgements and summaries were important in revealing how state sovereignty should be interpreted. For those opposed to the majority interpretation, the central was not about the power of the legislature to delegate as has been stated, but about state sovereignty. As one of the dissenting judges noted: 'The Aliens Act reflects the philosophy of the Nation State. Its major unspoken premise is that aliens have in general no right to be on the national territory. It cannot therefore be compared with normal legislation designed to reconcile the fights of the citizen with those of the State in the interests of the common good.'[19] In distinguishing the rationale of this case from Fajajonu (which will be discussed below), Justice Barrington noted that in the latter: 'The reasoning was developed to strike a balance between the rights of the individual citizen and the exigencies of the common good. But there is no such balance to be struck in the present case for the simple reason that, under our law, an alien has, generally speaking, no right to reside in Ireland.' He added: 'If one were to glean the policy of the Act for its terms it would appear to be that generally speaking aliens have no right to be in Ireland and may be excluded or deported at any time unless the Minister sees some reason for allowing them to remain.'[20] For Justice Keane the view remained that 'in the plainest language it [the Aliens Act] empowers the Minister to exclude and deport, not merely particular aliens, but whole categories of aliens determined by their nationality or "class".'[21]

The Irish State's failure to win this Supreme Court case resulted in the insertion of new clauses into the draft of the Immigrants Trafficking Bill of 1999. The Bill had initially been introduced to curb and deal with the trafficking of illegal immigrants but John O'Donohue introduced a number of significant amendments on the rights of non-Irish nationals. Section 5 of the Bill sought to reduce the period given to non-Irish nationals for accessing judicial review from 3 months to 14 days while section 10 of the Bill empowered the State to arrest and detain a person issued with a deportation order for a maximum period of eight weeks. Because of the controversial nature of these clauses, which may have been 'repugnant to the Constitution', the Bill was sent to the Supreme Court by the President under article 26 of the Constitution. The question was whether these changes violated the constitutional rights of access of persons to the courts or were in breach of the constitutional guarantee of equality before the law. It was claimed that non-Irish nationals were being treated unequally in accessing judicial review since they had to find a barrister to take their case, the system of legal aid was inadequate, they were housed in remote inaccessible direct provision centres, and because they sometimes needed translation services. However, none of the provisions was found to be unconstitutional. For Keane, 'nothing prohibits the person concerned from applying for an extension of the 14 day period before that actual 14 day period has elapsed.'[22] He argued that the State must exercise wide powers in the restriction and regulation of immigration as an inherent element of State sovereignty which had been recognized since the 'earliest times'. Mullally has rightly argued that as well as accepting the tacit equation of asylum and illegal immigration that was contained in the Bill the Chief Justice saw asylum and immigration as threats to the integrity of the territory of the State. Rather than recognizing international law or that the right to asylum was also enjoyed since the 'earliest times' he chose to accept a state-centred viewpoint.[23] The question of individual human rights, especially of non-Irish nationals, remained secondary to collective considerations of national-State sovereignty. Non-Irish nationals did not have the same constitutional rights as Irish citizens. As Keane asserted: 'in the sphere of immigration, its restrictions or regulations, the non-national or alien constitutes a discrete category of persons whose entry, presence, and expulsion from the State may be the subject of legislation and administrative measures which would not, and in many of its aspects, could not, be applied to citizens.'[24]

It is important not to overstate the Supreme Court's historical concern with defending individual rights. The limited protection of individual rights has in some ways always remained secondary to a concern to preserve the rights of the family as recognized in the ideologically loaded 1937 constitution. The family possesses an almost sacred quality in the constitution.[25] As the Supreme Court itself stated:

> The constitution clearly places the family as the fundamental unit of the State. The family is the decision maker for family matters – both for the unit and for the individual in the family. Responsibility rests fundamentally with the family. The people have chosen to live in a society where parents make decisions concerning the welfare of their children and the State intervenes only in exceptional circumstances.[26]

So that, as asserted in another judgement: 'the rights of the family are superior to those of the State itself'.[27]

A central issue that has dominated the juridical field with reference to migration has been birthright citizenship and the right of residency of non-Irish parents of children born in Ireland to stay with them in Ireland as a family unit. The role of families in migration is often overlooked both in terms of the decision of an individual to migrate, but also in relation to family reunification. The State has systematically aimed to prevent family reunification by placing a number of legal impediments in the way and by individualizing the migration process. This includes restricting the rights of non-EU migrants to family reunification. It even extends to Irish nationals with non-Irish spouses or partners, who cannot automatically have these family members join them.

The issue of whether non-Irish parents of Irish-born children could remain in the State with them was initially dealt with Fajujonu v. Minister for Justice, Equality and Law Reform in 1990. The case involved a Nigerian and Moroccan couple who were illegally resident in the State for several years but who had had 3 children during that period. Mr Justice Walsh and Justice Finlay decided that a child having been born in the State had a right to reside here. Both argued that under Article 41 of the constitution the child had inalienable and imprescriptable rights to the family unit which needed to be safeguarded and protected. As Justice Walsh asserted, the parents 'and their three children constitute a family within the meaning of the Constitution and the three children are entitled to the care, protection and society of their parents in this family group'. In concurrence Justice Finlay added that 'where, as occurs in this case, an alien has in fact resided for an appreciable time in the State and has become a member of a family unit within the State containing children who are citizens... there can be no question but that those children, as citizens, have got a constitutional right to the company, care and parentage of their parents within a family unit'.[28] Parents could only be refused residence if 'a grave and substantial reason associated with the common good' was evident. As a result of this decision, non-Irish parents of Irish-born children could apply to the Minister of Justice to remain in the State and were rarely refused.

In an almost identical case concerning L & O v. The Minister for Justice, Equality and Law, involving a Czech (Lobes) and Nigerian family (Osayandes), in February 2003, however, the Supreme Court decided on a 5 to 2 decision to restrict automatic residency rights for non-national parents of Irish-citizen children.[29] A foreign national parent of an Irish-born child did not, it was argued, have an automatic entitlement to remain in the State with the child. The rights of the child and family unity could be maintained outside of the State. It was now argued that non-Irish parents of Irish children could be deported in the interests of the common good: 'the rights of the family are not absolute. The State by its laws, made for the common good, may so order society as to restrict family life'.[30] The State was now entitled to deport in order to preserve the integrity of the immigration and asylum system. Even though the majority of judges involved argued this decision was in conformity with the previous Fajajonu judgement, the decision that parents of Irish children could now be deported from Ireland was a clear reversal of that decision. Given the interpretive elasticity permitted to judges and the poly-vocality of all texts, a distinction was made by them between the facts in the two cases:

> The cases are very different. First, the facts and circumstances are very different. Secondly, these cases call for analysis at a different time, they are to be analyzed under a different legislative scheme, a legislative scheme under which the applicants may apply and appeal, and a scheme giving the applicants more rights than existed previously. Thirdly, the State is now part of the Dublin Convention.[31]

Although there had also been a partial turnover in the composition of the Supreme Court, the change in decision between the Fajujonu and L & O cases reflected the fundamental socio-political changes that had taken place in Irish society during that period. The Fajujonu decision had not been based on individual rights per se but on the need to protect the child and maintain the family at a time when the Catholic Church still retained power in Irish society. However, by 2003 Ireland had moved away from Catholic dominance and had shifted from being a country of emigration with few non-Irish residents, to a country of net immigration. In addition, the late 1980s and early 1990s were still a period of emigration but by 2003 this had altered considerably. In the year prior to the decision there were over 11,000 applications for asylum, with the majority coming from Nigeria. Applications for residency on the basis of having an Irish-born child also increased dramatically and there were over 11,000 applications still outstanding in February 2003. This was also a central issue in the Citizenship Referendum of 2004, which will be examined in the next chapter.

With increasing numbers of asylum-seekers arriving in the State, negative media reporting and political discourses describing them as 'bogus' or as exploiting Ireland's generosity became widespread.[32] The State also began refusing applications to parents of Irish children if they had not been in the country for an 'appreciable time' – which was by definition a contested and arbitrary criterion. Discussions of immigration were now framed according to controlling the entry of asylum-seekers. This new context made a significant difference for interpreting immigration. These changes were acknowledged by some of the judges. As one put it:

> there is manifestly a distinction to be drawn between a situation where the number of persons seeking to enter the State in any one year is very low, for example 30 or 40, and the situation where many thousands seek to do so. In the latter situation, the… necessity of maintain the integrity of such a system n the interests of the common good is far greater than in the former case.[33]

According to the majority viewpoint the immigration system now had to be protected for the common good. Unregulated immigration challenged state sovereignty and represented threat to the social order so that Murray noted, 'the interests of the common good... includes the maintaining of true social order within its territory.[34] In making his decision Judge Keane noted the need for the immigration control system to be kept intact in changing circumstances:

> It cannot be right that this court should approach this case on the assumption, totally at variance with the facts known to us, that conditions in Ireland are as they were in the 1980s when there was a relatively high level of unemployment, many Irish people were emigrating to seek work abroad and there were relatively few immigrants or persons seeking asylum as refugees. I think it would be wrong for this court to approach the important issues which have arisen for resolution without having regard to the major changes in Ireland which have occurred over the past decade in this whole area... The legislature and executive cannot be expected to disregard the problems which an increased volume of immigration invariably creates, because of the strains it places on the infrastructure of social services, and, human nature being what it is, the difficulty of integrating people from very different ethnic and cultural backgrounds into the fabric of Irish society.[35]

The judiciary, he continued, had to support the State to ensure that strategic and opportunistic asylum-seekers did not take advantage of the State's generosity and protection of human rights: 'Ireland, like other States, has undertaken considerable obligations in relation to refugees or people who claim to be such. These responsibilities, undertaken in the name of the vindication of human rights, have now involved the State in providing for the hearing of 11,5000 such applicants each year.' However, 'the lengthy processing times meant that a female applicant may give birth in Ireland'. Taking as given the State's conceptual and political division between asylum-seekers and economic migrants the asylum-seeker was seen as an 'opportunistic reproducer'[36] who could be contrasted with hard-working economic immigrants. In a situation in which 'an orderly system in place for dealing with immigration and asylum applications should not be undermined by persons seeking to take advantage' the integrity of the immigration and asylum system had to be prioritized over the maintenance of the family unit.[37]

Similar concerns in maintaining state immigration controls at the expense of individual rights or the family was evident in the case of Bode v. Minister for Justice, Equality and Law Reform & Ors. In the Bode case the central question concerned whether constitutional and convention rights of applicants had to be considered within the creation of a new Irish Born Child Scheme. The establishment of the scheme followed the Citizenship Referendum and involved the creation of a once-off administrative measure in which parents of children born in Ireland before 1 January 2005 could apply for residency. In an earlier decision the High Court had argued that by denying Falajimi Bode the right to remain in the State with his daughter the Minister of Justice was in breach of the constitutional and legal rights of both applicants, particularly their family rights protected under article 40 and 41 in the constitution, and article 8 of the European Convention on Human Rights Act, 2003. The Supreme Court, however, overturned the High Court's decision stating that the scheme was a one-off generous scheme that allowed the Minister for Justice absolute discretion. Justice Denham, ordinarily considered one of the most liberal-minded judges, again articulated the principle of sovereignty and state integrity in a new context of immigration. Restating the Gannon ruling on the Osheku v. Ireland decision, she concluded:

> At no stage was it intended that within the ambit of the scheme the Minister would consider, or did the Minister consider, Constitutional or Convention rights of the applicants. Thus the terms of the pleadings and of the appeal relating to the Constitutional and Convention rights of the applicants were misconceived and premature. Applicants who were not successful in their application under the IBC 05 Scheme remain in the same position as they had been before their application.

The 'scheme was an exercise of executive power by the Minister. It did not purport to address nor did it address constitutional or convention rights.' It was a 'gift, in effect'.[38] And a generous gift should not undermine state sovereignty: 'In every State, of whatever model, the State has the power to control the entry, the residency, and the exit, of foreign nationals. This power is an aspect of the executive power to protect the integrity of the State. It has long been recognized that in Ireland this executive power is exercised by the Minister on behalf of the State.'[39]

Although the Bode decision was reversed in May 2008 following the cases of Oguekwe v. Minister of Justice, Equality, and Law Reform and Dimbo v Minister of Justice, Equality, and Law Reform, it demonstrated judicial views on state sovereignty and its correlation with the common good, even at the expense of an individual's human rights. The operation of the law in Ireland provides a false legitimacy to existing social and political power relations. It is part of the social totality at once shaping, and being shaped, by power relations. The State and migrant are not equal adversaries in search of justice. Nor are judges impartial mediators between them. As Burton and Carlen point out: 'Idealistic tautologizing demonstrates the absurdity of the notion of mediation. The Judge, the authorities rightly claim, mediates the law correctly because he, like the policeman or any other State official *is* the law'.[40]

The history of the treatment of migrants in the Irish juridical field registers a relative shift in its balance from protecting the family and individual rights towards favouring State views on sovereignty. Together with the State, the Supreme Court has in effect cooperated and contributed towards the reproduction of morally loaded frameworks for understanding and adjudicating migrants' presence and thereby supplemented State strategies of maintaining racial uniformity. Law's own description of itself as timeless, as above the petty concerns of day-to-day events activities, and politics is fictitious. Despite claims of autonomy, the Supreme Court has contributed toward the material subordination of migrants, structuring the rights of residence and access to resources. Periods of rapid social change or social 'crisis' have brought the constructed nature of the law in sharp relief. They show that decisions are not made without regard for context, but rather that context and ideological processes play a central role in structuring judicial decision-making at the highest level. For most people including immigrants and those working in the field of migration this is obvious and apparent, but it is less so for those working in the juridical field, who see their absolute autonomy from the state as a central facet of their profession.

Notes

1 See M. Bloch, *Feudal Society* (London: RKP, 1945).
2 Bourdieu, The Force of Law: Toward a Sociology of the Juridical field, *Hastings Journal of Law*, 38, 209–48.
3 D. Kennedy, Legal education and the reproduction of hierarchy, 32 *J. Legal Education*, 32, 591–615, Dec. (1982).
4 P. Bourdieu, The Force of Law, p. 820.
5 *Irish Times*, 12 June 2008.
6 'They', he stated, 'buy vodka or beer in the off-licence and are drinking in a flat when a row breaks out and one person reaches for a kitchen knife and stabs the other person'. Ibid.
7 P. C. Bartholomew, *The Irish Judiciary* (Dublin: Notre Dame, 1971), p. 36. See T. Ward, *Justice Matters, Independence, Accountability and the Irish Judiciary* (Dublin: ICCL, 2007).
8 B. Chubb, *The Government and Politics of Ireland* (London: Longman, 1982), p. 318.
9 M. Foucault, *The Archaeology of Knowledge* (London: Tavistock Publications, 1972), p. 50.
10 This is together with EU law and International Human Rights law.
11 Wittgenstein, *The Philosophical Investigations*. Rules can never determine their own application or be automatically applied to new cases as if the rule itself could suggest standard according to which it should be applied. See also H.L.A. Hart, *The Concept of Law* (Oxford: Clarendon Press, 1994) for a discussion between primary and secondary rules.
12 J. Keane, 1999 Minister for Justice v. Laurentiu, 118.
13 M. Oakshott. *Experience and its Modes* (Cambridge: Cambridge University Press, [1933] 1995).
14 J. Searle, *The Construction of Social Reality.*
15 J. Gannon, in Osheko v. Ireland, 1986 IR 733 at 746: Article 26 Referral of the Illegal Immigrants (Trafficking) Bill 1999 ([2000] 2 IR 360), FP v. Minister for

Justice ([2002] 1 IR 164) and AO and DL v. Minister for Justice, Equality and Law Reform ([2003] 1 IR 1).

16 Ibid.

17 J. Costello in Pok Sun Shun v. Ireland I.L.R.M 593 at 599 (1986).

18 J. Keane, Minister for Justice v. Laurentiu, 1999, 136. The Right of the State to control the entry of aliens, their activity in the State, and their departure is part of the sovereign rights of the State. S. Denham, 1999, Minister for Justice vs Luarentiu.

19 Barrington, J. Sorin Laurentiu v. Minister for Justice, Equality and Law Reform, Ireland and the Attorney General, 1999: 101.

20 Ibid., 84, 86.

21 J. Keane, 1999, Minister for Justice v. Laurentiu, 128.

22 J. Keane, Illegal Immigrants and Trafficking Bill, 2000.

23 S. Mullally, The Irish Supreme Court and the Illegal Immigrants (Trafficking) Bill, 1999, *International Journal of Refugee Law* 13 (2001) p. 356.

24 Keane, J., in Immigration Trafficking Bill, 2000, 50.

25 Women were conceived in the Constitution primarily as homemakers. See Lentin (1998).

26 North Western Health Board v. HW and CW 2001 3 IR 622, p. 722.

27 Fennelly L. and O. v. Minister for Justice, Equality and Law Reform [2003] 1 I.R. 1.

28 Walsh, J. Fajajonu v. Minister for Justice 91990, 2 IR 162.

29 *Reform* ([2002] IESC 109/02 and 108/02).

30 S. Denham, L. and O. v. Minister for Justice, Equality and Law Reform [2003] 1 I.R.

31 Ibid.

32 Pollack, A..'An Initation to racism? Irish daily newspaper coverage of the refugee issue' in D. Kiberd (ed) Media in Ireland the Search for Ethical Journalism, Dublin: Open Air Four Courts Press.

33 Ibid., pp. 86–7.

34 Ibid., p. 186.

35 Keane. J in Fajajonu v. Minister for Justice (1990) 2 IR.

36 J. Harrington, Citizenship and the biopolitics of post-nationalist Ireland, *Journal of Law and Society*, vol. 32 (1995), p. 442.

37 Keane, J. in Fajajonu v. Minister for Justice (1990) 2 IR, 39.

38 Supreme Court, S. Denham J., in Bode (A Minor) v. Minister for Justice, Equality and Law Reform and Ors [2007], IESC 62, 20 December 2007.

39 Ibid.

40 F. Burton and P. Carlen, *Economy and Society* 6, 4 (1977), p. 390.

Chapter 8

Citizenship in Ireland

This chapter examines the historical development of the concept of citizenship in Ireland. It discusses the 2 principal modes through which citizenship is conferred, *jus soli* – through soil, and *jus sanguinis* – through blood, and examines how these processes became reconfigured with the Citizenship Referendum of 2004. It examines the events leading to the build up of the Referendum before looking at the process of naturalization in Ireland.

Citizenship

In contrast to the power of the state to determine the entry of foreigners which is being increasingly subject to international law and supranational constraints, the conferral and acquisition of citizenship is entirely at the discretion of the state. It therefore provides a less mediated and clearer expression of national self-understanding and nationhood.

An inherent dualism and ambiguity at the centre of modern citizenship can be traced back to its origins in the French Revolution.[1] The Revolution both engendered the birth of the modern nation-state representing an expression of the will and interests of the people, and included within its compass broad strata of the population provided with equal legal and political rights. The enjoyment of rights and assuming of responsibilities and obligations conferred by membership to a political community was a profoundly radical idea carrying oppositional connotations within the context of the hierarchical privilege characterizing the feudal orders. Yet, this expansionary and universalist aspect of citizenship and statehood simultaneously embodied an exclusionary aspect expressed in the idea of a bounded nation-state selectively conferring membership to those it deemed eligible or worthy. Citizenship embodied a peculiar and contradictory mix of both inclusionary universalism and exclusionary particularism, egalitarianism and hierarchy, sameness and difference, natural law and conservative thought-styles. In order to establish the inclusion of some individuals as members, citizenship required the exclusion of others – whether as slaves or women as in the Greek city-states, or poor migrants in the contemporary nation-state.

In its modern incarnation citizenship, as Marshall points out, is linked *both* to membership of a nation and to capitalism's requirement of free and equal individuals.[2] Discussions about the institution of citizenship therefore simultaneously inflect debates about capitalism, democracy, and nation-states and nationhood. The modern institution of citizenship is tied to both *territory* and to *membership* of a nation.[3] As a social status it primarily refers to membership of free and equal individuals into a territorially bounded civic and political national community conceived as nation. The fundamental aspect of citizenship is the access it provides to a broad range of rights and resources. These include a complex array of civic, social, political, and economic rights, and even intangibles such as a feeling of belonging or identification. Yet, with rights and protection came obligations such loyalty and the availability for military service. The inclusion of the mass of the population into the nation therefore presupposed a social contract within which citizens, in exchange for rights, a minimal level of protection, and later, economic access to social welfare, became obligated to the state and available for conscription.

Nations and nationalism

The modern world of nation-states enmeshed within an inter-state system divided according to mutually exclusive citizenry and intra-state differentiations between citizens and foreigners is not only a historical artifact but a shifting construct. Long-term processes of state formation and nation-building characterized by intense power conflicts engendered two interconnected structural integration dynamics entailing territorial integration and strata integration.[4] State societies as nation-states emerged predominantly in Europe from around the second half of the 18th century.[5] Nation-building took place within an irreducible class context characterized by a rising industrial bourgeoisie and a declining aristocracy.[6] As Tilly notes, the top-down nationalizing efforts of European rulers created bottom up demands for autonomy and independence by political entrepreneurs.[7] In the French Revolution, for example, citizenship was given to anyone who claimed allegiance with the Revolution. The exclusionary aspect of nationalism emerged with the consolidation of the national capitalist class around its borders, its growing political hegemony and its need to cement layers of society to its world-view. Although of a different temporal order, nation-building, imperialist war, and capitalist industrialization later became inextricably linked. Rising liberalism, democracy, and pacification within the state engendered increasing national economic and political rivalries for new world markets, imperial wars, colonial conquest, between territorially bounded national forms of capitalism.[8]

The emergence of nation-states putatively constituting a political expression of the nation – conceived as a singular people – and their needs and interests was underpinned and shaped by the proliferation of nationalist ideologies. Processes of nation-state formation have always relied upon homogenized narratives constructing a singular dominant ethnicity, culture, and national identity.[9] Various ethnic markers symbolized by race, culture, language, or religion valourized and expressed through myths and selective memories served to create new self-understandings that functioned to mask the heretofore ethno-cultural diversity that characterized many states. The idea of the nation has also frequently combined cultural, ethnic, territorial, and biological constituents in order to draw boundaries between groups. In addition, human affects and emotions play a central role in collective forms of identification and in the construction of a national habitus.

Together with the emergence of national borders and states, such emotionally charged discourses of homogeneity grounded a reconfigured notion of belonging and not belonging, insiders and outsiders, legitimate and illegitimate members. The modality of exclusion has, however, shifted with historical context and political conjuncture. With the emergence of nation-states, earlier state or local juridical exclusions based predominantly on class, status, or economic grounds have become reconfigured, reinforced, and eventually partially supplanted by new status markers based on ethnicity, race, and/or phenotypical characteristics. In 'imagining' a national community in terms of national categories, the state orchestrates a wider *conscience collective* which is both descriptive and normative whilst reflecting and prioritizing the values of the dominant class and ethnicity.[10] States attempt to create a cohesive and homogenous nation through various narratives, categorizations, and rhetorical devices, but also in their practices. Nation-making is an ongoing process and states continue to go to great efforts to institutionalize nationalism and nationhood as part of a political project of 'group making'.[11] The administrative categories and classifications used by the state play an important role in defining broader discourses of identification and exclusion. An important aspect of this vision of divisions is the way that individuals are encouraged to identify themselves predominantly in narrow national terms both emotionally and cognitively.

Nationhood is not simply one way of thinking about the world or one mode of identity that can be chosen but the central form of thinking in modern life. It expresses the natural moral order. Culturally demarcated nationality serves as a basic cognitive and social category and organizing principle in everyday life, operating often unconsciously through the habitus and body. Nationalism is not something that is intermittently expressed at the periphery of social life but is an enduring condition reproduced on a daily basis through the whole complex of beliefs, assumptions, habits, and practices people draw upon in their lives.[12] These representations and practices are so familiar that they go unnamed and therefore remain tacit or unnoticed. To deny or challenge nationality is in effect to deny something natural and rooted in the embodied self's conception of the world.

Though consonant with wider structural and historical processes, nationalism in Ireland retained its own specificity, reflecting indigenous historical processes of social struggle. Moreover, it has not remained a stable ideology historically, assuming different forms depending on the context and dynamic of political relations. Initially predicated upon an Irish republican nationalism which sought to merge urban aspiring bourgeois Protestants with Catholics as in the United Irishmen, it later became defined in terms of a white Celtic/Gaelic, rural, and Catholic people or 'race' defined in opposition to British urban Protestant colonialism. This had its political roots in the mobilizing campaigns for independence from British colonialism and civic inclusion led by Daniel O'Connell and its cultural underpinnings in the work of Thomas Davis. It retained strongly progressive elements in terms of including workers' struggles that combined national and economic aspirations, mass mobilization, and strong support for the anti-slavery movement. The consolidation of these political and cultural components was followed by their reconfiguration after the 1860s in the wake of four major socio-economic ruptures: an agricultural and economic revolution entailing a shift to small and middle-sized farming; the rise of mass education in the 1860s; a devotional revolution led by the Catholic church; and an escalation in political mobilization and calls for independence led by Charles Stewart Parnell.[13] Expressions of Irish nationhood in post-independence Ireland of the 1920s were not the same as their articulation pre-independence. Yet, partition meant that Irish Republican nationalism, in a symbiotic relation with the Church, continued to employ British monarchical nationalism and Protestantism as a negative frame of reference. Nor were the claims to nationhood characterizing De Valera's national autarky and self-sufficiency during the 1950s comparable to nation claims in the Celtic Tiger and its embrace of global capitalism. Contingent historical factors played a strong role in shaping modern-day Irish nationalism. This included the contradictory approach of the Southern elite to Irish nationalism during the more recent Northern Ireland Troubles, and the increasingly reactionary nature of Irish nationalism as state power became consolidated.

The Citizenship Referendum

The Citizenship Referendum of 2004 demonstrated the Irish State's attempt to control the flow and ethno-racial composition of migrants entering the country and to thereby reassert its sovereignty in terms of reconstructing the nation by design.[14] Questions concerning who to admit into a bounded national territory or as a member of the nation-state came to the fore. In effect the Referendum served as a catalyst for a debate on ethno-racial inclusion and national identity.

Citizenship in Ireland can be acquired in 3 major ways: through birth – by *jus soli* and *jus sanguinis* criteria; through residence and naturalisation; and through marriage to an Irish citizen. The principle of *jus sanguinis* – right of blood – meant that every person born to an Irish citizen, including those born to Irish citizens living abroad, or whose grandparents were Irish citizens, could gain citizenship. Until 2004 the principle of *jus soli* – right of the soil – was unconditional, so that every person born on the island of Ireland could acquire citizenship. Citizenship could also be acquired through naturalization. If a person had lived in the country for 5 out of the previous 9 years, and was of good character, they could apply to the Minister of Justice, Equality and Law Reform for naturalization. Finally, citizenship could also be acquired through marriage with an Irish national. Post-nuptial applications for citizenship, however, ceased to be sanctioned in 2005 following allegations by the State that there had been a significant rise in the number of 'marriages of convenience' in the State.[15]

Although always bounded and restrictive, the mode and language through which exclusionary national citizenship is produced and reproduced varies historically and between states. For most states the ascription and acquisition of citizenship has been by birth through one or both of the principles of *jus soli* and *jus sanguinis*. According to Brubaker, these principles reflect radically different and shifting political world-views and conceptions for gaining citizenship.[16] In theory they represent two thought-styles pitting bourgeois rationalism against conservative romanticism, liberal political norms versus ethno-cultural values, or cosmopolitanism versus ethnocentrism and xenophobia. The choice of citizenship principles adopted by the state (or prioritized if both were employed), thereby provides an important insight into the state's vision of the social world and reflects its self-understanding and conception of nationhood. *Jus soli* has historically been associated with republicanism, universalism, and an expansive and outward-looking definition of the nation in which all children were equal at birth.[17] By contrast, *jus sanguinis* has been correlated with a conservative, differentialist, and exclusionary and inward conception of the nation. It has now become common practice to associate these two antithetical positions with French and German conceptions of nationhood respectively.[18] In France, citizenship and nationhood reflected the aims of the French Revolution. It was based on an abstract, republican, and secular definition of the nation that was coterminous with the territorial state and state formation. Political inclusion was predicated on the cultural assimilation of the individual so that second-generation immigrants could become French if they chose to internalize French civic values. By contrast, the German idea of the nation developed before state formation, was imposed from above, and tied to the particularity of the estate as a closed institution-reinforcing community, ethnic, and group belonging. The nation was seen as an organic ethno-racial community, culturally and linguistically homogenous, and sharply differentiated, for example, from Jews and Slavics. The German particularistic understanding of nationhood was *volk*-centred, exclusionary, and differentialist and citizenship was acquired through descent.[19] By shaping integration and naturalization into their national terrain in the 20th and 21st century the two different state-centred and cultural and differentialist notions of nationhood and citizenship had major repercussions for the inclusion, integration, naturalization, civic incorporation, and social trajectory of immigrant communities over the centuries. However, in practice, there is more ambiguity in the institutionalization, employment, and consequences of these two citizenship mechanisms. Though state formation plays an important role, other contingent empirical and historical factors have also been influential in determining which mode of citizenship is adopted. In Britain, for example, *jus soli* was tied to the feudal rather than republican notions, so that those born on British soil were seen as British subjects of the king. As Joppke has argued:

> only *jus sanguinis* was originally the quintessentially modern membership principle, because it made nationality law a 'right of person', according to which nationality was transmitted like the name of the family, through filiation, and could not be lost by an individual's contingent movements in space. By contrast, *jus soli* was then tainted by its feudal origins, because it derived from the ownership of the land by the Lord, its human elements included, who owed the Lord their 'allegiance'.[20]

Commonwealth countries which came within the ambit of the British Empire subsequently tended to operate with the *jus soli* tradition.[21] Second, the implications of these distinct and opposed expressions of sovereignty for the treatment of immigrants and their descendents, and the particularity of national models, should not be overstated.[22] The difference in their effects has been one of degree rather than of kind, and often more symbolic than material. As Brubaker was right to point out, if citizenship is to be internally inclusive it necessarily has to be externally exclusionary. Third, most countries, including France and Germany, and others, such as the UK, Australia, and Portugal – which introduced residence conditions into previously existing unconditional *jus soli* principles during the 1980s – utilize both citizenship criteria, though the balance between them varies. Principles of citizenship have therefore undergone major transformation since the rise of post-war migration, especially, though not exclusively, in Europe. The development of international human rights and norms geared towards eradicating discrimination, itself a consequence of a relative increase in functional democratization within and between states, has played a major role in this change.[23]

Citizenship in Ireland

The unique circumstances characterizing the birth of the Irish State – its ideological animosity yet material dependence on Britain, its membership of the Commonwealth, the role of partition, and its extensive history of emigration – meant that citizenship and nationhood in Ireland were capaciously defined to include both *jus soli* and *jus sanguinis* principles. Given its republican political ethos *jus soli* was foregrounded, yet its extensive and intensive history of emigration meant that *jus sanguinis* also played an important role.

Under article 3 of the Free Irish State Constitution of 1922, citizenship was conferred to those present in the area of the jurisdiction of the Irish Free State on 6 December 1922, and to persons either born in Ireland or to Irish parents resident there for at least 7 years. The Irish Nationality and Citizenship Act of 1935 further expanded the remit for acquiring citizenship by introducing an unconditional *jus soli* criterion. However, citizenship by descent could only be acquired if the parent of the individual was the father.

Under article 2 of the 1937 Constitution every person born on the Island of Ireland had entitlement to Irish citizenship and those born to Irish parents had an automatic entitlement to citizenship. One of the implications of partition in Ireland, however, was that citizenship was never defined in the Constitution. The Irish state under De Valera operated with the belief that the nation had not emerged in its entirety and retained an irredentist and a territorial claim over Northern Ireland. As a measure of inclusion towards Catholics living in Northern Ireland the 1956 Nationality Act legally enshrined the principle of *jus soli* to all those born on the island of Ireland, and citizenship through descent was possible if either parent was an Irish national.

Up to the 2004 Referendum, citizenship in Ireland had been primarily based on legislation. However, following the 1998 Belfast Agreement, Article 2 of the Constitution was altered so that anyone born on the island of Ireland could acquire citizenship as a constitutional right, over and beyond the control of the Oireachtas and statute law. The State sought to reverse this constitutional change through the Citizenship Referendum by re-empowering the Oireachtas to decide the circumstances and conditions under which individuals were entitled to acquire Irish citizenship and by implication come into the State.

On 11 June 2004 the Irish State held a Citizenship Referendum that endeavoured to reformulate the Irish State's norms for determining admission and residence. The government sought to end the automatic right of conferral of citizenship to all children born in Ireland, by markedly qualifying the unconditional principle of *jus soli*. The referendum aimed to shift citizenship based on birth, which had operated as the primary source of citizenship since the foundation of the State (and as a constitutional right from 1937), to citizenship based on ethnicity or blood ties. The implications of this shift were clear. It entailed reframing nationhood and the acquisition of citizenship from an expansive conception towards an exclusionary, restrictive, and ethno-racial conception based on descent. Irish citizenship, nationhood, culture, and national identity was to be primarily acquired through blood ties. Aside from its material implications, this shift constituted a profound alteration in the Irish State's self-understanding and sense of nationhood that had existed for the previous 80 years. The image of blood had served in nationalistic discourses primarily as a metaphor for sacrifice during independence; it was now to serve as a metonym for belonging.

Altering the acquisition of citizenship, however, was not an easy task. In legal terms it entailed an alteration of the Constitution, which meant holding a referendum. It also encroached on terms and principles that had been established in what was perceived to be a landmark historical achievement, the 1998 Belfast Agreement. Moreover, ideological and symbolic factors added further hindrances to changing citizenship. Although definitions of nationhood are generally conditioned and reproduced from above by state, economic, and media interests, they are always done so over time in interaction and negotiation with interests and forces from below. National consciousness cannot be altered automatically or simply according to instrumental needs. As conservative writers rightly acknowledge, tradition is ubiquitous and pervasive, so that collective memory together with past understandings of citizenship and nationhood are crucial normative resources in shaping and structuring future conceptions and everyday world-views.

The State's decision to hold a referendum was underpinned by the steep rise in the number of asylum-seekers and residency applications made in country. In 1996 applications to remain as a parent were given to 149 former or current asylum applicants; by 2000 this had reached 1,515, increasing to 8,620 applications in 2002.[24] Between 1996 and 2003 the Minister of Justice had granted almost 10,500 people leave to remain in the State, and in February 2003 a further 11,493 applications were still outstanding as individuals sought residency in the State on the basis of being parents of an Irish child. It was against this backdrop that the Referendum sought to re-establish sovereign control over the number of asylum-seekers and their families remaining in the State. The referendum would also facilitate the State to achieve other aims: it would allow the State to reassert its authority and sovereignty over those who could reside here; it would enable the State to regulate the entry of asylum-seekers whose presence was seen as depleting state resources, and challenging heretofore dominant conceptions of nationhood; it would allow a reconfiguration of the composition of migrants residing in the territory and maintain Ireland's association with whiteness. In effect it permitted the State to re-nationalize the nation.

The Referendum functioned as a State strategy to reproduce an ethnically exclusive national identity and idea of nationhood premised on race and racial hierarchies. The Citizenship Referendum was not simply about asylum-seekers coming to Ireland to give birth, but specifically about black Nigerian asylum-seekers coming to do so. However, the State was careful not to invoke xenophobic terms, to explicitly employ racially marked language, or use biological hierarchy in its campaign to associate race and national belonging. State discussions concerning the targeting and restricting of specific immigrant groups took place in a codified or euphemized discourse referring to nation and culture. The nation was represented in terms that were simultaneously biological and cultural. Differences in 'race' were expressed in differences in nation and culture. The Citizenship Referendum showed that 'national belonging and homogeneity... not only blur the distinction between race and nation, but rely on that very ambiguity for its effect.'[25] The invocation of citizenship and race drew attention to national frontiers so that the limits of race coincided with the limits of national boundaries. The Referendum was part of a new racism that was 'primarily concerned with mechanisms of inclusion and exclusion. It specifies who may legitimately belong to the national community and simultaneously advances reasons for the segregation or banishment of those whose "origin, sentiment, or citizenship" assigns them elsewhere.'[26]

Although the decision to hold the Referendum was attributed to the idiosyncratic inclinations of the Minister for Justice at the time, Michael McDowell, broader structural processes underpinned its logic. The Department of Justice had been conscious of the citizenship implications of the Belfast Agreement from the outset. A proposal on changing citizenship had initially been proposed in 2001.[27] Its re-emergence in 2004 followed 3 developments.[28] First, there was a sustained increase in the numbers of non-white asylum-seekers entering the State. The State used the Referendum as an opportunity to clamp down (and be seen to be clamping down) on non-EU immigration, especially of Nigerians. Second, challenging asylum-seekers' right to acquire citizenship allowed the State to appease a floating xenophobia and anxiety concerning immigration that it, along with the media, had fuelled. Third, the State had informally decided in 2003 to open its borders to workers from the EU 10. The move to do so was simultaneously inclusive and exclusive – extending entry to EU nationals while restricting it to those outside the EU. The former were essentialized as a body of white workers necessary for the economy, whereas the latter were conceived as Black welfare dependents.

Because it could not explicitly invoke ethno-racial or xenophobic considerations for the Referendum – and actually denounced those who voted for the Referendum on racist grounds – the State's agenda for holding the Referendum was masked behind a series of wavering rationales. It initially focused on material and moral arguments. It was argued that various masters of maternity hospitals in Dublin had approached the DJELR to complain about a large tide of pregnant asylum-seekers arriving in Ireland to give birth in their hospitals. The DJELR claimed that 25% of births in Dublin's maternity hospitals were to non-Irish nationals.[29] By exploiting a 'citizenship loophole', asylum-seekers were stretching the limited resources of the maternity hospitals and placing them in crisis. Moreover, those travelling in the late stages of pregnancy were also recklessly endangering the lives of their unborn children. Women getting pregnant in order to gain citizenship – 'citizenship tourism' – were not only exploiting the State's generosity, but using the sacred institution of childbirth for instrumental ends. The result of these discourses, readily amplified by the media, was the creation of a moral panic centred on a 'maternity crisis' in which hospitals were being inundated with African/Nigerian asylum-seekers and unable to cope.

However, the State's campaign to construct a moral panic was not without problems. The masters of the hospitals denied that they had specifically approached the Minister of Justice, or sought to restrict the number of non-Irish nationals arriving in the state to give birth.[30] In addition, the figures referring to the high number of non-Irish nationals coming to give birth were challenged in terms of both their accuracy, and the fact that they included EU nationals who were the largest group of non-Irish nationals in the State. In response to these criticisms the government shifted its argument by claiming that asylum-seekers were exploiting the liberal nature of the Irish migration system and challenging its 'integrity' as a whole. A more restrictive system of citizenship criteria needed to be introduced in order to align Ireland with all the other European states, and to prevent growing 'passport tourism'. Two further complementary arguments were also adduced. Providing citizenship to those who only had a tenuous connection to Ireland devalued what was a sacred institution.[31] In addition, a preliminary decision reached by the European Court of Justice in the Chen case allowed the mother of a child born in Belfast to a Chinese national a right to reside in the UK or any other EU state. This opened Ireland to further abuse, providing a backdoor to EU residency.

The State's response, though far from balanced, was nevertheless not surprising when viewed from a nation-state and sovereignty point of view. On an objective basis the State's rationalization for the Referendum was largely without a firm statistical foundation. It had not produced reliable figures on the number of pregnant women arriving to use maternity services nor could they be disaggregated to distinguish between EU nationals, those who were married to an Irish national, and those who arrived as 'passport tourists'.[32] However, it should be noted that despite the absence of hard evidence showing that asylum-seekers had arrived specifically to give birth in Ireland, it seems entirely clear that some were doing precisely this. The wide gulf in wealth between Nigeria and Ireland, and the establishment of social networks and trafficking links, meant that structural conditions generated such movement in some cases. Moreover, with restricted alternative opportunities to enter and remain in the Irish State, long delays and high refusal rates in processing asylum applications, and protracted waiting in direct provision centres, it could be argued that having a baby often served as a practical strategy to gain long-term residency. Migrating to have a child was therefore an eminently sensible option to take.[33] The State's argument that asylum-seekers were arriving was therefore not entirely fictitious or simply an ideological invention. However, the generalization and exaggeration of asylum-seekers as an abstract threat to the sovereignty and integrity of the nation-state through the construction of a 'crisis' certainly was.

Second, the crisis in the maternity hospitals was more plausibly explained not by the arrival of asylum-seekers but by the systematic underfunding of the health service. Ironically, poor conditions led to staff shortages which made the health service highly dependent on foreign workers in order to operate. Third, the Chen case did not allow unqualified settlement for a non-EU national but only gave Chen a right to citizenship because her considerable wealth allowed her not to be a burden on the state.[34] The Supreme Court judgement in the L & O case in 2003 had already established that the parents of Irish-born children had no automatic right to stay in the State. Fourth, the requirement for a long-term connection with the State as a basis for gaining citizenship conceived as a sacred institution was undermined by the operation of the doctrine of *jus sanguinis*, which allowed anyone who could show that they had an Irish grandparent born on the Island of Ireland, and even those whose great grandparents were on the register of births, citizenship. In addition, the State had, up to 2004, also been issuing passports to anyone willing to invest a substantial amount of money in the country.

Although nearly 80% of those who voted in the Referendum voted in favour of changing Irish citizenship policy, the result reflected a complex process.[35] The State's victory was aided not only by their rhetorical power, the use of a new political language, and the State's higher level of campaigning and financial resources, [36]but by their power, together with the media, to define the context of the Referendum via a moral panic underwritten by a simple moral binary: of closing a loophole that was being exploited by 'citizenship' or 'passport tourism'. Moral indignation at the transgression of a quasi-sacred institution of citizenship played a key role. Equally, longer-term negative characterisations of asylum-seekers in media and political campaigns as 'bogus', 'welfare spongers', or responsible for crime, were simultaneously prevalent. The panic and almost hysterical fear concerning immigrants in Ireland in 2004 was unprecedented. As Durkheim rightly highlighted in various essays, people are especially susceptible to the moral authority exerted by respected individuals and social groups. Conflating colour and cultural inferiority, political statements and fantasy images concerning asylum-seekers were amplified and extended through various radio and print media to create a moral panic, effectively criminalizing Nigerians who were seen as posing a threat to the social order. The creation of a moral panic allowed the State to elicit the people's consent to institute 'what was needed in the circumstances': a tougher and more restrictive citizenship policy. Moreover, for the first time in a long while, Ireland had become a country of great wealth, with something to protect. The country offered relatively high wages and acute labour shortages existed. Although migration had increased sharply at the end of the 1990s the majority of immigrants were EU 12 nationals, highly skilled workers migrating to work for multinational companies, and returning Irish migrants. However, the arrival of non-white Nigerian and other African nationals within a short time frame created a racially framed culture shock.

The Referendum was differently interpreted by differently positioned individuals and the vote may have reflected socio-economic and class processes tied to scarce material resources. Discourses that asylum-seekers were a burden on state resources and the welfare system, given priority on public housing lists, and had higher welfare payments, had become widely circulated in economically marginalized areas. Low-income constituencies characterized by high levels of social exclusion where competition for scarce state resources was acute, tended to produce a high 'yes' vote. The lowest level of support for the Referendum was in the most affluent constituency in the country, in the Dun Laoghaire/Rathdown at 71%; the highest level of support was in Longford – a poor region outside Dublin's commuter belt – standing at 84%. The class support for the Referendum was also demonstrated in the high percentage of those in the Labour Party and Sinn Fein who voted 'yes' – 55% and 57% respectively – despite both parties urging their members to vote 'no'. The State's success in imposing an authoritarian populist form of nationalism invoking xenophobia, race, and culture, and redefining themes of culture and identity, rightness, and fairness within a rhetoric of moral and social order, has partly to be seen in the context of a booming but unequal economy, characterized by a crisis in working class representation. The social partnership process effectively instituted a functional disconnect between political parties, the labour movement, and the working class. In a context of little discussion about immigration, this allowed a xenophobic and populist nationalism that complexly articulated race and nation to fill a political vacuum.[37]

However, although mediated by class factors, a populist exclusionary form of nationalism transcended class sentiment. Exit polls demonstrated that people voted 'yes' in the Referendum for a variety of reasons. In some cases it was not the specific referendum proposal about citizenship that was being evaluated, or voted upon, but rather broader concerns about immigration generally. Many voters did not understand the technical changes being discussed, or what was involved in these changes. The 'yes' or 'no' vote then functioned as a means for expressing a broader anti- or pro-immigrant sentiment. In one exit poll 27% of voters agreed with the statement that 'there were too many immigrants' in Ireland, while a third felt they were motivated to vote 'yes' by anti-immigrant feelings. 36% of voters also stated that the main reason they voted 'yes' was because they felt Ireland was being 'exploited by immigrants'.

The State's success in redefining migrants and altering citizenship by imposing a new vision of nationhood and national self-understanding indicated a historical shift in Irish nationalism. Citizenship was effectively to be allocated and withheld on racial and cultural grounds. As a political process for aligning national and social identity, the Referendum also represented a victory over competing more liberal definitions of the nation. Irishness and blackness were to remain exclusive categories. National self-understanding, although an ambiguous and contested political process, no longer used Britain primarily as its negative foil of reference, especially after the Belfast Agreement. In the new socio-economic context of the Celtic Tiger, black asylum-seekers became the negative markers of difference. With the end of Republicanism in the North, the imagined community in the South was to be narrowly constructed on racial and cultural grounds.

Citizenship and naturalization

As well as increasing the formal legal impediments to acquiring citizenship, the State has made the practical acquisition of citizenship through naturalization more difficult. At the end of 2005 the State determined that individuals could no longer apply for citizenship by marriage to an Irish national, claiming that it was being exploited by migrants using it to carry out 'marriages of convenience'. Naturalization policies also vary between states. In some, such as Germany or Switzerland, naturalization is a privilege that requires long residency periods, and operates entirely at the discretion of the state. In others such as the USA, Sweden, and Canada naturalization is a right and a formality providing certain residency criteria are met.[38] In Ireland, although the residency period is relatively short, and there are currently no citizenship tests or language requirements for gaining naturalization, the State has put a number of rigorous and time-consuming mechanisms for granting citizenship in place. There is a long application procedure averaging over 2 years – meaning an application for naturalization can take at least 7 years to acquire. However, even when all naturalization criteria are satisfied, the Minister for Justice still has absolute discretion in refusing an application and there is no right of appeal. This allows the State wide parameters of discretion and introduces a strong arbitrary element into the process, especially for discriminating on the basis of skill level and ethno-cultural difference.

There have been over 50,000 applications for naturalization during the past 10 years. The rate of application has also increased steeply and as of April 2009

Table 8.1 Naturalization applications 1999–April 2009

Year	Applications received	Certificates issued	No of apps refused / deemed ineligible
1999	739	416	79
2000	1004	125	57
2001	1431	1048	8
2002	3574	1332	135
2003	3580	1664	179
2004	4074	1335	779
2005	4527	1451	2428
2006	6813	1390	2191
2007	7616	1501	1612
2008	10885	3117	2795
2009	2179 to date	1054 to date	613 to date

there were still 16,847 applications waiting for a decision. In response the State has become increasingly restrictive in conferring citizenship, especially following the arrival of a relatively large number of accession nationals. In 2003 there were 179 refusals; by the end of 2004 this rose to 779, and to 2428 by 2005. The recessionary context further increased the State's refusal rate. In 2002, 9% of applications for citizenship were refused; by the end of 2008 this had risen to a refusal rate of 47%.

Conclusion

The hegemonic Irish identity and national self-understanding established during the 1920s and 1930s and reshaped in the 1950s and 1960s was radically altered following the rise of the Celtic Tiger. The 2 main pillars and reference points and influences on Irish cultural and political identity, the Catholic Church and British State, have both lost their importance. Through systemic media reporting of abuse scandals the media ensured that the Church lost its moral authority and cultural power, leaving the latter in steep decline. The peace process and Belfast Agreement led to a reassessment of the ideological animosity towards Britain and the nature of Irish identity. This new national identification took place in a fundamentally altered economic context characterized by rapid economic growth, pervasive consumer individualism, and conspicuous consumption, all driven by neo-liberal state policies.

Though established and taken-for-granted constituents of the sociological and political lexicon, citizenship and nationhood are highly contested and amorphous concepts that function as key variables for regulating *and* explaining social activity in modern nation-states. Materially, they constitute a vehicle *and* object of social closure used to prevent access to immigrants into the territory and its resources; ideologically they facilitate the operation of an emotionally charged distinction between those who belong and those that do not.

Migrants often expose the social and political faultlines of religion, ethnicity, class, gender, and culture which lie beneath the veneer of any 'imagined national community'. Ireland was no exception. The new articulation of nationalism with ethno-racial discrimination can be understood in terms of this new tension between the Irish community 're-imagined' in the 1990s and corresponding to a narrowly conceived sense of ethnic citizenship and the reality of increasing inequality and social diversity. National identity is defined by exclusions which mark its limit. Irishness defined in ethno-cultural terms has had no room for non-white, non-Celtic people and those who can't participate in its collective historical experience. The notion of the Celts still functions as a shorthand descriptor for Irish peoples and institutions, creating a strong biological undercurrent for narratives of who and who does not belong to the nation.

It is in this context that we can read the sub-text of government policy in the ongoing maintenance of a restrictive and exclusionary definition of Irishness as white and Catholic and also in the overt immigration policies which are straightforwardly aimed at deterring the entry of specific types of non-Nationals. The Citizenship Referendum was an attempt to introduce a peculiar ethnically determined notion of Irishness: one that had become increasingly Europeanized (with entry in European markets, accession state workers) but simultaneously racialized in terms of whiteness. The Referendum showed how ideologies of inclusion and exclusion, nationalism, and racism can morph into one another; and secondly, how class processes saturated by understandings of national self-belonging can operate, especially in a context of a working class crisis of representation.

Notes

1 S. Castles & A. Davidson, *Citizenship and Migration* (London: Palgrave, 2000); Joppke Immigration and the Identity of Citizenship,: the paradox of universalism, *Citizenship Studies* 12(6) (2008), pp. 533–46.

2 T. Marshall, *Citizenship and Social Class* (London: Pluto [1950], 1991).

3 R. Brubaker, *Citizenship and Nationhood and France and Germany* (Cambridge: Cambridge University Press, 1992), p. 31.

4 N. Elias, *The Germans*.

5 B. Anderson, *Imagined Communities: Reflections on the Origin and Spread of Nationalism* (London: Verso, 1983); E. Gellner, *Nations and Nationalism* (Ithaca: Cornell University Press, 1983); A.D. Smith, *The Ethnic Origins of Nations* (Oxford: Basil Blackwell, 1986); E. Hobsbawm, *Nations and Nationalism since 1780* (Cambridge: Cambridge University Press, 1990); Giddens, *The Nation-state and Violence*.

6 In such a context only the aristocracy conceived of themselves part of a 'nation' – not one correlated with national borders but part a broader European caste, with family members distributed all over Europe.

7 C. Tilly, The state of nationalism, *Critical Review*, 10,2 (1996), 299–306.

8 Hobsbawm, *Nations and Nationalism*.

9 Calhoun, C., *Nationalism* (Buckingham: Open University Press, 1997).

10 P. Corrigan & D. Sayer, *The Great Arch*.

11 Bourdieu, What makes a social class? *Berkeley Journal of Sociology*, vol. 22, pp. 1–18.

12 As Billig pointedly notes: 'nationhood provides a continual background for... political discourses, for cultural products, and even for the structuring of newspapers. In so many little ways, the citizenry are daily reminded of their national place in a world of nations.' M. Billig, *Banal Nationalism* (London: Sage, 1995), p. 8.

13 T. Garvin, National identity in Ireland, *Studies*, Issue 379, vol. 95, Autumn (2006).

14 A. Zolberg, *A Nation by Design* (Harvard: Harvard University Press, 2007).

15 Spouses of Irish nationals can instead apply for citizenship through naturalization, albeit after a reduced period of 3 years.

16 R. Brubaker, *Citizenship and Nationhood in France and Germany.*

17 Both concepts have a medieval pedigree. For example, right of soil and blood in the UK can be associated with regional clan and monarchical conceptions of group membership.

18 R. Brubaker, *Citizenship and Nationhood in France and Germany*, p. 4.

19 There were different approaches to naturalization in German states. It has been argued that the policies of Baden and Bavaria were more liberal than Prussia before 1914, though after this date the pattern became reversed. O. Trevisiol, *Die Einburgerungspraxis im Deutschen Reich 1871–1945* (Gottingen: V&R Unipress, 2006).

20 Joppke, 2003, Citizenship between de- and re-ethnicization, p. 435.

21 Other factors include the role of political economy, whether the country is a settler or non-settler country, or the role of empire. See T. Janoski, and E. Glennie, The integration of immigrants in advanced industrialized nations, in Marco Martiniello (ed) *Migration, Citizenship and Ethno-National Identities in the European Union* (Aldershot: Avebury Press, 1995), pp. 11–39. Classical countries of immigration such as the USA, Canada, or Australia (which are also ex-British colonies or members of the Commonwealth), have been especially marked by the principle of *jus soli*. By contrast other European states such as Switzerland or Austria have foregrounded the principle of *jus sanguinis* in their conferral of citizenship.

22 There have been structurally similar developments of inclusion and exclusion in most European liberal democratic states. Second- and third-generation French youth of Algerian descent are often still treated and defined as Algerians even though they formally possess French nationality and are *de jure* French. They are as equally marginalized as the Turkish youth living in Germany. In practice most migrants and their descendents have been *de facto* marginalized and socially excluded within both states in some form.

23 C. Joppke, *Citizenship and Migration* (Cambridge: Polity, 2009).

24 B. Ryan, The celtic cubs, p. 9.

25 P. Gilroy, *Ain't No Black in the Union Jack* (London: Routledge, 1995), p. 45.

26 Ibid.

27 *Irish Times,* 10 April 2004.

28 In a more restricted sense, the timing of the Referendum was also influenced by the fact that it took place on the same day as the European and local elections and the Fianna Fail/PD government was keen to revive what had become flagging support for government through anti-immigrant populism.

29 *Irish Times,* 23 April 2004.

30 *Irish Times,* 13 March 2004.

31 'The real issue is do we have a law in Ireland, alone of the EU member-states, which confers citizenship from birth and, by definition, under the European treaties citizenship of the European Union on anybody born in the island of Ireland no matter how casual or tenuous the connection of their parents with the Irish State.', M. McDowell, *Irish Times,* 9 April 2004.

32 Few EU nationals have sought to gain citizenship since it implies acquiring a limited amount of extra rights and entitlements.

33 See E. Luibhead and R. Lentin, Introduction, in Special issue of Women's Studies, *Women's Studies International Forum,* 27 (2004), pp. 293–300.

34 Brian Lenihan summarized these arguments by arguing that 'a yes vote in the Referendum will ensure that Irish citizenship is based on a real connection with Ireland and is not a flag of convenience for people from third countries wishing to enter the European Union... Ireland is now alone of the 25 members of the European Union in allowing an automatic right to... We know both from our own maternity hospitals and from the clear evidence of the Chen case that this is now a "pull" factor for non-EU citizens who want to get either Irish citizenship for their children or EU residency for themselves, or both... This referendum is not about human rights. It is not about statelessness. It is most certainly not about racism. This referendum is about how in the light of the real-life circumstances we find ourselves in, we shall regulate Irish citizenship for the future citizenship at birth.' *Irish Times,* 2 May 2004.

35 A high turnover for the Referendum of over 60% this showed a broad consensus among the electorate concerning the necessity of the changes determining rights to Irish citizenship.

36 Those arguing for a 'Yes' vote spent over €200,000 on their campaign while those arguing for a 'No' vote, with a deficit of resources, spent only €7,000.

37 See Gilroy, *Ain't No Black in the Union Jack* for a description of a parallel process in the UK.

38 Brubaker (ed) *Immigration and the Politics of Citizenship in Europe and North America* (Lanham: University Press of America, 1989).

Chapter 9

Stratifying the labour supply: labour migration and occupational segmentation

The majority of migrants who came to Ireland did so to work. This chapter examines the ethno-national segmentation and over-representation of migrant workers in specific industrial and occupational niches. This, it will be argued, is the outcome of a variety of multilayered and dynamic processes operating at a macro, meso, and micro level. They include global and domestic capitalist production imperatives, the state regulation of the labour supply, employer discrimination, the operation of social networks, gender, education, and migrant dispositions.

The segmentation of labour based on the ascribed characteristics of the worker rather than on human capital is not anomalous to the operation of the capitalist labour market, but appears to be an intrinsic feature of it. Segmentation can result in the marginalization of migrants and creation or reinforcement of ethno-racial divisions in Irish society.[1] Though segmentation is the conjunctural outcome and interplay of a number of contradictory social, economic, and historical factors, it is, above all, a political process. The regulation of labour to meet fluctuations in aggregate employment levels cannot simply be left to market price mechanisms in capitalism functioning as signalling devices. Rather, states are required to play a central role in overcoming this regulatory dilemma. The Irish state has regulated and calibrated the supply of labour through the construction of its immigration policy. This has simultaneously functioned to create a contingent and flexible workforce. These processes are subsequently mediated by non-state institutions that include employer hiring practices, migrant recruitment networks, worker supply chains, transport and communication links, international geo-political histories, and global inequality.

The Celtic Tiger

Western capitalist countries require migrant labour to fill jobs: just as the movement of capital is determined by profit, so too the movement of labour is conditioned by wages. This dynamic was perhaps no more evident than in the unprecedented joint arrival on Irish soil – in one of the most open and economically globalized countries in the world – of transnational foreign capital and foreign migrant labour.

The economic boom in Ireland from the mid-1990s had an enormous demographic impact on the size and content of the Irish working population. Various historical explanations have been posited for Ireland's rapid economic growth ranging from longer-term explanations pointing to Lemass's introduction of economic liberalization in the late 1950s and early 1960s, Irish membership of the European Economic Community in the 1970s, a broad economic shift towards fiscal prudence, low wages, public sector cuts, to explanations citing neo-liberal minimal state intervention and deregulation from the 1980s and 1990s. A major precipitating factor, however, was undoubtedly the arrival of US transnational corporations (TNCs) in the 1990s.[2] Their entry symbolized a shift from agribusiness and traditional manufacturing to a post-Fordist economy increasingly based on hi-technology and services. In 2006 in the three broad areas of economic activity, agriculture constituted a mere 5% of total employment, whereas industry constituted 24.7%, and services a staggering 71% of total employment.[3] The arrival of TNCs was by no means an accident but followed several years of a state developmental strategy involving various state-societal alliances, and global production and innovation networks led by agencies such as the Irish Development Agency.[4] Embedded firmly in the global market and international capital flows, the Irish economy was remarkably open even when measured against the standards of an increasingly neo-liberal international order. Foreign direct investment (FDI) companies were induced through an aggressive liberalization agenda that included low corporation taxes, the availability of a flexible, well-educated, English-speaking workforce, the existence of minimal labour regulation standards, and a gateway into the European market. The vast majority of FDI came from 3 main industries pursuing export-orientated economic policies: information technology, pharmaceuticals, and electronic engineering.[5] Even after many TNCs had left Ireland, the stock of foreign direct investment in Ireland in 2006 was still 5 times greater than the OECD average.[6] FDI precipitated an unprecedented growth in economic output, and subsequently underpinned the high levels of employment and huge growth in GDP and GNP. In alliance with FDI, rapid industrial growth and industrial upgrading was also based on other socio-political and economic factors varying in importance but including increased R&D spending, greater access of the population into third-level education, tightened wage restraint managed through the hegemonic institutionalization of social partnership, the expansion of the public sector, and increasing productivity and consumption all operating through a virtuous feedback loop.[7]

By the end of the 1990s the Irish economy was the fastest growing in the developed world with the best job creation record of any OECD country. Just over 1.1 million had been in the workforce in 1988; by the end of 2007 this figure had almost doubled to over 2.1 million with significant growth in export sector, public sector, construction industry, financial services, and personal and other services sectors.[8] Intransigent unemployment standing at almost 20% in the late 1980s fell to under 5% by the mid-1990s, reaching a mere 4.2% in 2006 – one of the lowest levels amongst the EU member states.

Between 1994 and 2000 almost half a million new jobs were created in the State.[9] Though foreign direct investment and export-oriented manufacturing stimulated economic growth it was in the broadly defined 'services sectors' where the largest amount of employment growth initially took place. Between 2001 and 2006 the Irish labour force grew by a further 17%, increasing from 1.8 million to 2.1 million workers.[10] The total employment of 2.06 million people in 2006 can be broken down into 11 main economic sectors (see Figure 9.1).

Following 2001, and in order to escape recessionary forces that had gripped many OECD countries, the government deregulated and stimulated investment to create an enormous property bubble in the property and housing market. Together with accelerated domestic consumption the result was a massive

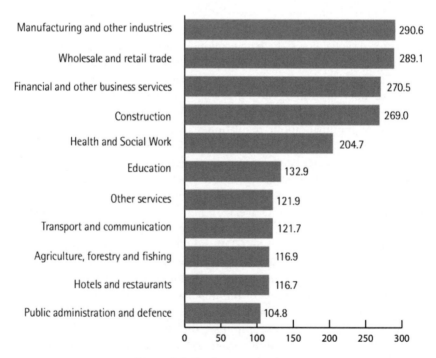

Figure 9.1 Employment by sector
Source: FAS, using CSO 2007:12.

growth in property development, house prices, and a rapid overall expansion in the construction sector.[11] Later employment growth was concentrated in the financialization and construction sectors – with 14% of the workforce estimated to be located in finance in 2008.[12]

Though by no means a straightforward picture, economic and employment growth became concentrated in certain sectors. Like other developed economies the Irish economy expanded rapidly away from Fordist mass production to post-Fordist service work. In *absolute* terms the labour market burgeoned not only in the export-orientated foreign capital sectors but more broadly in the health, education, and the finance and business sectors, while employment fell in agriculture. There was also a *relative* decline in manufacturing though absolute numbers remained high (see Figure 9.2).

Segmentation

Reflecting broader global patterns of labour market segmentation, the occupational uptake of migrants has differed considerably from the native Irish population. The occupational segmentation of visibly different groups whether

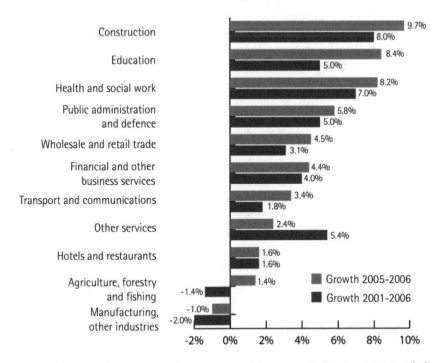

Figure 9.2 Annual average employment growth by sector 2005–6 and 2001–6 (%)
Source: FAS, using CSO

defined in terms of gender, ethnicity, race, or religion – that is, in terms of an individual's ascribed characteristics rather than their achievements – is a pervasive feature of all modern democratic (and supposedly meritocratic) societies. Horizontal and vertical segmentation invariably involves groups who are socially deemed to have tenuous or contingent ties to the labour market, that is, categories of individuals who are seen as not a 'proper' or 'normal' part of the workforce or are considered to have an alternative role outside of the workforce. This includes women who are perceived by the state, unions, and employers to be part of the non-paid domestic sphere, and migrants who are regarded as temporary workers in the state, and may also see themselves as such. These ideological conceptions are often justified by appeal to the innate natural or cultural differences between these groups and the adult white male population.

The concentration of immigrants especially into low-skilled occupational niches has largely been co-extensive with modern immigration. Labour markets are institutionally and geographically embedded, and systemically uneven and diverse institutions.[13] Nevertheless, despite this national and regional variability there are also some generic features characterizing all of them with regard to ethno-national segmentation. The majority of post-war immigrant workers in Western Europe have been concentrated in unskilled manual occupations, as natives moved increasingly into white-collar work. In the 1950s German *Gastarbeiter* (guestworkers) were disproportionately concentrated in agriculture and mining. Whilst during the 1960s as the economy shifted they moved into construction and vehicle manufacture; 75% of workers in Ford's Cologne plants were Turks. In France, during the 1960s, migrants were concentrated in construction, metallurgy, chemical manufacture, rubber, and asbestos, with one fifth employed as farm labourers.[14] Similarly, concentrations of immigrants in manual work characterized employment patterns in the UK.

More recently, in the USA, many Latinos have become concentrated in 3-D jobs (dirty, difficult, and dangerous) such as working in restaurant kitchens, cleaning, or as agricultural workers. While Puerto Ricans have taken up low-paid jobs in the declining manufacturing sector, including the garment industry, in building trade occupations, as well as food preparation and housekeeping. Within the context of an increasingly deregulated global capitalism the correlation between migrants and low-paid work shunned by native workers is becoming more common. As Harris notes:

> There is rarely a shortage of jobs. In London or Washington, at times of peak unemployment, there were shortages of unskilled labour; but at pay rates so low and in living conditions so bad, it would have meant self destruction for the native born worker to take them. It was implicit in the popular morality that no one should take them... In New York, in the 2 or 3 thousand garment shops in the high fashion garment industry there are perpetual vacancies. To work a 10 hour day at furious, piece rate governed pace, in dark and dangerous conditions for pay

which was at worst, in the 1980s, no more than $1 an hour (compared to a federal minimum wage of $3.35). Single mothers with dependent children could not take such jobs even if they lived close enough to avoid travel costs; but illegal immigrants could.[15]

In the context of intense global competition, many businesses could only survive by relying on (often undocumented) migrant workers. The garment industry in London, for example, was heavily reliant on Turkish, Kurdish, and Cypriot workers to work in its sweatshops during the 1990s. However, following the implementation of the Uruguay rounds of the world trade negotiations, and exposed to direct international competition from China, the industry collapsed.[16]

However, migrants do not only cluster into the secondary labour market. In the USA, entry of Latinos into working class occupations can be contrasted with the labour market access of Asian workers. 45% of Asians were in the managerial and professional category compared with 17% of Latinos in 2005.

Immigrants in Ireland

It was within the new context of unprecedented levels of economic growth, with annual growth rates averaging above 5%, that labour migration took place in the Celtic Tiger. Immigrant workers constitute approximately 1 in 6 of the labour force with about 352,000 estimated to be in employment in 2008. They not only differ from Irish nationals according to the type of jobs that they have taken up but also in terms of labour force participation, unemployment, levels of education, and earnings.

There is an overlooked class dimension to immigration in Ireland. The large numbers of migrants in the Irish workforce has led to a significant re-composition of class relations in Ireland tha has a number of undeveloped implications. Migrants have been funnelled exclusively towards certain industries, sectors, and occupations, thereby occupying different positions in the stratified and hierarchical labour market relative to native Irish workers.[17] Although the measurement of class has generally been a contested area in which a category of process is reduced to a thing, it has always been reluctantly applied in Ireland because of the country's predominantly rural character. These obstructions were redoubled by the arbitrary nature of the occupations classified within each of the CSO's Socio-economic and Social Class categories. Classification and the work of selection are social processes involving schemes of inference and judgements about what constitutes or falls within a category. They are also contested and ideologically charged processes. Occupations listed by the CSO in the socio-economic group within the highest socio-economic category, 'Employers and Managers', strangely include cashiers, bank and counter clerks, debt, rent and other cash collectors, glaziers, painters and decorators, cabinet makers, bakers and floor confectioners, chefs, and cooks; whilst the 'Managerial and Technical' category in the Social Class scheme includes petrol pump attendants and sales assistants. The effect of this is to markedly exaggerate claims of growth in the size of the middle class in Ireland.[18] Simultaneously such classification underplays the effects of de-skilling. Nevertheless, the CSO categories do provide some broad measure for comparing Irish and non-Irish nationals. They point to significant concentration of non-Irish nationals into the lower social classes. 63% of non-Irish workers were located in the bottom four social class groups – Skilled Manual, Semi-Skilled, Unskilled, and All Others Gainfully Occupied and Unknown – compared to 49% of Irish workers.[19] In terms of socio-economic groups, 25% of non-Irish nationals were in the top 3 socio–economic groups compared to32% of Irish nationals.[20] This concentration in the lower classes has occurred despite the fact that migrants in Ireland are generally well qualified, with 43.8% of non-Irish nationals aged between 25 and 44 holding a third-level qualification in 2006 compared to 41.3% of the corresponding Irish population.[21] Immigrants are less likely to be in high-level occupations even when age and education are taken into account, especially those from new EU member states.[22]

These developments point to crucial issues concerning the reconfiguration of the Irish working class. Class analysis in Ireland has to be rethought, recalibrated, and expanded within this new context in which migrants almost constitute a sub-proletariat with low wages, unskilled jobs, and insecure employment. This is made even more complex by the simultaneous feminization of work. The junction between gender, ethnicity, and class based issues of power entail a reconsideration of the simple analytical priority afforded to the contradiction between capital and labour for understanding social subordination. The combination of these categories points to an 'articulated ensemble of social relations structured in dominance'.[23]

At a more concrete level the class positioning of migrants is reflected in their occupational segmentation. This sectoral and occupational clustering points to the existence of a dual labour market consisting of a well-paid, secure and highly skilled primary sector characterized by career progression, contrasted with a secondary sector associated with low pay and poor working conditions. Migrants have largely been filtered into the latter. But there are exceptions including some German and Indian nationals.

According to CSO data, 38% of workers in the hotels and restaurants industry, 17.7% of workers in the construction sector, 19.4% of workers in Wholesale and retail trade, and 18.9% of workers in other production industries were non-Irish nationals. By contrast, very few were found in the education sector (7.1%) and only 1.6% of those working in public administration and defence were non-Irish nationals.[24] Within sub-sectors migrants have a near monopoly in certain areas in the Irish economy such as the red-meat, contract cleaning, domestic work, and mushroom sector.

Looked at in national terms over half of Polish males are in construction and manufacturing, while a half of all Polish females worked in shops, hotels, and restaurants, working predominantly as sales assistants (7%), building labourers (6%), cleaners and domestics (5%), and carpenters and joiners (4%). Similar sectoral and occupational clustering characterized Lithuanian workers who in addition also work in the food industry – especially as mushroom pickers.[25] Many filled gaps in the labour market especially in near-minimum wage industries including food, catering, agriculture, or manufacturing and production. This mirrors patterns in the UK where, at the end of 2007, it was estimated that 97% of such workers were earning between the minimum wage of £5.10 and £6 an hour.[26]

Nigerians have become concentrated in health services and business services sectors and their most common occupations were as care assistants and attendants (11%), security guards (7%), and sales assistants (7%), though some were also doctors (6%). There is also evidence of many becoming taxi drivers or opening shops as immigrant entrepreneurs. A large number of Chinese work in the hotel and restaurant sector (54%). Their most common occupations were as chefs and cooks (19%), and waiters and waitresses (9%) though some also worked as sales assistants (9%). Many are also students who work part time in these occupations.

Filipinos were narrowly concentrated in the health sector with 7 out of 10 females and 4 out of 10 males working there. The most common occupations were as nurses and midwives (42%) and care assistants and attendants (14%). In terms of Indians almost all the women were working in the health sector (88%) while for men business services dominated. Like the Filipinos, nursing (2,246) was the most common occupation followed by software engineers and programmers for men. However, other research shows many also work in the restaurant sector, and as sales assistants.[27] The main occupations of Brazilians were as butchers and meat cutters, builders' labourers, and food and drink operatives.[28] If nationality does play a significant explanatory role in occupational uptake it is evident in the employment of Germans in Ireland. The latter have a markedly different and preferential labour market composition in terms of social class than any other national group, including the Irish, with 46% working as managers or professionals with business services featuring as the main sector of employment for both males and females.[29] Their most widespread occupations were as general clerical workers (10%), computer analysts (4%), architects and town planners (3%) and managers of marketing, etc. (3%).

This ethno-national sectoral/occupational clustering, in which jobs of a particular type are linked with categorically distinct workers, has been shaped by a number of complex, overlapping, and sometimes contradictory processes. Occupational segmentation is not simply something that happens, but is 'made' through the intended and unintended actions of variously positioned social actors within definite social and contested relations of hierarchical power operating at a macro, meso and micro level.

Labour markets are not clearing houses where supply and demand meet through price signals. Instead they are characterized by categorical inequalities which are not incidental to their operation but created by them. Labour markets are socio-political constructions and their regulation and reproduction involve a number of non-economic factors embedded in cultural, social, and political structures. The factors underpinning occupational segmentation are complex, contradictory, and multilayered. They include global economic forces of supply and demand for labour, domestic economic processes including the demands and requirements of capitalist employers for a certain type of flexible and compliant labour, state regulatory processes and institutional factors, social networks, employer discrimination, trade union activity, and the culturally structured work expectations of immigrant workers. As Peck notes: 'the conflicting motivations, goals, and strategic practices of different groups in the labour market – which divide not only between capital and labour but also social fractions within these aggregates – call for a conception of the labour market as a socially constructed and politically mediated structure of conflict and accommodation among contending forces.'[30]

In Ireland, ethnic segmentation has been fundamentally shaped by a state regulatory regime, operating at the objectivity of both the 'first' and 'second' order. This includes the legal regulation of immigration policy and processes of state classification and discourses that construct a hierarchy of migrant statuses, and racialize migrants. It also involves social networks, discriminatory and pragmatic hiring practices, the indigenous historically established customs and expectations surrounding work, and the concrete characteristics of migrants including their nationality, region of origin, gender, class and qualifications, skill levels, language capabilities and socio-cultural expectations about work. The result of this articulation of processes contains a number of unintended consequences that shapes the labour market.

It is important to emphasize that rather than emerging spontaneously, the Irish State, together with employers and employment agencies, in the context of an acute shortage of labour, engendered a large number of migrations. Their intervention accounts for the timing of the migration flows and the specific countries and regions from where these flows occurred. Once initiated, however, these migrations became self-sustaining and cumulative through the development of migrant chains and social networks providing information flows between sending and receiving countries. These self-sustaining chains then became difficult for the Irish state – as a liberal democratic state – to fully control.

Capitalist demand

One of the major factors structuring labour market segmentation is the structure and type of labour demand in the national economy. The dynamics of international and domestic capitalism require flexible workers in order to maintain profit rates. Capitalism fundamentally structures the character, allocation and intensity of work. In modern differentiated economies increasing numbers of jobs involve 'the social processing of commodities and consumers [rather] than the processing of raw materials.'[31] A neo-liberal deregulatory agenda and various other socio-political and cultural factors, including social partnership, have strongly determined the shape and contours of the Irish labour market. The shift towards the neoliberal agenda constituted less of a retreat of the state per se than a strategic repositioning to meet the needs of capital at the expense of labour through deregulation, stripping away of market rigidities, and providing a flexible and compliant workforce. It is important, however, not to use 'neo-liberalism' as a catch-all explanation for the processes shaping labour markets. Though crucial for structuring the logic and unfolding of their current configuration of labour markets, welfare systems, and individualistic ideologies, labour segmentation and inequality were prevalent even during more corporatist and Fordist–Keynesian phases of economic development, if not centuries before.

As has been the case in a number of capitalist countries, labour demand in Ireland has entailed a polarized requirement for both high-skilled and low-skilled workers.[32] As one commentator noted with regard to the USA:

> In a period of about 30 years the workforce has been transformed in industrial and occupational terms. This was a polar development in which both very highly paid and poorly paid jobs grew, while many in the middle, including the lost manufacturing jobs, shrank. Professionals sporting credentials, the badge of their higher education and qualifications... composed 23% of the workforce... At the other end of the workforce were millions producing or performing services or selling or moving products for far less money and benefits. This reshaped labour force was polarized by race and gender as well.[33]

The expansion of both highly skilled, professional, well-paid jobs, such as those in computer and information technology, and the medical field, occurred at the same time as the growth of precarious, flexible, and part-time employment in traditional manufacturing and services in Ireland.[34] The need for well-paid, predominantly male, immigrant workers with productivity-enhancing skills working for a number of US investment companies in the hi-tech sector or doctors – in 2000 over a third of doctors in Ireland were foreign born[35] – could be contrasted with a similar requirement for poorly paid and exploited female workers in the mushroom industry. Despite their binary analytical contrast, skills and labour shortages are inextricably linked and complementary. As Harris notes:

> The highest skilled hospital physicians depend for their effectiveness on a legion of unskilled workers supporting them – cleaning, laundering, bed-making, cooking and serving, carrying and portering, manning telephones and security services… Indeed, the more highly skilled the labour force of the developed countries becomes, the greater is the need for unskilled support workers; and, in an open economy, many of these will come from developing economies legally or illegally.[36]

In Ireland as part of their increasing stylization of life, professionals have sought more and better restaurants, theatres, clubs and with more couples working they have also demanded crèche facilities or domestic maids for their children, better health care, and personal services as well as newly developed and exclusive housing and accommodation.

Both labour shortages and skills shortages existed in 125 occupations in Ireland in 2005[37] and many 'difficult to fill' vacancies that were distributed over various employment sectors remained even after the large-scale entry of accession state nationals (see Table 9.1).

This bi-polar development of work vacancies included an expansion in flexible working conditions and short-term contracts at both the top and the bottom of the labour market hierarchy as well as a widening of labour market inequalities. The occupational polarization generated both a reconfiguration of class relations, and inequality. Such a transfer of wealth from labour to capital was facilitated and solidified through the social partnership process.

The need for both highly skilled and lower-skilled workers, with less requirement for jobs that fall in the middle of the occupational hierarchy, can be examined in more detail below. Professional occupations were one of the fastest growing occupational groupings between 2001 and 2006.[38] Included in this category were vacancies for production managers in industry, but also other mangers and administrators, chemists, biological scientists, physicists, and natural scientists. In construction there were shortages of architects, town planners, and quantity surveyors. In the financial sector there were shortages in the areas of accounting, quantitative finance and compliance. Engineers were in demand

Table 9.1 Difficult to fill vacancies by sector, 2004–6

	2004	2005	2006
Construction	23%	20%	15%
Industry	37%	32%	48%
Retail	13%	13%	8%
Services	27%	34%	30%
Total	100%	100%	100%

Source: (FAS, ESRI, 2007: 12)

in all areas including civil/mining, mechanical, electrical, electronic, software, chemical, and planning and control engineers. In the health professions shortages were recorded for medical practitioners, pharmacists, doctors, dental practitioners, nurses and midwives, medical radiographers, physiotherapists, and occupational therapists.[39] The State's support and investment in R&D, as part of its attempt to create a 'knowledge economy', also led to an acute shortage of computer analysts and programmers. The Irish Director for ICT argued that Ireland was now 'facing into a crisis'.[40]

Although the state formally has repeatedly emphasized the need for high-skilled workers in its official discourse, and as part of its ideological construction of a 'smart' or 'knowledge' economy, the demand for low-skilled workers in Ireland has remained just as acute. Labour shortages in the low-paid secondary sector were just as severe as deficits in the primary sector. Labour requirements existed in catering, food preparation trades, in security and protective service occupations including security guards, in catering occupations for waiters and waitresses, and in health and care-related occupations including a desperate need for care assistants, domestic workers, and other childcare-related occupations. The Celtic Tiger economy was also marked by a shortage of office cleaners, personal services, dishwashers and fast-food operatives, agricultural workers, factory workers, builders, labourers, sales assistants, security guards, operatives in metal work, plant and machinery, assemblers, lineworkers and for staff to work in warehouses.

Many of these vacancies were for low-skilled, low-paid, low-status jobs that indigenous Irish people no longer wished to do. The difficulty of excessive labour turnover was compounded by the creation of more attractive occupational vacancies for native workers in addition to the weak incentive mechanism tying work and rewards in many of these occupations. With a decrease in the number of workers directly involved in production and the emergence of new service-oriented jobs there has been a shift in how jobs are evaluated. As Berger notes:

> the work involved in the new range of jobs is often frustrating and dehumanized. But it is not physically arduous, and the conventional values of society, re-imposed everyday by the media, confer an enviable social status upon the new jobs. The white collar offers membership of a higher division of labour. Higher because less physical. Higher because more abstracted. Higher because of the 'sophistication' of the equipment used. This new category of work has altered the remuneration expected for work in general. Remuneration now includes a life-style which, as it were, houses the wages even while being dependent on it.[41]

With local workers unwilling to take up such low-status work, and with female recruitment drying up in gender filtered occupations, migrants began filling these vacancies. Modern mass production and large parts of the services industry still require unskilled workers. The majority of work taken up by for migrants has been in 3-D low-status work. 75% of all applicants for work permits in 2000 were for unskilled work.[42] This can be seen in the need for labourers in construction, sales and services, cleaning services, and catering. As a FAS skills report noted these positions could only be filled by non-Irish nationals willing to undertake such low-grade labour: 'The changes in the nationality composition of the employment stock and the work permit data suggest that employers continue to source labourers from abroad, particularly in the services, agriculture and construction sectors; currently, Irish persons appear to be reluctant to take up jobs as labourers given the availability of alternative job opportunities.'[43] Migrants were also required in what is the largest occupation in the country (*pace* the 'knowledge economy'), sales assistants. Such work was also one of the most gendered, non-unionized, part-time, and contractual forms of employment. Although the value of retail services grew by a massive 43% between 2001 and 2007 based on the massive rise in conspicuous consumption and easily available credit, according to the Mandate union the average starting pay for retail workers stood at €9.09 an hour, slightly over the minimum wage.[44] Difficult-to-fill vacancies in food preparation for butchers and de-boners meant that the latter also had 'one of the highest proportions of non-Irish nationals employed. They appear regularly in the work permit data suggesting employers are having difficulty sourcing workers from the EU'.[45]

Without migrants, large sections of the Irish economy would not have been able to operate. Migrants served as an available labour force willing to work in such conditions and for such wages. However, the picture in Ireland is more complex than simple dual labour market theorists would suggest. Migrants have not only entered the secondary labour sector. The acute skills shortages in the IT and medical sector, for example, has meant that migrants also entered into the primary sector. These workers are 'flexible' in a different sense. They are sought by recruitment agencies and major multinational companies who place a premium on their skills. They are perceived as workers who carry their portable skills, knowledge, creativity and human capital with them. Rather than seeking long-term contracts, job-security, or promotion within internal labour markets, they pursue extremely high wages and job bonuses.[46]

Employers

Understanding occupational segmentation requires examining the role of employers in recruiting migrant workers. Some of the strongest support for migration in Ireland has come from employers and employers' organizations such as Irish Business and Executive Council and Irish Small and Medium Enterprises. Structural processes inherent to capitalism play a significant role in recruiting workers. Capitalist competition prevents employers from raising wages to attract native workers or improving their working conditions, especially in jobs not amenable to mechanization or where capital cannot be used to replace labour. Moreover, employers are also reluctant to raise wages because of what Piore calls 'structural inflation'.[47] Since occupational wage differences in capitalism confer status and prestige, raising one group or individual's wages may precipitate further calls for a wage increase from other groups. Although employers have a fundamental interest in the cost and productivity of labour power they also exercise, to varying degrees and depending upon the industry, a level of discretion over the kinds of workers they employ. They primarily require workers who are willing to work hard and to take low wages but who are also compliant, willing, and flexible. As Waldinger and Hecter note: 'Simply put, bosses want willing subordinates… They also prefer "cooperative" to "combative", and deferential over rebellious – in other words, a worker who knows her or his place.'[48] As another commentator notes: 'The migrant is in several ways an "ideal" worker. He [sic] is eager to work overtime. He is willing to do shift work at night. He arrives politically innocent – that is to say without any proletarian experience.'[49] Those in the primary sector ordinarily require certain clusters of scarce knowledge and skill sets. However, employers may also try to look for workers who possess soft skills for work in the service economy, which is primarily located in the secondary labour market: 'In the postindustrial service economy, the quality of the service interaction matters more and more, so it is no surprise that employers are also searching for workers with a "friendly" feel or approach… which to a large extent means the ability to keep a smile regardless of how unpleasant the customers or working conditions.'[50]

Rather than relying solely on human capital criteria as neo-classical economists argue, employers' choices of the suitability of 'appropriate' workers is often determined categorically on the basis of ascriptive criteria – gender, ethnicity, or race. Employers seek migrant workers precisely because they differ from the indigenous Irish population, because they are structurally disempowered in terms of citizenship rights; in terms of their subjective orientation and willingness to accept poorer working conditions and socially undesirable forms of work; and because they have negative ascribed characteristics. Their state-sanctioned socio-economic vulnerability is especially evident for those on work permits, those in the secondary labour market sector who have a lack of knowledge about their rights and entitlements, those with insufficient language proficiency, or those with an irregular legal status.

Put another way, legal status, background economic conditions, unfamiliarity with local standards of job intensity, rights and entitlements, lack of language skills, and need to provide remittances or repay debts, means that some migrants constitute part of a hyper-flexible workforce.

However, the simple picture of employers drawing on a flexible disempowered workforce needs to be qualified. In reality recruitment practices are more complex and contradictory. In contemporary capitalism not only are jobs ranked in terms of pay, stability, conditions, autonomy, and social status but so too are migrants and ethnic groups. Extant racial hierarchies based on skin colour, nationality, religion, and stereotypes of various nationalities are operationalized and used by employers when hiring workers. Employers operate with a mix of pragmatic considerations and stereotyped and sometimes xenophobic view of immigrants. This includes socially meaningful but arbitrary traits and racialized stereotypes shaped by long-term historical processes of colonial knowledge, and circulating and reproduced in state and media discourses. Thus for example employers may see Nigerians as lazy, dishonest, or confrontational; Poles as hard working and willing to take low wages; Germans as humourless, but reliable and good workers.

Many migrants are also forced into jobs for which they are overqualified. Although over a quarter of Poles had completed at least third-level courses only 9% found themselves in the top 3 occupational groups with 60% concentrated in the lower socio-economic groups. Equally although 23% of Lithuanians have a third-level qualification, only 2% are working as professionals. The elision between level of qualifications and type of occupation also indicates the operation of racial hierarchies in recruitment. The 2006 Census shows that although half of Nigerian nationals have completed a third-level course and had similar educational qualifications to Germans, only 25% were in the top 3 occupational categories as managers or professionals as compared to 46% of Germans. This anomaly can partly be explained in terms of the lower levels of language competence of some migrants.[51] However, other factors including a lack of recognition of qualifications and employer discrimination also appear to play a central role. One study found that employers faced with applications from candidates who were identical in all relevant characteristics other than their ethnic or national origin were twice as likely to call Irish applicants for interview as minority nationals.[52] Other studies have demonstrated that non-Irish nationals are 3 times more likely to report having experienced discrimination whilst looking for work than Irish nationals, and blacks 7 times more likely.[53] Again, this may point to different qualifications, the existence of discrimination as an explanatory factor is supported by interview data from other reports.[54] In one study, a Nigerian national who had a masters degree in human resource management and IBC status spoke of how he could only get a job as a delivery driver. He had made over 100 applications in the year but only been called to 1 interview with a car rental company. He talked about his experiences with the business sector. 'If I think about it, it has to do with stereotyping. Because you say you're Nigerian, that's why you can't get that job' (Peter, Nigeria). Another who had a degree in political science and a masters degree in transport and logistics noted: 'I see supply chain analyst, I apply for it, but no way. Supply chain administrator, they won't give it to me… Yeah. Because immediately they see my name they know they won't' (Akin, Nigeria).

Hence, although potentially a flexible and compliant category of workers, employer xenophobia and racism, especially against Nigerians, can sometimes trump economic considerations in hiring workers, particularly in small-size firms.

State regulation and classification

The asymmetrical power relation between employer and employee means that labour structurally remains at a power disadvantage in relation to capital. Despite an overall global shift from 'despotic' to 'hegemonic regimes', semi-coercive mechanisms are still required to retain and maintain workers in these jobs.[55] As we shall see these are created through state classification and policy measures.

The transnational economic forces operating on the demand side of the labour market are always conjoined with national processes of state regulation and institutionalization structuring the supply side. Notwithstanding the growth of economic globalizing forces that have partially undermined the sovereign power of nation-state, many states still possess considerable power in shaping economic processes. Despite a neo-liberal refrain about reducing government interference in the market generally, the Irish State has played a central role in planning and structuring labour market supply. The state has served as an adjustment mechanism for imbalances in the labour market supply. During periods of boom it has actively recruited workers directly from those on the margins of the labour market such as women or migrants. During the slump, it has increased punitive controls and restrictions on the labour market entry of migrants and increased the disciplining effects of the market.

In Ireland the State formally undertakes this labour market planning process through the interaction of state agencies with the social partners. In reality, however, it is employers that have had the most significant input in tailoring immigration policy towards their labour requirements.

This can be seen in the State's regulation of the labour supply during the Celtic Tiger boom. Within the context of unprecedented labour demand, the Tánaiste, Mary Harney, warned in 2000 that a failure to address the labour shortage could undermine the Irish Republic's economic growth since wage rates and the availability of skilled workers remained central concerns for multinational companies in relation to investment decisions.[56] Evidence of acute labour shortages was further underlined in the Small Firms Association employment survey in the same year. This stated that, of the 69% of companies which had vacancies, 91% were unable to fill them. A large source of demand came from unskilled sectors, such as hotels and catering, and other low-grade services, with 44% of employers in these areas claiming that they could not recruit, primarily as a result of the low rate of pay.[57] In addition, the government estimated that some 200,000 new workers would be needed by 2006 as part of the National Development Plan.

The Expert Group in Future Skills Needs (EGFSN) set up by the State in 1997 as part of the social partnership process also highlighted the significant skills and labour shortages in the State. The EGFSN, dominated by business elites, has played a central role in labour recruitment.[58] To remedy the shortfall it suggested encouraging greater participation in the labour force by married women, those who had taken early retirement, and those on social welfare who were unwilling to take up work because of the poverty trap. However, it acknowledged it would be difficult to recruit these categories because of the low rates of pay, poor working conditions, and greater range of opportunities available in other occupational sectors.[59]

The number of women entering the labour force in Ireland increased rapidly during the Celtic Tiger boom. In 1994, 40% of women were in the Irish labour force; by 2000 this had risen to 53%.[60] This was primarily determined by greater labour demand, but also the increasing necessity for Irish households to acquire 2 incomes in order to survive in a country characterized by a costly standard of living. Moreover, women predominantly entered into specific types of devalued occupations, seen as an extension of their domestic role, that were located in the secondary labour market – as sales workers, personal and protective service workers, and in clerical and secretarial work.[61] Though there were some exceptions, for example in the health sector, women's average income in 2002 was only 63% of that of men.

However, the scale of the Irish boom meant that despite the increased entry of female workers, labour shortages in various occupations remained. The Irish State also began actively to recruit Irish emigrants living abroad, especially in the UK.[62] As the Tainaiste noted rather optimistically at the opening of a Jobs Ireland recruitment fair in London:

> Research has shown many Irish people in Britain retain a strong desire to return to live and work in their own part of Ireland. They still buy their provincial newspaper, the *Irish Post* or browse their internet editions, avidly follow events back home and keep a keen eye on the fortunes of their local football and hurling teams. This wish to come back to one's own county or locality is perfectly understandable but until recently seemed to be an impossible dream for most Irish people living and working in Britain. However, this Government's commitment to spreading the benefits of Ireland's booming economy throughout the country means that, what was once wishful thinking is now a realizable goal for most people.[63]

The campaign was a huge success. Between 2002 and 2004 it is estimated that about 37% of immigrants in Ireland were returning Irish nationals.[64] However, this supply of labour began to dry up and with new expectations about work and changed values having lived abroad, the returnees did not necessarily wish to take jobs in the occupations in which the severest labour shortages were located.

The State also set about strategically targeting specific countries for the recruitment of non-Irish workers through work fairs and advertising campaigns. The first international jobs fair conducted by FÁS, in April 2000, was held in Newfoundland and was swiftly followed by others in London, Berlin, Cologne, Hanover, Manchester, Prague, Birmingham, Cape Town, and Johannesburg. In 2001, there were also visits to Poland, France, Croatia, Estonia, Australia, New Zealand, Russia, India, and, again, Canada and South Africa.[65] The targeted recruitment drive was predominantly aimed at non-African, non-Asian countries (with the exceptions of South Africa and India). These nation-states are generally populated by white Christians, who are, from the State's point of view, more easily 'assimilatable' into Irish society. The racialization of recruitment was part of a straightforward attempt by the State to regulate internal ethnic and religious diversity, which has both a historical and comparative precedent.[66]

In parallel with the State recruitment fairs, large companies also experiencing labour shortages, such as McDonalds and Tesco, also actively and independently sought to recruit workers from abroad. Tesco, for example, could easily source Polish workers for its stores in Dublin after it purchased 13 hypermarkets in Poland in 2002. Employment agencies also mushroomed, with the number of licensed agencies in Ireland increasing from 195 in 1987 to 447 in 1999.[67]

Hence, in contrast to the dominant theoretical viewpoint which presumes that individuals rationally choose to migrate to Ireland because of their knowledge of an income differential within the context of perfect information, these processes highlight a more structural explanations in which the State, as a proxy and support to capital, plays a central role in generating migration from poorer countries with a surplus of labour. Rather than arising spontaneously, some migration was systematically engendered though a strategic and selectively initiated search for new sources of labour. Such a strategy was commonplace among European countries after the Second World War. After the war the British recruited migrants from ex-colonies in the Caribbean, India, and Pakistan. Germans recruited Italians, Spanish, Greeks, Tunisians, Yugoslavians, and Turks in the 1950s and 1960s. The French recruited Tunisians and Algerians. Given the severe nature of labour shortages these states sometimes competed with one another for the same pools of labour by offering various incentives in order to secure these workers.

As well as immigrant policies located in what Bourdieu calls the 'objectivity of the first order', state classificatory processes operating through 'the objectivity of the second order' have been central to the process of state recruitment. A number of categorically distinct migration mechanisms and categorical schemas have been utilized to filter and differentiate the supply of migrant labour. The creation of different immigration statuses is inextricably bound up with national origin as a socio-cultural-political category. Differential legal statuses became articulated with different nationalities that in turn shaped access to specific forms of work. Such a process created a correlation between legal status, nationality, and occupation. This can be seen in relation to the different legal statuses that work permit, work visa, and EU nationals have, and their correlation with different occupational sectors.

Differentiating migrant workers

Work permits were the major mode through which non-EU nationals gained employment in the State. In 1993, only 1,103 work permits were issued. By the end of 2003 this figure stood at 47,551 – a 700% increase.[68] Up to 2003 the most rapid increase in work permits was in the agricultural sector (with the number of permits rising from 70 in 1998 to 7,242 in 2003) and in the catering and hotel industries (where the number of permits rose from 607 in 1998 to 11,548 in 2003)[69] (see Table 9.2). About 75% of these work permits went to unskilled sectors.[70] Such unskilled positions lack a career path and are characterized by wages that fall well below the national average.

Following the admittance of 10 accession states into the EU in May 2004 (which included Poland, Latvia, and Lithuania), the number of permits issued began to fall rapidly. By the end of 2007 23,604 permits had been issued, falling to 7,692 during the recession in 2009.

The demand for unskilled labour was matched by a demand for skilled workers. In 2000, business organizations and government bodies such as the

Table 9.2 Work permits issues and renewed by sector, 1998–2006

Sector	1998	2003	2004	2005	2006
Agriculture	70	7,242	3,721	2,139	1,952
Industry	705	3,376	2,174	1,680	1,676
Services	4,941	36,933	28,172	23,317	21,179
Medical, Nursing	620	2,709	2,469	2,683	2,852
Catering	607	11,548	8,306	6,976	5,842
Education	298	759	717	726	798
Domestic	59	944	772	684	631
Entertainment/Sport	264	1,172	1,191	1,175	1,261
Other services	3,093	19,801	14,717	11,073	9,795
Total	5,716	47,551	36,067	27,134	24,854

Source: ESRI, O'Connell & McGinnity, Immigrants at work, 2008:5

National Competitiveness Council and FÁS called for the creation of a fast-track work authorization/visa system. These fast-track visas/authorizations were introduced specifically to facilitate the recruitment of specialist categories of workers in sectors where acute skills shortages existed: professionals in information technology and computing, skilled workers in construction, and doctors and nurses in the medical field. In 2001, for example, of the 2,358 work visas issued 80% went to nurses and 10% to software engineers.

Despite the existence of these migration employment schemes for recruiting migrant workers to fill labour and skills shortages (which were altered in February 2007 with the introduction of the green card scheme), the largest numbers of workers that have entered Ireland to work are EU workers including accession state nationals.[71] Ireland was 1 of only 3 countries, together with the UK and Sweden (who also faced a labour shortage), to allow accession state nationals to immediately come and work following European expansion in May 2004.[72] There were a number of dimensions concerning the Irish State's decision to allow the entry of accession state nationals. As a member of the EU the Irish State had little control over the eventual entry of EU 10 nationals and since the UK had agreed their entry the CTA predisposed Ireland to do so as well. Simultaneously it also suited the State's racialized preference hierarchy of incoming migrants. The accession states were perceived to be socio-culturally closer to Irish nationals populated predominantly by white Christians that ameliorated concerns about skin colour and alien cultures. Although born as an anti-imperialist state, the modern Irish State fits easily into the ethnic and racial hierarchies that were ultimately created by the imperialist conquest of the world. Hence its desire for a flexible migrant labour force was mediated by a preference that they be white rather than brown or black, and also religiously or culturally similar. Most importantly, however, the decision to allow workers from the EU 10 to work immediately was a major benefit to Irish business.[73] It meant that Ireland had access to a pool of labour containing 208 million workers. Subsequently there was a sharp rise in the number of workers from Poland, Lithuania, and Latvia coming to Ireland. In 2003, 3,028 Personal Public Service Numbers were given to Polish nationals; in 2004 this increased to 27,295, rising to 93,787 in 2006. Similarly the number of Lithuanians applying for PPSNs increased from 2,379 in 2003 to 16,039 in 2006.

The arrival of a large supply of predominantly cheap EU labour to Ireland was a central part of the Irish State's immigration strategy. Human labour is a valuable economic resource and its transfer from poor to rich countries is of considerable benefit to the latter. From an economic point of view the State saves a considerable amount of money by not training migrants workers – a cost borne by the sending state – and can ideally dispose of these workers without them drawing on State benefits. These workers:

are coming to offer their labour. Their labour power is ready-made. The industrialized country, whose production is going to benefit from it, has not borne any of the cost of creating it; any more than it will bear the cost of supporting a seriously sick migrant worker, or one who has grown too old to work. So far as the economy in the metropolitan country is concerned, migrant workers are immortal: immortal because continually interchangeable. They are not born: they are not brought up: they do not age: they do not get tired: they do not die. They have a single function – to work. All other functions of their lives are the responsibility of the country they came from.[74]

From about 1999 to 2003 Irish labour migration policy and the regulation of the labour markets largely developed in a non-interventionist laissez-faire manner primarily designed to serve the needs of the economy. Immigration was 'employer led'. The State as we noted above operated a work permits system – loosely based on a 'guestworker system' – in which employers had to pass a formal labour market test by advertising jobs on the Irish market before applying for a permit. Work permits were rarely refused – as Junior Minister Noel Tracey explained: 'We have had a very liberal regime in place in relation to work permit applications where circa 95% of these were granted.'[75] In 2000 the State developed a more elaborate categorization system to indicate a more precise connection between social rights and marketable skills. A work authorizetion/visa system with greater rights and entitlements than the work permit system was introduced to attract more skilled employees who were in high global demand, to fill the acute skills shortages facing the Irish economy.

However, after April 2003, and in the context of a minor downturn between 2001 and 2002, the Irish State adopted a more interventionist and strategic approach to labour migration with the introduction of the Employment Permits Bill 2003.[76] This policy was predicated on a rigid binary classificatory division between EU and non-EU migration and based on the impending incorporation of new accession state workers. At the same time as allowing accession state nationals to enter into the workforce the State became more restrictive towards non-EU nationals. These restrictions included enforcing and imposing narrower interpretations of the labour market test which had heretofore generally been loosely adhered to by bureaucrats, raising permit fees, and increasing the number of jobs deemed as 'ineligible' for work permits. The State intervention was designed to ensure that overheating in the boom was minimized and that wage rates did not rise too greatly.

The shift from an ad hoc market-driven policy to a more managed interventionist approach to migration following 2003 continued to reflect the twin state concerns of providing a flexible workforce, whilst maintaining national homogeneity in the state. Although the Irish State is one of the most open global economies with regard to the free flow of capital goods and services, it has continued to regulate the ethno-national composition of the workforce. This contradiction between the free flow of goods and requirements of capital, and the need for a preferably white workforce, was forcefully expressed in the EGFSK Report on migrant labour, *Skills Needs in the Irish Economy: the Role of Migration* (2005). The report reasserted the need for a constitutive binary division between EU and non-EU migration as a core foundation in Irish migration policy. Based on the idea of a Community Preference policy, a codified notion of ethno-racial and cultural preference, it advocated that most or all unskilled vacancies in the Irish labour market should be filled by migrants from the expanded EU. A sufficient pool of potential migrant labour existed within the accession countries to fill unskilled vacancies and tapping into this pool needed to be prioritized over the entry of third-country nationals. Consequently, the work-permit system should be steadily closed off: 'Any work permit system should aim to further constrict the flow of low skilled or unskilled labour into the economy from outside the EEA. [This requires a] set of migration procedures that differentiate between the various categories of migrants and types of migration.'[77]

It has been estimated that 90% of skills shortages were being met from within the European Union.[78] CSO figures also showed numbers in employment from the 'rest of the world' declining.

Eschewing any belief in the volatility of supply and demand in global production and the fluctuating and unpredictable character of labour markets, the EGFSN attempted to predict almost 'soviet style' the exact number of jobs that would be needed in the country in the future.[79] The report argued that there would be a shortage of 606 computing graduates in 2006, 969 in 2007 and 1,217 in 2010 and that there would be a need for an extra 600 mushroom pickers in 2008.[80] If automatic prices mechanisms failed to provide an adjustment mechanism in the labour market, the Irish State's attempt to transcend this regulatory dilemma by predicting shifting labour demands in a complex economy was equally doomed to futility. These predictive measures were designed by the State to achieve a balance between 2 contradictory requirements – to ensure that wages would not rise because of a lack of labour supply, and to ensure that too many migrants did not enter the state over and above what was needed for the economy. As part of the community preference criteria the EGFSN argued that countries such as Poland and the Czech Republic, which had large labour forces and low wages, should specifically be targeted. Poland had the highest unemployment rate in the EU at 18.8%, which created a further 'pull factor' for workers. Average earnings in these countries were estimated to be less than 60% of those available in Ireland. However, although the accession states could provide a pool of unskilled labour, it was unlikely that they could provide graduate workers for the Irish workforce. This was because Ireland only offered the 14th highest graduate earnings across the EU within a context of intense global competitive demand for highly skilled mobile labour from the USA, Canada, Australia, and the UK.

However, although its wages were lower, the report argued that the State's high level of income inequality was a positive factor in attracting high skilled labour: 'In Ireland's case, our high level of income disparity may in fact offer an initial competitive advantage when competing for high skilled migrants... Since Ireland is considered to have the greatest income disparity in Europe, this may unintentionally make Ireland more attractive to highly skilled migrants than economies with greater income equality.'[81]

In addition the report suggested offering greater incentives to skilled migrants by introducing a green card immigration system. This would provide easier pathways to citizenship. In order to exclusively attract skilled workers, applications for the green card would be heavily restricted to occupations with high salary levels: those earning over €60,000 or more in all occupations, and only those earning between €30,000 and €59,999 in certain strictly delimited occupations would only be eligible to apply.

The result, then, of the State's strategy of categorizing migrants was the construction of an elaborate set of socio-legal categories that crudely constructed human beings according to their relative use for capital. A multi-tiered migrant work regime was created, conferring differential rights for highly skilled visa holders on the one hand, and lower-skilled work permit holders on the other. After the accession of new EU states in 2004 Eastern Europe was to serve as the main reserve for cheaper labour. A hierarchical 3-fold stratification of labour in terms of Irish native nationals, EU nationals, and non–EU nationals was underpinned by a tacit or unspoken racialization of that labour since many workers from non–EU countries are not white or perceived as culturally similar. Third-country nationals were in effect deemed by the State to be 'third class' nationals.

Social networks

As well as macro economic and state processes, occupational clustering in Ireland also entails the operation of social networks. Social networks provide conduits of information facilitating migrants who come to Ireland to secure work. The existence of networks accounts for the regionally circumscribed nature of migration to Ireland. For example, the large numbers of Chinese from Shenyang or the Fujian district or Indians from the Punjab or Kerala who arrived in Ireland did so as a result of social connections. Because recruitment takes place through word of mouth, certain industries can become dominated by certain nationalities, as the large presence of Brazilians in the Irish meat industry has demonstrated.

It is, however, important to avoid reifying historically broad abstractions and analytical economic concepts into substantive realities. The way for example sociologists divide society into 'economic', 'political', and 'social' spheres is problematic since these can refer to the same nexuses of events seen from different points of view. Production networks always intersect and presuppose nonproduction networks, ties based on friendship, kinship, ethnicity, class, school, political affiliation, sexual relations, etc.[82] Social networks operate within a global context of inequality and the nation-state's attempts to regulate borders and people. The role of social networks within a context of economic inequality was highlighted in a number of interviews in the ICI research project on integration. For example, the difficulty of getting a job and living in a low wage economy following the recession in Lithuania in 1999 was an important factor prompting many Lithuanians to leave the country. As one interviewee noted there were few jobs available and there was a need to work in more than one job in order to make ends meet: 'In Lithuania some people can have 2 or 3 jobs for a salary and work 70–80 hours' (Gabrius, Lithuania).

Finding work in another country can be difficult for migrants for a variety of reasons: because of language competence, an unfamiliarity with local knowledge and practices required to access work, or because of discrimination. The central role played by social networks and social capital in finding work has long been recognized.[83] This is especially the case for low-paid work. A report on low-paid work in London for example noted that two-thirds of migrants secured work through a friend.[84] In the context of poor language skills, low-skill levels, discrimination, or an undocumented status, word of mouth plays the central role in recruitment. The pattern of discovering jobs through word of mouth or from friends employed in low-wage service occupations was identified by a variety of migrants: 'It happens… usually in those circles where people don't speak English… a friend would go through a friend or they would work in the same factory together' (Ada, Lithuania). Another Lithuanian respondent who had a friend managing a petrol station stated that: '[I] got a phone call from a friend who had been here four years [and was] a manager of a garage' (Barbora, Lithuania). Three weeks later she was on a plane to Ireland.

Social networks not only provide information about jobs, but also a place to stay, information about the country and how to manoeuvre through its bureaucratic impediments:

> A lot of the time it's connections because of the difficulties in securing an accommodation. And somebody goes there and says OK I can talk to my landlord and he can give you a house… So, it kind of pulls you towards that very point. Or you're looking for a job, you say oh there's a job very close to IBM and I can help you get a job in IBM. And now you can get housing in Blanchardstown then and I get a job in IBM, that will be fine. So, different elements are pulling people around. (Niva, Nigeria).

A large number of migrants in Ireland were also directly recruited through employment agencies. Such agencies link labour demand from specific countries with specific sources of labour supply, thereby filtering workers from specific countries into specific jobs and solidifying processes of occupational segmentation. Employment agencies can be seen as institutionalized forms of social networks. Recruitment agencies in Ireland and abroad – such as the World Lithuanian Agency, or nursing agencies in India bringing nurses from Kerala to work Dublin hospitals for example, also played a significant role in recruiting workers. Hence, if a migrant didn't know about Ireland as a destination they were encouraged by the agencies to travel and work there.

Earlier migrants mediate between employers and other co-national migrant workers. Information about job availability provided on migrant networks and through word of mouth suits employers since it decreases the time and effort in recruiting and searching for a 'suitable' employee, especially for entry-level or low-status work. It saves the employer utilizing resources on advertising or trying to find a worker for a job shunned by native workers because of its low pay and conditions. Existing workers simultaneously act as informal referees on the suitability of the candidate recommended. The rise in outsourcing and subcontracting in Irish employment contracts has increased the use of existing kinship and friendship relations so that 'subcontracting, chain migration, segmented labour markets, and job monopolies reinforce each other'.[85] The high level of informality also allows employers to use ascriptive rather than human capital characteristics in choosing employees, allowing the employer to sidestep employment rights and formal contractual agreements which may characterize the formal recruiting and selection procedures of larger firms. This is especially the case in hotel and restaurant work.[86] With the exception of health and construction sectors migrants have generally been located in industrial sectors and occupations where union membership has been low, and informal forms of recruitment and exploitation high.

Social networks therefore play a vital part in structuring occupational segmentation. Tilly and Tilly summarize their role well:

> Despite the illusions of census occupational statistics and economic theory, all real labour markets segment radically; any firm maintains effective access to only a fraction of the workers who could, in principle, fill its jobs, while any potential worker maintains effective access to only a fraction of the jobs she could, in principle, fill. Newspaper advertising, employment agencies, and school placement offices mitigate the particularism of labour markets, but fall far short of eliminating the central importance of prior contacts, direct or indirect, between employers and potential workers. Hiring within restricted networks theoretically diminishes the efficiency of markets in matching people (or the 'human capital' they embody) with jobs. However, it also reduces the costs of collecting information on either side, speeds up the spread of news about openings, expands the tacit knowledge shared by fellow workers, permits exchanges of favours that will serve future opportunities, and provides some guarantees to both parties that the other will meet commitments implied by the hiring.[87]

For migrants with poor language skills and a lack of local knowledge and 'know-how' about securing work, social networks play the fundamental role in finding employment. An unintended effect, however, is the solidification of ethnic segmentation.

The social meaning of work

Accounting for labour segmentation also means examining the dispositions and intentions of the migrant actors who get jobs. This in turn involves a more complex and more rounded view of humans than has hitherto been accepted in explanations of economic behaviour. Rather than taking the rational individual of neo-classical economics as the starting point people need to be seen as profoundly social beings who are mutually susceptible to one another. Humans are socially interactive creatures embedded in social relationships, immersed in social ties and contexts within which they act. Their work practices are situated, meaning-bound, and take place within structured sets of community and family relationships which shape the interaction order and their sense of self. Though it is commonplace for conventional economic theory to employ an asocial and reductionist conception of work the social dimension and meaningful nature of work are also absent from some Marxist accounts of labour which otherwise paradoxically take the social nature of production as a first principle.[88] Both theoretical positions emphasize income differentials exclusively in their explanations. However, work not only provides a source of income and material interest but also constitutes an important social role in terms of symbolic prestige and identity. Jobs provide roles through which social individuals define and see themselves and try to gain respect from others within a peer group, community, or nation.[89] Occupational uptake is therefore not simply shaped by wage differentials but also by social status, honour, and the social esteem attached to various jobs.

However, the social values accruing to jobs are themselves arbitrary institutionalizations of contested socio-political and historical processes involving social closure. Jobs are classified and stratified according to status and income and are usually ordered on the basis of efforts to monopolize 'ideal or material goods and opportunities' so that certain jobs confer 'a special social esteem'.[90] The socially valued characteristics of the jobs and the status they carry, as well as the wage levels, play a crucial role in deterring or encouraging Irish workers from taking them up.

Recruitment for low-skilled jobs in advanced and expanding industrial economies with increasingly educated workforces and higher social expectations constitutes a basic structural problem for many of these economies. Higher levels of education have resulted in higher social and economic expectations regarding work and made it increasingly difficult to fill lower ranked jobs in

Ireland. In 1999, 27.1% of the population in Ireland aged 25–34 had a third-level education; by 2007, this had increased to 41.3% – the joint second highest in the EU 27.[91] Many increasingly educated Irish workers have left these low-grade factory jobs for white collar work only to be replaced by migrant workers.

Migrants are not only structurally positioned differently in legal status, but also have a different socio-cultural background and habitus from native Irish workers. Their different dispositions and self-perception as temporary workers can engender a different frame of reference and set of expectations from Irish workers with reference to judging and evaluating work and employment. With a foreshortened temporal horizon, migrants may conceive of themselves as target earners for whom work in another foreign country becomes a means to an end. Without work in their country of origin or in extremely poorly paid jobs, wages in Ireland are, by their standards, high. Moreover, work also becomes disconnected from the position it held in the status hierarchy in the community of origin. Migrants are thereby able to divorce themselves from the status of the job because it is removed from the evaluating national social context and peer reference group. This does not necessarily mean that migrants do not recognize the stigmatized status of the work that they are taking up. Rather, because the work is conceived as a temporary commitment – for quickly making money, acquiring savings, or sending remittances, 3-D poorly paid jobs are not automatically shunned as they may be by the indigenous workforce. Saving as much money as quickly as possible allows the worker to envisage a different future for him or herself and their family. Just as the migrant worker is expendable from the State and employer's point of view, so the worker sees his alien present as expendable for a different future. As Berger writes: 'While working he lives only the present of things exterior to him. In this his experience is similar to that of many indigenous workers. The difference is that when the migrant worker clocks-out he does not re-enter his own present.'[92]

The effect of low-status stigmatized jobs becoming filled by stigmatized migrant group is complex and can redouble and solidify the negative status of the occupation and its ranking, and also those who fill these positions. After time, native workers may become reluctant to fill what have become stigmatized as 'immigrant jobs' taken up by inferior workers. This may reinforce the structural demand for immigration.[93]

Piore is correct to assert the importance that the meaning and status that a job has as a motivation for taking it: 'it is basically the accumulation and maintenance of social status, and not income, that induces people to work. People work, in other words, either to advance up the hierarchy of jobs (and hence, of social status) or to maintain the position they have already achieved. Such a view implies that there will be acute motivational problems in… jobs at the very bottom of the social hierarchy, because there is in effect, no position to be maintained.'[94] However, his opposition between income and status with the latter as carrying all explanatory weight is overstated. Equally, his view that migrants' 'social identity is located in the place of origin, the home community'[95] allowing them to take demeaning jobs is also exaggerated. Migrants take low-skilled 3-D jobs not simply because they see themselves as temporary workers outside of their peer community of evaluation, but because they need the income. Income has more weight than Piore acknowledges. In an increasingly unequal world, the material position of migrants means that a large majority take up 3-D work from the necessity of having to sell their labour power. Wages in Ireland are estimated to be up to 5 times higher than they are in Poland and this undoubtedly plays a role in the willingness of the latter to take up low-grade work. Migrants would obviously prefer better-paid jobs with higher social status, promotion opportunities, and meaningful characteristics but are, inter alia, structurally prevented by state classifications and employer discrimination from accessing them. They perceive 3-D work as an unavoidable necessity. The interplay between economic and status factors in explaining the take up of jobs can be complex. As one Nigerian interviewee stated:

> At the age I came to Ireland it was difficult for me to do certain jobs. The kind of jobs I had to do, you know were horrible, were not the kind of jobs I was used to... Menial jobs, cleaning jobs, house keeping jobs, all kinds of jobs which in my country I was paying people to do for me. You know? I couldn't contemplate myself doing them. Considering my level of education. And all my life I have been taught to use my brains to earn money, not my hands, and my brawn you know. And I find the situation where I am getting used to it now though. (Akintunde, Nigeria)

It is because of their different expectations and their socio-economic structural disempowerment that migrants are sought by employers. However, as we have noted, not any migrant will do. Migrants are racialized by employers and can suffer discrimination in various employment sectors.

The acceptance of low-status work by migrants is not a given but may only be temporary. As the notion of a temporary stay becomes temporary, and migrants begin to settle and form communities, they may become more unwilling to accept the inadequate nature of the work they do and its stigmatized status. Given the length of time needed for community formation, this shift in attitude, however, may mean that they don't refuse these 3-D jobs for themselves but for their children. Moreover, Irish nationals have become more willing to take up certain low-skilled work. Jobs that were shunned during a period of boom have been taken as acceptable during the recession when a different world-view about the nature and availability of work exists. However, this shift is only within certain parameters. Nor does it mean that all jobs will be filled in a recession. Recessionary economies can still be characterized by labour shortages in certain occupations.[96]

Labour markets are complex, historically variable entities that have often been characterized by ethnic occupational segmentation. It has been argued that the labour segmentation of migrants can be explained by a number of factors. The changing nature of the labour market; supply and demand factors; state classification in constructing immigration statuses; state regulation of permit allocation; employer discrimination; employment agencies; social networks; and migrant dispositions all play a role. In addition, the regulation of the Irish labour market; been strongly affected by various contingent historical and institutional factors including economic and state policy decisions and the unintended consequences ensuing from these. It has also integrally involved the hegemonic incorporation of labour through the social partnership process.

Taking Irish jobs?

The Irish States's labour market migration policy which aimed to attract highly qualified non-EEA workers to fill skilled occupational vacancies and EEA workers to fill lower-skilled jobs contained 2 related aspects: an economic aspect and a national-cultural aspect. One of the overriding assumptions behind state policy has been that migrants should not become a burden on the Irish exchequer. This led to restrictions on the entry of 'dependents'. Simultaneously this policy was underwritten by the belief that highly skilled migrants would be easier to integrate partly because of language skills which would again reduce social costs.

State institutions, agencies and state bureaucracy have intervened to regulate the flow of immigrant labour for the needs of Irish capital. Irish State policy has construed migrant workers largely in terms of economic criteria: the need to meet the labour demands of the economy. The increase in work permits, visas and entry of migrant workers has been one method for reducing wage pressure to benefit business interests. However, this narrow economic concern has always been mediated by the State's restricted notion of Irish nationhood and security, in which the Irish government expects workers to return (voluntarily or otherwise) to their country of origin once their labour is no longer needed. Such a standpoint echoes the restrictive policy of other European nation states and effectively denies the reality of long-term immigration. The result, then, of the State's legislative and classificatory strategy is the construction of an elaborate set of social categories which crudely construct human beings according to their relative use for the needs of Irish capitalism. A multi-tiered migrant work regime has been created with differential rights for highly skilled visa immigrants, on the one hand, and lower-skilled work permit immigrants. The Irish State has wedded a state developmentalist and intervention project with a neo-liberal policy of deregulating markets. It has aimed to combine a minimalist

Table 9.3 Nationality of non-Irish in employment, 2005–7

	2005	2007
UK	24.5%	16.6%
Rest of EU 15	14.0%	11.2%
EU 10	31.8%	48.6%
Rest of the World	29.7%	23.6%

Source: CSO/ McCormack FAS

neo-liberal approach in relation to the flow of goods and services with a highly interventionist regulation of labour supply.[97]

The new employment system therefore continues to operate and reproduce a tiered work regime with different rights and entitlements allotted to different categories of workers on the basis of pay and skill levels. As a result of their concentration in low-paid jobs a new media and populist discourse centred on migrants lowering indigenous wages or displacing Irish workers began to emerge, especially after the GAMA controversy and the Irish Ferries dispute in 2005. These discourses were often articulated with or contained negative cultural national evaluations of migrants. The mix of national cultural stereotypes with economic concerns is by no means new and even articulated by sociologists. For example, Weber, who, in his nationalist economic concerns about the wages of the German working class being undercut by Polish workers, ruefully noted that: 'there is a certain situation of capitalistically disorganized economies, in which the higher culture is not victorious but rather loses in the existential fight with lower cultures.'[98]

Within a politically charged context it has become commonplace in academic and media discussions to assess the value, contribution, consequences, and impact that immigrants are making to Irish society.[99] This assessment is largely framed within a quantitatively orientated discourse of costs and benefits. The founding principle is that from the point of view of the state and the economy, immigration and the immigrant have no meaning and *raison d'être* unless they 'brought in' more than they 'cost'.[100] This constituted a self-evident problematic. A follow-up question facing policy makers is how to maximize the 'profits' (primarily economic) while minimizing the 'costs' (economic, but also social, cultural, and national). However, as Sayad (1999) has rightly pointed out in his discussion of France, the very accounting conventions that determine what are 'costs' and 'benefits' in these discussions are ideologically loaded.[101] The failure to establish what is 'a cost' or 'a benefit' stems from the difficulty of reaching a shared consensus on a number of questions: the frame of analysis – whether one takes humanity as a whole as reference, the receiving nation-state, or the sending country; identifying and ascertaining what constitutes 'skill level' and its impact; and where, and if at all, direct competition with natives took place. Consequently, there is no consensus on the effects of immigration on economic efficiency and local wages. The majority of writers in the field have nevertheless indicated that the effect of immigration on wages of the indigenous population is minimal.[102] For immigrants to displace workers they need to be competing for and actively seeking the same jobs. However, evidence suggests that migrants often compete with other migrants for jobs. As is the case in many other countries sectoral employment trends in Ireland reflect the fact that rather than taking up indigenous jobs, migrants have been concentrated in certain employment sectors: largely in lower skilled occupations, which increasingly better educated Irish people with higher expectations, are no longer willing to do. Rather than competing with indigenous workers, migrants have tended to possess different skill sets and expectations, allowing them to undertake essential complementary work that facilitates, underpins, and generates work done by Irish nationals. The largest level of competition has largely been between immigrants workers. By undertaking work in areas of labour shortage, of skills shortage and complimentary work, migrants have contributed, it is argued, significantly to the Irish economy. Their segmentation and the fact that they do not take indigenous jobs but jobs that Irish people don't want to do or cannot do, points to the fact that there may still be a continuing need for migrants, even in a recession.

However, it would be too simplistic and convenient to argue that the entry of migrant workers, especially those that have been systematically disempowered through the work permit system, but also those from Eastern Europe, with low levels of English proficiency, has had no effect on the wages and conditions of the Irish labour force. Given the context of the boom there was generally little job displacement, but there were a number of cases of migrants being paid lower wages than Irish workers. Migrant labour was in many instances being used to push down indigenous working conditions by employers, and this was facilitated by the State. This generally occurred in specific employment sectors. There is little evidence to suggest that migrants, taken as a whole, have lowered the overall wages of Irish workers in the economy. The availability of cheap and flexible labour was one of the major reasons that employers' organizations such as IBEC, the Chamber of Commerce, and Irish and Small and Medium Enterprises have generally been sympathetic to the presence of migrant workers. Few, however, as we shall see in the next chapter, campaigned to secure them equal workplace rights.

Notes

1 WRC, *Issues and Challenges in the Recruitment Selection of Immigrant Workers in Ireland* (Dublin: PAS, 2009), p. 11.

2 D. O' Hearn, Macroeconomic policy in the Celtic Tiger: a critical reassessment, in C. Coulter and S. Coleman (eds), pp. 34–55.

3 CSO, *Principal Social and Economic Results* (Dublin: Government of Ireland, 2007) p. 14.

4 S. O'Riain, *The Politics of High-Tech Growth* (Cambridge: Cambridge University Press, 2004).

5 D. O'Hearne, Macroeconomic policy.

6 T. Killeen, speech at the Launch of Jobs Ireland, New York. Friday 20 October 2006. www.entemp.ie/press/2006/20061020c.htm.

7 S. O'Riain, *The Politics of High-tech Growth*, p. 47.

8 CSO, *Principal Social and Economic Results.*

9 S. O'Riain and P. Murray, Work transformed: the two faces of the new Irish workplace, in *Contemporary Ireland: A Sociological Map* (Dublin: UCD Press, 2007), pp. 248–64.

10 FAS, National Skills Bulletin 2007 (Dublin: FAS, 2007), p. 10.

11 By 2006 this employed 9% (269,000) of the total workforce and grew at a rate faster than any other industrial sector, accounting for a quarter of net jobs generated in 2006.

12 Allen, *Ireland's Economic Crash* (Dublin: Liffey Press), p. 40.

13 Peck, *Workplace: The Social Regulation of Labour Markets* (New York: Guildford Press, 1996), p. 85.

14 N. Harris, *The New Untouchables*, p. 10.

15 Ibid., p. 19.

16 Shelley, *Exploited*, p. 24.

17 The exception here is migrants from the UK whose distribution is similar to Irish nationals.

18 See Allen's sharp criticism of David McWilliams claims in *The Pope's Children* (Dublin: Gill and MacMillan, 2006); K. Allen, Ireland: Middle Class Nation, *Edudes Irelandais* 32: 3, 2007.

19 CSO, Principle Social Economic Results, p. 66.

20 Ibid., p. 62.

21 Ibid., p. 22. There is, however, some variation between nationalities with almost three-quarters of persons from the EU 15, excluding Ireland and the UK, educated to third level, and over 50% from the rest of the world.

22 Barrett, Kearney, & McCarthy, 2006.

23 Hall, S. (1980) Race articulation and societies structured in dominance, in UNESCO, *Sociological Theories: Tace and Colonialism* (Paris: Unesco, 1980).

24 CSO, *Quarterly Household National Survey*, 2008, quarter 1,

25 CSO, *Non-Irish Nationals Living in Ireland* (Dublin: Government of Ireland Publications, 2008).

26 See Home Office, Accession monitoring Report, May 2004–March 2007 (London: Home Office, 2008)

27 ICI, *Getting On.*

28 *Non-Irish Nationals living in Ireland.*

29 *Non-Irish Nationals living in Ireland*, p. 54.

30 Peck, *Workplace*. 2000: 4–5.

31 Berger and Mohr, *The Seventh Man*, p. 120.

32 S. Sassen, *The Global City* (Princeton, Princeton University Press, 1991); Castells, *The Rise of Network Society* (Oxford: Blackwell, 1997); K. Moody, *US Labour in Trouble and Transition* (London: Verso, 2007).

33 K. Moody, *US Labour*, p. 43.

34 P. Breathnach, Occupational change and social polarisation in Ireland: further evidence, *Irish Journal of Sociology*, Vol 16., pp. 22–42 (2007).

35 OECD, *International Migration Outlook, Annual Report 2007* (OECD: Geneva, 2007), p. 165.

36 Harris, *The New Untouchables*, p. 25.

37 *Expert Group on Future Skills Needs: The Role of Migration* (Dublin: Forfas, 2005). These included occupations in science, engineering occupations, IT professional occupations, business and financial occupations, healthcare occupations, education, care occupations, legal and security occupations, construction professional occupations, construction craft occupations, other craft occupations, arts, sports and tourism occupations, transport and logistics, library and clerical, sales occupations and as operatives. It is commonplace for state agencies and economists to make a distinction between skills shortages and labour shortages. The distinction has been more pithily expressed as that 'between jobs people won't do, and jobs that they can't do'. There are also questions tied to the retention *and* replacement of workers.

38 FAS *National Skills Bulletin* (Dublin: Forfas, 2007).

39 Ibid.

40 *Irish Business Review*, October 2008, p. 15.

41 Berger and Mohr, *The Seventh Man*, p. 120.

42 *Irish Times*, 5 July 2001.

43 FAS, National Skills Bulletin, 2007, p. 73.

44 Dail Debates, 25 February 2010.

45 FAS, National Skills, 2007, p. 8.

46 O'Rian and Murray, Work Transformed, p. 252.

47 M. Piore, *Birds of Passage* (Cambridge: CUP, 1979), p. 33.

48 R. Waldinger and M. Hechter, *How the Other Half Works* (Berkeley: University of California Press, 2003), pp. 15, 16.

49 Berger and Mohr, *A Seventh Man*, p. 138.

50 R. Waldinger and M. Hechter, *How the Other Half Works* (Berkeley: University of California Press, 2003) p. 16.

51 ICI, *Getting On*.

52 F. McGinnity, J. Nelson, P. Lunn and E. Quinn, *Discrimination in Recruitment – Evidence from a Field Experiment* (Dublin: Equality Authority, 2009).

53 P. O'Connell and F. McGinnity, *Immigrants at Work: Ethnicity and Nationality in the Labour Market* (Dublin: Equality Authority, 2008), p. x.

54 WRC, *Issues and Challenges in the Recruitment Selection of Immigrant Workers in Ireland* (Dublin: PAS, 2009).

55 M. Burawoy, *The Politics of Production: Factory Regimes under Capitalism and Socialism* (London: Verso, 1985).

56 *Irish Times*, 22 December 2000,

57 *Irish Times*, 22 January 2001.

58 K. Allen and S. Loyal, Rethinking immigration and the state in Ireland, in R. Lentin and R. Lentin (eds), *Race and State* (Dublin: Cambridge Scholars Press, 2006).

59 *Expert Group in Future Skills Needs 1999* (Dublin: Forfas 2000). p. 7.

60 CSO, *Women and Men in Ireland 2003* (Dublin: Stationery Office, 2004), p. 16.

61 CSO, *Women and Men*, p. 20.

62 Loyal, Welcome to the Celtic Ireland; for an extended discussion see K. Hayward and K. Howard, Cherry-picking the diaspora, in Fanning (ed.) *Immigration and Social Change in the Republic of Ireland* (Manchester: Manchester University Press, 2007) pp. 47–62.

63 Mary Harney, speech at FAS jobs fair, London, 13 May 2000, at www.entemp. ie/press/2000/130500.htm.

64 M. Ruhs, *Managing the Immigration and Employment of non-EU Nationals in Ireland* (Dublin: Policy Institute, 2005); NESC, 2006: 7.

65 *Irish Times*, 22 December 2000.

66 C. Joppke, *Selecting by Origin: ethnic migration in the liberal state* (Cambridge, Massachusetts: Harvard University Press, 2005).

67 K. Allen, Double Speak: Neo-liberalism and migration, in Fanning (ed) *Immigration and Social Change in the Republic of Ireland*.

68 Ruhs, *Managing the Immigration,* p. 15.

69 O'Connell and McGinnity, *Immigrants at Work*.

70 Ruhs, *Managing*, p. 17.

71 According to the 2006 Census of the 420,000 non-Irish nationals in the State, 276,000 are from the EU with 144,000 of these from outside the EU 25. Some 120,00 are from the EU 10.

72 Thus prior to May 2004 nationals from the 10 new accession countries were regarded as third country nationals – Czech Republic, Cyprus, Estonia, Hungary, Latvia, Lithuania, Malta, Poland, Slovenia, and Slovakia.

73 As the EGFSN 2005 noted: Indeed the availability of a large stock of European labour all of whom are entitled to move to Ireland without any administrative procedures, permits or restrictions on family reunification offers a significant resource for Irish employers.

74 Berger, *A Seventh Man*, p. 64.

75 Noel Tracey, Address to the Expert of Supply Chain Professionals, 2001, www.entemp.ie/press/2001/091101.htm.

76 M. Ruhs, *Managing the Immigration*.

77 *Expert Group on Future Skills Needs 2005*.

78 Conor Lenihan in *The Irish Times*, 27 February 2008.

79 K. Allen, Double Speak: Neo-liberalism and migration.

80 Ibid., p. 93. Allen highlights the paradox of this approach which aims to combine the free movement of goods and services with a command model of labour market supply.

81 Ibid.

82 Tilly and Tilly, *Work under Capitalism* (Boulder: Westview Press, 1998), p. 79.

83 A. S. Massey et al., Theories of international migration, p. 448.

84 Y. Evans et al., Making the city cork: Low paid employment in London, *Queen Mary: University of London*, November 2005, p. 5.

85 Tilly and Tilly, *Work under Capitalism*, p. 29.

86 MRCI, *Exploitation in Ireland's Restaurant Industry* (Dublin: MRCI, 2008).

87 Tilly and Tilly, *Work under Capitalism*, p. 26.

88 Here the motivation underpinning work is singularly the necessity to sell one's labour power. Although true, this tenet should only form a point of entry into a broader analysis that examines how mutually susceptible social individuals attach meaning to work practices and who view and evaluate work differently.

89 R. Sennett and J. Cobb *The Hidden injuries of Class* (London: Faber and Faber [1972] 1993).

90 M. Weber, *Economy and Society*, p. 935.

91 CSO, *Measuring Ireland's Progress* (2008), p. 50.

92 Berger and Mohr, *A Seventh Man*, pp. 164, 186.

93 Massey et al., *Theories of International Migration*, p. 453.

94 M. Piore, *Birds of Passage*, p. 33.

95 Ibid., p. 54.

96 N. Harris, *Thinking the Unthinkable: The Immigration Myth Exposed* (London: IB Taurus, 2002).

97 K. Allen, Double Speak: Neo-liberalism and migration.

98 Cited in H. James, *The End of Globalization* (Cambridge, Massachusetts: Harvard University Press, 2002): p. 16.

99 See for example Ruhs, *Managing the Immigration*.

100 A. Sayad, The suffering of the Immigrant, p. 76.

101 A. Sayed, 'Costs' and 'benefits' of immigration, in P. Bourdieu et al. (eds), *The Weight of the World* (Cambridge: Polity, 1999).

102 B. Chiswick, *The Economics of Immigration: Selected Papers of Barry R. Chiswick* (Cheltenham: Edward Elgar, 2005).

Chapter 10

The migrant as worker

Global capitalism is not just a system of economies but also a geo-politically mediated, plurality of interacting, rival, and competing states. As we noted in Chapter 2, states are complex and contradictory entities that are both internal to and external from the logic of capital. Nation-states play a critical role in instituting strong private property rights, guaranteeing accumulation, underwriting capitalist rules of competition and free trade, and constructing markets.[1] Within this global nexus of capital, state, and labour and the specific configuration it has taken on in Ireland, a number of migrant workers have experienced degrees of super-exploitation characteristic of earlier capitalist labour regimes. This chapter examines how these forms of exploitation have manifested themselves in accordance with different migrant statuses, varying employment sectors, and gender. It situates this exploitation within the context of global and domestic economic processes, and in the workings of a neo-liberal Irish State that has sought to increase labour productivity by restructuring and creating a flexible labour force. This restructuring has entailed employing more female and migrant workers, often on a part-time, contractual, or agency basis.

The changing face of global production

The abrupt end of the post-war boom following the onset of the 1973 recession engendered a number of profound changes in the global economy. A long-term fall in the rate of profit, and intensifying global and local competition, forced developed capitalist enterprises to initiate a series of fundamental transformations in the production process in order to sustain and bolster profit levels. These changes were underpinned by a correlative shift in the political vision of nation-states entailing an ideological acceptance of minimal state intervention in the operations and effects of the market. Keynesian national-interventionist economies began to yield control to the logic of global capital and many states came under sustained pressure to do so from structural adjustment programmes initiated in the 1980s. These processes were rationalized under an ascendant neo–liberal ideology promoting market fundamentalism. As the market became increasingly disembedded from its social underpinning, national autarky and economic protectionism gave way to sustained patterns of deregulation and denationalization and to the removal of obstacles and impediments to the global flow of capital, goods, and services.

The introduction of various liberalization agreements and the growth of free trade, ideologically underpinned and promulgated by organizations such as NAFTA and the WTO, not only indicated a shift in the balance of various national-class forces, but also resulted in a fundamental alteration in the world division of labour. Because high costs tied to labour-intensive forms of production led to declining rates of profit, large companies were compelled to shift to developing countries where labour and production costs were cheaper. The movement of manufacturing production to the 'Asian Tigers' – South East Asia, Japan and China – was indicative of such a geo-economic shift in production as manufacturing moved to the global South while services moved to the North. The production vacuum created in developed economies by the loss of manufacturing became filled by an expanding service-oriented economy. In the USA, for example, a loss of over 5 million jobs in manufacturing between 1979 and 2004 was matched by the growth in service employment of just over 3 million jobs during the same period.[2]

A global division of labour incorporating a dichotomy between manufacturing-oriented developing economies exporting to service-dominated developed economies, should, however, not be exaggerated. Hence, even today when current global employment in manufacturing is estimated to be between 150 million and 200 million, about 50 million of these jobs are still estimated to be in the G7 industrialized countries.[3]

Nevertheless, increasing global economic interdependence, expressed through the development of international cross-border production chains and foreign direct investment, constitute a central facet of the modern global economy. Industrial production abroad has been a major US economic strategy since the Second World War. More recently it has been manifested through Foreign Direct Investment. Between 1973 and 1993 US Foreign Direct Investment grew tenfold.[4] Ireland with its low corporation taxes and Irish-Development-Agency-led agenda became a major beneficiary of this US policy. However, other altered forms of production aimed at lowering costs, increasing profits, and intensifying output have also been introduced both globally and in Ireland. Increasing outsourcing, in which chains of supplier firms involved in mass production became extended in order to acquire cheaper, less unionized, workers from secondary supplier firms and thereby lower production costs, has been one manifestation of this. In the USA, for example, General Motors reduced its in-house work from 70% in 1990 to 49% only a few years later.[5] Outsourcing and a lengthening of production chains also resulted in the establishment of new forms of 'just-in-time' production.

In modern capitalism the organization of work has always been shaped by the introduction of technology that has often displaced and deskilled workers. This, combined with the development of lean production techniques originating in Japan during the 1960s, have also transformed the workplace as Taylorist work practices disappear.

The decline of economic boundaries between countries with unregulated economies open to globally competitive, shifting, and precarious contexts of production, has increased pressure on workers to produce more, to produce quicker, and to produce cheaper. Pressures to produce more involve strategies such as extending the number of hours worked, mechanization, and employee participation schemes often measured through the implementation of benchmark metrics and key performance indicators. These processes have also had a profound affect on the composition of the labour force. There has been a dramatic growth in the employment of contingent, part-time, flexible workers on short-term contracts who often fall outside the purview of labour law. Other manifestations of these contractual shifts in the capital and labour relationship include the introduction of irregular hours, an increase in overtime, a fall in real wages, concessionary wage cuts, the implementation of two-tier wage schemes, erosion of paid pensions, the reduction and removal of social state protections, the naturalization of long-term unemployment, lower union participation rates, and union avoidance in the workplace. The cumulative effect of these processes has been to lower pay and working conditions and to heighten social and economic inequality.

Universal economic processes expressing the logic of capital have to be constructed through particular cultures. Global capitalism is always locally situated and has to draw on local values at the same time as it dislocates them. There is, moreover, a tension between the global mobility of capital and relative fixity of labour – that is, in the relation between people and things. Despite neoclassical assertions, humans are not commodities like any other. Such a view ignores both the social nature of humans, and the reproduction of labour. Because it sees these processes in terms of its own vested interests this difference, paradoxically, becomes inverted by the state. States view migrant workers as temporary disposable commodities. However, because humans create communities, develop social ties, and thereby become geographically embedded, migrants often become a permanent feature of the national landscape – their temporary migration is a 'temporary that lasts'.[6] By contrast, states view foreign capital investment as an enduring national asset, whereas capital, especially its manufacturing, financial, and technological variants embedded in a global production network and expansive information flows, is relatively mobile and increasingly moves in search of new markets and profits.

The move by Dell from Limerick to Lotz in Poland can only be understood in this context. In Limerick, Dell employed over 3,000 workers with the average industrial Irish wage for a worker stood at €37,500; in Lotz the average industrial wage stood at €7,500, and corporation taxes were even lower than those in Ireland.[7] Dell's rationalization for the move was to realign its business by increasing competitiveness and costs by reducing headcount; the massive economic and social repercussion for community life in Limerick was simply collateral damage.

Notwithstanding this realignment, a free and unfettered movement of capital to cheaper production zones exists more in theory than in practice. In reality there exist numerous obstacles and limitations on the movement of capital: international competition causes companies to maintain high rates of investment in fixed capital – in equipment and structures – and these may be relatively immobile; many forms of production cannot be moved abroad easily since they are either location-specific such as construction, or their provider needs to be physically present, such as personal services such as crèche-facilities, cleaning services, and security services.

As was noted in Chapter 1, the dislocation and growing world inequality that ensued from the accelerated global economic integration of capital, goods, and services following trade liberalization and deregulation under the auspices of the WTO, increased structural adjustment programmes aimed at eradicating years of job protection, geo-political trade and investment alliances, and neo-liberal ideology has increased the pressures on people throughout the globe to migrate. When combined with social networks, state demand for labour, geo-political ties, and transport connections, mass immigration has often ensued.

Shifts in Irish production

One of course has to be careful not to extrapolate from a global and universal unfolding logic of capital to historically specific processes that characterized Irish economic development. The development of Irish capitalism has embodied both universal aspects of the unfolding logic of capital and specific historical, political, and cultural factors. According to the AT Kearney Globalization Index, Ireland has the second most globalized economy in the world, whilst the Heritage Foundation and the Wall Street Journal have rated it third in the world on their indices.[8] Moreover, Ireland has for the last 30 years provided a pro-business environment for companies to grow and for neo-liberal ideology to become enshrined. The country is characterized by a remarkable permeability and reciprocity between state elites, politicians, and business and corporate elites. This is manifest both at State level through development agencies such as the IDA, Enterprise Ireland, and Forfas, but also in the lobbying power of organizations such as IBEC, ISME, Chamber of Commerce Ireland,

and the Construction Industry Federation. Such lobbying and networking have produced one of the lowest corporation taxes in Europe, standing at 12%. The State has subsequently given free rein to market logic and competitive capitalism, resulting in certain classes accruing vast levels of wealth and to greater national inequality. It has been estimated, for example, that in 2007 the top 5% of the population owned 40% of the country's wealth.[9]

The development of the Celtic Tiger can be characterized by two main phases with distinct growth rates and differentiated investment patterns. The first phase took place between 1995 and 2002 and was fuelled by US investment in manufacturing, computing, and pharmaceuticals geared towards exports. Attracted by low corporation taxes, and various productivity promises made by the IDA, Irish industry became heavily reliant on US investment. High wages and increased productivity ensued. Following a recessionary turn in the USA in 2001 a second phase of economic growth was focused on the services sector. A new regime of accumulation centred on finacialization and the banking industry, but also on construction and property investment, emerged. Both sectors exhibited high levels of deregulation.

By operating within a small open economy exposed to the fluctuating market demands of competitive capitalism, and characterized by weak employment protection, especially in the private sector, and threadbare capital regulation, Ireland has been particularly exposed to global competition and to the global restructuring of the workforce that was sketched above. In such a context Irish employers have sought to increase productivity per worker without significantly increasing unit labour costs. Though pressure on productivity varies according to sector, it has essentially entailed a three-dimensional strategy: increasing capital investment through the introduction of machinery and technology; making workers work harder and for longer hours; or by reducing their level of remuneration and their range of entitlements. Irish employers have been remarkably successful in increasing worker productivity despite constant refrains from the State, economists, and employers about a lack of worker competitiveness in the Irish economy. Productivity has grown annually by 4%.[10] Irish productivity growth based on per-hour criteria has always been very high even when compared to countries such the USA. Analysis carried out by the National Competitiveness Council (NCC) shows that since 1990 and using GDP as the base for calculations, Ireland's average productivity increased from just two-thirds of the US output per hour in 1990 to exceed US performance in the late 1990s.

In 2008 productivity in Ireland measured as GDP per person employed was the second highest in the EU 27.[11] The pressures to increase productivity – to produce more, to produce quicker and to produce cheaper – are invariably shaped by a number of factors, for example, the nature of the employment sector, the type and variety goods and services produced, as well as how these

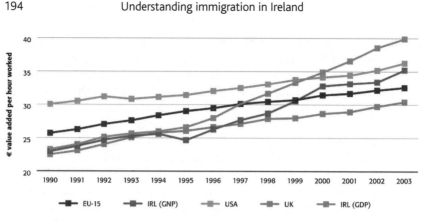

Source: Forfas, 2007

Figure 10.1 Output per hour worked in selected economies, 1990–2003 (€)

industries and occupations are linked to global competition, state subsidies, and trade union membership. Technology often plays a significant role in reducing unit costs; however, given the nature of what is produced or supplied, certain industries are unsuited for increased capital investment. If moving abroad to cheaper production zones is debarred for various reasons, replacing 'standard' forms of labour with more flexible and precarious labour at home provides an alternative option. Irish employers, especially those located in the private sector, have thereby sought to replace full-time workers with job security and pensions, with cheap fixed-term contract or atypical agency workers, who do not have to be paid for time that has not been fully worked, including holiday pay, pensions, fringe benefits, overtime, etc.[12] This has often been facilitated and sanctioned by the State and various EU Directives and has taken place under social partnership processes emphasizing national development, at the expense of labour protection. In certain vulnerable industries Irish employers have set about reducing costs by replacing full-time male workers by part-time workers. As Robinson notes: 'By replacing one full-time sales assistant with two or three part-timers, employers can save as much as eight man hours per week.'[13] The increase in the number of part-time workers in Ireland has been significant: in the year up to the first quarter of 2008, part-time work accounted for 66% of overall employment growth. Such forms of work pay less per hour than full-time work, providing fewer benefits with flexible hours usually determined and allocated by the employer. Average hourly earnings for full-time workers in 2006 were €20.11 compared to an average of €14.76 per hour that part-time workers received.[14] Moreover, growing numbers of temporary contracts were being given to workers. The 'flexibilization' of the Irish workforce has also involved a growth in the number of temporary agency workers. The industry is one of the largest worldwide private employers of workers, today employing over 9.5 million workers on a daily basis and generating revenue of over €230 billion.[15] Employment agencies as mediators of labour have thereby functioned as 'purveyors of flexibility'.[16] The number of licensed agencies working in the Irish market has similarly grown dramatically. Although exact numbers are difficult to ascertain, according to the DETE there were 195 agencies in the State in 1987, 447 in 1999, and 650 in 2007, falling to 615 in 2009 after the onset of the recession.[17] Although agencies are by law required to acquire a license under the 1971 Employment Agencies Act, many do not and a large number in Ireland remain unlicensed. Moreover, there are numerous employment agencies located outside of the State that are not subject to national employment laws. For example, there are an estimated 770 employment agencies in Poland alone.[18]

There is very little data available on those engaged in agency work in Ireland. The European Foundation for Improvement of Living and Working Conditions, while noting that agency work had the fastest growing form of atypical employment in the EU in the 1990s, and that agency workers earned only 68% of the wages of their directly employed colleagues, placed Ireland as the country with the highest percentage of employees with a temporary employment agency contact in the EU.[19] It is estimated that there were about 35,000 agency workers in the State in 2009, having risen from 4,000 in 1997.[20] However, rather than numbers, which remain small, it is the type of work contract they are gradually insinuating on a more general basis that is significant.[21] The use of disposable temporary workers is particularly suitable for adjusting to the inherent structural tendency of capitalist market booms and recessions and is often championed by business associations. The majority of contracts in Ireland were from 1–3 months' duration and the existing legislation meant that neither the agency nor the company that hired the workers were legally deemed to be the employers, making workers especially vulnerable to exploitation and flexibilization. As the Director of IBEC explained: 'A flexible labour market is a prerequisite to economic success... Agency work can often offer a level of flexibility with regard to working hours and location... Business will oppose any measure that will make it more difficult to get a job and keep a job, including any attempts to make the labour market less flexible.'[22]

Ireland was only 1 of 3 states, together with Hungary and the UK, that did not legislate for the equal treatment, pay, and conditions for agency workers who did similar work to regular employees. Instead it steadfastly maintained a 6-year block on the Temporary and Agency Workers EU directive.

In conjunction with changing the nature of employment contracts, many firms have also sought to acquire cheaper, more vulnerable labour – that is, labour considered to have an alternative position outside the national labour market: female and migrant labour. This form of labour, when combined with the profound change in the nature of employment contracts, has produced a highly flexible set of workers. Their existence and demarcation as ascribed groups are not aberrations, but central to the overall composition of the workforce. As Corrigan notes:

> These allegedly distinctive strata, as Max Weber recognised some time ago, share their market position with any member of the working class. Their unfree or ascriptive economic and social relations are the precise pedestal for the (relatively) more free, seemingly 'achieved', relations of others within the working class. Ascription is not, as it were, antagonistic to effective social or technical division of labour (the rationalist thesis in brief); but is the manner in which that division and circulation is accomplished. Status relations are the mode of achieving contractual relations; the contradiction between formal and substantive rationality is permanent and coextensive with capitalism.[23]

Exploitation of migrant workers

Depending on the industry, part-time female workers and temporary agency workers have in turn been supplemented or replaced by migrants in a serried process which underscores an incremental shift away from the employment of relatively empowered, though always class mediated, male workers with citizenship rights to those at the bottom of the socio-legal hierarchy in terms of power, status, and legal rights and entitlements. Although employers do not create the categorical differences between immigrants and natives, which are overwritten by ethno-racialized state categorizations and classifications, they certainly manipulate and employ them.

In some ways the super-exploitation of migrant workers as a social fact only exists for the population when through a work of representation the media talks about it. Cases of labour exploitation of migrant workers, though increasing, rarely make newspaper headlines and on the whole remain invisible. There are, however, some exceptions. In 2006 a Filipino beautician, Salvacion Orge, employed on a 6-month contract to work on an Irish Ferries ship, was found to be receiving an hourly rate of just over €1 while working 12-hours a day, 7 days a week on a total salary of €354 a month. A more recent case involved a Pakistani national on a work permit who worked in a restaurant from 2001 to 2006. Despite working excessive hours and having no days off, the employee was paid €150 per week of which €100 was deducted for accommodation. The employer held his permit, passport, and threatened to have him deported and render him homeless if he complained. When he did he was summarily dismissed.

Though extreme examples, these cases were emblematic of the logic of capital and state regulation of the labour market. Together with other cases in Ireland they can be mapped on a broad spectrum of workplace exploitative practices that range from a failure of employers to give holiday pay to working highly excessive and unsocial hours at below minimum wage rates, through to forms of quasi-bonded labour. Such forms of exploitation are of course not peculiar to Ireland but express more global processes. But they point to the existence of differentiated and stratified labour regimes in Irish society.

The number of cases that the Labour Relations Commission Rights Commissioner Service has processed involving foreign workers has continually increased. In 2002, of the 5,692 cases processed only 2% involved migrant workers; in the first 8 months of 2004, migrant workers brought 8% of all cases processed.[24] Investigations into employment violations included a variety of recurring offences: the employment of migrant workers with unequal pay and conditions in comparison with other Irish or EEA staff; failure by employers to pay workers prearranged wage rates; workers being paid below the minimum wage and being subject to excessive working hours; illegal pay deductions, with recruitment costs to be borne by the prospective employee; unfair dismissal; and the non-payment of overtime or holiday pay. In 2007 over a quarter of the 6,000 migrants who accessed the Migrant Rights Centre Ireland service for advocacy and support stated that they had experienced some form of workplace violation.[25] These workplace violations occurred irrespective of nationality, immigration status, gender, and employment sector, though these variables were of significance. Immigrant workers were earning up to 18% less than Irish workers despite the fact that they were generally better qualified.[26] Many were therefore also not employed in occupations commensurate with their educational status, having thereby undergone a process of deskilling and negative social mobility.[27]

Explaining the exploitation of migrant workers is a complex issue that needs to be unpacked in each of its manifestations. The relation between wage labour and capital has to be situated simultaneously within the competitive relation between individual capitalists. Within the broader context of a global supply of labour and the global and domestic pressure exerted by capital and employers to reduce wages to increase profit margins, there are at least 5 major analytically distinct though substantively interlocking explanatory processes that modulate the treatment and level of exploitation of migrant workers. These include: firstly, vis-à-vis state policies and classification, the limited nature of migrant worker social, political, and economic rights; secondly, the structure and context of the employment and occupational sector; thirdly, processes intersecting with class and ethnic relations involving gender and patriarchy; fourthly, the level of trade-union and labour activity; and fifthly, the government's regulation of various employment sectors in terms of maintaining labour standards, fining employers who exploit their workers, and employing labour inspectors. In addition, there are a number of complex structural, contingent, and local factors and mechanisms. These include the role of employment agencies; societal levels of racialization, racism, and discrimination; the meanings, practices, and dispositional characteristics of the migrant in terms of their economic, cultural, and social capital and what types of work and conditions they are willing and able to accept; and the migrant's temporal perspective – that is, their sense of being a short-term target earner or long-term resident. We can look at these five broad processes below.

Creating a bonded worker: work permits

In modern nation-states individuals are positioned in terms of specific social roles and statuses through forms of state classification and categorization. Using the institution of citizenship as a benchmark, states categorize and classify individuals conferring different civic and political rights upon them. States simultaneously homogenize and disempower migrants as a collective category, and individualize and differentiate them according to stratified legal-political and ethno-national statuses. State categorizations of migrant status create different classes of workers with different rights that determine residency in the territory, access to employment, eligibility to social welfare protection, and family reunification. Complex divisions and distinctions are produced between asylum-seekers, holders of work permits, work visas, and green cards, as well as international students and 'old' European and new EU accession state nationals. The cumulative effect of this process is that migrants are not only accorded different social, political, and economic rights and entitlements, as compared to Irish citizens, but they also become stratified in terms of their susceptibility to exploitation.

Work permit holders

The main instrument through which immigrant labour was brought to Ireland between 1999 and 2004 was the work permit system. Falling under the jurisdiction of the Department of Enterprise, Trade, and Employment, permits were non-transferable, tied to specific jobs, renewable on a yearly basis, and would only be dispensed following a labour market test in which employers had to demonstrate that it had not been possible to fill the vacancy with indigenous Irish or EEA workers. In order to discourage excessive use of the system employers also had to pay for the permit – initially €159 (£125) but following signs of an economic slowdown in 2001, €500. In theory permit charges could not be passed on to the employee, though in practice they invariably were. To minimize the arrival of immigrants above the level of labour market demand, family reunification was severely restricted. Permit holders could apply to the DJELR for family members to join them after 1 year, at the Minister's discretion, but there was no guarantee their family would be allowed to come.

From 1999 to 2007 over 120,000 *new* work permits were issued; the number of renewals was considerably higher. Although permits were issued to individuals from over 150 countries, the top 5 countries accounted for 41.3% of work permits in 2002.[28] Up to 2003 the majority of the permits that were given out went to individuals from Latvia, Lithuania, the Philippines, and Poland (9.8%, 9.6%, 8%, and 7.8% respectively). Following EU expansion in 2004 a significant change took place in the composition of nationals claiming permits. In 2007, for example, the majority of permits were given to individuals from India (4,068) and the Philippines (3,885), followed by the South Africa, Ukraine, and the USA.

Although initially open to a wide variety of occupations, reflecting the broad endemic pattern of labour shortage in Ireland, as demand became concentrated in certain sectors, and specific occupations became more difficult to fill, the state deemed a number of occupations ineligible for securing a permit. A large source of demand came from unskilled sectors, such as the services and catering sectors, with 44% of employers in these areas in 2001 claiming that they could not recruit, primarily as a result of the low rate of pay.[29] 75% of all applicants for work permits in 2000 were for unskilled work[30] and have remained so.

Modelled on the guest-worker system devised by the large industrial powers after the Second World War, the permit system was designed to meet the needs of employers for cheap labour, and of states for temporary labour. Emblematic of these recruitment programmes was the *gastarbeiter* system in Germany. In describing the latter, albeit exclusively from a male perspective, Berger noted:

> What distinguishes this migration from others in the past is that it is temporary. Only a minority of workers are permitted to settle permanently in the country to which they have come. The migrant comes to sell his labour power where there is a labour shortage. He is admitted to do a certain kind of job. He has no rights, claims, or reality outside his filling of that job. While he fills it, he is paid and accommodated. If he no longer does so, he is sent back to where he came from. It is not men who immigrate but machine minders, sweepers, diggers, cement mixers, cleaners, drillers, etc. To re-become a man (husband, father, citizen, patriot) a migrant has to return home. The home he left because it held no future for him.[31]

The Irish system was similarly constructed on the premise that migrant labour should be construed as a commodity, recruited on a temporary basis to meet economic needs, and discharged once no longer expedient. To that extent migrant workers constituted a labour reserve that could be laid off during an economic downturn with no political consequences.

The work permit system was designed to simultaneously meet the twin symbiotic needs of state and capital. However, this was primarily at the expense of the migrants. Work permit holders, because they lacked important social and political and economic rights, constituted cheap, flexible labour. Given the precarious and non-unionized status of those employed in the unskilled sector, exploitation in these areas was rife as the number of cases reported to the MRCI demonstrated.[32] Work permit holders were earning less than indigenous workers, even though they were better qualified.[33] The permit system effectively tied workers to a particular employer facilitating worker exploitation. Migrant workers accepted lower wages and poorer conditions for a number of reasons, but primarily because of the difficulty of moving between jobs on a work permit. As one Indian national explained in an interview:

> I personally felt they were paying wages below the industry average and I wasn't happy about that. But the thing is that, because the work permit is so difficult, I saw people from India working in the company because, with a work permit, you're stuck, you can't change. It's a hold on you and they're making it tougher every year and you can't change it. (Inderjit, India)

The non-transferable nature of the permit, which was usually held by the employer, meant that employers could threaten workers with deportation or with not renewing a permit if the latter made complaints about pay or working conditions. Two Lithuanian interviewees who had come before the expansion of the EU vividly conveyed how the permit constrained the worker:

> It's ownership. You get a work permit for a year and its ownership… you have to be good enough so it would be extended. You cannot talk against anyone, you cannot even say what you want sometimes… The work permit only works for that company, if you leave it, you have to struggle… it never stopped anyone coming here getting a job… It left you vulnerable of course. (Adomas, Lithuania)

As another noted, his employer regularly threatened to not renew his permit or send him back to Lithuania: "'we will send you back if you do this"… Somehow people thought we were envelopes and they could send us back' (Gabrius, Lithuania).

The inability to complain was compounded by the fact that work permit holders had few avenues along which to pursue rights protections or to seek redress for exploitation.

The permits system essentially constituted a state-sanctioned form of structural disempowerment designed to provide employers with a highly flexible and industrious migrant labour force. In addition to a lack of access to social welfare this skewered power relationship between employer and worker was reinforced by an information deficit on rights and entitlements, minimum wage levels, or going rates for jobs. Having incurred high levels of debt to family and friends or to recruitment agencies to travel to Ireland, and constrained by obligations to send remittances back to family members, effectively made migrants bondaged workers.

Work visas/authorizations/green cards

In 2000 the Irish State also introduced a work visa/authorization system for specialist categories of workers as a result of continuing skills shortages. Work visa/authorizations gave the worker more rights and entitlements than those provided by work permits, allowing the recipient to move between jobs, albeit within a similar occupational category. They were also renewable on a 2-year basis, allowed applications for family reunion after 3 months, and were easier to obtain since the employer did not have to undergo a labour market test or pass through DETE bureaucracy.[34] Between 2000 and 2007 over 13,000 work visas/ authorizations were issued. After February 2004, and following a pressure from Irish Nurses Overseas Organization to secure family reunification rights, spouses of workers under this scheme were given an automatic right to work.[35]

This binary work permit/work visa system, however, was modified following shifts in the dynamics of the Irish labour market and the entry of accession state workers. In February 2007, as a central part of the implementation of the Employment Permits Act 2006, a 'green card system' was introduced. The new system was designed to replace the work visa/authorization system and modify the operation of the work permit system. Under the scheme a green card would be granted to the employee for an initial period of 2 years, after which time it would 'normally be renewed indefinitely'. The permit allowed the employee to apply for family reunification immediately, and after 2 years, to apply to the Department of Justice for long-term residency of 5 years. The fee for the green card of €1,000 for a new permit and €1,500 for an indefinite permit was to be paid by the applicant. who could either be the employer or employee. Those securing a new work permit were required to stay with the employer for at least 12 months. The fees for work permits were also increased – €500 for a permit of up to 6 months, €1,000 for a 6 month to 2 year permit and €1,500 for a 3 year permit. The spouse and dependents of work permit holders could apply for a spousal work permit. The introduction of bi-annually renewable permits, and for the permit to be held by the employee after 2007, was designed to temper the exploitative relationship between employer and worker.

The launch of the green card system followed recommendations given by the Expert Group on Future Skills Needs Report (2005) and discussions between the social partners. In order to facilitate the in-migration of highly skilled workers from outside the EU, the EGFSN favoured a 'green card' system which would be available to non-EU workers. However, this system contained an important number of restrictions. The business-dominated EGFSN wanted the state to carefully control the flow of skilled migrants claiming it was necessary to 'be able to amend eligible sectors, occupations, salary levels or qualifications on a regular basis, in accordance with the changing needs of the enterprise sector'. To do this, it advocated a system where decisions could be made on an 'administrative' rather than legislative basis, thereby effectively by-passing equality legislation. It also proposed that family reunification should only take place when the migrants had sufficient earning capacity and that 'the duration of the period during which the migrant remains tied to their initial employer ought to take account of the time it would take an employer to re-coup their investment in that migrant', and that this would normally take one year. Despite agreeing in principle that skilled migrants ought to be able to obtain some form of long-term residency, the EGFSN qualified this by recommending that 'The Minister should retain discretionary powers to either refuse or cancel permanent residency'. The Employment Permits Act 2006 – which came into effect in February 2007 – more or less incorporated all of these EGFSK's proposals.

Hence rather than providing greater protections against exploitation, as the state claimed, the Employment Permits Act 2006 was designed to facilitate flexibility in the economy, cut out the bureaucratic impediments facing small businesses, deport or repatriate migrants whose permits had expired and simultaneously to encourage the arrival of highly skilled migrants. As the EGFSN noted:

> While the extremely flexible procedures outlined above have served many companies well, in some instances, particularly for some small and medium enterprises, the system has proved somewhat difficult to navigate and burdensome. The absence of clear guidelines and criteria for fast-track applications, the *ad hoc* nature of many of the procedures, and the lack of consistency in decision-making leaves the system vulnerable to potential abuses. …Additionally, the requirement for a labour market test (which can take four to five weeks) imposes a significant constraint on companies, particularly when the vacancy in question is for specialized personnel. The permit system as it currently stands makes little provision for the repatriation of migrants upon the expiration of their permits; most permits are renewed with little or no validation of continued economic need. This gives the impression that the work permit system which was designed to facilitate temporary migration only, can be used to acquire permanent status.[36]

The Act therefore failed to strengthen the protection of migrant workers against exploitation in a number of ways. Firstly, green card and work permit holders are in theory allowed to move between jobs, but the DETE has very rarely sanctioned this in practice. Few migrants have been permitted to move from one job to another. Migrant workers are also obligated to remain with their employer for 12 months. Most evidence from the Labour Court and Equality Commission suggests that exploitation of workers occurs from the outset of the employment contract rather than after a significant duration. The legislation actually marked a regression from the work visa system since it made it more difficult for the worker to change employer.

In addition, although employers are obliged to pay the national minimum wage there is no obligation to pay industry-specific established 'going rates' or 'standard working week remuneration'. The 2006 Act also misleadingly refers to a 'green card' scheme which is assumed to mirror the American visa scheme. However, the Irish green card does not confer immediate or permanent residency; rather, green cards need to be renewed two years after being conferred and they only provide 'long-term residency', which has to be renewed after 5 years.

European expansion

Recent revelations about abuses suffered by migrants are not accidental, but are rather an intrinsic part of a neo-liberal economic system designed to serve employer interests. Consequently as Berger perceptively notes:

> What determines a person's position in the social hierarchy is the sum of his [sic] abilities as required in that particular social and economic system. He is no longer seen as another man, as the unique centre of his own experience: he is seen as the mere conglomerate of certain capacities and needs. He is seen, in other words, as a complex of functions within a social system. And he can never be seen as more than that unless the notion of equality between men is re-introduced.[37]

After the accession of new EU states in May 2004 the permits regime was re-modelled to reduce the number of work permits given to non-EU Nationals and to use Eastern Europe as the main reserve for cheap labour. It subsequently became state/bureaucratic procedure to hierarchically and preferentially distinguish between EU 15, EU 10, and third country nationals. 'EU' and 'non-EU' refers not only to nationality, but to immigrant status. However, despite this binary distinction, there is no clear-cut dichotomy in practice between citizens and non-citizens in Western migrant states, but rather a continuum of statuses, with those in the centre sometimes referred to as 'denizens'.[38]

With the exception of the right to vote, European workers have similar rights to Irish nationals. Although migrants whose immigration status changed after 2004 noted that the level of exploitation they endured had diminished since they no longer required a work permit. However, some, especially those in the unskilled sector, still highlighted the fact that they were not getting the same pay as Irish workers, or being treated differently at work. As one perceptively noted:

'Here you are not an employee, you're a foreigner' (Gabrius, Lithuania). There remained a 10–18% difference in income between immigrants from the new member states and natives.[39] As the CSO noted, employees with Irish nationality had the highest average hourly earnings of €19.86, while employees from EU Accession States had the lowest at €11.52 per hour.[40] Gender and language also played a significant role in pay differentials so that non-Anglophone, East European, women workers could be earning as much as 30% less than their Irish counterparts.[41]

The smooth political and economic incorporation of former socialist states – characterized by business-friendly fiscal regimes, weak or non-existent labour movements, low wages – into post-Cold-War European capitalism has been a remarkable achievement by any measure. Their entry into the comity of free nations characterized by free speech, free occupational choice, and freedom to travel was not only an immense political and ideological victory for capitalism, but simultaneously provided the older European states with a pool of cheap labour capable of exerting pressure on wages and conditions in the West. What German workers experienced in relation to the entry of new Slovakian workers in the EU according to Anderson, is broadly emblematic of pressures on pay in Ireland:

> The archetypal case is Slovakia, where wages in the auto industry are one eighth of those in Germany, and more cars per capita are shortly going to be produced – Volkswagen and Peugeot in the lead – than in any other country in the world. It is the fear of such relocation, with the closure of factories at home, that has cowed so many German workers into accepting longer hours and less pay. Race to the bottom pressures are not confined to wages. The ex-Communist states have pioneered flat taxes to woo investment, and now compete with each other for the lowest possible rate: Estonia started with 26%, Slovakia offers 19%, Romania advertises 16%, while Poland is now mooting a best buy of 15%. The effect of the enlargement has essentially been much of what the Foreign Office and the employers' lobbies in Brussels always hoped it would be: the dissension of the EU into a vast free-trade zone, with a newly acquired periphery of cheap labour.[42]

The Posted Workers Directive, which facilitated the free movement of labour, demonstrated in a number of high profile cases including the Lavalle, Viking, Rouffert, and Luxembourg cases in Sweden, Denmark, Germany, and Luxembourg, that a European race to the bottom was underway.[43] Equally, the consistent thread behind the changes in Irish migration policy has been to create a highly flexible workforce.

Though legal and immigration status has been a significant factor structuring the susceptibility of migrants to exploitation, in terms of disempowering them, it is not exclusive in determining their inferior treatment; other factors involving discrimination in terms of race, ethnicity, or nationality have also played a role. The effect discrimination has in marginalizing ethnic groups, even when that group has full citizenship rights, can be seen in the case of travellers in Ireland. Equally, during the 50s, many migrants in the UK who had arrived from former colonies with *de jure* equivalent of English citizenship rights still found themselves at the bottom of the social hierarchy because of the operation of state and individual racism.

Employment sector

A spectrum of employment conditions for migrants both between industries and within them also plays a role in explaining the differences in wages and conditions between migrant and native workers. According to the 2006 National Employment Survey non-Irish nationals only earned between 77% and 86% of Irish employees in all employment sectors with the exception of the wholesale and retail sector.[44] Recorded abuses of workers' rights tended to be prevalent in most employment sectors sometimes irrespective of legal status. However, certain employment sectors, especially low skilled sectors and/or those requiring little English language competence, showed significantly higher levels of exploitation than others. These include the horticulture, hotel and catering, and the construction industry, as well as the domestic service sector.[45] Between 2005 and January 2007, almost 63% of those who came to the Migrant Rights Centre Ireland for support having experienced exploitation were from the agricultural sector, as were 48% of domestic workers, 36% from the hotel and catering, 35% from construction, 28% in services, 23% in manufacturing, 20% in cleaning and maintenance, and 8% in business and IT.[46] The National Employment Rights Authority detected a similar concentration of breaches in specific sectors with 76% of employers in catering, 90% in contract cleaning, and 64% in construction found to be in breach of employment terms and conditions.[47]

Agriculture

The Irish agricultural sector contributes approximately €5 billion a year to the Irish economy yet it has been in a steep long-term decline. About 37% of the labour force was located in this sector in 1960 but this fell to only 5.7% of the labour force by 2008. Despite the decline the industry has suffered from acute labour shortages. As the EGFSN (2005) noted: 'The continuing decline in numbers of people engaged in agriculture presents a serious challenge to the viability of the industry in Ireland at its current scale.'[48] Changing demographic patterns in Ireland including an increase in rural–urban migration has depleted many farms of a local labour supply. This shortfall has been exacerbated by the spread of dominant urban values into rural areas, further reinforcing the demeaning status attributed to agricultural work. However, perhaps of greatest significance in accounting for the labour deficit are the low wages and poor working conditions characterizing the sector. Agricultural work is predominantly unskilled and interchangeable. In 2001 the average agricultural worker earned €333 per week, compared to industrial workers who earned €508 per week and unskilled workers in the construction industry who earned €592 per week.[49] In 2003 average family farm income amounted to just €15,054 per year, a figure well below average national incomes across all other sectors of the economy.[50] As a traded sector open to the global economy and with new forms of transport allowing food goods to be delivered rapidly, agriculture has faced intense competitive pressures from international firms, forcing employers to reduce wages and cut costs. This has been redoubled by pressures exerted by domestic supermarkets to improve efficiency and for Irish growers to lower prices through mechanization, rationalization or work intensification.[51] The nature of the product has, however, set limits on the levels of mechanization and technological innovation that can be introduced into the production process, rendering the sector labour-intensive, with relatively low output per unit of labour. About 7% of those working in Irish agriculture, forestry and fishing are non-Irish nationals, and a significant number of these are female.[52]

Within the sector the commercial horticultural industry is estimated to have a farmgate value of approximately €380 million, and contain over 6,000 in its labour force.[53] Mushroom production is partly responsible for its high value, constituting about 40% of all horticultural production with an output value of €110m.[54] Declining profit margins in the context of intense competition have led to the closure of a number of small horticultural businesses though a significant number of small-scale producers still exist in the industry, with many located in Leinster and Munster. Teagasc estimates that there are about 580 growers in the country and about 14,000 agricultural workers on farms producing about 50,000 tons of mushrooms per annum. The low rates of pay, the demeaned status attached to the work, and labour shortages in the sector have led many Irish employers to turn to migrants to fulfil their labour needs.[55] A large majority have been sourced through work permits from Eastern Europe prior to EU accession, with many coming from Lithuania, Latvia, but also from other Baltic states such as Estonia and Belarus, as well as China. For migrants, agricultural work may be the only work available. Moreover, the work requires minimal language competence, training, or skills, and is seen as providing a short-term foothold into employment in Ireland. The cash-in-hand nature of farm work also means that there are always a number of undocumented workers prepared to work in the sector.

The seasonal nature of agricultural and mushroom production, fluctuating demand, combined with fierce sectoral competition, has a number of implications. The structure of the sector means that employers require a flexible and compliant workforce who can harvest at short notice. They seek temporary and legally precarious workers who do not have to be compensated for work that they do not do, including holiday pay, weekend bonuses, etc. Piece rates are imposed in place of hourly rates – a practice that is prevalent in horticultural sectors worldwide.[56] This allows employers to increase worker productivity, work intensity, and pay below the minimum wage.[57] It also encourages the use of employment agencies and labour contractors to supply workers.

Given the structural configuration of the horticultural and mushroom sector, exploitation has been rampant and poor working conditions accepted as the norm. Those working in the mushroom sector were not only being paid wages below the industry's going rate (set by the Agricultural Workers Employment Regulation Order), but also significantly below the statutory minimum wage. Some workers were being paid as little as €2.50 an hour, about a third of the minimum wage at the time.[58] Other stories of workers having delayed payments, not receiving overtime pay, paid annual leave, or preferential rates for bank holiday and Sunday pay were common. Some were not given contracts, pay slips, or excessive deductions were made for accommodation or PRSI.[59] For example, following investigations by the Department of Social and Family Affairs in 2007 over 500 employers out of a total of 4,853 who were inspected were not meeting their obligation to pay their share of PRSI contributions for employees.[60] In 2007 €250,000 was recovered in judgements and settlements from 20 farms alone pertaining to the exploitation of 100 migrant workers in the horticultural sector in Ireland.[61]

In 2006 14 female workers, mostly from Lithuania and Latvia, were dismissed from Kilnaleck Mushroom Farm after complaining about a change in work procedures. They claimed they had been working at least 80 to 100 hours per week for an average of €2.50 an hour. The women also worked bank holidays, including Christmas day, as a normal day. Although the employer had made deductions they could not receive social welfare since PRSI contributions had not been made, and they had not been habitually resident for 2 years.[62]

In parallel with wage exploitation there have also been a number of health and safety implications for migrant workers. The shift from standard working weeks to rotation work has had severe consequences for workers' health. Infrequent irregular hours, followed by intense and physically demanding bouts of work and work rotation, tend to severely disrupt the body's natural circadian rhythms. Health and safety issues relating to the use of toxic chemicals and pesticides were especially acute. Exposure to dangerous chemicals used to treat mushrooms had potentially adverse long-term effects on the lungs of workers, and implications for the reproductive health of women. The lack of provision of health and safety training exacerbated the information deficit on health procedures caused by a lack of English.[63] One Lithuanian worker, Anna, vividly described her experience of working on a farm to the MRCI:

> I was picking mushrooms on the farm, collecting crates, mixing chemicals to spray on mushroom disease, and watering mushrooms. I got paid a piece rate when I picked mushrooms and paid per hour when I did all the other jobs on the farm. I didn't have any idea that there is an agricultural pay rate for the job I was doing. There was only one Irish lady picking mushrooms with us. I don't know was she paid different or the same as us. I got pay slips with my wages but I never knew when pay day was... I could work as little as 2 hours a day or up to 16 hours day – it all depended on the mushroom flush. When mushrooms where picked we could be finished any time of day or night. That didn't matter on the farm. As far as I know my employer paid my taxes and PRSI. €45 was taken out of my wages every week for accommodation. I never got paid overtime, Sunday pay or public holidays. When I got sick I still went to work as I couldn't take day off. I could have day off only if there where no mushrooms to pick but as I was living in a mobile home on the farm my employer could came in and ask me to do other jobs on the farm if there was anything else to be done. Girls who lived in town had days off and he didn't call them to come in for two 2 work as they needed to pay for a taxi, but I was there 24/7. As far as I was concerned we were slaves at his farm with no feelings allowed. I was told if I came to work I must work and if I want to complain I can leave as there are hundreds of others behind the gates who will be more than happy to do my work. That is what I believed was true... I wasn't told anything about Health and Safety at the farm and no masks were given to us when we picked mushrooms or when we mixed chemicals for disease spraying. I suffer from bad eyesight now, long coughs in the mornings and get breathless. That is all after I worked on the mushroom farm. And the other two girls who I shared the caravan with suffer from similar health problems... My English is not very good and it is hard to communicate with people in the local community. I don't feel very comfortable around Irish people and I don't have any friends from my home country to mix with only the two girls who I am sharing house with. Most of time I spend in the house.[64]

The provision of cheap, and usually poor-quality accommodation to migrants by employers increased the latter's power and control over the workers in several ways. It permitted surveillance of the worker, allowing the employer to know their availability in order to pick flushes of mushrooms, which could take place at any time of the day or night. On-site accommodation also functioned to minimize contact between the indigenous population and migrant workers, rendering them invisible. But most importantly, the provision of accommodation dramatically increased the employees' structural dependence on the employer for fear of being made homeless.

Processes of exploitation, though sometimes undoubtedly the result of individual unscrupulous employers, point to broader structural mechanisms in the horticultural supply-and-demand chain. Within Ireland's open economy, global competition combined with the dissolution of EU protectionism have merged with domestic pressures on small-scale farmers from labour contractors mediating between them and supermarkets to lower costs. By outsourcing, sub-contracting and increasingly elongating supply chains, supermarkets are able to simultaneously secure cheap goods and divest themselves of responsibility in relation to labour conditions. Profits that accrue to supermarkets at the expense of exploited migrant workers are by no means negligible, for example, in 2008 Tesco Ireland announced profits of €2 billion.

Although EU enlargement has benefited businesses generally to the extent that it increased the potential supply of cheap labour and kept wage pressure down, the move also reduced the availability of constrained workers on permits to the detriment of employers in the agricultural sector:

> During the course of this research, consultations with stakeholders in the agricultural/horticultural sector highlighted a number of challenges facing that sector. The horticultural sector has been a significant beneficiary of the current work permit system. The enlargement of the EU has provided increased access to skilled operatives and supervisors for the sector. However, the free movement of labour from within the ten accession countries has also meant that migrants who previously availed of work permits now have increased opportunity to move employment and, as a result, there has been increased turnover of labour within the horticultural sector. Teagasc and Bord Bia say that to maintain an adequate and stabilized workforce of skilled labour in the horticultural sector, it is no longer possible to meet these needs from within the EU and that the experience of growers has demonstrated that staff sourced outside of the EU under work permits provide a much more stabilized workforce than EU employees.[65]

Migrants on permits have been particularly vulnerable to employer pressures to increase productivity per unit by intensifying the work process. There are, however, other factors apart from their structural–legal position that keep them locked into such poor work conditions. Threats of deportation or dismissal if complaints are made, their dependence on employer accommodation, the informality between employer and employee characterized by the absence of employment contracts, and the lack of union presence compounds their vulnerability. The geographically dispersed and isolated nature of the workplace in rural areas often means a lack of workplace support, and restricted access to redressing employment abuse. This inability to complain about conditions is compounded by language difficulties, lack of work rights information, minimal levels of alternative work in rural areas, and financial commitments to family members to remit wages.

As we shall see later, in terms of exploitation there are a number of striking parallels between the agricultural and the domestic work sector. Like domestic work, agricultural work is heavily gendered, there are high levels of informality between employer and employee, and the workplace remains hidden from public gaze so that the workers are generally 'invisible'. These problems are exacerbated by the seasonal nature of agricultural work, which leads to high levels of labour turnover and make trade union recruitment difficult.

Construction

The construction industry saw dramatic worldwide growth over the past decade, accounting for astonishing 7% of global employment.[66] It also played a central role in Ireland's economic and employment growth. Even when it began to decline after 2007, construction still accounted for 10% of Irish GNP, generating €38.5 billion.[67] Following 2001 the government radically deregulated the sector, initiating a large property bubble based on unsustainable speculation. This led to a huge expansion in the number of new houses built between 2001 and 2006. A sharp increase in the number of state infrastructure projects was matched by a protracted move away from local authority and social housing towards a housing system geared towards the market. The housing boom meant that employment in construction rose by over 40% between 2002 and 2008, and accounted for 13% of total employment in 2007.

In the context of rapid growth the sector suffered from both severe levels of labour and skills shortages. The structure of the industry has demanded a certain type of worker. Based on seasonal building projects that have to be completed according to strict deadlines, and in various dispersed locations, the industry requires flexible, temporary, mobile labour, sometimes at short notice. High numbers of migrant workers, in both skilled and low-skilled positions, have entered the sector. In 2007 it was estimated that about 17% of those employed in construction were non-Irish, with nearly three-quarters of these from the Accession States.

The construction sector was characterized by high levels of self-employment and sub-contracting with large building sites in Ireland containing workers from several different contractors. Deregulation in the sector not only resulted in property speculation, but engendered high levels of immigrant worker exploitation. Almost 20% of all cases taken at the Labour Relations Commission in 2006 were by East Europeans located predominantly in the construction sector.[68] Most claimants were in low salary employment (between €301 and €400). The employment violations they suffered included the non-payment of wages, of holiday pay, unfair dismissal and unfair treatment and harassment, and issues related to holidays, excess hours, and insufficient rest periods.

Table 10.1 Estimated nationality of workers in construction 2006–7 fourth quarter

	2006 Total employment	Construction sector		2007 Total employment	Construction sector	
Unit	000	000	% of total	000	000	% of total
Irish*	1,786.0	234.5	13.1	1,804.2	231.0	12.8
Non-Irish nationals: of which:	286.0	50.2	17.6	334.7	48.0	14.3
United Kingdom	51.3	7.5	14.6	51.4	6.4	12.5
EU15 excl. Irl. and UK	32.7	1.5	4.6	34.5	1.5	4.3
Accession States EU15 to EU27	124.2	34.2	27.5	167.7	35.1	20.9
Other	77.9	7.0	9.0	81.0	5.0	6.2
Total	2,072.1	284.6	13.7	2,138.9	279.0	13.0

Source: Construction and Housing in Ireland 2008.

Includes 'not stated'

Note: Data may be subject to sampling or other survey errors, which are greater in respect of smaller values or estimates of change

Exploitation in the construction sector, although rife in the private sector, has also been recorded in a number of public building projects. In March of 2006, 3 cases of employment exploitation involving construction companies and state projects in the energy sector emerged simultaneously. Over 66 Polish workers at an ESB power station in Moneypoint were found to be paid just €5.20 an hour, less than one third of the legal minimum going rate of €18.97 set by the construction industry's registered employment agreement (REA). The German company Lentjes had subcontracted the work to ZRE Katowice (Ireland) Construction. In a second case, almost 200 Serbian workers employed as part of ESB's €3 billion renewal of the electricity network had arrears to the value of €4 million. Many were paid under €5 and some only paid €3.21 an hour, instead of the REA rate of €18.97. Again the main contractor, Dublin-based Laing–O'Rourke Utilities, one of the largest construction companies in the State, blamed subcontractors Energoprojekt Oprema. A third and similar controversy involved Hungarians employed at Spencer Dock.[69] In all the cases subcontracting and outsourcing to non-resident contractors became a central factor accounting for employment abuse, allowing companies to deny responsibility for treating and paying workers in line with legal standards.

However, perhaps more than any other case, the 2005 Gama controversy represented the exemplary manifestation of the logic of migrant worker exploitation in the Irish construction sector. Gama was the second largest construction company in Turkey, employing over 10,000 workers in Europe, Asia, and the Middle East. It was invited to Ireland by the then Minister for Enterprise, Trade and Employment, Mary Harney, following a trade delegation to Turkey in 1998 as part of facilitating the 1999 National Development Plan. Arriving in 2000, the Irish subsidiary of Gama contained over 1000 Turkish employees. Although work permits were deemed ineligible for non-EU construction workers, approximately 1000 were issued 'liberally and quickly' to Gama between 2004 and 2005.[70]

Between 2000 and 2005 Gama secured nearly €200 million worth of state contacts, and €120 million of private contracts.[71] In 2001 it secured the Ballincog bypass contract with a bid that was €15m lower than its nearest rival. This was made possible by lowering wages and introducing highly exploitative employment practices. Many of Gama's migrant employees were housed in barrack-like dormitories with poor living conditions. This not only ensured disciplinary control over the workforce, but also separated Turkish from Irish workers, who were on different pay scales. A large number of Turkish workers were being paid between €2 and €3 an hour for an 80-hour week, even though the minimum wage stood at €7 and the minimum registered employment agreement industry rate for operatives stood at €12.96. Other immigrant workers in the Ballinicog project for example, were working up to 84 hours a week and only receiving €3.30 for overtime and €4.40 for working on Sundays.[72] When the Labour Inspectorate began their investigation in 2004, Gama began to harass and intimidate workers living on site by threatening them with deportation or repatriation if they spoke out. Gama also took out a successful high court injunction preventing the publication of the Labour Inspectorate report.

The company eventually admitted underpaying workers by 8% though pay-slips indicated more serious levels of exploitation with workers receiving €1,000 for 330 hours' pay instead of €4,200. Many of the pay-slips displayed incorrect data on wages and indicated unwarranted deductions made for national insurance and tax. In addition, it later emerged that large parts of these wage entitlements were being transferred to a secret bank account based in Amsterdam – up to €40 million in wages from many as 2,000 past and present Gama workers.

The Gama controversy again highlighted the lack of adequate protection for work permit holders in Ireland. Despite legislation guaranteeing migrant workers the same rights including minimum wages, statutory rest breaks etc., their pay was heavily cut and withheld. Moreover, many were members of the SIPTU union and Gama had formally agreed to accept legally binding building-sector pay rates.

Several factors underlay the exploitation of the Gama workers including their inability to complain, poor enforcement of labour standards, a lack of knowledge of rights, including minimum wages and going rates, the employer holding their passports and legal documentation, language barriers, a fear they would lose their jobs, dependence on accommodation, and finally State indifference. Despite knowledge of these recorded employment violations the government still awarded Gama the Clontibret–Castleblayney bypass contract in 2005.

Providing care: gender and migrant workers

Domestic workers

The increasing feminization of migration has been a remarkable global phenomenon: over half of the world's migrants are now women. In line with this global shift 47% of non-Irish nationals in Ireland are female.[73] However, the gender ratio varies markedly according to nationality: only 35% of Polish and Pakistani migrants were female compared to approximately 60% of Swedish and Filipino migrants.[74]

Increasing female global mobility does not automatically equate with increasing female equality. The combination of a number of processes including more women entering the labour force, low European fertility rates, and an ageing population in developing OECD countries has resulted in increasing dependency ratios and to a shortage of people to look after children, the elderly, and the infirm. These factors are compounded by the limited penetration of technology that is permissible in the care sector.

With men generally refusing to take on these negatively valued, gendered roles – symbolically representative of unproductive and taken-for-granted women's work – the result has been a rapid increase in global demand for female domestic workers. Domestic work is one of the largest occupations driving international labour migration.[75] A large majority of female migrants are undertaking domestic work as a straightforward extension of the gendered and unpaid work carried out in the household. Formerly unpaid work has become increasingly commodified and brought under the sway of the market. A class and developmental component overwrites this gendered process as women from poorer developing countries increasingly replace middle-class women in developed countries as primary carers. As part of a 'global care chain',[76] working women in developed economies in the North 'solve' their childcare and domestic responsibilities by passing this work over to disempowered women from developing countries in the South, in effect subcontracting the problems created for them by the 'second shift'. In many cases the migrants themselves have left their own children behind, usually to be cared for by grandparents or extended family members as part of the pooling of family resources so common in poor developing countries. The high demand for domestic workers is set to continue as Asian, Latin American,

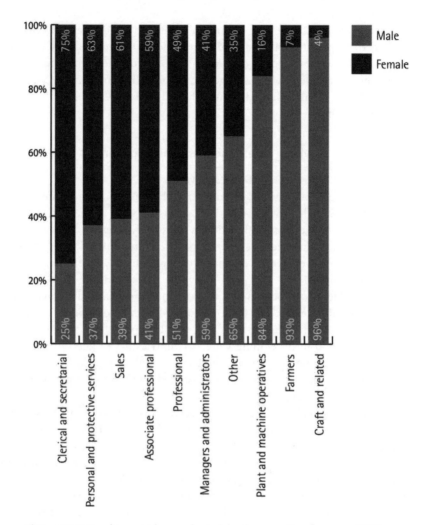

Figure 10.2 Employment by gender in broad occupational groups, 2006

Caribbean, and African domestic workers migrate to affluent East Asian countries, the Middle East, North America, and Western Europe. Female domestic migrant workers include Sri Lankans going to the Middle East, South Americans going to Spain, Ethiopians travelling to Lebanon and Italy, and Filipinos migrating to Ireland.

In Ireland the rapid growth in the economy saw a rapid increase in female participation in the workforce from 45.9% in 1997 to 60.3% in 2007.[77] This increase has, however, been structured according to a gendered division of labour and characterized by unequal pay.[78]

Increased female labour market participation has not yet seriously challenged the widespread view that women retain primary responsibility for childcare – the state continues to position this as an issue of private responsibility.[79] The increase in labour participation of married women did, however, lead to the emergence of dual-income couples with an increased combined income. For some couples, especially those working in the professional or the higher social classes, dual incomes permitted not only rising consumption, but in the context of increasing crèche costs for childcare, allowed the employment of domestic and care workers including au pairs, nannies, or housekeepers. The result was a sharp rise in demand for domestic workers. In 2004 approximately 62,000 persons were employed in care work, constituting just over 3% of national employment in Ireland.[80] The majority of domestic workers in Ireland are women from the Philippines, though Ukrainian, Latvian, and Sri Lankan nationals are also present. In 1999, 80 work permits were given to those in the domestic sector and by 2002 this had risen to 788, falling to 644 in 2005 after the entry of accession state nationals (see Figure 10.3).

A large number of workers were recruited through employment agencies. The Philippines, for example, has approximately 1,000 agencies for overseas workers, the majority of which are geared towards recruiting domestic workers.[81] Some of these charge very high fees and severely penalize workers for leaving contracts. The position of domestic workers can be characterized by multiple levels of structural and psychological dependence. The combination of unequal power and intimate social relations – especially for live-in workers – increases the worker's precarious social position. Working in the private sphere, in someone's home, has two major consequences: informality and invisibility. The conjunction of informality and invisibility

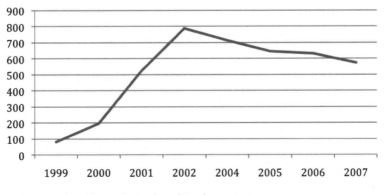

Source: Department of Enterprise Trade and Employment

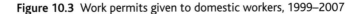

Figure 10.3 Work permits given to domestic workers, 1999–2007

renders domestic workers especially vulnerable to super-exploitation. Anderson has usefully highlighted the contradictory social relations that structure domestic employment.[82] On the one hand the private sphere is considered to be governed by informal values of mutual dependence and affectivity, which though hierarchical, are nevertheless reciprocal relations of duty between employee and employer. For domestic workers these become fused with a formal labour contract entailing abstract instrumental market values. The notion of duty can then be used to make employees work beyond what is stated on their contract – longer hours, for no remuneration, or for carrying out contractually unspecified tasks. This is exacerbated by the fact that the work they do is devalued as 'women's work' and therefore does not possess 'proper' market value. Emotional blackmail can also be used to make workers work harder by reframing a formal social power relationship between employer and employee into an informal reciprocal relationship between an adult and child.

In terms of invisibility, domestic workers cannot be seen in the sense they reside and live behind the closed doors of people's homes. Isolated from other workers and sometimes from friends and social networks, they are exposed to emotional manipulation and threats. Yet simultaneously, because they are in the employer's home, they are under constant surveillance and scrutiny by their employer.

In Ireland, migrant women have generally experienced double disadvantage in terms of earnings. Not only are their earnings lower than men generally, but they are also 14% lower than of those of native females.[83] This fact, conjoined with the low status and prestige attached to domestic work, has meant that the lowest weekly wages given to work-permit holders went to those working in private homes in Ireland.[84] The average wage received by domestic workers after deductions in 2004 was approximately €250 a week, a figure equivalent to the minimum wage.[85] Since domestic workers are generally outside of the gaze of protective labour legislation, and given the unique and unequal power relation with the employer, the result is low pay, excessive hours, and illegal pay deductions. Isolation from other employees and friends, a lack of knowledge of employment rights and social entitlements, little access to complaints mechanisms, but also the structural dependency of the work permit, underpinned these employment violations. Given the high level of informality between employer and employee, threats concerning non-renewal of work permits and ultimately deportation often arise in the sector. Live-in domestics who depend on accommodation are particularly vulnerable to these threats. The worker may also owe fees to an agency, have incurred a high level of debts coming to Ireland, or as is often the case, have a family depending on remitted income.

Nurses

Another heavily gendered occupational sector in Ireland is the nursing sector. However, in contrast to domestic work there is a predominance of relatively skilled workers, high levels of unionization, and consequently lower levels of exploitation. Nursing is the third largest occupation in Ireland following sales assistants and farmers, constituting a central part of the gendered division of labour. It is estimated that more than half of all new nurses registered in the State in 2006 came from outside the EU.[86]

Given its unsuitability to mechanization and an ageing population, global demand for nursing has remained high. Already existent labour shortages created by the sector's expansion have been exacerbated by the emigration of Irish nurses for more attractive working conditions in Canada, the USA, the UK, Australia, and the Middle East. Between 1999 and 2000 it was estimated that for every 1,600 non-Irish nurses that registered in Ireland, half that figure of Irish nurses left or had intended to leave.[87] In 2000 the health sector was estimated to be short of over 1,800 nurses.[88] The State responded by recruiting agency nurses from abroad. Many of these were recruited initially from the EU but as supply fell they were subsequently drawn from Asia. This acute shortage also partly prompted the introduction of the work visa system. Between 2000 and 2006 some 9,441 nurses were issued with work authorizations or visas. The vast majority – over 90% – were nurses from the Philippines or India,[89] though others arrived from South Africa, Australia, and Nigeria.[90] Many were recruited through Irish-based globally connected employment agencies. However, other unlicensed agencies in Ireland, plus indigenous agencies in the Philippines, were also involved, some of which charged exorbitantly high fees for bringing nurses to Ireland, effectively keeping many nurses in severe debt.[91]

The case of Filipino nurses offers a microcosm of the complexity of migratory processes, highlighting the interplay and connection between emigration and immigration, global economic inequality and social processes, entailing transnational family connections, remittances and economic development.

The Philippines remains one of the poorest countries in the world. With the disappearance of male formal employment opportunities, the burden of survival has fallen increasingly on women's shoulders. It has been estimated that nearly 9 million Filipinos live abroad.[92] The Filipino government has actively promoted a culture of emigration. The government has long been producing and training a surplus of gendered workers, with women associated with the care sector and men working abroad as seamen. It has been estimated that about 85% of the country's nurses have left the Philippines.[93] Competition for the 4-year nursing degree is intense, and the cost high, resulting in many families making financial sacrifices to fund family members. The decision to migrate is usually a family decision. When the worker leaves to work abroad the extended family network, including grandparents, often take on the role of looking after the migrant's children. As a result migrants have a substantial degree of pressure to send remittances back to support and sustain a dependent family, and to save enough money to improve their children's upbringing.

In 2005 the top 6 destination countries included Saudi Arabia, the United Arab Emirates, Britain, Taiwan, Ireland, and the USA. When Filipino nurses started arriving through the work visa system in 2000, a staff nurse in Manila could earn approximately $200 per month, compared with approximately 10 times that in Ireland.[94] In addition to higher wages, Ireland also offered greater opportunities for career advancement, entry into Europe, and an English-speaking and Catholic culture that was cemented through connections with Irish missionaries. Filipinos in Ireland have the highest labour force participation rate of any group in Ireland. About 70% work in the health sector as nurses, midwives, and care assistants.[95]

Despite a similar national background and equally gendered form of work as domestic workers, there have generally been few reports of nurses experiencing workplace exploitation, though issues involving securing promotion exist.[96] The discrepancy can be explained by a number of factors. By contrast to domestic workers, nurses are in high skilled occupations, predominantly in the public sector, were on work visas (prior to green cards) that were given a 'stamp 4', had high levels of membership in strong unions such as the INOU, and their work is publicly visible. Moreover, they generally have English language competence and are informed of their rights and entitlements before they arrive in Ireland.

However, nurses have experienced forms of extra-workplace discrimination, particularly in relation to family life which, plays a central role in Filipino culture. Many were prevented from having their families join them in Ireland. Moreover, problems in securing work remained for those who had brought their spouses. The operation of dense transnational networks sharing information about these impediments to family life encouraged many Filipinos to emigrate elsewhere, particularly to countries offering better working and family conditions. This forced the Irish State and employment agencies to find an alternative source of labour, principally from Kerala in Southern India. Kerala also contained a large number of Catholic, English-speaking nurses willing to emigrate. This shift in sourcing is evident in the distribution of work visas given by the State which, after sourcing enough Filipino and Indian nurses, began to restrict the number of permits to non-EU workers after 2005 (see Figure 10.4).

Continuing pressure by Filipino and Indian nurses about family reunification rights eventually forced the State to allow spouses of those on work visas the

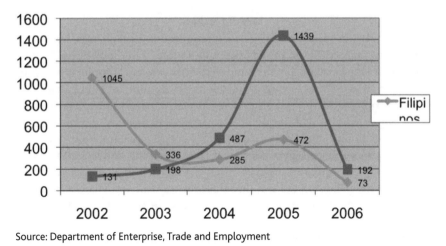

Source: Department of Enterprise, Trade and Employment

Figure 10.4 Share of non-agricultural incomes

right to work in 2004. Although spouses of visa holders did not have to undergo a labour market test they still had to acquire a work permit and wait several weeks for it to be processed. This deterred employers, who needed to fill a vacancy quickly, from giving them jobs. One Indian nurse commented about the difficulty of her husband finding a job: 'Yeah it's a big problem after coming here you know if you get some job in the papers and will advertise some jobs, so if we apply for that and if he gets selected sometimes the work permit is the big problem. So, my friend told me that her husband got a job as a security officer... but the problem was no work permit, so they refused the job' (Kumal, India). Family life for nurses on work visas was also problematic because of growing children. When a child reaches 18 they no longer qualify as dependants and have to leave the country.

Within the context of aggressive recruitment campaigns and better working and living conditions offered abroad, a recent study found that only 1 in 7 of those nurses interviewed intended to remain long-term in Ireland, with the majority citing issues such as citizenship and immigration procedures as the main reason given for leaving.[97]

State regulation and the enforcement of employment standards

A further factor shaping the level of migrant exploitation has been the State's failure to maintain and enforce labour standards, to employ an adequate amount of labour inspectors, to sanction and fine employers, and to provide accessible systems of redress for exploited workers.

Seeking redress

Migrant workers face a variety of factors preventing them from leaving an exploitative employer or reporting exploitation. This includes a lack of alternative employment, physical and verbal threats and intimidation by the employer, fear of not having a permit renewed and/or being deported, financial obligations to recruitment agencies or family members, lack of knowledge of rights and entitlements, language deficiency, dependence on accommodation if supplied by an employer, working in an individualized and isolated work context, lack of social and family support, and lack of financial resources for self-support. However, a lack of state support and protection plays a central role, including the inability to acquire a bridging visa if a permit is not renewed, or to claim social welfare because of the Habitual Residence Condition.

Migrant workers are unlikely to complain about employment violations for a number of reasons, because they are not in unions, or they are undocumented, or because of fear of reprisal,[98] especially if they work for smaller employers. Consequently those that seek redress usually do so after they have left their employment. Settling a complaint can be a long, protracted, and stressful process involving complex legislation.[99] A hearing for example, can involve 5 Acts or more including the Terms of Employment (Information Act) 1994 and 2001; Unfair Dismissals Acts 1977–2001; Employment Equality Act 1998 and 2004; Minimum Notice and Terms of Employment Acts 1973–2001; National Minimum Wage Act 2000; Organization of Working Time Act 1997; and Payment of Wages Act 1991. There are also a number of judicial bodies designed to deal with complaints including The Labour Relations Commission, The Equality Appeals Tribunal, The Labour Court and the Equality Tribunal. If a case is not informally resolved or settled it goes to a hearing, where the claimant usually requires a representative, sometimes translation facilities, and may need a (willing) witness and documentation that is difficult to secure. Although most cases are usually settled in favour of the claimants, the acute stress and time-consuming nature of the process dissuades many migrants from taking a case or seeing it through to the end. In a sample of 69 cases analysed by the Migrant Rights Centre Ireland, 17 took 6 months to one year and 30 over one year, to be finalized. A handful took over 2 years.[100] The waiting period for accessing redress in the Equality Tribunal has been exacerbated by the absence of language interpretation mechanisms in the Labour Relations Commission and Employment Appeals Tribunal. In addition, the need to financially support oneself during this period meant that some migrants withdrew their claims.

The main agency responsible for maintaining labour standards until 2007 was the Labour Inspectorate, then part of the DETE. However, as a state institution its investigating powers remained stiflingly weak. With inadequate staffing levels

– in 2001 there were only 17 inspectors – and a shortage of resources, morale in the Inspectorate was reported to be low. The Inspectorate pointed to a lack of staff, high staff turnover, a deficit of resources, inadequate training, lack of clarity in their role, poor legal support, and complex legislation as hampering their pursuit of exploitative employers.[101] Cases of employment abuse could also take up to 2 years to process.[102] This was recently highlighted in a case involving a migrant Bangladeshi working in a restaurant. When the worker, who was working 12 to 14 hours a day, paid 70 pence an hour, and sharing accommodation provided by his employers with 10 other waiters, made a complaint, the case took 2 years for the Inspectorate to investigate. In 2006 there were effectively only 14 inspectors working in the State, covering a workforce of over 2 million. The 50 dog wardens and 700 tax inspectors employed at the same time were indicative of the State's lack of concern in regulating employment standards.

Despite a growing number of reported cases of exploitation the number of inspections taking place has consistently fallen. In 2002 there were 8,323, inspections; by 2003 this had fallen to 7168, and 5160 by 2004. Moreover, these numbers exaggerate the number of workplace inspections actually taking place since investigations into an employer's records take place under various headings – such as the Minimum Wage Act or Organization of Working Time Act – so are therefore recorded as separate inspections. Hence of the 4225 inspections that took place in 2005 less than 1,800 employers were actually visited by the Inspectorate.

The Inspectorate also only has limited powers to sanction violating employers. The maximum fine it could impose on an errant employer in 2006 was €3,000[103] Rather than being mandated to fine or prosecute exploitative employers the main objective of the Inspectorate was instead to seek compliance and rectification of employment violations. Consequently, very few companies are fined or prosecuted. In 2002 from the 8,223 inspections carried out only 25 prosecutions were initiated; in 2003, 7,168; by 2004 this fell to 5,160 inspections

Table 10.2 Employment rights compliance inspections and prosecutions initiated, 2002–7 (to date)

Year	Inspections/Visits	Prosecutions Initiated
2002	8,323	25
2003	7,168	20
2004	5,160	14
2005	5,719	25
2006	15,885	8
2007 (to 12/10/07)	7,849	15

Source: Parliamentary Questions Vol. 640, No. 2, question 90: 24/10/2007

and 14 prosecutions, and despite an increase in inspections in 2006, only 8 prosecutions were initiated.

The number of prosecutions initiated and those carried to their conclusion also differed. Thus in 2006 despite 104 detections of companies found to be paying below the minimum wage only one actual prosecution took place.[104]

The lack of a punitive deterrence enabled companies to pay below minimum or standard wages until they were caught doing so, effectively fostering a culture within companies of 'wait and see'. Combined with the forces of capitalist competition this meant that if one company failed to pay statutorily agreed rates others were compelled to do so also in order to compete in market conditions, thereby precipitating 'a race to the bottom'.

The operation of business and political pro-business interests in the State ensured that the Inspectorate remained a powerless entity. Thus in 2004 following repeated calls for more manpower the Minister for Finance offered funds for the employment of 8 extra inspectors. However, the Minister for Enterprise, Trade and Employment, Mary Harney, a prominent Progressive Democrat, had this reduced to 4 extra inspectors, effectively turning down 4 extra workers for her own Department.[105] The State's pro-business agenda and low prioritization of labour rights was also reflected in the decision of the Minister of Enterprise, Trade, and Employment, Michael Martin, not to allocate additional resources to the Inspectorate immediately after the GAMA controversy. Instead, the budget of the Competitions Authority and Consumer Affairs was dramatically increased, the latter by 76%.[106]

However, following the Irish Ferries dispute, and in the context of signing a new social partnership agreement – Towards 2016 – the Irish Congress of Trade Unions demanded a major restructuring of the Labour Inspectorate. As a result, the Labour Inspectorate was replaced in February 2007 by a new independent agency, the National Employment Rights Authority (NERA). As part of the transformation the number of labour inspectors was to be increased to 90 and the maximum fines for employment transgressions increased to €250,000 and/or 3 years in prison. In addition to placing NERA on a legal footing, protective legislation for workers in terms of safeguarding the minimum wage and protecting them from unfair dismissal was to be implemented in the Employment Law Compliance Bill 2008 (ELCB). Celebrated by the union movement as a new era of rights for workers, the Bill incorporates many of the weaknesses affecting the Labour Inspectorate. By contrast to other European countries such as Spain, France, Germany, and Belgium, where employment rights are not based on immigrant status, monies owed to undocumented workers cannot be reclaimed by the Inspectorate. NERA also continues to operate with the policy of recovering monies owed to employees by issuing Compliance Notices rather than sanctioning employers with fines or penalties. Consequently in cases of exploitation: 'the inspector's main priority is to have the matter rectified.'[107] This effectively means that employers who fail to pay employees thousands of euros may not be fined for doing so. Moreover, employing 90 inspectors still does not provide an adequate number of staff to deal with a working population of over 2 million people.

The lack of monitoring by the state of employment violations, the effect of its work permit system in promoting exploitation, and its failure to create a fair and facilitative system of redress are manifestations of the State's consistent standpoint towards labour. With sustained resistance from employer organizations such as IBEC, the ELCB looks increasingly likely not to be passed, especially in a recessionary climate. Moreover, the number of labour inspectors has actually declined over the last two years with only 71 inspectors in place in 2010, a figure that is not set to rise because of a moratorium on recruitment.[108]

Trade unions

The politics of worker organization and trade unionism also plays a central role in explaining migrant labour employment and exploitation. In Ireland, the union movement has been indelibly shaped under the aegis of social partnership. The power and composition of unions has thereby changed dramatically over the last 30 years. The intensely competitive international economic context where average levels of pay and productivity differ between states, and where production is becoming increasingly outsourced, moved abroad, or new technologies developed, has been both shaped by and affected by union membership and activity. Global capitalist competition has necessarily engendered resistance and struggle in various places. However, despite an underlying ideology of internationalism, in practice unions have been organized predominantly on a national or sub-national level so that it has been increasingly difficult for them to get a foothold in processes unfolding at a transnational level.

In addition, the corporatist state that existed in a neo-Keynesian Fordist economic environment in the 1960s and 1970s has been replaced by a new increasingly neo-liberal state.[109] In the earlier phase trade union recruitment of migrants in European countries entailed a political struggle involving the equalization of the rights and entitlements of migrant workers with native workers. In the present conjuncture of lean production, global outsourcing, and a weakening in the potency of union strength, it has been in the opposite direction with indigenous workers moving towards the diminished rights and entitlements of migrant workers.

The Irish Ferries dispute in 2005 was emblematic of a process involving the use of migrant labour to undermine wages and conditions in the Irish economy. In 2004 Irish Ferries announced its plans to re-register its ships under a flag of convenience and to replace 543 staff on union rates with mostly eastern European workers from Latvia earning below the minimum wage. By laying off more than 400 workers and paying workers approximately €3.60 an hour the company sought to make €11 million in savings.[110] The move was rationalized in terms of increasing competition from airlines and other ferry services. However, its owners, Irish Continental, had an operating profit of €24 million in its ferries division and the company's 3 executive directors were paid a total of €1.25 million plus generous share options.[111] The company's attempt to generalize this cost-cutting package on its other ships in 2005 led to a series of strikes and the occupation of 2 ferries by crew members. With the agreement of Siptu, 400 Irish seafarers were nevertheless laid off and replaced by East European agency workers, recruited through a Cypriot-owned agency, and paid at the minimum wage of €7.65 – almost a third less than what they had been paid before. The company also received €4.3m towards the cost of redundancy payments from the Irish State. By acquiring a 'flag of convenience' from a country where labour laws were weak and minimum wages low, crew members became subject to that country's labour laws.[112]

The major interlocutors in the displacement debate were not only populist politicians, but also broadly left and liberal commentators. The then leader of the Labour Party, Pat Rabbitte, asserted: 'Displacement is going on in the meat factories and it is going on in the hospitality industry and it is going on in the building industry… we need to know more about the numbers coming here, the kind of work they are engaged in, the displacement effect, if any on other sectors.' He added: 'The time may be coming when we will have to sit down and examine whether we would have to look at whether a work permits regime ought to be implemented in terms of some of this non-national labor, even for countries in the European Union… There are 40 million or so Poles after all, so it is an issue we have to look at'.[113] Backed by unions,[114] a call to stop 'the race to the bottom' ensued that framed subsequent discourses about migrants. Such populist discourses referring to displacement often gave rise to feelings of racism and resentment in the labour movement.

The factors that made migrant workers vulnerable to exploitation and susceptible to accepting wage levels below the going rate remained undiscussed. This included their immigration status, knowledge of rights and entitlements, language proficiency, the wages and conditions in the country of their origin, and the low level of trade union representation and recruitment that existed in various sectors of employment. Rather, they were simply represented as a threat to Irish workers.

Union membership in Ireland is in steep decline dropping from 37.5% in 2003 to 31.5% in 2007. Despite falling union densities, it is primarily within sectors and occupations characterized by a trade union presence, that the de-socializing effects of capital have been partially mitigated. In Ireland there is generally a correspondence between wage levels in employment sectors, social protection, and trade union activity, particularly in the public sector.

The low level of migrant worker recruitment by Irish trade unions has been a crucial factor in explaining the high levels of exploitation effecting migrant workers. Despite constituting 1 in 6 of the workforce union recruitment of migrant workers has generally been low, though it is growing. Whereas union membership for Irish nationals stood at 36% in 2007 the corresponding figure for non-Irish nationals was only 13%.[115] The reasons for this uneven distribution are complex but a central factor is the location of migrants predominantly in the private sector where union membership has historically been low – 20% of those in the private sector in 2005 were in a union as compared to 85% in the public sector. But it is also an effect of labour migrant segmentation into specific occupational sectors, especially in secondary labour markets. These are sectors and occupations that are exposed to the harshest aspects of international competition, open to the vagaries of fluctuating labour supply and demand, and consequently characterized by poor incomes and working conditions. They are also sectors characterized by high staff turnover and temporary contracts and include agriculture, domestic work, food-processing, and the hospitality industry. Hence, the wholesale and retail, hotel and restaurants, and agriculture, forestry, and fishing sectors all have relatively high levels of a migrant presence, yet low levels of union density at 17%, 8% and 8% respectively.[116] Conversely, public sector employment in public administration and defence and education, for example, record low levels of migrants but high union density. The highest level of trade union membership was recorded in the public administration and defence sector, where almost 80% of employees were union members in 2007. Education had the second highest level of unionization standing at almost 60%, and also had one of the highest levels of annual earnings.

These patterns point to important questions concerning migrant recruitment. A number of structural and dispositional factors impact upon migrant membership of trade unions. State classification of legal status that produces differentiations between migrants and native workers can divide workers. The pervasiveness of state nationalistic discourses, banal forms of nationalism, and employer strategies can also solidify into caste-like relations that may cut across union attempts at fostering social solidarity, as can employer strategies:

> Migrant workers do the most menial jobs. Their chances of promotion are exceedingly poor. When they work in gangs, it is arranged that they work together with other foreigners. Equal working relations to indigenous workers are kept to a minimum. The migrant workers have a different language, a different culture and different short-term interests. They are immediately identifiable – not as

Table 10.3 Employment sector, migrant sectoral presence, union membership, and salary

NACE economic sector	Migrant sectorial presence (Census 2006)	Union membership (QNHS 2006)	Salary (National Employment Survey)
Agriculture, forestry and fishing	6.7%	7.1%	*
Other production industries	14.9%	33%	*
Construction	14.1%	23.8%	42,190
Wholesale and retail trade	12.5%	16.7%	28,813
Hotels and restaurants	31.7%	8.9%	22,139
Transport storage and communication	9.7%	46.3%	40,719
Financial and other business services	7.7%	21.2%	50,092
Public administration and defence	2.6%	78.7%	43,098
Education	5.8%	61.5%	45,792
Health	11.6%	48.3%	33,603
Other services	11.8%	16.9%	27,236

individuals, but as a group (or a series of national groups). As a group they are the bottom of every scale: wages, type of work, job security, housing, education, purchasing power.[117]

Indigenous workers can often therefore see migrants as inferior and different. As Berger notes, 'Different to the point of being unknowable'. This is not simply a strategy of divide and rule.

The presence of migrant workers, seen as intrinsically inferior and therefore occupying an inferior position in society confirms the principle that a social hierarchy – of some kind or another – is justified and inevitable… Once accepted, the principle of natural inequality gives rise to a fear: the fear of being cheated out of one's natural and rightful place in the hierarchy. The threat is thought of as coming from both above and below. The working class will become no less suspicious of the bosses. But they may become equally jealous of their privileges over those they consider to be their natural inferiors… When the indigenous worker accepts inequality as the principle to sustain his own self-esteem, he reinforces and completes the fragmentation which society is already imposing upon him.[118]

The concentration of migrants in 3-D sectors such as agriculture, construction, and hotel and restaurants characterized by seasonal work, or boom periods that are conducive to high staff turnover, can also prevent unions organizing. Language barriers, and the view that migrants are only here on a temporary basis – held both by the unions and the migrants themselves – also plays a key role. A fear of retribution from employers may also affect union membership. Finally, depending on their country of origin some migrants, especially those from former socialist states such as Poland or China, may be distrustful and suspicious towards what they associate with a repressive state apparatus.

It can be argued that the concentration of migrants in low unionized sectors may also result from social closure effected by native Irish workers in order to monopolize social and material resources in cases where migrants may be seen as threatening wages and conditions. There is some anecdotal evidence for this in the taxi industry, but this has to be contextualized within the context of profound levels of state deregulation and the ensuing competition this created. It is not, moreover, significant enough to generalize about on a national scale. Nevertheless, these processes point to the fact that the trade union movement in Ireland is a diverse and varied social institution with an ambiguous relationship to migrants. Although guided by an ethos and rhetoric of internationalizm, trade unions have in practice operated principally according to nationalist concerns. Over time European union movements have realized that such a strategy of 'blaming the migrant' is counterproductive, if not morally dubious, and have since been more willing – or seen it as a necessity – to include more migrants in their membership base.[119] In Ireland both ICTU and SIPTU have diverted resources towards recruiting migrants. The latter has appointed non-Irish nationals as union organizers and recruited over 15,000 migrants. The Irish Nurses Overseas Union has also successfully recruited a large number of migrant nurses through an active recruitment programme. Attempts are also underway in SIPTU to shift union recruitment towards a US SEIU model. In the US the SEIU recruited by stepping outside of the workplace and entering migrant community meeting places, such as churches and cultural organizations, where migrants tended to congregate, mix, and where relations of trust could be built. They also systematically targeted their recruitment in low paid and employment sectors with concentrations of migrant workers. Despite criticisms of a rigid, top-down approach, the SEIU has been at the forefront of successfully recruiting and representing undocumented workers. This entails an ideology in which exploitation in the workplace was seen as exploitation no matter whether the individual was an indigenous worker, on a work permit, or undocumented. However, other smaller unions in Ireland have been less willing to recruit migrants for a variety of reasons including a lack of political will, bureaucratic and organizational inertia, or because of a shortage of resources.[120]

Immigrants are not passive effects of processes of exploitation but, depending on their position in social space and social, cultural, and racial attributes, are positioned differently in terms of disempowerment. Although not collectively organized on a broad national scale or within a social movement, a number of migrant-led-organizations have formed.[121] There has also been a significant move of migrants into politics. In 2009 over 40 foreign candidates from over 13 countries stood in the Irish local elections. At the same time however, political mobilization has been extremely varied often depending on the country of origin of the migrant with moderately high levels of political organization of Filipino, Nigerian, and Polish nationals for example, as compared to migrants from China. Such levels of organization may alter over time.

Conclusion

Not all migrants experience exploitation. Nor are they passive dopes without agency. Nevertheless, because of the specific power configuration a considerable number, especially those in the lower skilled employment sectors, have suffered exploitation. It has been argued in this chapter that there are several complex and interlocking processes engendering and structuring the specific contours of migrant exploitation including capitalist competition, state classification, immigration status, but also trade union organization, gender, and ethno-racial discrimination.

Both the Irish State and the economy have undergone significant alteration over the past decade in terms of shifting towards a neo-liberal agenda. In order to attract investment and businesses the Irish State aggressively set out to cut taxes. In 2006 the business tax rate was just 12.5% while capital gains were taxed at 20%. There were no property taxes, and by international standards social security contributions were remarkably low.[122] Despite its increasing global openness to capital and market mechanisms the State has played a central role in constructing a flexible labour market. As the Minister of State with special responsibility for trade and commerce acknowledged when addressing the poor level of rights given to workers:

> It is important to get the balance right between rights and employment to ensure we are competitive so that the economy can grow and prosper, and create opportunity and employment. For that reason we need flexibility, which we have with the model we have with regard to the voluntarist approach and until recently a strong social partnership model that allowed us to sit down and discuss in a very mature fashion how to address workers' pay and conditions in addition to legislative support. On the other side, we need to be competitive in a globalized economy where there is competition coming from all over the world and from within the

EU itself. We need to strike that balance to ensure we have in place rights and protections, but we do not burden business to the point where it cannot compete and we lose jobs.[123]

The hierarchical stratification of migrant labour in terms of limited rights has been central to this. It is this paradox and fundamental structural contradiction between low taxation, free movement of goods and services, and the regulated and controlled movement of foreign workers which provides a necessary, though not sufficient, framework for understanding the broad factors underpinning migrant exploitation.

Social partnership has shifted the ideological terrain on which state, capital, and labour negotiate in favour of the former. At a structural level it has consolidated neo-liberal state policies. This can be seen in terms of the share of economy allocated to wages which fell from 78% between 1960 and 1970 to 62.3% between 1991 and 2000, falling even further to 54% between 2001 and 2007. Moreover, the share of the economy going to capitalists, the self-employed and landlords increased at the expense of wage earners between 1987 and 2004 (see Table 10.4).

Through conferring various legal migration statuses based on economic needs and sovereignty, the State has made migrant workers vulnerable to exploitation. What the existence of coerced migrant labour points to is not an aberration or a residue from former modes of production, but what Corrigan describes as a 'crucial supporting machinery for free wage labour' that is central to capitalism and its expansion.[124]

If the social state has failed to protect workers, by proving sufficient rights, resources, and information, then it becomes necessary for the labour movement to do so. However, migrants are largely located in sectors which are characterized by low levels of union density. Unions are only beginning to develop new forms of recruitment, but new conceptions of the role of migrant workers also require a strong move away from existing nationalist ideologies. As Harris notes:

> there is never a solid argument for a robust and unsentimental internationalism, an acknowledgement that the material conditions of life of the native-born depend upon the work of foreigners. At best there is a plea not to be unpleasant. Those with material concern with internationalism, the global businessmen and bankers,

Table 10.4 Share of non-agricultural incomes

	1987	1997	2004
Profits, rent and self employed earnings	30.7	43.7	48.1
Wages, pensions and social security	69.2	56.3	52.1

Source: CSO, National Income and Expenditure Annual Results for 2004

are not trusted to do more than advance their own narrow interests. Those who historically championed worker internationalism, the Marxists and socialists, have all too often retired into defending the old nationalism as the only way to defend the poor.[125]

It therefore remains a challenge for the labour movement to undertake a fundamental structural shift in its world-view and to see migrant workers as part of its future.

Despite the differences in the experiences of migrants many are generally at the bottom end of the socio-economic ladder. They share similar racialized disadvantages in terms of housing and educational opportunities, experience low standards of living, poverty, and social exclusion, and are equally targets of informal and institutional racism, discrimination, and hostility. As experience from elsewhere shows, migrants who are socially excluded or who are treated as second-class workers may retreat into self-enclosed ethno-national communities. These processes will be examined in the next chapter.

Notes

1 D. Harvey, *A Short History of neo-Liberalism* (Oxford: Oxford University Press, 2005).
2 K. Moody, *US Labour in Trouble and Transition*, p. 37.
3 P. Martin, The Recession and Migration, International Migration Institute, University of Oxford Working Papers 2009, p. 8.
4 K. Moody, *US Labour in Trouble and Transition*, p. 16.
5 Ibid.
6 A. Sayad, *The Suffering of the Immigrant*.
7 K. Allen, *Ireland's Economic Crash*, p. 38.
8 K. Allen, Double Speak: Neo-liberalism and migration.
9 The Bank of Ireland (2007), The Wealth of Ireland, www.eapn.ie/eapn/wp-content/uploads/2010/04/Bank-of-Ireland-Wealth-of-Nation-Report-2007.pdf.
10 P. Tansey, *Productivity: Ireland's economic Imperative* (Dublin: Microsoft, 2005) Tables 20 and 21.
11 CSO, *Measuring Ireland's Progress, 2008* (Dublin: Stationery Office, 2009).
12 ESRI, Layte et al., 2008.
13 Cited in Harris, *The New Untouchables*, p. 29.
14 CSO, *National Employment Survey 2006*.
15 CEITT, Annual report, *The agency work industry around the world* (2009), www.ciett.org/fileadmin/templates/ciett/docs/Agency_work_industry_around_the_world_-_2009_Edition.pdf.
16 Peck, J and N. Theodore, Flexible recession: the temporary staffing industry and mediated work in the United States, *Cambridge Journal of Economics* 2007, 31, 171–92: p. 172.
17 Dail Debates, 25 February 2010.
18 Siptu, *Justice for Agency Workers* (Dublin: Siptu, 2007), p. 5.

19 Conroy and Pierce, *The European Foundation's for Improvement of Living and Working Conditions*, 2006, p. 2.

20 Debates, 25 February 2010.

21 Peck, J. and N. Theodore, Flexible recession.

22 Brendan McGinty, Director IBEC, *The Irish Times*, 20 February 2008.

23 Corrigan, Feudal relics or capitalist monuments, p. 73.

24 Labour Relations Commission, Migrant Workers and Access to the Statutory Dispute Resolution agencies, October 2005, p. 12.

25 MRCI *Annual report, 2007*.

26 A. Barrett and McCarthy, The earnings of Immigrants in Ireland, Results from the 2005 EU Survey of Income and Living Conditions (Dublin: ESRI, 2007).

27 Barrett and McCarthy, The earnings of Immigrants in Ireland, Results from the 2005 EU Survey of Income and Living Conditions, ESRI, p. 1.

28 M. Ruhs, Managing the immigration, p. 15.

29 *Irish Times*, 22 January 2001.

30 *Irish Times*, 5 July 2001.

31 *A Seventh Man*, p. 58.

32 MRCI, *Annual Report 2006*.

33 E. Quinn and G. Hughes, *The impact of Migration on European Societies: Ireland* (Dublin: ESRI, 2004).

34 Under the system a work visa could be acquired abroad from an Irish embassy or consulate by producing a valid job offer from an Irish employer.

35 Spouses of visa holders had to apply for a work permit though they did not have to undergo a labour market test.

36 2005: 33.

37 Berger, *A Seventh Man*, p. 141.

38 T. Hammar, *Democracy & the Nation State*.

39 Barrett, McGuinness, O'Brien, 2008: 1.

40 CSO, *National Employment Survey 2006*.

41 ESRI, 2007.

42 P. Anderson, *The Old New World* (London: Verso, 2009) p. 55.

43 J. Costello, *Irish Times,* 19 March 2009.

44 CSO, *National Employment Survey 2006*.

45 Labour Relations Commission, *Migrant Workers and Access*, p. 13.

46 MRCI, *Annual Report, 2006*, p. 10.

47 NERA, Quarterly, issue 4: 2008.

48 EGFSK, The role of migration, p. 91.

49 Ibid.

50 Calculations published by the Department of Agriculture and Food.

51 This has been with the support of Teagasc and Bord Bia and grants from the Department of Agriculture and Food.

52 CSO QHNS, 2008.

53 Bord Bia, www.bordbia.ie/industryinfo/hort/pages/default.aspx.

54 MRCI, *Harvesting Justice* (Dublin: MRCI, 2006), p. 4.

55 Ibid.

56 S. Ortiz and S. Aparicio, Management response to the demands of global fresh fruit markets: Rewarding harvesters with financial incentives, *The Journal of Development Studies*, vol. 42(3), pp. 446–68, April (2006).

57 B. Rogaly, Intensification of work-place regimes in british horticulture: the role of migrant workers, *Population, Space and Place*, 14 (6) (2008) p. 504.

58 MRCI, *Harvesting Justice* (Dublin: MRCI, 2006).

59 Ibid.

60 *Irish Times*, 7 April 2007.

61 MRCI, 2008.

62 *Irish Times*, 19 January 2006.

63 In 2005 a 14-year-old boy died of hydrogen sulphide poisoning while visiting his mother on a farm in Co. Cavan. MRCI, *Harvesting Justice*.

64 Ibid., p. 20.

65 EGFSN, 2005.

66 P. Martin, The Recession and Migration, p. 7.

67 CSO, Construction and Housing, 2008.

68 Labour Relations Commission, Annual Report 2006 (Dublin: LRC, 2007).

69 *Irish Times*, 28 March 2006.

70 *Irish Times*, 15 March 2005; Mick Barry, *We Are Workers, Not Slaves – The Story of the GAMA Struggle* (Dublin: Socialist Party, 2006).

71 *Irish Times*, 18 May 2005.

72 M. Barry, *We are Workers*, p. 16.

73 CSO, Census 2006.

74 Ibid.

75 United Nations, FPA, 2006: 24.

76 A. Hochschild, Global care chains and emotional surplus value, in Hutton, W. and Giddens, A. (eds) *On The Edge: Living with Global Capitalism* (London: Jonathan Cape, 2000), p. 130.

77 CSO, *Women and Men in Ireland, 2007*.

78 Women's income in 2005 was around two-thirds of men's income. CSO Women and Men, 2007.

79 S. O'Sullivan, Gender and the workforce, in S. O'Sullivan (ed), *Contemporary Ireland: a Sociological Map*, 2007.

80 EGFSN, 2005.

81 Human Rights Watch, 2004a.

82 B. Anderson, Discussion paper: illegality and domestic work. Centre on Migration, Policy and Society, University of Oxford, COMPAS, April (2005), www.compas.ox.ac.uk.

83 Barrett and McCarthy, 2007, The earnings of Immigrants in Ireland, results from the 2005 EU Survey of Income and Living Conditions, ESRI, 1.

84 M. Ruhs, *Managing Immigration*.

85 MRCI, *Private Homes: A Public Concern: The Experience of 20 Migrant Women Employed in the Private Home in Ireland* (Dublin: MRCI, 2004) p. 14.

86 *Irish Times*, 13 February 2008.

87 NESC, p. 179.

88 *Irish Times*, 3 March 2000.

89 *Irish Examiner,* 13 February 2008.

90 *Irish Times*, 13 February 2008.

91 P. Conroy and M. Pierce, p. 22.

92 *Irish Times*, 29 January 2008.

93 *Irish Times*, 23 January 2008.

94 *Irish Times*,18 July 2000.

95 CSO, *Non-Irish Nationals in Ireland.*

96 *Getting On.*

97 *Irish Times*, 13 February 2008.

98 Comhairle, 2006 Employment Rights: 6.

99 MRCI, *Accessing Redress for Workplace Exploitation: The Experience of Migrant Workers* (Dublin: MRCI, 2007), p. 21.

100 Ibid., p. 23.

101 *Irish Times*, 8 May 2005.

102 *Irish Times*, 10 June 2003.

103 *Irish Times*, 20 March 2006.

104 See Parliamentary Question No. 112 answered with Question No. 79, 24 October 2007.

105 *Irish Times*, 15 April 2005.

106 *Irish Times*, 18 November 2005.

107 http://www.employmentrights.ie/en/media/Guide%20to%20Inspections%20pdf.pdf.

108 *Irish Examiner*, 12 January 2010.

109 Harvey, *A Short History of Neoliberalism.*

110 *Irish Times*, 15 December 2005.

111 *Irish Times*, 3 December 2005.

112 As Shelley notes: 'The shipping industry is rife with extreme exploitation and, indeed, forced labour. By its nature the industry is international, and ship owners have been able to use this to their advantage. A vessel may be owned in one country, "flagged" in another, operated by a company in a third country, and crewed by an agency based in a fourth using seafarers from a number of countries. It may then ply its trade between a whole different set of countries. This makes the enforcement of minimum labour standards a challenge.' *Exploited,* pp. 86–7.

113 *Irish Times*, 3 January 2006.

114 The President of Siptu, Jack O'Connor, welcomed Rabbitte's remarks as 'helpful' and 'timely' (040106).

115 CSO, QHNS, 2008.

116 CSO, QHNS, 2008.

117 Berger and Mohr, *A Seventh Man*, p. 139.

118 Ibid., pp. 140–1.

119 R. Penninx, R. and J. Roosblad (eds) *Trade Unions, Immigration, and Immigrants in Europe, 1960–1993. A Comparative Study of the Attitudes and Actions of Trade Unions in Seven West European Countries* (New York/Oxford: Berghahn Books, 2000).

120 T. Krings, Equal rights for all workers: Irish trade unions and the challenge of labour migration, *Irish Journal of Sociology*, 2007.

121 A Feldman, Immigrant Civic Mobilisation, in B. Fanning (eds) *Immigration and Social Change in the Republic of Ireland* (2007).

122 Tony Killeen, Minister of State for Labour Affairs, speech at the launch of jobs Ireland New York, 20 October 2006.

123 Dail debates, 25 February 2010.

124 P. Corrigan, Feudal relics or capitalist monuments, p. 63.

125 N. Harris, *The New Untouchables*, p. 20.

Chapter 11

Racism and integration in Ireland

This chapter examines two closely related processes in Ireland, integration and racism. It begins by looking at the problematic nature of racism, how it has been theorized and how it can be understood in the Irish context. The second part of the chapter then provides a socio-genesis of the concept of integration before looking at ideological problems associated with the concept and suggesting how, if at all, it might be operationalized.

Racism and ethno-racial domination in Ireland

As is the case in most European states immigration has not been welcomed by everyone. It has been argued by some commentators that it is immensely unpopular, with only 19% of Europeans seeing it as good for their country and with 57% of Europeans arguing that there are 'too many foreigners'. In Ireland 78% want to reimpose restrictions on Eastern European immigration.[1] Tensions between in-groups and out-groups are a sociological universal. The levels of racism in Ireland should not, however, be exaggerated. A far-right anti-immigrant party has yet to emerge and unlike nearly all other European and North American states, Ireland has not been strongly affected by post 2001 anti-Muslim rhetoric. However, racism and discrimination against travellers has been a long-standing feature of Irish society. Despite Ireland's tourist-orientated national self-image as a welcoming, hospitable nation, levels of racism directed towards migrants undoubtedly exist.

The murder of a Chinese language student in Dublin in 2001 was considered to be the first fatal death resulting from racism, the death of a Nigerian boy in 2010 the most recent. In a survey carried out in the same year, almost 80% of individuals from black or ethnic minority groups living in Ireland claimed they had experienced some form of racism or discrimination whilst living here.[2] Many of these discriminatory attacks were not one-off or incidental occurrences.[3] Rather, they constituted a feature of everyday life occurring in a multiplicity of social situations: in pubs, from neighbours, in banks, on buses and taxis, with regard to housing, at school, and even at the cinema.[4] More recent reports have suggested that this level of discrimination has not diminished.[5] A study carried out by the EU's Fundamental Rights Agency in 2008 found that Ireland was among the worst 5 countries in the EU when it came to racial discrimination and abuse. It also noted the operation of racial hierarchies. 73% of those surveyed from Sub-Saharan Africa stated they had experienced racism in Ireland, as opposed to 25% of those from central and Eastern Europe.[6] Cases taken on race grounds have also been increasing. In 2005 there were 82 such cases lodged with the Equality Tribunal. In 2008, 359 such cases were lodged out of a total of 842. Racism affects adults and children alike. A survey by the Teachers Union of Ireland found that 1 in 4 teachers were aware of racist incidents in their school over a period of a month.[7] More qualitatively orientated studies have confirmed the statistical prevalence of racism in the country.[8] As one immigrant from Nigeria noted: 'If they could find a means of hijacking you and sending you back to your country, they would have done it. Just imagine when we go for shopping, they will come and meet you. "You f**king black stupid thing, get out of this place, you go back your f**king country"' (Abassi, Nigeria). Though a large amount of racism is directed at Africans, immigrants from Asia, including China and India, also noted significant levels of racism: 'If I walk in O'Connell Street in the middle of the night, maybe some drunk man will shout at you, "Chinese b******d" (Ho, China).[9] In research on the integration of Indian nationals one Sikh student from India, wearing a turban, reported experiencing abuse every day of the 3 years he had spent in Ireland.

There is also a significant degree of underreporting of racism. A European-wide survey found that 82% of respondents who said they had been discriminated against did not report their experience of racism and had various reasons for not doing so: a feeling that nothing would happen or change by reporting the incident, a belief it was too trivial and that it happened so often that it was normal, a fear of negative consequences of reporting, the bureaucratic inconvenience involved, language impediments, insecurities including having an undocumented status, and not knowing how or where to report the incident.[10] In Ireland there are few formal mechanisms in place to report experiences of racism; the closing down of state agencies such as the NCCRI, which was one of the few national mechanisms for recording incidents of racism, compounded the problem. Moreover, the high level of discrimination experienced from the Gardai to whom migrants are expected to report racist abuse has also acted as a deterrent.[11] The 2001 Amnesty report indicated Gardai were the second highest source of racist discrimination and the European Union Minorities and Discrimination Survey (2009) found that Sub-Saharan Africans were twice as likely to be subject to police stops as other members of the public, the highest stoppage rate in the EU.[12]

Migrant workers have also been hindered from accessing employment and certain occupations because of racism and discrimination. Non-Irish nationals are 3 times more likely to experience discrimination while looking for work, while it is estimated that black people are 7 times more likely.[13] Moreover, once in the workplace, non-Irish nationals are twice as likely to experience discrimination as Irish nationals.[14] 32% of work permit holders reported experiencing harassment and insults in the workplace, constituting the second most common form of discrimination.[15]

Explaining racism is inordinately complex and difficult. There are perhaps fewer areas in the social sciences where the degree of political and ethical involvement in the sociological stance is as high. Given the history of violent practices and forms of domination which have resulted from racist or discriminatory ideologies and the liberal moral opprobrium that has subsequently become attached to racism, few individuals or groups, including political parties and social movements, willingly accept the label 'racist'. Emotionally charged discussions also involve contested definitions and applications of the term racism, which has changed meaning through time and history. Though first used in the 1930s the term is inextricably tied up with the notion of 'race' that emerged in the 16th century. 'Race' originally referred to lineage, breed, or common descent, and identified a population with a common origin and history.[16] Its meaning changed significantly following the development of scientific discourses utilizing the term as an explanatory concept in the 18th century. The hierarchical division of humanity into a number of races paradigmatically expressed in Linneaus's four-fold classification introduced in *Systema Naturae* in 1735 was premised on a form of biological determinism in which race determined an individual's social, psychological, and cultural characteristics and capacities. For most of the late 18th century and early 19th century race classifications were based on the phenotypical characteristics that included skin colour, hair type, size of lips, and nose shape, but also an emphasis upon the dimensions of the skull.[17] Although the number of races varied, reflecting and rationalizing an age of imperialism, colonialism, and slavery, Africans were invariably placed at the bottom of the racial hierarchy. In its starkest formulation dark-skinned Africans associated with negative moral traits were contrasted with white-skinned Europeans correlated with virtue and civilization. These conceptions of race, reproduced in the work of various influential philosophers such as Kant, Lock, Hume, and Herder, fed into, reinforced, and became interchangeable with exclusionary notions of nationhood and ethnicity.

A major shift in the understanding of racism following the Second World War, Nazism, and the emergence of post-colonial discourse. Together with the rise of population genetics there occured an expansion and proliferation of liberal democratic values emphasizing formal equality, equal opportunity, and colour blindness. It has been argued that modern forms of racism are less concerned with fixed and hierarchical biological and somatic criteria but rather cultural processes and attributes. 'Race' is no longer explicitly mentioned but its biological associations are instead presupposed in the background of a national–cultural discursive formation[18] and in coded discussions of nationhood. 'Race' has become what Whorf calls a 'hidden category' that is re-encoded into national and cultural differences. Old biological conceptions of race are now increasingly articulated through new forms of cultural racism.[19] Although there has been a tilt in the balance between these 2 forms of racism the conceptual and sequential distinction between biological superiority and culture differentialism racism is overstated in most academic discussions. Although scientifically discredited the concept of race and phenotypical markers continue to demarcate races in everyday discourses. As Rattansi argues:

> generalizations, stereotypes and other forms of cultural essentialism rest and draw upon a wider reservoir of concepts that are in circulation in popular and public culture. Thus, the racist elements of any particular proposition can only be judged by understanding the general context of public and private discourses in which ethnicity, national identifications, and race coexist in blurred and overlapping forms without clear demarcations.[20]

The concept of racism has therefore become increasingly expansive. Its current usage remains analytically indistinguishable from prejudice, discrimination, ethnocentrism, and xenophobia. Moreover, in academic discussions it has merged with debates concerning ethnicity, ethnocentrism, identification, and belonging. Because of this proliferation in meanings some commentators have suggested that rather than a singular form of racism, historical evidence points to the existence of a multiplicity of racisms that manifest themselves in complex and varied ways.[21] However, others have suggested that the term should be abandoned outright and replaced for example by 'an analytics of racial domination'.[22] For Wacquant, this would disaggregate some of its confused overlapping mechanisms including:

> categorization (including classification, prejudice, and stigma), discrimination (differential treatment based on imputed group membership), segregation (group separation in physical and social space), ghettoization (the forced development of parallel social and organizational structures), and racial violence (ranging from interpersonal intimidation and aggression, to lynching, riots and pogroms, and climaxing with racial war and extermination).

He adds: 'these basic mechanisms of *ethno-racial subordination* enter into mobile combinations in different societies and during different periods within the same society so that at any point each group is confronted with a particular profile *of racial domination*'.[23]

Wacquant's important theoretical intervention reflects both the proliferating unreflexive use of the term 'racism', and an increasingly culturally orientated understanding of it. Equally, discussions of ethno–racial domination in the sociology of race in Ireland have been dominated by questions of culture, subjective identity, and representation or what can be labelled 'culturalism'. In the social sciences historical analyses of social relations and material processes have correlatively receded since the late 1970s, following what Gustav Bergmann calls the 'linguistic turn' in philosophy. Two developments have been of special significance: first, the development of cultural studies, which had its roots in the work of Richard Hoggart, E.P. Thompson, and Raymond Williams, and reached maturity in the work of Stuart Hall and the Birmingham School of Cultural Studies. Second, philosophical discourses have converged in espousing a 'differentialist turn', challenging the centralizing and homogenizing claims of the nation-state and Western Enlightenment universalism and natural law thought styles. Radical post-structuralist, deconstructive analyses, and postcolonial theory (for example in the work of Bhabba, Said, Weivorka, Henry Gates, and Spivak) became hegemonic during the 1990s. Though acknowledging material social relationships (the British cultural turn was heavily influenced initially by Gramsci, and post-colonial thinkers such as Spivak readily acknowledge Marx), there has over time been an increasing emphasis on textualism, signification, semiotics, encoding, and decoding. This is reflected in the emergence of a new conceptual vocabulary which emphasizes difference, diversity, hybridity, syncretism, intersectionality, alterity, cultural pluralism, identity, and Otherness.

There were, of course, social and intellectual reasons for this intellectual shift. The rise of new social movements, as well as the collapse of the USSR, led to a new focus on identity politics. There were also attempts to move away from what were considered essentialist and class reductionist analyses of social life. But these twin processes were overlain by what Bourdieu (1979) calls the 'scholastic view' or *skole*, resulting from a failure to engage in sociological reflexivity. There was no acknowledgement that the intellectualist bias inherent in the scholarly gaze of the modern academic was being imposed onto the object studied – hence a preoccupation with language, symbols, and meaning. These were the essential tools and components of the academic standpoint but they had a distorting effect once substituted for an analysis of the broader world of social practices. The new writing on racism and immigration in France and the USA particularly, borrowed heavily from abstract French post-structuralist philosophy. The concept of 'Otherness', for example, has its intellectual roots in Husserl's discussion on the impossibility of gaining access to another's consciousness in the fifth Cartesian Meditation, before being developed by Levinas in *Totality and Infinity*, and later incorporated within Derrida's discussion of 'violent hierarchies' which was itself shaped by the Algerian War.[24] Rather than adopting a sociological reflexivity towards these concepts (as opposed to the self-reflexivity involved in acknowledging one's social position and location in the social world in terms of gender, ethnicity etc.), writers and migration experts in Ireland uncritically adopted this framework in their analyses and understandings of racism and immigration. Consequently, a large number of the articles and chapters in a variety of major edited works on racism and immigration in Ireland focused on the discursive construction of a narrow sense of Irishness and identity, and its concomitant engendering of Otherness.[25] These analyses have tended to concentrate on interrogating the homogenous and exclusionary construction of national discourses of Irish identity as white, settled, and Catholic. Such a restrictive notion of identity, it is argued, militates against the construction of a more inclusive and encompassing notion of a multi-ethnic Ireland by stigmatizing or racializing an 'out-group' or 'Other'. The solution to such exclusionary definitions and processes is to either reduce power differentials in Irish society, or to celebrate diversity, difference, and hybridity. The majority of the various theoretical frameworks contained in these works can be accommodated within 2 broad positions: first, those post-modern positions which rightly emphasize power and racialization; and second, those liberal positions which focus on the importance of celebrating diversity, multiculturalism, and pluralism.[26] Notwithstanding their divergent conceptual frameworks in relation to power, both of these broad positions share an emphasis on difference and diversity and also an analytic framework which approaches racism through a Self–Other, Us–Them dynamic. Thus, typically, it is suggested that 'Othering – denying equal legitimacy to individuals and cultures that do not conform to one's own arbitrary, ever shifting criteria of normality – is a two sided coin. On the one hand it creates a clearly defined undifferentiated "them"… On the other, it forges a bond of solidarity.'[27] Or that 'we cannot understand Irish racism, or the Irish racialization of the Other, without understanding the racialization of the Irish self'.[28]

The singular emphasis on the construction of Irish identity, Otherness and diversity is problematic for a number of reasons. First, such an analysis fails to explain why these self–other or 'us–them' processes emerge in the first place, and therefore remains at the level of description rather than explanation. Although questions of racialization as a subset of themes of Othering are insightfully discussed, there seems to be little analysis of the rationale underlying these processes of group-making and the socio-historical triggers which engender this. There are some exceptions which are found in the most interesting of the available works, but these rationalizations for group formation are pitched at a very high level of generality and point to endemic tendencies in the broad abstraction of 'modernity' to exclude Others,[29] or to restrictive forms of ethnic nationalism.[30] All European societies as modern societies which need to 'Other' are simply painted as racist without examining the different racial inequalities between these societies and the concrete socio-economic mechanisms which explain these differences. Processes of racialization are uneven, complex, and historically determined. Earlier processes of racialization had a significant class dimension so that peasants and workers had been racialized as an inferior race or a 'breed apart' by middle-class and aristocratic groups in their construction of racial typologies. Whether and which groups are racialized, and the intensity and extent of negative evaluative judgements associated with a race, vary historically. Who is included in racial categories, and the number of categories that exist, has also shifted over time. And a group racialized in one context may become de-racialized in another, as the experience of Irish and Jewish immigrants in the USA shows. Post-modern and liberal standpoints have disarticulated the social and economic conditions of the emergence of forms of signification and racialization. As Hall himself noted in his earlier writings: 'the question is not whether men-in-general make perceptual distinctions between groups with different racial or ethnic characteristics, but rather, what are the specific conditions which make this form of distinction socially pertinent, historically active'.[31] Signification of 'Otherness', as a basis for racialization and racism, can have effect and meaning only within determinate economic and political relations of social domination. Such perceptual and cognitive distinctions are made by embedded individuals in the real world, in their practices and in their struggles over symbolic and material resources. Language as a practice, as Wittgenstein rightly notes, is always embedded in other, broader practices or forms of life.[32]

Secondly, the exclusive focus on difference and Otherness in these analyses ignores the contradictory attitudes – or what Gramsci calls contradictory common sense[33] – which many in the indigenous population have towards immigrants. Far from a general fear about difference, these include more specific concerns about competition for scarce resources, maintaining status and distinction, jobs, and pay levels. But these can often co-exist with feelings of mutual identification and humanitarian concern towards asylum-seekers and migrants and their social condition. Resentment built up through people's own experience of employment finds an outlet in attacks on 'spongers' who are defined precisely by their ability to escape the constraints of work. However, the generalized identification of immigrants – rather than, say, tax-avoiding entrepreneurs or establishment politicians – as 'spongers' is itself a function of a specific political conjuncture. The crucial point here is to avoid analytically transmuting the complex and contradictory attitudes of the indigenous population into a flattened metaphysical formula about a 'fear or dislike of the Other' – but rather to analyse these responses empirically within their specific social context.

Thirdly, there is also often a prevalent and unwarranted idealism in the focus on racism conceived as a 'discourse' or 'narrative', rather than seeing racist discrimination as a manifestation of material and symbolic practices, embedded simultaneously in institutions and bodies.[34]

Fourthly, some of these approaches have tended to focus singularly on questions of individual prejudice: how some individuals have a pronounced dislike of other individuals be it because of ignorance or seeing them as a social threat. However, what is perceived at the individual level has to simultaneously be understood at the group or social level in terms of group stigmatization.[35] Stigmatization of individual migrants presupposes migrants have considered collectively as inferior. The need and ability to treat migrants as inferior to themselves and to engage in collective national identification through social closure are not explicable by looking at the individual personality structure of those who discriminate, but has to be understood in terms of broader material and social processes.

There are also specific problems with each of these in positions. In terms of the post-modern standpoint, power is seen as de-centred into a host of social spaces. As a result, there appears to be little common ground from which to develop a strategy to oppose racism that involves the majority of the indigenous population. With reference to the standard liberal positions, state, church, and media discourses emphasize the values of diversity and pluralism while packaging it within the framework of 'interculturalism'. Interculturalism was the National Consultative Committee on Racism and Interculturalism's preferred term to designate cultures which interact with one another. This body, predominantly funded by the DJELR before its very recent abolition, stressed the idea of a partnership between NGOs, employers, the unions, and the state to challenge racism. There was, however, little recognition that some of these groups might actually benefit from racism. Thus a recent NCCRI publication on diversity at work simply assumes that the business 'community' has an automatic interest in eliminating racism. It was further assumed that a harmonious immigration policy could be created which took into account 'the long term (as opposed to event driven) national security concerns; the broad socio-economic concerns of migrants and broad human rights/equality concerns… and the medium to long term needs of the economy (as opposed to annual fluctuation).'[36] Equally the National Action Plan against racism operated largely on a discursive level far removed from everyday concrete struggles and racist encounters. The State's insistence that it is acting as an agent for eliminating racism was systematically undercut by the exclusionary and racist policies and practices it produced at the same time.

Instead of following these approaches, an analysis attentive to the practices of division and the mechanisms that ensure the reproduction of ethno-racial subordination and domination in Ireland is necessary. This entails a stronger focus on economic and state processes. However, this is not to simply reverse the continuing shift away from the economy, politics, culture, and identity. One would have to problematize these clear-cut analytical distinctions in the first place. Rather, it is to understand these processes within capitalism as a *whole*, and in all their interconnections. The aim is to shift the paradigm for understanding processes of ethno-racial domination towards a more broadly conceived and multilevelled cultural materialist framework that acknowledges the role of economic power, but one that also recognizes struggles for status and recognition.

Loosely stated racism can be defined as any beliefs or practices that attribute negative characteristics to any group or persons either intentionally or unintentionally on the basis of their supposed 'race' or ethnicity within the context of differential relations of power. The notion of racism then functions as a generic concept: it suggests what particular social actions and practices may have in common. The term refers to the representation of the cultures and ways of life of black and ethnic minorities as inferior, or as a threat to the culture of the dominant group in society. In this sense, racism can also be seen as an exclusionary practice which occurs when a specific group is shown to be in unequal receipt of social and material resources and services. Processes of racism also often intersect with other forms of discrimination based on gender for example.

Central to the relations between established indigenous white Irish citizens and migrant newcomers is not the characteristics of the groups themselves – given the wide range of differences and similarities, the selection of what is deemed similar or different is relatively arbitrary though historically physical or normative-cultural differences have dominated as markers of distinction – but the difference in the power ratio between these groups, the way they are bonded together, and their degree of organization.[37] It is the configuration of their social relationships as aspects of a power differential, and not their physical characteristics per se, that explains the relationship of domination. Social stigmas are transformed and reified through material stigmas relating to the body, skin-colour or innate biological characteristics or pinned on cultural traits. These are then given force and articulated through nationalist discourses which themselves draw on collective fantasies and emotional forms of identification. In Ireland a specific variant of Irish nationalism developed into Irish racism. The state, media, and various intellectuals were especially important in facilitating this through an authoritarian populism expressed in campaigns that vilified asylum-seekers or portrayed immigrants as threatening Irish identity and culture or displacing jobs.

It is useful to analytically distinguish between overt individual or group racisms and institutional racisms. Racism operates at an individual or group level, and an institutional level. It is simultaneously an attribute of social structures and personality structures. Individual or direct forms of racism, we highlighted above, can range from verbal name-calling to violent physical abuse. By contrast, institutional forms of racism refer to the intentional and unintentional effects of institutional actions, i.e. policies and practices that are discriminatory towards or indifferent to the needs and requirements of minority ethnic groups including migrant workers. Institutional racism entails examining discrimination at the level of the state, its structure, its cultural and institutional assumptions, and how it operates – including state inaction which can de facto lead to discriminatory and racist outcomes. In Ireland, there is increasing evidence of racism in the delivery of public services.[38] This is not only from state frontline service providers, especially those working in immigration, the police and GNIB in terms of law enforcement and a disproportionate attention focused on individuals from minority ethnic groupings, but also in social and welfare offices that have high levels of discretion in issuing welfare payments and in applying the Habitual Residence Condition.

The distinction between the two structural and individual processes is somewhat arbitrary and variable, but the two are integrally linked since they both presuppose differential power relations and individuals socially positioned in differentiated ways. Groups that have the power to define the social world including politicians, businessmen, state bureaucrats, and the media have a strong influence in shaping how racism emerges on the ground so to speak. The 30-year delay between signing the CERD (UN Committee on the Elimination of Racial Discrimination) convention and is ratification is an indication of the Irish State's indifference to racism.[39] Its unwillingness to produce anti-racist legislation, and its discriminatory and selective immigration policy and practices, the racial profiling effectively sanctioned in the Immigration Act of 2004, and a failure to systematically collect basic data on racist incidents, are more indicative of its stance towards racism than its ill-conceived and under-funded National Action Plan Against Racism launched in 2005, which had little practical effect and which remained at variance with more general state practice.

Racial distinctions permit the creation of not only symbolic and material barriers, but also emotional barriers rigidifying the antagonistic relations between groups. Social superiority engenders the gratifying euphoria and emotional rewards that go with the consciousness of belonging to a group of higher value or possessing a higher status. The power differential allows the stigma to stick without counter-assertion, and for the discrimination to have added effect or to 'bite into' the immigrants.[40] Racial discrimination is not targeted exclusively to 'people of colour'. Yet, the hierarchical racial ordering of different human categories in Ireland means that racial domination and its operation is varied. There are elements of intra-racial and ethnic hostility and discrimination between the immigrant nationalities such as that between Polish and Chinese nationals, or Lithuanians and Nigerians. For example, as one Lithuanian interviewee talking about immigrants and social welfare stated: 'Give someone a chance. There was a moment in Ireland when people from Nigeria were coming here giving birth, to 3, 4, 5 kids and living on social benefit' (Anna). There is, as Wacquant rightly notes, an inadequate sociological understanding of:

> the differential impact of racial imposition upon the collective psychology of the
> dominated and of the suffusive sociological ambivalence characteristic of the

position and disposition of intermediate groupings. It is as if revealing that subjugated categories also have their own ethno-racial distinctions would tarnish them and blunt their critique of racial domination. This tendency is particularly pronounced today due to the reviviscence of populist epistemologies that accord on principle a privileged cognitive status to the putative concerns and viewpoints of the subordinate.[41]

The socio-dynamics underlying processes of social closure in which more powerful groups have a self-image of themselves as better has both a material and symbolic dimension. We therefore need to examine dynamic and shifting concrete socio-historical processes to understand the underlying rationale for various forms of group-making and boundary construction based on ethnic and racial boundaries. This involves looking at state discourses and symbolic classifications. But it also entails examining and explaining broad socio-economic forces and class conditions, as well as the concrete and material relations and practices through which racial division and ranking and inequality becomes inscribed and embedded in the social order. Sociological analysis needs to move away from phenomenal forms of analysis that focus simply on racialisation and skin colour. The focus instead needs to be on broader underlying social and power relations including class relations. This does not mean ignoring race as a social marker but involves looking at its articulation with class conditions.

The recent development of contemporary Irish society is inherently paradoxical. At the same time as producing unprecedented wealth, it has created extreme forms of poverty and social marginalization. The growing gap between rich and poor has also been reflected in other social processes, for instance the emergence of a two-tier health system and growing numbers of homeless people. Government policy with respect to taxation and the wage restraint agreements negotiated under the rubric of 'Partnership 2000' have seen corporate profits rise while the poorest have slipped further behind. Almost 70% of workers in 2007 earned less than the average industrial wage while it is estimated that the richest 5% own 42% of wealth in the country. The economic boom has had massive social, political, and cultural repercussions for Irish society, including the realignment of notions of ethnicity and class. The Celtic Tiger signifies an emphatic shift in the context for the reception and integration of would-be immigrants. It is important, therefore, to acknowledge, in opposition to the liberal view of a society composed of sovereign, equal, individuals, a more radical view which emphasizes the processes of racialization emerging within, but not wholly reducible to, a broad context of cultural and economic differences in power, scarce resources, and social domination.

It is largely by reference to this context that we can attempt to understand the growth of ethno-racial discrimination at least at the individual level in

Ireland. Although this may take the form of a relatively coherent theory, it can also appear in the form of a less coherent assembly of stereotypes, images, and attributions, and as an explanation that is constructed and employed by individuals to negotiate their everyday lives. As Miles notes, discrimination can be characterized as practically adequate, in the sense that it refracts, in thought, certain observed regularities in the social world and constructs a causal interpretation which is presented as consistent with those regularities.[42] Such images and stereotypes rarely emerge spontaneously and often arise from state and media discourses, given their monopoly over the powers of governance, diffusion, and representation. Thus, refugees in Ireland, and Europe generally, are often represented as being responsible for a number of social and economic problems (which usually existed well before their arrival), such as housing shortages, unemployment, and the general lack of adequate statutory provisions. For many disempowered sections of the population, often embedded in atrophying housing estates, racist discourses often constitute a description of, and explanation for, the world they experience on a day-to-day basis. Ethno-racial discourse provides an ideological account of the social world which recognizes and offers an explanation for the housing crisis, for the lack of jobs, for the continuance of poverty – experiences which many marginalized groups face. As a correlate of racialization, it therefore serves to make a causal link between observed, material differences in Irish society and signified phenotypical and cultural differences of black and ethnic minorities. It helps to make sense of the economic and social changes accompanying poverty, urban decline and social exclusion, as they are experienced by sections of the working class within the context of a booming Celtic Tiger economy. Such a process indicates a crisis in working-class representation and the inability of the indigenous poor to access political representation. Wacquant's discussion of the tensions that arose from the accelerated deproletarianization of the working class and their residential proximity with concentrations of immigrants in disadvantaged areas in France is equally applicable to Ireland: 'Spatial segregation intensifies hardship by accumulating in isolated urban enclaves downwardly mobile families of the native working class and immigrant populations of mixed nationalities who are young, economically fragile and equally deprived of readily marketable skills in the core of the new economy.' He adds: 'territorial stigmatization encourages among residents sociofugal strategies of mutual avoidance and distancing that exacerbate processes of social fission, feed interpersonal mistrust, and undermine the sense of collectivity necessary to engage in community-building and collective action.'[43]

In a study carried out by Amnesty International in 2002, 44% of respondents believed that asylum-seekers were depriving indigenous Irish people of local authority housing, and 15% believed that asylum-seekers could obtain grants to buy cars, while 10% believed that they were given free mobile phones.[44] In research carried out by the Irish Refugee Council, many asylum-seekers referred to the hostility they encountered from other excluded and marginalized groups.[45] It was felt that such indigenous excluded groups often perceived asylum-seekers and refugees as welfare scroungers, or as preventing them from receiving certain scarce social resources: 'I think Irish people... are racist people but I think the racist people are from Ireland's cities, the people who are getting Social Welfare. I really think that educated people are not racist... even if in their roots they have some racism they learn to control it or they learn what it is to be racist.'[46] 'In inner city areas these people are thinking that refugees and asylum-seekers are their competitors, or in competition with them.'[47]

Such explicit, potentially violent hostility concurs with 'popular' definitions of discrimination as well as those definitions used by the media and government. However, this view occludes the more silent but equally pernicious and powerful forms of discrimination in institutions which operate through state organizations, bureaucracies, and are enshrined in state practices and classifications. And, of course, asylum-seekers are more likely to encounter such overt racial hostility from inner-city working-class communities because of their similar social and geographical position – immigrants tend to move to poorer neighborhoods because of the supply of cheap housing and because these are areas in which co-nationals tend to live. It is within the over-determined material and spatial context of growing inequality between rich and poor, a symbolic space of stigmatization, degradation, and a crisis of working class representation, that populist language of us and them, and narrow and exclusionary notions of the nation and who belongs and who doesn't have proliferated and taken hold.

It is important not to oversimplify or homogenize the causes of ethno-racial domination in Irish society over the fight for scarce material resources: that is to flatten out manifestations of socio-power differences on an economic anvil. Though class processes help to illuminate and structure ethno-racial processes of domination and racial politics, racism and racial domination are irreducible to the contradiction and struggle between capital and labour. We need to understand humans in a more rounded sense as social and meaning-driven creatures, and racial subordination as part of this more complex picture. Symbolic and emotional factors also play a role in racism and discrimination. Socio-psychological processes with a structure and discernible dynamics, involving transference, group-fantasies, labelling, and a search for distinction, status, and recognition are important explanatory variables too. As Elias rightly argues, struggles for the satisfaction of such human requirements may become more protracted when the certainty of material needs becomes established. Non-economic factors relating to status may also become increasingly important where power balances are less uneven.[48] Thus, processes of racialization and ethno-racial domination are heterogeneous, contradictory and uneven, and cannot simply be reduced to a consequence of the practices of state, media, and capital. The argument that is proposed here is merely that these practices have been particularly important in understanding *some* forms of racial subordination which have emerged in modern Irish society. Other sites where such domination operates and is reproduced also need to be acknowledged. These include playgrounds, streets, classrooms, hospitals, and the workplace. As Rattansi argues, such sites often embody racialized power relations which are tied to various power/knowledge configurations.[49] However, in contrast to many post-modern approaches – the importance of the state and the economy should not be downplayed. Processes of immigration and ethno-racial domination in Ireland need to be understood within a framework which includes concepts of social relations of capitalist accumulation, cultural nationalism, social closure and status, and state regulation and control. The importance of concrete historical, material, and social relationships need to be reasserted both as furnishing a more realistic explanatory framework, and as providing a more viable basis for challenging and explaining immigration and ethno-racial domination than theories of hybridity and a unqualified celebration of diversity.

Racism and ethnic differentiation are not absolutely defined or rigidly fixed, nor are the social divisions they create. Immigrants are not passive subjects or merely victims in this process. The short-term nature of Irish immigration has meant that immigrant mobilization has been uneven and based predominantly around nationally exclusive organizations. Though they are individualized through state immigration categorizations and often lack a common history, culture, and language which consequently presses them towards social fragmentation and generates different perceptions of self interest, an immigrant social movement or organization based on acquiring civic rights and challenging racism and discrimination may be developing. In the long-term, and depending on various contingent factors such as the role of the labour movement (but irreducible to it since racial divisions and mobilizations transcend or cut across class divisions) a fully fledged social movement or pressure group based on promoting collective interests, challenging discrimination, and claiming civic, political, and economic representation may emerge. In the context of pursuing actual livelihood strategies unequal stratified immigration statuses and discrimination may produce a potent counter-process around which immigrants organize.

The recession has created a structural, conjunctural, and national ideological economic crisis which has in turn engendered a crisis in the social partnership process and resulted in a crisis in working class representation. The outcome of these processes will significantly shape the development and intensity of popular and institutional forms of racism. The disconnect between the labour movement and the working class, its grassroots activity and experience, and its ability to be represented by partnership, has on occasion allowed an authoritarian nationalist populism and racism to arise as was especially evident in the Citizenship Referendum. This may also become re-expressed in the context of an ailing recessionary economy. In other cases social partnership facilitated the formation of relatively ineffective pro-migrant agencies such as the NCCRI, state projects such the National Action Plan Against Racism, and the development of a Ministerial Office for Integration Policy all paying lip service to migrant needs but where rhetoric was rarely matched by concerted action.

Integrating immigrants

The accommodation of socially and culturally distinct migrants into Irish society has become a major political, media, and populist concern. Although this process has been controversial and contested there are a number of positive aspects that need to be highlighted. Considering the rapid time-frame within which migration has grown, Ireland's reception of migrants has at one level been positive. On a political front, allowing migrants to vote and stand in local elections has been of enormous value in providing a sense of belonging and democratic access. Nevertheless, the process of including migrants into a host nation has been a complex one, freighted with a number of conceptual, ideological presuppositions and contradictions. Concerns about the inclusion of the migrant and how we conceptualize it elicits a number of important related questions entailing a conceptual examination of integration, multiculturalism, diversity, and interculturalism. One of the terms, if not the central one, presupposed within these discussions is culture. Yet, culture, as Williams reminds us, is one of the most difficult concepts to define in the language.[50] In its broad anthropological sense as a way of life, comprising community, language, tradition, kinship, symbols, it has become in the contemporary context a site of conflict and contestation. In recent decades bourgeois liberal forms of thought-style articulating conceptions of universal shared values as a basis for establishing a common ground upon which to resolve humanity's social and political problems, have ceded ground to more conservative thought styles, emphasizing the particularity, and fractious nature of incommensurable cultures. However, it is possible both to overestimate and to underestimate the role that culture plays in explaining social life. As cultural materialists show, culture does not explain everything.[51] Discussions of culture are simultaneously discussions of power. Culture is a place where political power can weave itself into people's everyday lives. And it is precisely because state power has to dissolve itself into and be expressed through a nationally defined culture that states see multi-cultural societies as problematical.[52]

Questions about immigrant incorporation and minority ethnic community formation will remain central concerns over the coming years as most states come to recognize that immigrants are not temporary sojourners, but tend to remain or settle in the host country. Concerns about recognizing migrant cultures reflect current political preoccupations; they would have been unimaginable in earlier periods where straightforward policies of assimilation dominated. Assimilation receded under a growing tide of multicultural thinking that emerged during the 1970s. Liberal states that are procedurally required to protect individual rights, enforce non-discrimination, and maintain public neutrality became challenged by a discourse of multiculturalism arguing for the state recognition and protection of distinct identities and minority cultures.[53] Close to a conservative thought-style, multiculturalism blended a romantic emphasis on particularity, organicism, and authentic community, with a liberal espousal of the formal equality of all cultural values in the tradition of Herder, Montaigne, or Montesquieu. Multiculturalism fundamentally entailed what Charles Taylor calls a 'politics of recognition'.[54] However, an ideological reaction to multiculturalism in the 1990s as an official policy followed from what were perceived to be its endemic failures as a normative discourse and policy. It was attacked from the right because of its focus on groups and collectivities requiring state aid and intervention in the context of a dominant neo-liberal orthodoxy championing individualism, minimal state, and responsibility. From the left it was criticized for failing to address power inequality, its preoccupation with surface differences in consumption and lifestyle practices, and its exclusive preoccupation with cultural and religious differences at the expense of material processes and class stratification. For both ends of the political spectrum it also entailed an unsustainable belief in value relativism.

The displacement of multiculturalism as an ideology has come in the wake of a reassertion of state policies emphasizing socio-economic integration and placing a stronger emphasis on immigrant adaptation. These processes have essentially been manifested in two distinct philosophies of incorporation – assimilation and integration – that have varied between the USA and Europe. Unlike the USA, which is an immigrant settler country, and where the notion of what constitutes a minority is constantly shifting, European states have never seen themselves as immigrant societies and have sought to retain a deep-seated nationalist culture.

However, despite the ubiquity of the term, especially in Europe, no one is really clear what integration exactly means. The concept remains a highly contested one, with continual slippages in definition, and in its normative and ideological implications.[55] Its meaning can vary between countries, alter over time, and is frequently based on the interests, values, assumptions, and perspectives of specific groups involved in the migration process. Its usage is also inconsistent. It can be used to refer to both a process and a state, and it can be employed in contrast to assimilation and multiculturalism, and at other times as a generic concept of which the former are variants.

Integration's current dominant usage is as a two-way process in contrast to multiculturalism and assimilation. In this sense it offers a political and moral consensual position between the two extremes. That is, it offers a third way between (overstated) characterizations of assimilationism in which the migrant is expected to give up her values, customs, and traditions, and multiculturalism in which these values and practices are officially recognized and valourized; between anti-immigrant sentiment and anti-racist discourses; between closed borders and open doors; and between enforcing the rights of migrants often guaranteed at an international level and government and right-wing populist calls for the expulsion of migrants or their containment as secondary citizens at a national level. However, the utility and popularity of integration does not simply derive from its 'two-way', 'democratic' and consensual connotation, but also from its capaciousness and vagueness.[56] Given so many conflicting interests and voices involved in the process of migration and settlement – states, public officials, political decision-makers, employers, NGOs, trade union officials, migrants, host populations, workers, service providers – as well as the different levels of policy application – individual, family, local, national – the term offers a suitable compromise for all.

There are, however, a number of problems with the concept of integration. Integration is not a neutral descriptive referring to a mutual process of social and cultural accommodation but an ideologically loaded quasi-performative concept. It views society as an internally coherent, organic, and integrated unity at once depoliticing it and masking and screening fundamental structural inequalities. The putative two-way relation between the individual immigrant and the state is one characterized by asymmetric power relations and rarely involves equal compromise on both sides. The enormous weight of the state can hardly be compared to the power of migrants who are 'individualized' through state forms of categorization. Most discussions of integration start from the state's view of what the phenomenon should be. This of course has to do with their greater power relation, their ability to impose and shape systems of classification and categorization, and the symbolic prestige and truth effects that follow from phenomena given an 'official' stamp. Despite claims to the contrary, integration remains, in practice, a process attempting to *re-nationalize* and assimilate migrants.

Moreover, the term fails to outline what immigrants are meant to be integrated into in the first place. It is deployed with an underlying assumption that the host society consists of a set of shared core values – a belief which implicitly looks to untenable nationalist discourses containing essentialized notions of national culture. It also fails to acknowledge that values are in flux and that members of the host society are changing too. Discussions of integration often operate with a reified non-processual view of the social world and culture. Equally, there is a tendency to focus on values, ideas, and norms rather than social practices. People adapt and learn not as autonomous individuals reading books, but participating in a multiplicity of social practices.

In many cases State discussions of integration often presuppose a methodological nationalism in which the bounded nation-state is seen as the container for processes of immigrant life. Transnational connections in which many immigrants maintain extensive and sometimes intensive links and networks with their country of origin though remittances, telephone, and email communication become downplayed or ignored. Finally, there is a fundamental problem with any discussion of multiculturalism, integration, or inclusion imposed by the very confines of its immanent world-view. Measures of integration are applied only to immigrants and minorities who are then judged according to these criteria and found wanting, when in fact a number of these measures could not be even achieved by the majority of people within the host nation-state. Thus issues of poverty, inequality, and access to employment affect a broad range of individuals who are not immigrants. Integration stops short in acknowledging that migrants are being inserted into a conflict-ridden, unequal, and exploitative form of capitalism. For some on the left this means that integration can be read as synonymous with conformism, reflecting an ideology of adjustment and identity thinking. Here immigrants are required to conform and adapt to a commodified cultural lifestyle and world-view. Hence, even when immigrants are included within specific spheres of society, the yardstick of measurement is a host population which itself is excluded from various aspects of social life in the absence of economic and cultural democracy.

In Ireland, 2 government reports, *Integration: A Two-Way Process* (1999), and *Planning for Diversity: National Action Plan Against Racism* (2005) were especially important for facilitating the introduction and establishment of the term in the national agenda. The appointment of Conor Lenihan, as Minister for Integration Policy in 2007, though a surprise choice given his earlier description of Turkish workers as 'kebabs', was a further indication of the State's move towards an integration agenda. Both reports on integration defined the term in a way that was close to multiculturalism, making them particularly attractive to NGOs and immigrant support groups. *Integration: A Two-Way Process* stated that: 'Integration means the ability to participate to the extent that a person needs and wishes in all of the major components of society, without having to relinquish his or her own cultural identity.'[57] The report, however, was exclusively concerned with the access of state services for refugees. The National Action Plan (NAP) held a similar, though more broadly applicable, multiculturalist view:

> The term 'integration' is widely used in a policy context at both national and
> European level. Integration is commonly understood to be a two way process that

places duties and obligations on both cultural and ethnic minorities and the State
to create a more inclusive society. In the context of the Plan 'integration' simply
means a range of targeted strategies for the inclusion of groups such as Travellers,
refugees and migrants as part of the overall aim of developing a more inclusive and
intercultural society.[58]

These reports constructed the State as a benevolent provider and protector of
vulnerable migrants. Both documents, however, failed to discuss what resources
and material infrastructure would be provided to facilitate such integration,
placing the emphasis and responsibility on the individual migrant to adapt
instead.[59] Though issues of racism were discussed, little (for obvious reasons)
was said about state-generated forms of racism and exclusion. Even less was
discussed about how such conceptions of integration were directly being
undermined by the State's policy of differentiating migrant statuses, impeding
family reunification, passing restrictive immigration legislation, and by
politicians' populist attacks against migrants. These reports were emblematic of
state discussions of integration. They were discourses at the level of rhetoric
rather than practice. A small but revealing and illustrative example of this
fundamental gap between what is said and what is done was evident in the
Gardai turban controversy in Ireland. On 6 October 2005, as part of the Gardai's
attempt to recruit individuals from minority ethnic backgrounds into an
increasingly multicultural and diverse Ireland, it was stated that the Gardai was
committed to adapting its uniforms, dietary practices, and working practices to
suit recruits from Muslim, Jewish, and Sikh backgrounds. Superintendent John
Grogan noted that 'it is a problem that has been solved in every other police
force and An Garda Siochana will be no different in that regard'.[60] However,
when a Sikh actually came forward to enter the Gardai Reserve, and asked the
Gardai to adapt its uniform by allowing a turban, the Garda commissioner, Noel
Conway, in a sharp U-turn, stated that this would not happen. The Minister for
Integration Policy, Conor Lenihan, rationalized the decision by drawing a facile
analogy, stating that when Government high officials made temporary visits to
the Middle East, they adapted to their socio-cultural and religious requirements,
and Sikhs needed to do the same. A similar uncompromising position was
initially taken in relation to religious freedom and Muslim women wearing
headscarves in schools.

As a 'treacherous metaphor',[61] integration offers no basis for measuring or
discerning the degree to which societies are already integrated, nor does it
provide any clear principles and criteria of what immigrants are to be integrated
into, and therefore how to operationalize the term. Nevertheless, even
recognizing that obtaining a criterion for assessing integration or incorporation
is limited, and that the term itself is ideologically loaded, it is still sociologically
useful to try to ascertain how immigrant experiences and treatment in various

aspects of society compares to that of the host population. It is not the concept per se that is problematical but how it is defined. In order to evaluate and assess the level or degree of migrant inclusion it is important to develop loose yardsticks against which to assess integration relative to the life chances of the host or non-migrant population bearing in mind earlier criticisms. This includes achieving public outcomes within employment, housing, education, health etc., that are equivalent to those achieved within the wider host communities. It also involves a subjective dimension – a sense of belonging and recognition in a given society.[62]

The inclusion of immigrants needs to be understood in terms of differential power. But it also has to be understood as involving their inclusion into a number of overlapping processes and spheres which follow diverse paths and possess their own logic and temporality. Social formations are broad complex structures composed of interdependent, conflict-ridden, and autonomous fields or configurations. Migrants engage in some fields and practices but may be structurally barred from others. When included they enjoy the same rights and opportunities as the host population; when segregated they have low-skilled 3-D jobs, low-grade housing conditions, and lack of access to public services. Rather than following a linear or developmental logic, social integration or inclusion may often take a 'nested'[63] form involving virtuous and vicious circles: access to a language school may facilitate access to a community, which in turn may allow access to various forms of information and shared knowledge and jobs.

It can be argued that 4 broad interconnected processes have significantly shaped and account for the patterns of incorporation or integration of various migrant groups in Ireland: firstly, the mode of entry and legal status of the migrant; secondly, the conditions of reception in the host country, including racism and discrimination from the State and general population; thirdly, the characteristics, background, and outlook of the migrant (including, age, gender, ethnicity, socioeconomic background, language proficiency, etc.); and fourthly, the shape of government policies towards migrants in terms of providing language classes, recognizing qualifications, but also the State's policy to the resident population as a whole in terms of providing a basic economic infrastructure. These are analytically separated here but in reality are interlinked and overlapping. I have already discussed the second of these processes involving racism above. The third refers to the migrant's background. The worldwide growth of urban populations *viz-a-viz* rural populations has meant a partial shift in the outlooks and expectations of migrants generally. Nevertheless, a large number of migrants who arrive in Ireland still originate from rural areas. Although it should not be overstated and only used as a non-static conceptual device implying a continuuum, sociological dichotomies such as Tonnies typology of the differentiation between 'Gemeinshaft' and 'Gesselschaft' or Maine's between 'status' and 'contract' do have some validity in characterising the different mode of life, mentality and behaviour in these contrasting social worlds. As Bourdieu demonstrates in his early work in Algeria, adapting to a new life, where the primary group, family or household is no longer present and where there is a deficit of knowledge in local mores, know-how, folkways, and language can be a difficult experience for migrants. The arrival of migrants with rural backgrounds to the urban context of Dublin City can result in a strong sense of dislocation and a profound feeling of uprooting. As a result some migrants, as a defensive measure, may retreat into the familiar culture and lifestyle of national-migrant networks and groupings, especially if they experience racism or hostility but also as a default position for maintaining a national habitus. Here various Churches in Ireland have served as locations for co-national migrants to interact.

The explanatory implications of legal status for integration are also crucial. All countries of immigration classify and assign migrants to specific legal and political categories according to their mode of entry. These legal categories in turn shape rights and opportunities for migrants and thus have significant effects on their paths to inclusion. Socially structuring processes of official classification condition the level and trajectory of integration for all migrants as well as creating variations within the category of migrant. Thus whether migrants arrive and are classified as asylum-seekers, refugees, on work permits, on work visas, as students, as dependents of legal entrants, as EU nationals, as third country workers, returning immigrants, as skilled workers, or become undocumented workers, will have implications for their future integration, inclusion, and settlement. Immigrant status also determines the rights of immigrants to have family members join them. For migrants, having close family members, especially spouses or siblings, functions as a means to pool economic resources and also provides social support in a context where they may otherwise feel lonely and isolated in a foreign country. Families play an important role in shaping a migrant's inclusion by structuring their perception of belonging, reducing isolation, and their access to various monetary and social resources.

Legal status also structures access to employment. Although migrants generally have high employment levels compared to the Irish population they are excluded in other ways. Thus for example in research on the integration of Chinese, Indian, Lithuanian, and Nigerian nationals into Ireland there was considerable variation between the national groups in terms pf economic activity as a result of their immigration status.[64] Lithuanians, who as EU nationals have unrestricted labour market access, and Indian respondents (many who came on work visas to work in high-skilled jobs) recorded very high levels of employment whereas employment levels for Chinese and Nigerian nationals were significantly lower with only a little over half of Nigerian respondents being currently employed. Many Chinese nationals were students and could only work 20 hours if they were registered on a full-time course; similarly many Nigerians were asylum-seekers who had no entitlement to work.

As well as the 'objective' effects', in terms of structuring migrant's access to resources, and immersing them into a bureaucratically ordered world, the administrative categories and classifications used by the State play an important role in defining subjective processes of migrant self-identification. The system of state classification and categorization plays a central role in reproducing relations of power and domination by generating classifications enshrining social divisions between ethno-racial groupings. The production of concepts is central for the production of groups.

Immigration is unpopular in all European countries, albeit to different degrees. The classification of people and how this affects the people classified are of immense sociological importance.[65] Both dominant and marginalized groups can come to define themselves and each other through such categorizations: As Bourdieu notes in *Distinction*: 'Dominated agents, who assess the value of their position and their characteristics by applying a system of schemes of perception and appreciation… tend to attribute to themselves what the distribution attributes to them… adjusting their expectations to their chances, defining themselves as the established order defines them.'[66] The effect of state classification, as Sayad notes is especially influential on disempowered migrants in shaping their self-perception:

> Making a virtue out of necessity, and to a large extent because of the dominated position he [sic] occupies in the structure of symbolic power relations… At times, he must, as an immigrant (when he is at the bottom of the social hierarchy within the world of immigrant), assume the stigmas which, in the eyes of public opinion, create the immigrant. He must therefore accept (resignedly or under protest, submissively or defiantly, or even provocatively) the dominant definition of his identity.[67]

Notwithstanding the situational and contextual nature of national and ethnic identification, there is a complex and dialectical interplay between the image that people have of themselves and the images which others have of them.[68] However, the naming or imposition of an official classification can change the person named. Official taxonomies and census categories also shape the social relations between indigenous groups and as well as structuring interactional relations between ethno-racially differentiated migrants who may also racialize and stereotype one another. These classificatory schemes, which all individuals are compelled to refer to when talking about immigration, are used by individuals to give meaning to their social world.

State categorizations therefore provide master statuses in terms of which the individual migrant is defined and treated. Individuals can sometimes become caught in frame traps. The process is, of course, complex and contradictory.[69]

Migrants may accept the dominant definition given of them but not subjectively identify with it. 'Immigrant', 'asylum-seeker'and 'illegal' are negative attributions and referents. The fact of being seen by others as anomalous or even 'at fault' because of carrying an immigrant status in the established national order can become internalized and adopted as a central part of the migrant's self-definition. However, self-designation often depends on social position. It is because of its stigmatized status that many people from EU 15 countries do not regard themselves as 'immigrants.' However, for others the disposition acquired in the position occupied leads to an adjustment to 'a sense of one's place'. It is because of these morally charged accusations of deviancy and the implications they have for their treatment that migrants employ 'defence-accounts', devices which are 'designed specifically to avoid or reduce blame allocations'.[70]

According to Sayad, both strategies mean that the migrant as a 'being who exists for others' experiences his or her identity in a contradictory manner: on the one hand as a defence or under protest to the dominant definition, and on the other as submission or resignation to that definition. The question in the context of these social struggles between the immigrant and the host society is not whether the immigrant can conquer or recapture a 'legitimate identity', whatever that may mean, but of the possibility of the migrant constructing his own identity and of evaluating it in relative autonomy.

Conclusion

Within the context of increasing diversity the question of how Ireland will adapt to accommodate new socially and culturally distinct migrants and how migrants will adapt to Irish society will remain a major concern in the future. The nature of the uneven balance of power between the migrant groups and other interest groups including the labour movement, the State, and capital is not fixed but changing. Through mobilization and functional integration, outsider groups which had formerly accepted their inferiority and low position in the social hierarchy, and the requirement to shed socio-cultural values, may come to gain a more equal access to various power resources in a dialectic of oppression and counter-oppression, resistance and negotiation. Over the long term, depending on the level and degree of migrant group-making, power differences may lessen between established and outsider groups as the fantasy-laden collective 'we-images' of social superiority characteristic of the former may begin to diminish. As migrants organize more effectively and the power balance in Irish society shifts they may be in a better position to retaliate to stigmatization and discrimination.

Migrant domination is not a given but the result of social struggles. Racial and ethnic subordination depends on the outcome of ongoing political and ideological struggles involving capital, state, labour, and increasingly, the immigrants themselves. At a structural level challenging racism means simultaneously confronting the relations of power entailing economic inequality and the state. As one commentator rightly notes in relation to the latter, 'the form of the state structures the form of political struggles. Where state institutions impose racial categories, the struggle against racism will be a struggle against the state.'[71] It also involves daily struggles involving challenging media representations and everyday populist misinformation which takes more or less hold depending on the political and economic conjuncture. In order to have any purchase in this context, anti-racist struggles will have to be carried out at a number of different levels. Exclusionary forms of nationalism and racism cannot be simply replaced by anodyne notions of integration or by calls for more inclusive forms of national identity, which leave unequal forms of power in place. Nor can material shifts towards economic equality through the challenging of private property be secured without major ideological shifts which relate to classification, social recognition, and the valourization of difference.

Notes

1 Caldwell, *Reflections on the Revolution in Europe*, pp. 8–10.
2 E. O'Mahony, S. Loyal and A. Mulcahy, *Racism in Ireland: The Views of Black and Ethnic Minorities* (Dublin: Amnesty International, 2001).
3 Ibid.
4 The overwhelming majority of these racist incidents took place in public spaces. Over 44% of the experiences of racist abuse took place on the street, 24% in shops and 23% in pubs.
5 In a follow-up survey based on a different methodology an ESRI report found that reports of racism taking place in a variety of contexts had continued. F. McGinnity, P. O'Connell, E. Quinn and J Williams, *Migrants' Experience of Racism and Discrimination in Ireland: Survey Report* (Dublin: ESRI, 2006).
6 Fundamental Rights Agency, European Union Minorities and Discrimination Report, 2009), p. 6, http://fra.europa.eu/fraWebsite/attachments/eumidis_mainreport_conference-edition_en_.pdf.
7 *Irish Times*, 17 April 2009.
8 ICI, *Getting on*, in P. O'Connell & F. McGinnity, *Immigrants at Work: Ethnicity and Nationality in the Labour Market*.
9 *Getting on*, pp. 122–3.
10 Ibid., pp. 8–9. 36% indicated they did not report the incident because they did not know how to go about doing so or where to go.
11 The amnesty report shows the high proportion of racist incidents (25%) experienced at the hands of the Gardaí, the second highest source of racist incidents overall, despite both the introduction of new racial and intercultural instruction at the Garda training centre and the Employment Equality Act.
12 O'Mahony et al., Racism in Ireland, *The Irish Examiner*, 10 January 2010.
13 P. O'Connell & F. McGinnity, *Immigrants at Work: Ethnicity and Nationality in the Labour Market* (Dublin: Equality Authority, 2008).

14 Ibid.

15 *Migrants' Experience Of Racism And Discrimination In Ireland.*

16 M. Banton, *The Idea of Race* (London: RKP, 1975).

17 R. Miles, *Racism* (London: Routledge, 1989).

18 M Omni & H. Winant, *Racial Formation in the United States from the 1960s to the 1980s* (New York: Routledge and Kegan Paul, 1986); A. Rattansi, *Racism: A Very Short Introduction* (Oxford: Oxford University Press, 2007).

19 M. Barker, *The New Racism* (London: Junction Books. 1981).

20 Rattansi, p. 105.

21 P. Gilroy, *Ain't No Black*; A. Rattansi, *Racism.*

22 L. Wacquant (1997) For an analytic of racial domination, in *Political Power and Social Theory*, Vol 11, pp. 221–34.

23 Wacquant, For an analytic of racial domination, p. 230.

24 J. Le Sueur. *Uncivil War: Intellectuals and Identity Politics During the Decolonisation of Algeria* (Pennsylvania: University of Pennsylvania Press, 2001).

25 P. Cullen, Identity, emigration and the boomerang generation, in R. Lentin (ed) *Emerging Irish Identities* (Dublin: Trinity College Dublin, 2000); P. Gillespie, Multiple identities in Ireland and Europe, in R. Lentin (ed) *The Expanding Nation* (Dublin: Trinity College, 1999); B. Gray, Steering a course somewhere between hegemonic discourses of Irishness, in R. Lentin (ed) *The Expanding Nation*; R. Lentin, Introduction – Racialising the other, racialising the us: emerging Irish identities as processes of racialisation, in R. Lentin (ed) *Emerging Irish Identities*; Lentin & McVeigh, *Racism and Anti-Racism in Ireland* (Belfast: Beyond The Pale, 2002); McDonagh, The web of self-identity: racism, sexism and disablism, in R. Lentin & R. McVeigh (eds) *Racism and Anti-racism*; O'Toole, Green, white and black: Race and Irish identity, in R. Lentin (ed) *Emerging Irish Identities*; Sinha, The right to Irishness: implications of ethnicity, nation and state towards a truly multi-ethnic Ireland, in R. Lentin (ed) *The Expanding Nation*; E. White, The new Irish story-telling: media, representations and racialised identities, in R. Lentin & R. McVeigh (eds) *Racism and Anti-racism.*

26 Farrell & Watt, Responding to racism in Ireland: an overview, in *Responding to Racism in Ireland* (Dublin: Veritas, 2001); MacLachlan & O' Connell, *Cultivating Pluralism* (Dublin: Oak Tree Press, 2000); K. Monshengwo, The potential of public awareness programmes, in F. Farrell & P. Watt, *Responding to Racism in Ireland.*

27 S. Ni Shuinear, Othering the Irish (Travellers), in R. Lentin & R. McVeigh, *Racism and Anti-Racism in Ireland*, p. 177.

28 R. Lentin, Introduction – racializing the Other, p. 3. Lentin has shifted towards a different position in later work on the racial state and 'crisis racism'.

29 Ibid., p. 8; Gray, Steering, p. 66.

30 B. Fanning, *Racism and Social Change.*

31 S. Hall, Race, articulation and societies structured in dominance, in *Sociological Theories: Race and Colonialism* (Paris: UNESCO, 1980), p. 338.

32 L. Wittgenstein, *The Philosophical Investigations.*

33 A. Gramsci, *Selections from the Prison Notebooks* (London: Lawrence and Wishart, 1973), pp. 323–43.

34 Wacquant, For an analytic of racial domination.
35 Elias and Scotson, *The Established and Outsiders*, p. 22.
36 P. Watt and Farrell, Responding, p. 14.
37 Elias and Scotson, *The Established and Outsiders*.
38 MRCI, *Realising Integration* (Dublin: MRCI, 2006).
39 L. Bearne & V. Jaichand, *Breaking Down Barriers* (Dublin: Amnesty Irish Section, 2006).
40 Ibid.
41 Wacquant, For an analytic of racial domination, p. 226.
42 R. Miles, *Racism* (London: Routledge, 1989).
43 Wacquant, *Urban Outcasts*, pp. 29–30.
44 Opinion poll for Amnesty International (Dublin: Lansdowne Marketing Research, April 2002).
45 B. Fanning, S. Loyal and C. Staunton, *Asylum Seekers and the Right to Work in Ireland* (Dublin: Irish Refugee Council, 2000).
46 Ibid., p. 20.
47 Ibid., p. 21.
48 Elias and Scotson, *The Established and Outsiders*.
49 A. Rattansi, Just framing: ethnicities and racisms in a 'postmodern' framework, in L. Nicholson (ed), *Social Postmodernism* (Cambridge: Cambridge University Press, 1995), p. 262.
50 R. Williams, *Keywords* (London: Penguin, 1977).
51 T. Eagleton, Marxism and culture, paper given at Marxism Dublin, December 2009.
52 Ibid.
53 C. Joppke and E. Morawska (eds) *Toward Assimilation and Citizenship: Immigrants in Liberal Nation-states* (London: Palgrave, 2003).
54 C. Taylor, *Multiculturalism and the Politics of Recognition* (Princeton: Princeton University Press, 1992).
55 R. Bauböck, Rainer, *The Integration of Immigrants* (Strasbourg: The Council of Europe, 1994); A. Favell, *Philosophies of Integration: Immigration and the Idea of Citizenship in France and Britain* (London: Macmillan, 1998); A. Favell, Integration policy and integration research in Europe: a review and critique, in A. Aleinikoff and D. Klusmeyer (eds) *Citizenship Today: Global Perspectives and Practices* (Washington DC: Brookings Institute Carnegie Endowment for International Peace, 2001), pp. 349–99.
56 A. Favell Integraiton Policy and Integraiton research, pp. 3–4.
57 Ibid., p. 9.
58 DJELR, *The National plan Against Racism, 2005–2008* (Dublin: DJELR, 2005), p. 39.
59 B. Gray, Migrant integration policy: A nationalist fantasy of management and control?, *Translocations* Vol. 1: issue 1, August 2006; G. Boucher, Ireland´s lack of a coherent integration policy, *Translocations*, Vol. 3: issue 1, September 2008.
60 www.breakingnews.ie/2005/10/06/story224192.html.
61 M. Banton, Michael, National integration in France and Britain, *Journal of Ethnic and Migration Studies*, 27, 1: 151–68 (2001).

62 *Getting on*, p. 3.

63 H. Troper & M. Weinfeld, *Ethnicity, Politics and Public Policy: case studies in Canadian Diversity* (Toronto: University of Toronto Press, 1999), p. 15.

64 ICI, *Getting on*.

65 I. *Hacking Historical Ontology* (Massachusetts: Harvard University Press, 2002).

66 Bourdieu, *Distinction*, p. 471.

67 Sayad, *The Suffering of the Immigrant*, p. 286.

68 N. Elias and J. Scotson, *The Established and Outsiders* (Dublin: UCD Press, 2008), p. 197.

69 R. Jenkins, *Rethinking Ethnicity, Arguments and Explorations* (London: Sage, 1997).

70 M. Scott and B. Lyman. Account, deviance and social order, in J. Douglas (ed), *Deviance and Respectability* (New York: Basic Books, 1970). 1970: 138–139.

71 Gilroy, P. *Ain't no Black in the Union Jack*, pp. 33–4.

Chapter 12

Conclusion

This book has tried to provide a cultural and materialist analysis of immigration in Ireland, examining both the process of migration and the discourses attached to it and by integrating social interactionist analyses within a framework of political economy.

The short, condensed time-span within which Ireland became a country of immigration having been a country of emigration for so long is remarkable. In some ways Ireland offered a quasi-laboratory situation for examining the impact of migration upon a nation-state. However, analysing migration in all its complexity has not been easy. Migrants are from a diversity of backgrounds, have migrated for a variety of reasons, and have had a range of differentiated experiences living in Ireland. Moreover, as Burke rightly highlighted in his conservative critique of Paine, one of the most significant distinctions in the social world is between what is said and what is done. What the Irish State has posited abstractly though its immigration law and its various migration schemes, including its policy of integration, and how these have been applied and interpreted on the ground by various bureaucrats, judges, government officials, service providers, and migrants does not necessarily coincide.

This book has tried to highlight the economic, social, and political structures that generate and structure migration, as well as to a lesser extent the agency, lived experiences, and self-definitions of the migrants themselves. It has proposed a theory of migration that looks at the globally unequal material and economic contexts that engender migration as well as the role of social networks and families in facilitating that movement. The book has persistently emphasized the social nature of migration. The State has mediated and structured both the economic context and the operation of social networks through its immigration and labour market policy and its classificatory schemas. Standing both inside and outside the logic of capital the state has played a fundamental role in reconfiguring the labour market to bring in cheap and flexible labour to meet Ireland's economic needs. Rather than emerging spontaneously, the Irish State, responding to employer and business interests, shaped and induced a large number of migrations. This intervention accounted for the timing of the migration flows and the specific countries and regions from where these flows occurred. Once initiated, however, these migrations became self-sustaining with the development of migrant chains and social networks providing information flows between sending and receiving countries. They also became partly autonomous from state control and regulation.

The book has tried to highlight the contradictory roles of the state. As well as recruiting and constructing a flexible workforce the Irish State has simultaneously played an indispensable role in trying to maintain a racially, ethnically, and culturally homogenous population and regulate the social order. Moreover, its treatment of asylum-seekers has differed considerably from that of labour migrants. The asylum processing system and the regime of direct provision demonstrate its attempt to control and regulate the presence of certain categories of migrants in the country. Its construction of various legal impediments to family reunification, increased policing of borders and surveillance, and powers to deport are a further manifestation of a policy aimed at maintaining national homogeneity.

Notwithstanding broader social relations, it is impossible to understand the emergence of immigration in Ireland without invoking the Celtic Tiger and the neo-liberal market model it was based on. The Celtic Tiger created an insatiable labour demand. With an unemployment rate of almost 4%, and only 1.4% in long-term unemployment, Ireland proportionately had the best rate record of job creation of any OECD country during the early part of 2000. However, despite the increase in tax expenditure the proportion of money being spent on social welfare as a percentage of GDP fell on a yearly basis. In 1995 social welfare expenditure was 10.2% of GDP; by 2005, a decade later, it had fallen to 7.6%. From the 1980s the Irish State pursued a broader ideological shift towards neo-liberalism and deregulation. The retrenchment of the state was reflected in a decline in investment in social housing, low investment in the health service, and the privatization of various public utilities. Rapidly rising profits and income created a level of class inequality that was previously unknown in modern Ireland.[1] Of the 19 OECD high-income countries in the Human Development Poverty Index, Ireland came 18th. According to the UN Development Report the poorest 20% in Ireland receive 7.4% of total income whilst the richest 20% receive 42%.[2] A Bank of Ireland report on wealth in Ireland painted an even starker picture with the top 1% holding 20% of wealth and the top 5%, 40% of national wealth.[3]

A neo-liberal policy aimed at opening the social state to market mechanisms and increasing the volume and velocity of capital flows was paradoxically complemented by persistent state intervention in the regulation of the labour supply. Neo-liberalism is not a withdrawal of state regulation as something opposed to laissez faire, but a move towards a different type of state intervention. As a result, labour market expansion continued to be dependent on non-Irish workers. Large sections of the Irish economy cannot function without immigrant workers and the economy, as a whole, remains highly dependent upon them. According to the QHNS, in the first quarter 2008 non-Irish workers accounted for 90% of the net addition to employment.[4]

Unlike most other EU states the arrival of asylum-seekers preceded that of labour migrants so as to frame the issue of immigration in a specific way. The year 2004 marked a dramatic policy watershed in Irish immigration policy with both the Citizenship Referendum and EU expansion taking place. A shift from state and media discourses focused on 'bogus' asylum-seekers to discussions centred on the displacement and replacement of indigenous workers by migrant workers also took place.

Rapid economic growth created a structural tension between the logic of capital accumulation and that of political nationalism. The 'imagined community' which emerged during the early years of the Republic embodied a highly restricted notion of citizenship and ethnicity which, despite undergoing significant modification during the economic boom, has remained essentially exclusionary. The free and accelerating movement of goods and capital across national borders has not been matched by the free movement of people. Despite the acute labour needs of the Irish economy, the Irish government remained cautious with regard to the entry of non-Irish and especially non-EU nationals.

Since the foundation of the State, Irishness and citizenship had been correlated with whiteness and Catholicism, which implicitly acted as the measure against which social difference was constructed. However, this restricted, hegemonic, view of 'Irishness' came into conflict with the labour market imperatives of the increasingly globalized Tiger economy. Hence, there was a need for immigrant labour, yet also a hierarchical racialization of that labour. To this tension between historic nationalism and a contemporary economic revival can be added the issue of Irish constitutional liberalism. As a small state with a history of neutrality and a commitment to democracy and to the international rule of law, and coloured by its own experience of colonial oppression, Ireland has voiced strong support for the United Nations, and, specifically, the 1951 Convention Relating to the Status of Refugees, though this support has been more in terms of self-image than practice. Since the emergence of the Celtic Tiger, the Irish State has increasingly interpreted international protocols and legislation relating to migration in an increasingly illiberal spirit, and failed to adopt a number of international laws relating to human rights, workers rights, and racism. This liberal internationalization further complicates the political response to what is, for Ireland, a new problem of immigration. Here we see the overdetermination of a structural contradiction between, on the one hand, nationalism – closed, Janus-faced, insular, selective, discriminating, and particular – and, on the other, capitalism – open, expansionary, indiscriminate, global, and universal.

Migration and recession

The current global recession – which created a new *gestalt* within which immigration in Ireland is interpreted – represents the most serious crises in capitalism since the Great Depression. The Irish economy officially went into recession in September 2008. Prior to the recession it was the fourth most affluent country in the OECD. However, following its onset it was one of the most adversely effected countries in terms of economic contraction in Europe. The collapse in the financial sector, banking sector, and construction together with the disappearance of debt-fuelled consumer spending and credit have left the country in one of the most precarious economic positions internationally. Figures indicate that the recession is widespread and prevalent in most sectors of the economy. Curtailed construction and manufacturing output and employment have been matched by a contraction in employment in the services sector. In the last quarter of 2008 construction employment fell by 45,900 or 16.5% over the year.[5] The economic problems ensuing from the acute credit crunch, and inadequate general taxation regime, have resulted in a massive shortfall in public finances. Mounting job losses operating through a negative feedback loop have been both a cause and effect of this fall in consumer demand. The scale and rapidity of job losses in the recession have been unprecedented. According to redundancy data from the Department of Enterprise, Trade and Employment over 300 people each day were being made redundant during February 2009, and 13,034 notifications of redundancy were received in the first two months of 2009 – an increase of 132% on the same time in 2008. The Irish Live Register for January 2009 registered 326,100 individuals constituting the largest yearly rise since 1967. The unemployment rate doubled in less than a year, reaching over 10% in 2008, 12.5% in 2009, and stood at almost 14% by mid-2010.[6]

The Celtic Tiger provided one context for migration. The recession in Ireland has provided another. Patterns and flows of immigration have differed markedly. The recession has meant a dramatic slowdown in the volume of immigration. There was a dramatic 40% drop in immigration from the accession states in 2009 compared to 2008, as well as a steep fall in the number of work permits and Public Personal Service Numbers (PPSNs) issued. In 2008, 127,695 PPSNs were allocated to foreign nationals, down almost a third compared to 2006.[7] In the first 2 months of 2010, the number of work permits was more than 60% lower than in the first 2 months of 2008 (1,441 compared to 3,837).

The recession has also led to the re-emergence of patterns of Irish emigration. In September 2009, more people began to leave Ireland than to enter it for the first time in 15 years. The number of emigrants in the year leading up to April 2009 was estimated to have increased by over 40%. Of the 65,100 who emigrated during that time almost half were accession state nationals and almost 30% were

Irish nationals. Immigration of all non-Irish groups showed a decline, with those from EU 12 countries showing the biggest fall.[8] Rather than going to the traditional emigrant destinations including the UK or USA, whose economies were also in poor shape, early evidence suggests that Irish emigrants were leaving for Canada and Australia in increasing numbers.[9] Ireland has come full circle. In 2010 Ireland once again had one of the highest rates of emigration in the EU.

It is unclear how many migrants will stay or leave. The government's attempt to prevent and discourage migrants from settling permanently in Ireland often accords with the migrants' own desires to return to their country of origin. Figures in Ireland indicate that more than half the foreign nationals who registered for PPSN numbers in 2004 no longer appeared in employment or welfare statistics in 2008, suggesting that many had left the country.[10] There are a number of factors impinging on the decision of foreign nationals to stay or leave, including whether economic opportunities are better at home. One of the paradoxes of free movement between states is that it encourages circular migration – since there is no visa, workers can come and go as they choose, and the cost of returning and travel is usually small. By contrast strict border controls tend to trap people within a country since they are unwilling to leave because they believe that they will not be let back in if conditions improve. However, the global nature of the recession has meant that even many of the EU nationals who can leave and re-enter without restrictions are unwilling to leave Ireland, because of the costs of returning, the nature of family ties, and the future economic prospects of their country of origin. For example, many Polish migrants were cajoled into returning to Poland by the Polish Government after the country had begun to suffer from labour shortages which could no longer filled by Ukrainian, Belarusian, and Chinese migrants. Some migrants feel integrated not only economically, but socially, politically, and culturally and a large number see Ireland as their home. Those who have had families or children here may also be less willing to return – over 43,000 pupils of different nationalities were attending primary school in 2006/7, and there were 21,000 newcomers in post-primary education in 2007/8.[11] Migrant status also plays an important role in their decision to leave.

The implications of the recession for immigrants in Ireland

Since reaching its peak of wealth creation in the first quarter of 2007, Ireland's economy has contracted by almost one-quarter. Since January 2008, government debt has doubled to €75 billion and is expected to double again to €150 billion by 2014. An average of 18 companies a day have closed over the past two years.[12] Job losses are still mounting and unemployment increasing. Although the recession has had negative consequences for employment and living conditions for everyone in Ireland, migrants were made trebly vulnerable.

They are especially susceptible to exploitation; redundancy and poverty; and to racism and discrimination.

Even during the boom numbers of employers, operating within a small open economy exposed to the fluctuating market demands of global competitive capitalism, sought to increase profit margins often by exploiting migrant workers made vulnerable through the conferral of disempowering immigrant statuses. With the increase in global and domestic competitive pressures on wages and conditions during the recession, employers have attempted to reduce migrant workers' pay and working conditions even more.

Although job losses have been pervasive throughout the State, migrants have been especially prone to unemployment because of their concentration in certain low-paid occupations that have been most severely affected by the recession, and because of their precarious immigrant status. This follows global patterns in which low-paid workers are more likely to lose work during a recession.[13] Over half of the Polish and Lithuanian males, 2 of the biggest groups of non-Irish nationals in the State, were employed in construction and manufacturing, many working as building labourers or in factories, while half of all females were in shops, hotels, and restaurants.[14] There have been large decreases in employment for non-Irish nationals precisely in these sectors. In 2009, the employment of non-Irish nationals in construction more than halved, while in the wholesale and retail trade employment fell by 18%.[15] In addition, factors such as their concentration in cyclically sensitive industries, legal status, non-unionization, language barriers, and a policy of 'last hired first out', make migrant workers particularly vulnerable.

Nationals from the EU 15, who have been concentrated in different employment sectors, tend to have been less adversely affected by the recession than other immigrants. Data on UK nationals remains opaque. Their geographic distribution and demographic details are very similar to Irish nationals. Immigrants from outside the European Union have also experienced high levels of unemployment.

As a result, the unemployment rate for non-Irish nationals is higher than that of Irish nationals.[16] According to figures, although the number of people claiming either jobseeker's allowance or jobseeker's benefit[17] rose by more than half for Irish nationals, it tripled from 8,000 to 25,000 for non-Irish nationals in the year leading up to December 2008.

Unlike native nationals, restrictions on welfare access through the HRC have forced many migrants into acute poverty and social exclusion. Fewer than 5,000 individuals were refused on HRC grounds in 2005 but more than 10,500 were refused in 2009. Moreover, claiming social welfare often means that an application for citizenship or long-term residency is refused.[18] For this reason many migrants do not apply. Undocumented migrants in Ireland also face acute problems during the recession.

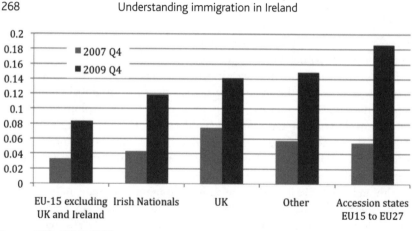

Source: CSO, QNHS 2010

Figure 12.1 Unemployment rates by nationality, 2007 and 2009

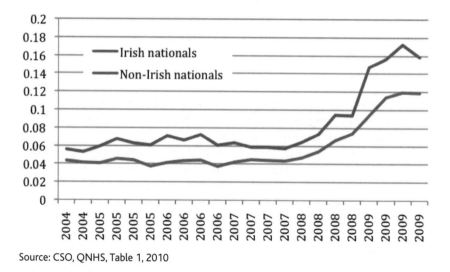

Source: CSO, QNHS, Table 1, 2010

Figure 12.2 Unemployment rates for Irish and Non-Irish nationals, 2004–9

Fear of job losses, increasing competition for resources, and heightened feelings of insecurity, have led to the scapegoating and to increased racism towards migrants for 'taking Irish jobs'. Due to sharp rises in unemployment and with household budgets sharply contracting, there has emerged a generalized fear in the country about future employment prospects and the threat of job losses. Even during the boom period immigration was a contested issue sometimes framed in erroneous emotive terms or through common-sense misunderstandings. The State responded to the recession by dismantling the equality infrastructure established over the past decade and increasing restrictions on migrants. In terms of the former the budget of the Equality Authority, which had dealt with numerous claims from migrants, was cut by over 40%, while the Irish Human Rights Commission suffered a 24% cut. The NCCRI was abolished and the number of English language support teachers was drastically reduced. In terms of the latter, restrictions on non-EEA students and on the entry of work permit holders, and their rights and entitlement once they arrived here, were augmented. After 1 June 2009 new permits for jobs paying under €30,000 were no longer given. In addition, the numbers of job categories ineligible for work permits were expanded and the duration of the labour market test was also doubled – a job had now to be advertised on EURES/FAS for at least 8 weeks and in a national press advertisement for 6 days. The State justified the increased employment permit restrictions by arguing that Irish nationals needed to be prioritized for jobs. However, this policy change affected only those on work permits – about 1.5% of the workers in the country – and therefore was more symbolic than practical.

Rather, these new restrictions fed into a populist discourse that served to apportion blame for the lack of jobs onto migrants. Within the context of a recession, where people have fears about their future employment, these policies ratcheted up a regressive and outdated form of nationalism. The call on a clampdown on work permits and the creation of tougher permit rules were called for by a vociferous group of populist politicians. As Fianna Fail TD Ned O'Keefe declared: 'I don't believe we should be giving permits to foreign workers – we must look after our own – we have to give priority to Irish workers and Irish jobs – the country can't afford it – every beginning starts at home'.[19] Another Cork TD Noel O'Flynn remarked: 'What in the name of God are we doing bringing workers in when we haven't work for our own people?'[20] He also called for greater checks to detect fraudulent claims on social welfare, a move echoed by Mary Hanafin, the Minister of Social and Family Affairs in July 2009. Leo Varadkar, the Fianna Gael spokesperson on Trade and Enterprise and Employment suggested migrants be paid to leave the country. Their views were also echoed by local politicians. In November 2009 the Fianna Gael Mayor of Limerick called for the cutting of social welfare payments and deportation of immigrants, including EU nationals, who were abusing Ireland's generous welfare system or who could not find work in Ireland. Although these politicians argued they were expressing the concerns of their constituents, they were actually contributing to the very xenophobia they attributed to the general population. This 'crisis racism' also served to divert attention away from the structural and policy factors, and political decisions, which created the recession in the first place. Local fears amplified by politicians were evident in a national poll carried out at the end of 2009, which found that 72% of respondents wanted either to see a reduction in the number of non-Irish migrants, or for some or all migrants to leave the country.

However, policies and practices have been contradictory, and not all have been restrictionist, especially as a result of lobbying by various NGOs. Work permit restrictions introduced in June were dropped in September 2009. The length of time migrants had to find a new job was doubled from 3 to 6 months in August 2009. Moreover, those who had worked for over 5 years in the work permit system did not have to renew their permit but could instead apply for permission to live and work in Ireland on a yearly basis without acquiring a new permit (as long as they were in employment and could support themselves).[21] In addition, after persistent lobbying by various NGOs and interest groups, a bridging visa was introduced in October 2009 so that unauthorized migrant workers who had become unemployed because they were made redundant or suffered workplace exploitation could apply for 4 months' residence permission in order to re-enter the permit system.[22]

The migration process in Ireland contains a variety of differentially positioned actors including employers, the state, politicians, the labour movement, NGOs, and the churches. The outcome of these ideological struggles structured by the relative power position of the actors has produced a contradictory and differentiated national immigration policy. At a national level Irish migration policy, for the most part, has been formed in the triangulation of the separate interests of state, capital, and labour. States by their very nature seek to impose restrictive borders. Though in principle business interest groups and employers support the free movement of capital, and some in Ireland have been sympathetic to pro-immigration policies, with a few exceptions, on both a global and national level, very few support open borders,[23] indicating that they benefit from the state stratified supply of cheap labour. Moreover, despite the supposed international character of the labour movement, few trade unions have called for less restricted movement, rallying instead to protect the short-term interests of their members' wage levels.

There are overwhelming moral and broad humanitarian grounds for accepting the long-term reality of migration. Migration and settlement in Ireland will continue in the future, though probably on a much smaller scale and on a different trajectory. Though patterns of emigration have re-emerged, and Irish workers are more willing to take on low-status, low-paid jobs that they once shunned, this is not an absolute shift and the persistence of 3-D jobs including cleaning, farming, and working in the meat sector, as well as high-skilled jobs such as IT or nursing, continue to require migrants to fill them. Moreover, in the longer term a demographic transition entailing falling birth rates, an ageing population, and shrinking workforce will put strains not only on the sustainability of Irish pension and social protection systems, to which migrants contribute, but also on businesses, and on government finances. In its recent Population and Labour Force Projections 2041 the CSO noted that by 2041, 25% of the population will be 65 and over, and that without sufficient net migration the domestic labour market will not be able to supply enough workers to support the economy's long-run growth potential even up to 2021. However, immigration is not a long-term solution to ageing populations since the immigrants themselves will age.

Although many immigrants will continue to arrive as migrant workers, issues such as family reunification will almost certainly also become prominent. In addition to family reunification, ethno-racial concerns involving social exclusion and issues relating to immigrant second-generation children will almost certainly play a central role in the future development of Irish immigration policy. Tensions may arise with the growth of family reunification as people come to live in Ireland rather than to work.

These processes will probably play themselves out within a context of a relative shift in power within the state apparatus from the DETE and its concern for labour needs to the DJELR and its restrictionary agenda. This has already been evident with the publication of the Immigration, Residence and Protection Bill, 2010. As well as increasing powers to deport and restrict entry, the Bill's rationale is expressed in what is absent in relation to immigration issues as much as what is present. As a result it fails to safeguard basic human rights through primary legislation; it fails to discuss integration issues and integration services such as language provision; it fails to stipulate the underlying criteria upon which ministerial authority can be exercised, allowing excessive discretion; and it fails to acknowledge immigration as a permanent feature of Irish society despite discussing a long-term residence policy which allows immigrants to stay in Ireland for 5 years.

Not only will there be a continuing need for migrant labour in the long-term, but the conditions which engender migration – including economic differences between developed and developing countries and global political instability – are unlikely to disappear anytime soon. The need for migrants to support family members through acquiring work and sending remittances will remain. In a 2-year period between 2004 and 2005 it was estimated that over €100 million was remitted to developing countries from Ireland.[24] In 2008 a massive €654 million was remitted to EU 27 countries and another €100 million was sent to non-EU countries.[25] Understanding world processes in global terms instead of through a national prism is important, and can help see the reality and factors underpinning migration. Moreover, using humanity as the frame of reference for understanding processes of migration in contrast to nation-states makes a fundamental difference in understandings of social justice. The social suffering caused by migration restrictions can be lessened by the implementation of open borders. Sufficiently cogent moral, humanitarian, and economic arguments based on rational arguments have been adduced for introducing open borders even though such policy generally has a strong counter-intuitive and threatening aspect in the public mind, and is currently not on, nor is likely to be on, the policy agenda of most states.[26] This does not mean that relatively more open borders should not be introduced immediately both for workers and for asylum-seekers. This has to be achieved in conjunction with greater information about immigrants, why they migrate, and their contribution to society, as well as shifting toward a more equal material context within which their presence is evaluated.

The specific role of the Irish labour movement in shaping migration is contingent upon the continued existence of social partnership. The hegemonic role partnership played for business has become destabilized in the context of the recession. And the emergence of migrant organizations will add to the complexity of these social processes involving state capital and labour. If the State's agenda has been to minimize the social rights of migrant workers through ethnic filtering, and to facilitate the exploitation of those deemed the weakest members of the migrant working class by marking and treating them as visibly different, anti-racist struggles based on re-asserting these rights will need to become stronger.[27] Such a strategy will need to reassert an international humanism and radical equality that does not reify migrants simply into factors of production. It also involves an increasingly transformative role for trade unions beyond their contradictory nationally orientated position. As Berger rightly notes:

> The only possible way beyond these contradictions would be for the trade unions to contest the migrant's inferior status by demanding right of promotion, right of political activity, right of residence for as long as he wishes, right of entry for his family. Yet to make these demands would be to alienate the majority of union members who have accepted their natural superiority over the migrant. It would also involve the unions in a head on confrontation with government and management, who argue that the national economic interest – which includes the interest of the national working class – depends upon immigrant labour being used exactly as it is.[28]

The actions and social struggles of differently positioned actors will determine the fundamental migratory challenges facing Irish society in the future and their outcome depends on the balance of the contesting forces both in Ireland, but also globally – capitalism is after all a world market phenomenon incorporating an international division of labour. The Celtic Tiger is dead and the relation between Irish State and capital is undergoing political reorganization in the recession. The dominant neo-liberal orthodoxy, entailing privatization, deregulation, tax cuts, and short-term economic practices, is under revision, although a return to the protectionism of the past seems highly unlikely. The contradictory field of forces will ensure that debates concerning immigration into Ireland and immigration policy will remain central concerns as Irish society continues to undergo renewal and change. One thing is certain, however: long-standing Irish socio-cultural and national homogeneity and the capital–labour relation have irrevocably been transformed by migration. Ireland has become an island of migration in an increasingly global age.

Notes

1 O' Hearne, Macroeconomic policy in the Celtc Tiger, p. 47.

2 UN Human Development Report, 2007 (Geneva: UN, 2008) p. 24.

3 Cited in Fintan O'Toole, Rich elite due a dose of patriotic punishment, *Irish Times*, 28 October 2008.

4 CSO, Quarterly National Household Survey, 2008.

5 Ibid.

6 In the fourth quarter of 2008 there were 2,052,000 persons in employment, an annual decrease of 86,900 or 4.1%, representing the largest annual decrease in employment since the Labour Force Survey was first undertaken in 1975. QNHS, 2008.

7 CSO Foreign Nationals: PPSN Allocations, Employment and Social Welfare Activity, 2008. 23 December 2009.

8 Immigration from EU 12 countries dropped from 33,700 in April 2008 to 13,500 in April 2009, according to CSO, Population and Migration Estimates, 2009, www.cso.ie/releasespublications/documents/population/current/popmig.pdf.

9 *Irish Times*, 29 December 2009. Also CSO September.

10 CSO, *Foreign Nationals*.

11 Office of The Minister of Integration: www.integration.ie/website/omi/omiwebv6.nsf/page/statistics-overview-en.

12 Daniel McConnell, Our economy has fallen off a cliff, *Sunday Independent,* 28 March 2010, http://www.independent.ie/national-news/our-economy-has-fallen-off-a-cliff-2114878.html.

13 M. Fix et al., Migration and the global recession, Migration Policy Institute, September 2009. www.migrationpolicy.org/pubs/MPI-BBCreport-Sept09.pdf. In Spain for example, unemployment has reached 14%, and now stands 20% for non-EU foreigners.

14 CSO, *Non-Irish Nationals*, 2008.

15 Calculations from QNHS, Table A2, *Estimated number of persons aged 15 years and older in employment (ILO) classified by nationality and NACE economic sector*, www.cso.ie/qnhs/calendar_quarters_qnhs.htm. Among the 39,000 non-Irish nationals making new applications for unemployment benefits in the first quarter of 2009, manufacturing workers accounted for about one fifth, and workers from a further three sectors – wholesale and retail, construction, and transportation – accounted for 14% each. Finance and insurance accounted for another fifth of the total. Statistics provided to the author by Central Statistics Office.

16 CSO, Live Register, March 2009.

17 Jobseeker's Benefit (JB) is a social insurance scheme. It is paid weekly to insured persons who are out of work. Jobseeker's allowance (JA) is a means-tested payment made to people who are unemployed and who do not qualify for Jobseeker's Benefit or whose entitlement to Jobseeker's Benefit has expired.

18 Immigrant Council, Citizenship processes in need of overhaul (new release, 7 May 2009), www.immigrantcouncil.ie/press_detail.php?id=9.1.

19 *Irish Times*, 9 February 2009.

20 *Irish Independent*, 7 February 2009.

21 Irish Naturalization and Immigration Service, New Provisions for Non-EEA workers who are made redundant (news release, 28 August 2009).

22 Irish Naturalization and Immigration Service, Undocumented Workers Scheme, October 2009, www.inis.gov.ie/en/INIS/Pages/Undocumented_Workers_Scheme.

23 The most prominent of these are the Cato institute, the *Economist* magazine, and the *Wall Street Journal*.

24 NESC, *Managing Migration* (Dublin: NESC, 2006), p. 183.

25 Dail Debates, Written answers, 23 February 2010.

26 N. Harris, *Thinking the Unthinkable*, 2002; T. Hayter, *Open Borders* (London: Pluto, 2000); J. Moses, *International Migration: Globlization's Last Frontier* (London: Zed, 2007). On moral grounds see J. Carens, Aliens and citizens: the case for open borders, *The Review of Politics*, 49 (spring 1997).

27 Allen, Double Speak: Neo-liberalism and migration, p. 97.

28 Berger and Mohr, *A Seventh Man*, p. 146.

Index